Mussolini's
NAVY

The battleship *Cavour* at Genoa, May 1938. On the right, the destroyers *Usodimare* and *Da Noli* of the 'Navigatori' class and, partially visible on the left, the battleship *Cesare*. Both *Cesare* and *Cavour* were extensively rebuilt in 1933–7. This photograph was taken in late May 1938 when the Italian battle fleet made a visit to Genoa after the 'H Review' in the Gulf of Naples on 5 May. (From an original print by Studio Calì, Genoa; Author's collection)

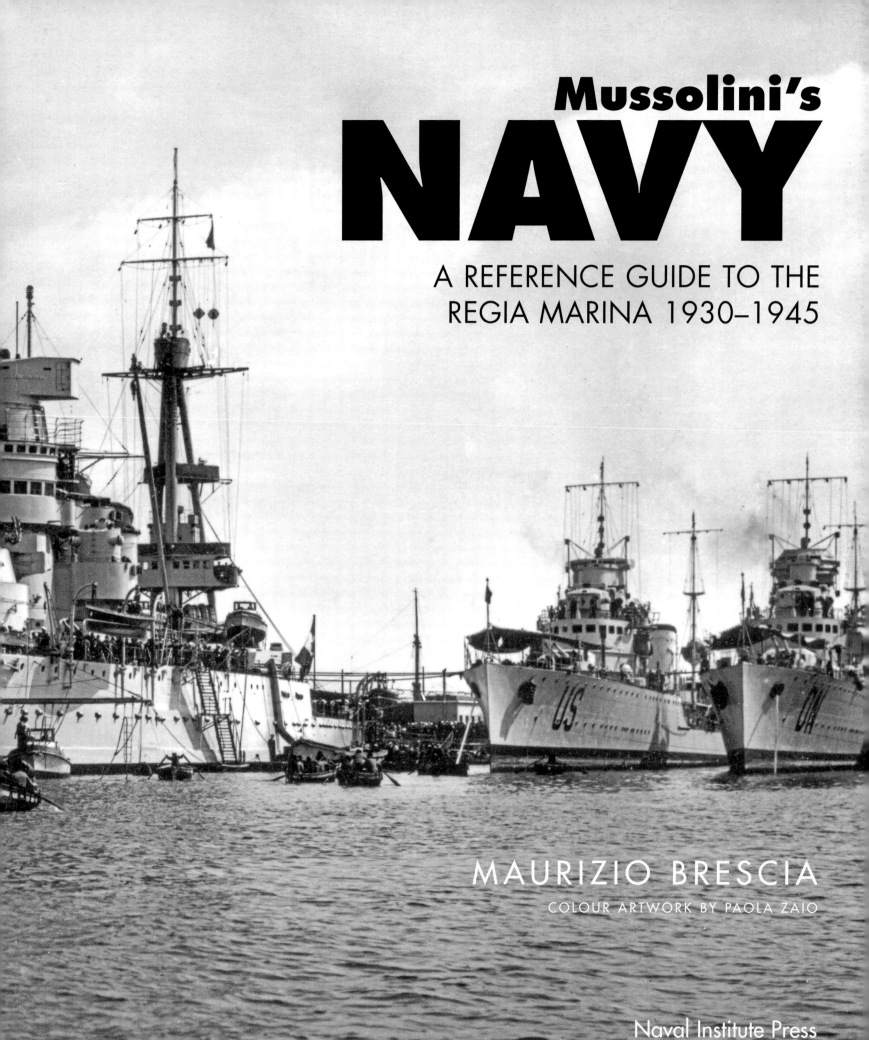

Mussolini's NAVY

A REFERENCE GUIDE TO THE REGIA MARINA 1930–1945

MAURIZIO BRESCIA

COLOUR ARTWORK BY PAOLA ZAIO

Naval Institute Press

This book is dedicated to the memory of my maternal grandfather, Giovanni Olivieri (1894-1970), who served with the Regia Marina during the First World War aboard the seaplane tender *Europa* and who – above all – was instrumental in instilling in me my passion for the study of history and the technical aspects of the ships of the Italian Navy.

Copyright © Maurizio Brescia 2012

First published in Great Britain in 2012 by
Seaforth Publishing
An imprint of Pen & Sword Books Ltd
47 Church Street, Barnsley
S Yorkshire S70 2AS

www.seaforthpublishing.com
Email info@seaforthpublishing.com

Published and distributed in the United States of America and Canada
by the Naval Institute Press, 291 Wood Road, Annapolis, Maryland 21402-5034
www.nip.org

LOC number: 2012941595
ISBN 978-1-59114-544-8

Typeset and designed by Ian Hughes, Mousemat Design Ltd
Printed and bound in China through Printworks International, Ltd

Contents

Foreword

DESPITE THE TITLE OF this volume, the Italian Navy was never particularly fascist. This does not mean that the Regia Marina's officers and men were opponents of the Mussolini regime, just that they were no more Fascist than the rest of the Italian population, especially in the 1930s – although the traditionally monarchist officer corps was somewhat more critical of the regime. This is perhaps indicated by the fact that only two battleships (*Littorio* and *Impero*), two destroyers (*Camicia Nera* and *Squadrista*) and a few other minor vessels bore Fascist names.

Between the two world wars, the Italian navy undertook an expansion programme which, despite the strain it imposed on the state finances, brought it almost to the same level as the French navy, its traditional rival, which is to say to fourth or fifth place in the navies of the world. However, when Italy declared war on France and Great Britain on 10 June 1940, this programme was still two years from completion. Nevertheless, on that date, the Regia Marina had two modernised battleships in commission (two similar ships and two modern '35,000-ton' battleships of the *Littorio* class were fitting out), seven heavy cruisers, twelve light cruisers, almost sixty destroyers and thirty-five modern torpedo boats, as well as a large underwater arm with 115 operational submarines. This was a balanced group of well-built ships, robust and of recent design but the Italian Navy

lacked aircraft carriers which, despite studies in the 1920s and 1930s, were never built because of the mistaken estimation (in particular within the navy itself) of their operational effectiveness in the restricted waters of the Mediterranean.

The lack of aircraft carriers – and of an adequate naval aviation arm – was not the Italian Navy's only shortcoming in this period. Development of radar and sonar equipment had been neglected, the problems this caused being exacerbated by the limited effectiveness of anti-aircraft and other guns designed before the mid-1930s. Hull designs and machinery were, however, generally excellent, granting high speeds but at the cost of endurance owing to high rates of fuel consumption. These deficiencies were not solely due to bad planning by the Regia Marina but largely because of problems in Italian industry, not least the almost 'cottage industry' state of the electronics sector.

At the same time, the Regia Marina was also expanding and upgrading its dockyards and naval bases both in Italy and the colonies, but shortage of money prevented this expansion from meeting actual requirements. Likewise, coastal defences could not be upgraded to the extent required. On the other hand, the naval training establishments were expanded, providing excellent training for officers and ratings: at the beginning of 1940 the personnel of the Regia Marina reached the

considerable number of 140,000 men (officers, petty officers and ratings), similar to the levels at the end of the First World War.

All this – and much more – is addressed in this volume, representing a wide-ranging descriptive analysis of the Italian Navy, its ships and its organisation in the Second World War. All the ships, from battleships to the small yet effective human torpedoes and assault craft, as well as naval bases and major support infrastructure, are described in this book, enhanced with an impressive number of high-quality photographs and specially-commissioned drawings.

This is certainly the first 'companion' of this kind presented to English-language readers who have in recent years demonstrated a growing interest in the Italian Navy whose ships and men, despite frequent bad luck and facing superior numbers, fought gallantly between June 1940 and September 1943.

Erminio Bagnasco
Editor of the Italian monthly magazine
STORIA militare

Aboard the battleship *Cesare*, on the afternoon of 7 July 1940, the ship's CO, Capt. Angelo Varoli Piazza, and two ensigns carry the battleship's battle flag and ensign from the officer's quarters (where they were usually stowed) up to the signal bridge and to the conning tower shortly before the ship's departure on the mission that would conclude with the Battle of Punta Stilo on 9 July 1940. (E Bagnasco collection)

Introduction and Acknowledgements

THE ACTIVITIES, ORGANISATION AND ships of the Regia Marina in the Second World War have been until recently somewhat neglected – outside Italy – by authors and publishers of books on the naval history of the conflict between 1939 and 1945. Although many often excellent Italian volumes on this subject have been published, beginning soon after the end of the war, foreign publishers had understandably shown less interest in it, largely due to lack of widespread knowledge of Italian – necessary to access the primary sources and the best books available, either published by the Ufficio Storico della Marina Militare (USMM – the Italian Navy's Historical Dept.) or by several private firms as well.

However, interest in Italian naval affairs has recently increased, particularly in English-speaking countries. An example of this was the publication by Seaforth of E Bagnasco and A De Toro's *The Littorio Class – Italy's Last and Largest battleships 1937-1948* (published in 2011 as the English translation of the original *Le navi da battaglia classe 'Littorio' 1937-1948* of 2008) which has been received with undoubted interest by the English-speaking readership and – almost simultaneously – other publishers, albeit with books and pamphlets addressing a less specialised audience, have produced further works relating to the most important ships of the Regia Marina in the Second World War.

However, there was still no general and all-encompassing work in English on the key technical, operational and organisational aspects of the Italian Navy covering a period necessarily longer than the war itself, including the preceding decade during which the Regia Marina, despite difficulties and setbacks, reached a strength and size unparalleled in its 150-year history.

In view of all of this, this book's title – *Mussolini's Navy* – could not avoid addressing a particular moment in Italian history (and the individual who affected almost all of its aspects between October 1922 and July 1943) although, as LtCdr. Bagnasco has already highlighted in his lucid introduction, the prevailing sentiment in the Regia Marina was monarchist, and the officers in particular regarded the royal family as an expression of higher authority and national continuity, rather than sharing the political sentiments of the times or firmly embracing the ideals of the Fascist regime.

We have thus tried to create a true 'companion', to furnish readers with a comprehensive guide containing information on the ships, dockyards, organisation and activities of the Regia Marina between 1930 and 1945, with additional thumbnails (and perhaps something more…) on camouflage, uniforms, flags, naval aviation and other related subjects. Like all such books, *Mussolini's Navy* is an introduction to the subject, and as much information and data as possible has been included: for further detail readers will have to refer to the extensive bibliography at the end of the book, largely relating to works and studies that – although almost all in Italian – have in several cases been published recently or are nevertheless still available.

Of course, such a book as this cannot ignore illustrations, so we decided to accompany this book with the greatest number of carefully selected high-quality images that it was possible to fit in the volume's format. The over 400 images in the book are, themselves, sometimes even more important than the text or data tables: even a less-than-perfect photograph may often 'tell' much more than a written page so, in several cases, it has been decided to couple significant photographs with comprehensive and detailed captions. As will be specified later, all of the images – other than those from the author's collection – come from the archives of the most important Italian naval researchers and collectors (as well as from several foreign naval enthusiasts) and from Foundations, Institutions and Museums, both public and private.

For the most part, original photographs have been scanned specifically for use in *Mussolini's Navy* and – when needed – the files have been appropriately restored and treated with computer graphics software, in order to make the book's illustrations one of its main features. At the same time, with the book's introductory and descriptive nature always in mind, the use of footnotes and

The destroyer *Espero* manoeuvring in the Gulf of La Spezia in the early 1930s; note the Union Jack atop the mast, probably hoisted to salute visiting British ships. (Author's collection)

other similar references has been avoided; nevertheless, the author and the publisher have always intended this book to be comprehensive and – therefore – we do hope that the readers will appreciate this 'dual approach' that has been adopted.

★ ★ ★

A book of this scope could not have been created without the contributions of many people who have collaborated with the author for more than a year in an effort of continuous and unselfish support which has proved to be both critical and invaluable.

Above all I wish to thank Robert Gardiner of Seaforth Publishing, for having believed – from the beginning – in my project for a possible 'companion' to the Regia Marina in the Second World War: he has accepted *in toto* my ideas, suggesting unquestionably important elements and coordinating the editorial work that has led to the creation and printing of this book.

Lieutenant Colonel Ralph Riccio, US Army, Retired (the knowledgeable and capable translator of the book *Le navi da battaglia classe 'Littorio' 1937-1948*) has worked continuously, showing great friendship, on editing all the chapters of this book, facing the unenviable task of reviewing and correcting the text that I did my best to write straight into English. In more than a year, we exchanged countless e-mails that, not infrequently several times a day, crossed the Atlantic in both directions to hone a sentence, choose the more appropriate term or decide the form and consequences of the language chosen and the literary consistency of the book. Beyond any doubt, I have found in Ralph not only a knowledgeable and careful language and editorial reviewer but also a true 'friend and colleague' who I hope one day to be able to meet in person, given the numerous interests (not only in the naval field) that we now share.

LtCdr. Erminio Bagnasco has, for many years, been one of the most prominent and active Italian naval authors and, certainly, the one who has written the greatest number of books, monographs, articles, photographic essays and studies on Italian naval ships of the Second World War. Since 1993, he has been the editor of *STORIA militare*, a monthly magazine which is a leader in Italy in the field of military history publications, for which I have the honour of being a member of the editorial board. The collaboration with Erminio has proved absolutely fundamental for my 'training and formation' as a naval author, and in the specific case of *Mussolini's Navy* has always been a primary influence on its structure and content, as only a true friend and teacher provide. Last but not least, several of the images illustrating this volume come from his huge and comprehensive collection.

Very special thanks are due to Paola Zaio, who contributed with dedication and professionalism to the creation of the colour profiles and tables that illustrate the most important forms of Italian naval camouflage for the 1940–5 period; she also proved to be an invaluable collaborator in the management and filing of the large amount of photographs from which those actually used in the book have been chosen.

Ensign Andrea Tirondola (Supply Corps, Italian Navy) helped for the short biographical notes on the most prominent Italian admirals and naval officers of the Second World War.

Finally, I wish to remember with emotion and gratitude Cdr. Aldo Fraccaroli (who unfortunately passed away recently, in March 2010) whose work is well known worldwide: he was not '*an* Italian naval photographer' but, more properly, '*the* Italian naval photographer' *par excellence*: not only a true expert in the field of naval photography, but also a fully prepared naval historian, with a deep and specific knowledge of the world's navies, and of the naval editorial field, for the last seven decades. A Regia Marina officer (and also an official naval photographer) from 1940–3, he has the great merit of having maintained the continuous and active presence of the 'Italian school' of naval photography in a crucial period in twentieth-century history. Many of his beautiful wartime photographs have been included in this book but – even more importantly – his courtesy, skills, preparation, elegance and helpfulness have always helped to focus the research and studies of many 'new generation' authors – including myself – in the vast field of naval history and of its related publications.

In addition to photographs coming from the author's collection, for publication in *Mussolini's Navy* several more have been provided – and generously shared – from the following Italian and foreign collectors and researchers: Attilio Albergoni (Palermo), Guido Alfano (Turin), the late Elio Andò, Giorgio Apostolo (Milan), Alessandro Asta (Trapani), Franco Bargoni (Rome), the late Arrigo Barilli, Enrico Buzzo (Genoa), Joseph Caruana (Malta), Mario Cicogna (Trieste), Stefano Cioglia (Cagliari), the Cocchi Family (Santa Margherita Ligure), Zvonimir Freivogel (Berlin), Marco Ghiglino (Genoa), Giorgio Ghiglione (Genoa), Franco Harrauer (Milan) Enrico Leproni (Milan), Bertrand Magueur (Toulon), the late Tullio Marcon, Carlo Martinelli (Genoa), the late Aureliano Molinari, Giorgio Parodi (Genoa), Aldo Petrina (Trieste), Fulvio Petronio (Trieste), Mario Piovano (Bergamo), the late Achille Rastelli, Nicola Siracusano (Messina), Aldo Starace (Trieste), Gianpiero Vaccaro (Piombino), Adm. Giovanni Vignati (Rome), and Evgeni Zelikov (Krasnodarski Kr., Russia).

Finally, I wish to thank the many organisations, museums, institutions, photographic studios, magazines and periodicals that have provided documentation and photographic collections: Archivio Storico Ansaldo (Genoa), Photo Marius Bar (Toulon), Photo De Siati (Taranto), Gruppo di Cultura Navale (Bologna, with its President Gino Chesi), Gruppo ANMI Milano, Gruppo ANMI Savona, Imperial War Museum (London), Istituto Luce (Rome), *Life*, 'A. Maj' Library (Bergamo, custodian of the 'Occhini Bequest', run with passion and professionalism by Mario Piovano), Museo Storico Navale (Venice), Naval History and Heritage Command (Washington, D.C.), *Rivista Marittima*, Società Capitani e Macchinisti Navali (Camogli), *STORIA militare*, Ufficio Storico della Marina Militare – USMM (Rome), US National Archives (Washington, D.C.), and the USAF Museum (Wright-Patterson AFB, OH).

To all these people and institutions go my thanks and gratitude, and they also should be given great credit for the completion of this volume. Inaccuracies and oversights are of course attributable only to myself, and I will indeed be grateful to readers who will report such errors for their correction in any future edition.

Maurizio Brescia
June 2012

Officers of a *Zara* class cruiser, probably the *Fiume*, during a ceremony in the mid-1930s.
(Author's collection)

CHAPTER 1

The Regia Marina from 1861 to 1939

The Early Years

Following the end of the Second War of Independence and the exploits of Garibaldi in Southern Italy in 1860, the Italian Navy was formed by the amalgamation of the former Navy of the Kingdom of Sardinia, the Bourbon Navies of Naples and of Sicily and the naval forces of the Papal State and of the Grand Duchy of Tuscany. The decree promulgated by Garibaldi at Naples on 7 September 1860 sanctioned – at least from a political point of view – the unification of the Sardinian and Bourbon Navies, whose vessels made up 75 per cent of the new Italian Navy.

On 17 March 1861, with the proclamation of the Kingdom of Italy, the Navy of the Kingdom of Sardinia had already been renamed the Regia Marina (Royal Navy) even though two previous decrees, in November 1860 and in January 1861, had already abolished the Bourbon Navy Ministries at Naples and Palermo. The Count of Cavour (briefly Minister of the Navy from 17 March until 4 June 1861) carried out a series of measures to give the newly-born Regia Marina a skeleton structure. First of all, the Navy Departments at Genoa and Naples were maintained, and a new Department in Ancona, with jurisdiction over the Adriatic, was created; at the same time, it was decided to maintain the Naval Schools of Genoa and Naples and to improve the organisation of the Naval Engineering Corps. Moreover, the Naval Supply Corps was created, along with the Consiglio dell'Ammiragliato (Admiralty Council – an administrative and command structure with duties quite similar to the Royal Navy's Board of Admiralty).

The process of the creation of the new Regia Marina (given the limited technical and operational value of the Papal and Tuscan navies) had to deal with the difficult situation arising from the need to amalgamate officers and crew from both the Sardinian and Bourbon navies. Antagonisms between officers with different training, personal grudges, conflicting political sentiments (either monarchist, republican, democrat or reactionary) caused unrest and rivalry, enhanced by misguided Cavour's mistake of replacing the commanding officers of several ships of the dissolved Bourbon Navy with officers from the Sardinian Navy. Another similarly difficult situation was also created when officers of the former Bourbon Navy joined the new Italian Navy with ranks superior to those granted earlier by Garibaldi (unquestionably already too generous and arbitrary) to men of the Sicilian Dictatorial Navy, which was also incorporated into the new Regia Marina.

After the death of Cavour, General Menabrea was appointed as Minister of the Navy, and he planned the construction of twelve sailing ships of the line with auxiliary steam machinery, and the same number of frigates and corvettes: types of ships that were almost ten years out of date by then. Luckily, after the fall of the Rattazzi government, the new Prime Minister Ricasoli appointed as Minister of the Navy Adm. Carlo Pellion di Persano, who gave impetus to a renewal programme for the Regia Marina that – even if only partially – prevented its decline. Between 1861 and 1863 the French armoured iron-built ships of the *Maria Pia* class were commissioned, among the best Italian ships of that period. At the same time, the steam frigate *Principe di Carignano* was built in Genoa, but her hull was wooden-built, and the armour was fitted only later. The two ironclads *Re d'Italia* and *Re di Portogallo* were built by the Webb Yard of New York, but with poor machinery and insufficient armour. Before 1866, further orders for ironclads followed: the *Palestro* and *Varese* (in France) and the *Roma* and *Messina* (in Italian shipyards), and – in Britain – the revolutionary 'ram' *Affondatore* but, except for the latter and the *Palestro*, none of the other ships were ready for the naval campaign of the 'Third War of Independence'.

In the years immediately following unification, the Regia Marina mostly used naval bases in the Tyrrhenian Sea, but the changing international situation and growing enmity with Austria increased the importance of the Adriatic theatre. As Taranto was rather remote, the base at Ancona became the main focus for Italian naval planning from 1861 to 1865. However, the events of the 'Third War of Independence' exposed the new-born Italian state's lack of military preparedness, particularly at sea, where the Regia Marina was defeated at the Battle of Lissa on 20 July 1866 by the Austro-Hungarian fleet commanded by Admiral Tegetthoff, losing the ironclads *Re d'Italia* and *Palestro*.

On 17 November 1869 the Suez Canal was opened to traffic and consequently Italy's geo-strategic position changed, its central position in the Mediterranean making it a focus for the major naval powers' commercial and naval activities. However, until the occupation of Rome in September 1870, Italian naval policy was still suffering from a lack of self-consciousness and national ideals: the occupation of the Papal State prompted a positive course of events that, with renewed priorities in economic and foreign policy, also included a strong impetus for the renewal, reconstruction and expansion of the Regia Marina.

Until 1871, the Italian Navy had to face a decrease in the number of its ships (losing more than twenty vessels), when Augusto Riboty – Minister of the Navy between 1868 and 1873 –

The steam frigate *Borbona* of the Bourbon Navy, laid down in 1857 and launched on 18 January 1860, was incorporated in the Regia Marina in 1861 and renamed *Giuseppe Garibaldi*. She ended her days serving between Massawa and Assab as a hospital ship, being broken up in 1899. (Ufficio Storico della Marina Militare)

The ironclad *Regina Maria Pia* in the 1880s. Together with the other ships in the class (*Ancona*, *Castelfidardo* and *San Martino*) she fought at Lissa but, at the time this photograph was taken, only *Castelfidardo* had been extensively modernised, while the other ships retained much the same appearance as in 1866. (Author's collection)

The old armoured frigate *Formidabile*, here at La Spezia in the 1890s serving as a gunnery training ship. Built at the Forges et Chantiers de la Méditerranée (La Seine sur Mer), she fought at Lissa in 1866 but was not stricken and broken up until 1904. (Author's collection)

The battleship *Lepanto* at La Spezia in the early 1890s. She took seven years to build (laid down on 4 November 1876 and commissioned on 17 March 1883), so she and her sister-ship *Italia* were almost obsolete when they finally entered service with the Regia Marina. Nevertheless, they were among the largest battleships of their day and had long service lives, the *Lepanto* being broken up in 1914 and the *Italia* not until 1921. (Author's collection)

was finally able to co-ordinate the construction of new ships, which in number and capabilities were finally adequate for the real needs of the Italian Navy. On 12 March 1873 the Minister of the Navy Admiral de Saint Bon, who took over Riboty's post at the end of his second term in the Department, presented the designs of the two new battleships *Caio Duilio* and *Enrico Dandolo*. These were revolutionary ships that, with a hull 109m long and displacing over 12,000 tons, with 7,710hp reciprocating engines (on two shafts) could steam at a maximum speed of 15 knots, absolutely remarkable for the era when they were built. The main armament consisted of four 17.7in/20 muzzle-loading guns, located in two revolving armoured turrets offset to port and starboard amidships. The design of these two ships, which gave the Regia Marina a position of prominence among naval powers, was due to the Director of the *Genio Navale* (Naval Engineer Corps) Benedetto Brin, who deserves to be

The armoured cruiser *Varese* of the *Garibaldi* class fitting out at the Orlando Shipyard, Leghorn, on 19 November 1899. The Regia Marina commissioned two other ships in the class (*Giuseppe Garibaldi* and *Francesco Ferruccio*), and seven more were sold to foreign countries: four to Argentina (*General Garibaldi*, *General Belgrano*, *Pueyrredon* and *San Martin*), two to Japan (*Kasuga* and *Nisshin*) and one to Spain (*Cristobal Còlon*). (Author's collection)

remembered not only for his influence on naval shipbuilding in the last quarter of the nineteenth century, but also for his contribution to the development of Italian naval strategy and doctrine in that period.

In 1878 Riboty pushed through the Italian parliament the law establishing the Naval Academy that – with the abolition of the Scuole di Marina in Genoa and Naples – would finally unify the training and education of all Regia Marina officers. After no more than three years, on 6 November 1881, the Academy was inaugurated, proving in a few years to be one of the foremost naval schools in Europe.

Later, for almost seven years, from 30 March 1884 until 9 February 1891 Adm. Benedetto Brin held the post of Minister of the Navy, but even before this appointment he had designed important new capital ships for the Regia Marina. In particular, in 1876 the battleships *Italia* and *Lepanto* had been laid down, reaffirming the originality of the Italian naval engineering school that began with the *Duilio*s. The main armament consisted of four 16.9in/27 breech-loading guns, again offset to port and starboard in barbettes amidships. Their maximum speed exceeded 18 knots, but it should be noted that developments in gunnery (both in firepower and in rates of fire) very quickly rendered the ships obsolete.

In his seven years as Minister of the Navy, Brin worked at the design of two additional battleship classes: the *Ruggero di Lauria*s and the *Re Umberto*s. With displacements ranging from the 11,000 tons of the first group of ships to the 15,000 tons of the second, these ships began the

trend – characterising most Regia Marina construction for almost half a century, until the late 1930s – that favoured speed over armour protection. Moreover, Brin's naval programmes allocated considerable funds for the building of several protected cruisers and of large numbers of torpedo boats.

A few figures may help to show the financial burden on the State's budget of the funds allocated to the Regia Marina in the years when Brin was Minister of the Navy. In 1884, for example, the ordinary appropriations for the Navy rose to 98 million Lira, but the approval of further additional allocations brought the total to 132.6 million Lira; moreover, the 1884 budget also provided 78.4 million Lira to be allocated to the additional expenses of the budgets for 1885, 1886 and 1887.

In the last years of his life, Benedetto Brin returned to his original activity as a naval architect, designing a class of two ships that may be considered the last Italian 'pre-dreadnoughts' and, on his death in 1898, by Royal Decree of 29 May that year the first ship of the class, then building at the Castellammare Shipyard, was named after him.

Regarding naval doctrine and strategy, Brin actively participated in the debate that – between 1870 and 1895 – saw the participation of the most qualified representatives of Italian naval thought. His technical and ideological contribution in what was then called the 'Questione delle Navi' ('The Ships Problem', i.e. the national need for a blue-water Navy, capable of more than just coastal defence) was crucial and – today – makes Benedetto Brin one of the most important Italian naval thinkers and strategists.

Among the European Powers

The fifteen years following the Battle of Lissa allowed the Regia Marina to renew its ships and its technical and organisational structure as well; at the same time, the Kingdom of Italy was consolidating its position in the international arena, taking on a greater political importance in Europe and in the Mediterranean and formulating its own colonial policy.

In 1881, with the French occupation of Tunisia, Italy was for the first time involved in a Mediterranean crisis with a strong naval character, as the importance of the naval base at Bizerte had been enhanced by increased funding granted to the Marine Nationale by the French state since 1878.

The policy of the German Chancellor Bismarck, intended to isolate France in Europe, led to the formation of the Triple Alliance, signed in Vienna on 20 May 1882 between Austria, Germany and Italy. The latter, although angering irredentist anti-Austrian sentiments, pragmatically gave more importance to the confrontation with France in the Mediterranean, in particular because of the defensive aspects of the Alliance between the three powers. At the same time, Anglo-German rivalry led to the Entente Cordiale between Great Britain and France in 1904, and to the birth of the Triple Entente in 1907 which also included Russia. Britain could thus influence both the Franco-Russian policy and institute – if needed – a formidable naval blockade against the continental powers of the Triple Alliance.

Paradoxically, in particular for Italy, the first

The battleship *Sicilia* in the Gulf of La Spezia, c. 1910, in a photograph taken by Studio Pucci of La Spezia. The three ships in this class (*Re Umberto*, *Sicilia* and *Sardegna*) were commissioned between 1893 and 1895; already obsolete at the beginning of the First World War, they were employed in various second-line duties during the conflict, and were stricken and broken up in 1919–20.
(Photo Pucci, La Spezia; Author's collection)

A view of the innermost basin of the La Spezia Dockyard in the early 1900s, looking east, with torpedo boats at bottom right, battleships and cruisers. The presence of a *Regina Elena* class battleship fitting out – in the centre of the image, to right of the chimney – allows this photograph to be dated to between 1906 and 1908, when the two battleships of this class built at La Spezia (*Regina Elena* and *Roma*) were being completed. (Author's collection)

Naval Convention of the Triple Alliance was not signed until in December 1900, eighteen years after the initial signing of the Treaty. The agreement provided the division of the seas within the 'substantial interest' of each party: Germany would control the North Sea, Baltic Sea and Atlantic entrances to the European continent, with the western Mediterranean assigned to Italy and the Adriatic to the Austro-Hungarian Empire. The eastern Mediterranean was to be shared between Austria-Hungary and Italy.

Italy could now devote less resources to its eastern coast, being now able to deploy more freely against France, but the Adriatic continued to be an ever-increasing source of friction between Italy and the Austro-Hungarian Empire. In particular, in 1908, the annexation of Bosnia and Herzegovina by Austria-Hungary led to a crisis in relations between Rome and Vienna, and the Italo-Turkish War of 1911–12 – with the resulting Italian territorial acquisitions in Libya and in the Aegean – made the Adriatic 'truce' between the two powers even more fragile.

The pre-dreadnought battleship *Regina Margherita* in the Canale Navigabile at Taranto, bound for Mar Grande, probably in the winter of 1912–13. (Author's collection)

While the renewals of the Triple Alliance (and its naval conventions) were signed, the world's navies worldwide were living a moment of great transformation due to the advent of the all-big-gun battleship. Until the early twentieth century, battleship armament was composed of guns of different calibres, so only a few of the most powerful guns could be carried aboard any one ship. The concept of a battleship whose main weapons were to be exclusively guns of the largest calibre practical, originated from a study by the Italian naval engineer Vittorio Emanuele Cuniberti and published in the 1903 edition of the already authoritative *Jane's Fighting Ships*.

Initially, the Regia Marina showed no particular interest in the *Dreadnought* and its successors, and it was not until 1909 that the first Italian 'dreadnought' was laid down: this was the *Dante Alighieri* which had some innovative features particularly with respect to armament, as the twelve 12in/46 guns of the main armament (manufactured at the Armstrong factory in Naples) were grouped into four triple centreline turrets, thus allowing all the heavy guns to bear in broadside fire. The *Dante* was followed, between 1910 and 1916, by the three *Cavour* class (*Conte di Cavour*, *Giulio Cesare* and *Leonardo da Vinci*) and the two *Duilio* class (*Andrea Doria* and *Caio Duilio*) which – apart from the *Leonardo da Vinci*, lost during the First World War – were modernised in the 1930s and served throughout the Second World War.

In 1908 the Austro-Hungarian Navy also laid down a class of four 'dreadnoughts', armed with twelve 12in/45 and twelve 5.9in/50 guns; this was the *Tegetthoff* class, from the name of the first ship to be launched (the others being *Prinz Eugen*, *Viribus Unitis* and *Szent Istvan*). These were quite similar to those of the Regia Marina, but with less powerful machinery and thus a slightly lower speed, nevertheless balanced by a more rational layout of four turrets, two forward and two aft, with 'B' and 'C' turrets superimposed over 'A' and 'D'.

When Italy left the 'Triple Alliance' and joined the 'Triple Entente' on the declaration of war on 24 May 1915, the Italian and Austro-Hungarian navies hade five and three dreadnoughts in commission respectively, as the *Andrea Doria* and the *Szent Istvan* would not be completed until 1916.

The Regia Marina in the First World War and Naval Operations in the Adriatic

The rivalry between Italy and Austria-Hungary in the Adriatic and the Balkans had in the meantime continued, assuming an ever greater importance when – on the outbreak of the war in Europe in August 1914 Italy, in accordance with the terms of the Triple Alliance, remained neutral.

It is not necessary here to dwell on how Italy completely changed its international position, leaving the alliance with Germany and Austria-Hungary and becoming one of the Entente powers. However, it must be remembered that the Treaty of London of 26 April 1915 with the Entente finally allowed the Kingdom of Italy to support nationalist and irredentist anti-Austrian policies, long espoused by the vast majority of the population, particularly among the middle class where the nationalistic ideals of the Risorgimento were more strongly rooted. The naval conventions of the Treaty of London, signed on 10 May 1915, gave Italian command of operations in the Adriatic, linked to the territorial compensations promised to Italy in case of victory against the Central Powers. Early in the war, the Regia Marina thus had five dreadnoughts in service, along with eight older pre-dreadnoughts; the Austro-Hungarian battle fleet numbered nine similar pre-dreadnoughts, as well as the three dreadnoughts mentioned previously.

However, in the Adriatic there was little opportunity for the capital ships of both sides to engage against each other: even before May 1915 the French navy had suffered significant losses there, with two battleships sunk and a third damaged by torpedo boats and submarines. Thus action in the Adriatic was like a 'guerrilla' campaign typified by clandestine operations punctuated with audacious coups by relatively few men in small, fast craft. The stalemate in the Adriatic can also liken it to the stalemate of the

trenches on land.

The Regia Marina had the following tasks during the war:

- Protection of the right flank of the army on the Isonzo line (and defence of the coastal front after the defeat at Caporetto).
- Strategic blockade of the Adriatic with the Otranto Straits barrage.
- Convoy protection.
- Defence of the Adriatic coast (with coastal batteries, railway guns, mine barrages etc).

A photograph the like of which will never be taken again: the Gulf of La Spezia in 1910, with a large number of ships of the Italian Navy. Destroyers and torpedo boats are in the foreground, and in the background several major ships: among them, some *Garibaldi* class armoured cruisers and battleships of various classes (*Re Umberto*, *Emanuele Filiberto*, *Regina Margherita* and *Regina Elena*). (Photo Pucci, La Spezia; Author's collection)

On 29–30 November 1916, bound to Corfu for a month-long deployment, as seen from aboard a 'three-stacker' destroyer. From right to left, a *Cavour* class battleship, the *Dante Alighieri*, another *Cavour* class battleship and a *Doria* class battleship. The capital ships of the Regia Marina (as well as those of the Austro-Hungarian Navy) were never employed in fleet operations and, for the most part of the conflict, remained idle at anchor in the naval bases of southern Italy. (A Fraccaroli collection)

port during attacks by motor-torpedo boats (the *Wien*) and human torpedoes (the *Viribus Unitis*), and one (the *Szent Istvan*) was torpedoed and sunk at sea by two motor-torpedo boats. The main supporter of the use of destroyers and small, stealthy craft was the Chief of Staff of the Navy, Admiral Paolo Thaon Revel, who had an opportunity to put these theories in practice when, between October 1915 and February 1917, he was the commander of the northern Adriatic Department and of the Regia Marina's headquarters at Venice.

On 29 December 1915, in the southern Adriatic, one of the few naval battles of the conflict between larger units took place, when the Italian scouts (light cruisers) *Bixio* and *Quarto* – escorted by several destroyers – engaged the enemy scout *Helgoland* and some destroyers and torpedo boats. In 1916 the opposing fleets made an ever-increasing use of destroyers and torpedo boats: the Regia Marina would attack the port of Durazzo (7 June), the Gulf of Parenzo (12 June) and the port of San Giovanni di Medua (16 June) with such vessels.

On 15 May 1917, between Brindisi and Durazzo, an Italian-British naval squadron intercepted some Austro-Hungarian ships going to attack the Otranto Straits barrage: in the action, the scout *Helgoland* and *Saida* were damaged, and on the Allied side, the Italian destroyer *Borea* was lost and the British cruiser *Dartmouth* damaged. By the end of 1917, after the defeat at Caporetto (and the stabilising of the front up to the River Piave, with Venice as an immediate secondary line), the activities of the Regia Marina initially consisted in supporting the Army operations on the coast, both in the Venetian lagoon and at the mouth of the Piave. On 11 November, two motor-torpedo boats (under Cdr. Costanzo Ciano and Lieut. Berardinelli) attacked the Austro-Hungarian battleships *Wien* and *Budapest* off Cortellazzo, forcing them to break off their bombardment of Italian positions on the coast. On 10 December, Lieut. Luigi Rizzo (CO of *MAS 9*), along with another boat, got into the port

Both sides clung somewhat rigidly to the dual strategy of maintaining a 'fleet in being', whilst attempting to attack the enemy in their bases, as is shown by the fact that both lost three battleships but none in action with ships of their own type. The Italian battleships *Benedetto Brin* and *Leonardo da Vinci* sank while moored in harbour (the first on 27 September 1915 at Brindisi, and the second at Taranto on 2 August 1916) both from internal explosions caused by sabotage. The *Regina Margherita* was lost at Valona (Albania) on 11 December 1916 after hitting a mine. Similarly, two Austro-Hungarian battleships were sunk in

One of the most famous Italian naval photographs of the First World War: the *MAS 7*, with Lieut. Gennaro Pagano di Melito in command, at Brindisi in summer 1916. The ships in the background are, from left to right, the armoured cruisers *Pisa* and *San Giorgio* and, at right, the salvage ship *Anteo* recovering the hulk of the battleship *Benedetto Brin*, sunk by sabotage on 27 September 1915. (E Bagnasco collection)

of Trieste, sinking the battleship *Wien*. This was one of the first real harbour attacks attempted by the Regia Marina which, by the end of the war, would inflict heavy losses to the Austro-Hungarians and which can be ranked among the most daring and glorious naval actions of the First World War. On 10 June 1918, Luigi Rizzo himself (by now promoted to LtCdr.) commanded a pair of motor-torpedo boats in an action against an enemy naval squadron off the island of Premuda, in which *MAS 15* torpedoed and sank the battleship *Szent Istvan* (and from then on, 10 June has been celebrated as Navy Day in Italy). As will be detailed in the chapter about assault craft, Capt. Costanzo Ciano, Inspector of all the Regia Marina's MAS, ordered a new 'self-propelled torpedo' to be built and – with this innovative craft – two divers attacked the port of Pola on the night of 1 November 1918, sinking the Austro-Hungarian battleship *Viribus Unitis* that, only a few days earlier, had been transferred (even if only administratively) to the newly-constituted Yugoslav Navy.

This brief account of such small craft operations would not be complete without mentioning the action of 11 February 1918 known as the 'Beffa di Buccari' (i.e. 'the Buccari Jeer'). The *MAS 96* (CO LtCdr. Luigi Rizzo, with the famous poet and patriot Gabriele D'Annunzio aboard), *MAS 95*, and *MAS 94* left Venice along with several escorting vessels, each of them towed by a torpedo boat. Upon arrival in the Gulf of Quarnaro, near the island of Cherso the boats slipped their tow and penetrated into the Gulf of Buccari. The facts are well known and – although none of the enemy ships at anchor in the area was sunk – the action had enormous propaganda value, also thanks to the famous message hand-written by D'Annunzio himself, and launched in a bottle in the waters of Buccari, with which D'Annunzio mocked the ' … more than cautious Austrian Fleet endlessly brooding in safe harbours the very small glory of the battle of Lissa…'.

The sea war ended, as on the eastern Italian land front, on 4 November 1918, but – from an ideal point of view – the final act of the First World War in the Adriatic took place on 24 March 1919, when the battleships *Tegetthoff* and *Erzherzog*

Franz Ferdinand, the scout *Admiral Spaun*, several destroyers and torpedo boats and four submarines, once flying the flag of the Austro-Hungarian Navy, arrived as war prizes in the lagoon of Venice with Italian crews, welcomed by the cheers of the Venetians.

The Regia Marina 1919–1939

At the end of the First World War, facing an unfavourable economic situation and having to cope with the impact of large-scale demobilisation, the budget for the Regia Marina in the immediate post-war years was drastically reduced.

The first consequence was that three of the new *Caracciolo* class battleships under construction were scrapped on the building ways. These ships, laid down during the war, would have been armed with eight 15in guns in twin turrets, and the hull of the namesake of the class – the *Francesco Caracciolo* – was launched solely to free the slip to build other ships; on the other hand, the technical characteristics of these ships and, in particular,

The launch of the light cruiser *Alberto di Giussano* at the Ansaldo Shipyard, Genoa, on 27 April 1930. Note the location of the aircraft hangar at the base of the forward superstructure, with the large aperture that will be later closed by a sliding door. (Author's collection)

The heavy cruisers *Pola* (foreground) and *Zara* at Venice in 1933–4. Note the Cant AR 25 seaplane on *Pola*'s quarterdeck; notice also that the forward and aft twin 3.9in/47 guns still have to be fitted. (Photo Baschetti, Venice; Author's collection)

their underwater protection would have been rather poor, and the Italian Navy never complained that they were abandoned. So, in the early 1920s only a small number of ships already laid down between 1915 and 1918 were completed (the three scouts of the *Leone* class), and a few auxiliaries were built, the most notable being the submarine tenders *Pacinotti* and *Volta*, the seaplane tender *Giuseppe Miraglia*, some small water and gasoline tankers and various miscellaneous shipyard craft.

In 1922, with the signing of the Washington Naval Treaty, Italy was allowed a parity with France even if – particularly on the Italian side – new ships were not immediately laid down; on the contrary, the Marine Nationale started construction almost at once of the *Duguay Trouin* class light cruisers and of the large destroyers of the *Jaguar* class, these latter ships being later (and only partially) balanced by the Regia Marina laying down the four *Sella* class destroyers.

The otherwise unimpressive Italian naval programme of 1922–3 did allow funds to be allocated for construction of the first 'Washington'-type heavy cruisers (*Trento* and *Trieste*), but these two ships – commissioned in December 1928 and April 1929 respectively – reflected all the features (and defects) of the first generation of cruisers built in accordance with the Treaty requirements. Following the two *Duquesne* class cruisers, the Marine Nationale had in the

meanwhile decided to build the four *Suffren*s (with more balanced features compared with the previous couple of ships), and the increasing French commitment to the construction of heavy cruisers convinced Mussolini's government to authorise the four *Zara* class cruisers – built between 1929 and 1932 – that, with a good balance of weapons, protection and armament, turned out to be the best Italian ships of this type. Similarly, after the first six light cruisers of the two early series of the 'Condottieri' type were built, they were followed between 1931 and 1937 by the improved four light cruisers of the two *Montecuccoli* and *Aosta* classes, and then by the two larger and more powerful *Giuseppe Garibaldi* and *Duca degli Abruzzi*.

Meanwhile, as the debate (or, rather, argument) between the Regia Marina and the Regia Aeronautica about the need to build and operate one or more aircraft carriers ended with the Air Force as the winner, the further expansion of the French Navy – which had meanwhile laid down the fast battleship *Dunkerque*, later followed by the similar *Strasbourg* – caused the Italian Navy to plan and implement the rebuilding of the two dreadnoughts *Cesare* and *Cavour*. The reconstruction of these two vessels, fully described in their section in Chapter 4, provided a technical result of remarkable consistency even though, when in wartime service, the two battleships exhibited all their structural, technical and

Gunner's mates and other ratings during an exercise with empty shell cases in the late 1930s. Note the summer working dress, with canvas jumper and trousers, but with a blue beret instead of the white canvas sailor's hat. (Author's collection)

operational limitations.

At about the same time, however, considerable importance was given to the destroyer component of the fleet, with the construction of the twelve scouts of the 'Navigatori' class and of the eight destroyers of the *Freccia* and *Folgore* classes. Moreover – taking advantage of the opportunity granted by the Washington Treaty that did not restrict the number of ships with a standard displacement of 600 tons or less – starting with the torpedo boats *Spica* and *Astore* a building programme was begun that, by the second half of the 1930s, would lead to the commissioning of thirty-two ships of this type. Finally, as will be discussed under submarines in Chapter 4, the Regia Marina was by this time concluding the building of small classes of boats and single prototypes and beginning the series production of both coastal and ocean-going submarines in a programme that would result in the Italian navy deploying no less than 100 boats at the outbreak of war in June 1940.

Up to the mid-1930s, the French Navy continued to be regarded as the only real 'opponent' of the Regia Marina and, consequently, in January 1934 the official announcement was made of the laying down of the first two Italian '35,000-ton' battleships, to be named *Littorio* and *Vittorio Veneto*. At the same time, the Italian Navy's CinC Adm. Domenico Cavagnari – who consistently opposed the construction of aircraft carriers – also favoured the design and construction of the *Pegaso* class escorts and also instituted the first studies that would lead (in the late 1930s) to the building of the small, fast cruisers of the 'Capitani Romani' class.

In the same period, the Fascist government started a major programme of industrial and technical co-operation with the USSR that – initially – led to the construction of the six large destroyers (or 'flotilla leaders') of the *Leningrad* class, built in 1936–40 and partially inspired by the 'Navigatoris' and similar French vessels as well. The collaboration between Italy and the USSR also influenced the design of several classes of Soviet destroyers like the type 'VII' and 'VII U'

ships, which closely resembled the *Freccia* class ships of the Regia Marina. After the completion at Ansaldo, Genoa, of the two patrol vessels *Kirov* and *Dzerdzinskji* (1933–4), the same shipyard provided considerable engineering and technical assistance for the design of the cruisers of the *Kirov* and *Chapaev* classes, each composed of six ships, built in the naval shipyards at Leningrad, Komsomolsk and Nikolaiev in 1935–9. Finally, between 1937 and 1939 the Orlando shipyard at Leghorn built the fast 'super destroyer' *Tashkent* that, according to the Soviet Navy's initial plans, was to have been the first of a twelve-ship USSR-built class, never completed because of the outbreak of the war, but whose design greatly influenced that of the 'Capitani Romanis'.

With the outbreak of war in Ethiopia in 1935, the Regia Marina began to face the possibility of a clash with the Royal Navy's Mediterranean Fleet that in September 1935 could muster up to five battleships and two aircraft carriers (although these were divided between Gibraltar and Alexandria). Because of the expense of further classes of destroyers – the four *Oriani*s and the twelve 'Soldatis' – that were to have been commissioned by the end of the decade, very little remained for the construction of additional larger ships, with the exception of the two battleships *Littorio* and *Vittorio Veneto*, whose construction was already underway. In the second half of the 1930s, in fact, the Regia Marina laid down no new cruisers, spending the funds allocated to ships of greater displacement to rebuild the other two remaining dreadnoughts (the *Doria* and the *Duilio*). The reconstruction of these two battleships can be considered a technical achievement on an even greater scale than that of the two *Cavour*s, but once recommissioned *Doria* and *Duilio* also denoted more or less the same deficiencies found in the two rebuilt *Cavour*s, showing that the large amount of money spent on their reconstruction would have been better spent on other types of ship for which there was greater need or at least to speed up the completion of the third and fourth *Littorio* class battleships, *Roma* and *Impero*, which had been laid down in 1938 at

The two IMAM Ro 43 seaplanes of the light cruiser *Raimondo Montecuccoli* during the ship's Far Eastern cruise of 1937–8. (Courtesy Cocchi Family)

Ansaldo, Genoa and at CRDA, Trieste, respectively.

The Italo-German alliance (which, on 22 May 1939, would lead to the signing of the Pact of Steel between Rome and Berlin) had, in the naval sphere, an official 'consecration' on 5 May 1938 when – during the visit to Italy by Adolf Hitler – the famous 'Rivista H' ('H Review') was held in the Gulf of Naples in honour of the German dictator. Almost all of the major units of the Regia Marina took part in the review (with the exception of the four *Montecuccoli* class cruisers), engaging in spectacular manoeuvring, target practice and simulated attacks by MAS, submarines and aircraft.

However, the specific manoeuvres and exercises carried out in the 'H Review' reflected the conceptual, strategic and operational limitations that would affect the operations of the Regia Marina in the imminent conflict. Hulls and equipment of generally good quality were negatively affected by machinery built for high speeds and, therefore, with high rates of fuel consumption and often prone to breakdowns. Accuracy of gunnery was reduced by factors such as twin guns mounted in single cradles and excessive muzzle velocities, frequently resulting in excessive salvo dispersion; moreover, equipment, ammunition and above all training for night fighting were almost non-existent.

The Regia Marina, which was for the first time in its history about to face the Royal Navy, was equipped and trained for a 'decisive' fleet action against a similarly-equipped opponent, while the upcoming war in the Mediterranean was to be of an entirely different nature. In fact, until just

The battleship *Littorio* being launched at the Ansaldo Yard in Genoa on 22 August 1937. *Littorio*'s launch was an important event at the time, being attended by King Vittorio Emanuele III and other members of the royal family, and widely covered by the media. (Courtesy Archivio Storico Ansaldo, Genoa)

before the war, very little work had been done to develop radar and sonar equipment, and build the escort vessels that would prove indispensable for convoy work and which had to be hastily produced after Italy entered the war.

The lack of aircraft carriers and – above all – of a genuine naval air arm (as all flying operations were left to the Regia Aeronautica) was badly felt, especially during the first two years of war; deficiencies in reconnaissance led to missed encounters with enemy formations, to losses of ships and to a general inability of naval forces at sea to operate efficiently and rapidly against the enemy, as it was not possible to find out their exact location, composition and movements in a timely manner. Submarines, as we shall see, were to be employed 'statically' – thus greatly limiting their operational potential – even though the Regia Marina's boats had been equipped with efficient and up-to-date torpedoes from the late 1930s.

Nevertheless, in spring 1940 the Regia Marina displayed an impressive fleet: the fifth largest in the world for surface ships, and the largest for submarines, with 115 boats in service. On 10 June 1940, when war against Great Britain and France was declared, the Italian Navy had two operational battleships (*Cesare* and *Cavour*) and four more were to join the fleet by the end of the summer (the two rebuilt *Doria*s and the modern '35,000-tonners' *Littorio* and *Vittorio Veneto*), and an additional two *Littorio*s were building. There were seven heavy and twelve light cruisers in commission, fifty-nine destroyers, and thirty-three old and thirty-five modern torpedo boats (the thirty *Spica* class, the four *Pegaso* class escorts and the submarine chaser *Albatros*). The training and motivation of both officers and men – albeit oriented more towards the tactics and strategic situations of the past rather than the present – was undoubtedly excellent, to some extent compensating for the Regia Marina's technical deficiencies.

Finally, one of the most significant problems the Regia Marina would face between 1940 and 1943 would be the Italian shipbuilding industry's inability to replace war losses (which totalled two battleships, thirteen cruisers, thirty-nine destroyers, a large number of torpedo boats and about sixty submarines). In fact, during the war – with the exception of the few foreign vessels acquired as war prizes – the Italian Navy was able to build and commission only three light cruisers, five destroyers and less than twenty submarines. On the other hand, it must be noted that the effort to designing and building escort vessels gave good results, with the construction of the destroyer escorts of the *Ciclone* class and in particular the numerous corvettes of the *Gabbiano* class, several of which served with the Marina Militare Italiana for many years after the end of the Second World War.

With this nonetheless considerable surface and submarine fleet, the Regia Marina was about to face the Royal Navy in a 39-month war that would end in Italy's defeat, but in which the Italian ships and crews served with courage and steadfastness, not only during the war itself but also the dramatic events of the Armistice. In doing so, the Regia Marina earned the respect of its enemies and the gratitude of the entire Italian nation, and for this too has gone down in history with a positive balance.

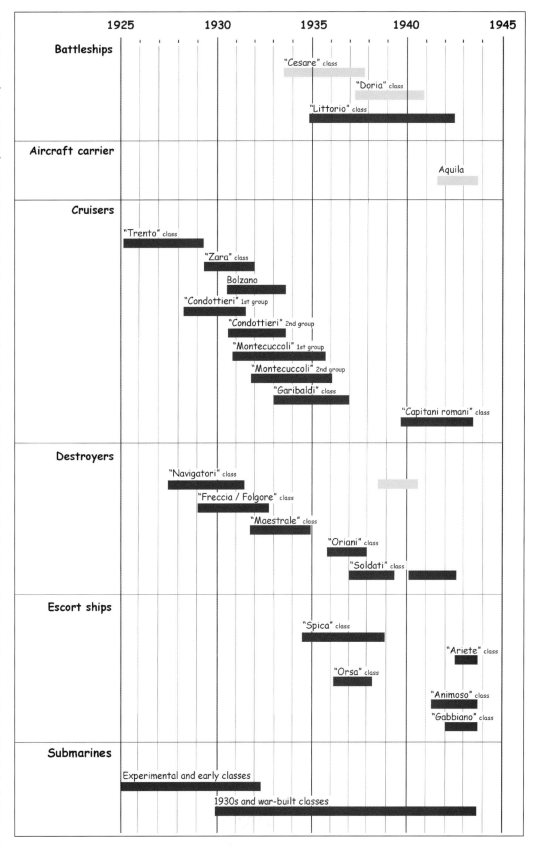

This table shows, for the period 1925–45, the series of Italian shipbuilding programmes for surface warships and submarines. Between 1925 and 1935 great emphasis was laid on the construction of cruisers and destroyers, while in 1935–40 the bulk of available funds went on the construction of the *Littorio* class battleships, with a consequent reduction in funds devoted to other types of vessels. The black lines indicate the construction of new classes, and the grey lines indicate the modernisations (or even the reconstruction) of some classes or of single ships.

CHAPTER 2

Dockyards, Naval Bases, Ports, Shipyards and Coast Defences

THE SHEER LENGTH OF the Italian coastline (more than 7,400km – about 4,000nm) can be seen as a strategic advantage, granting the potential for naval bases to be established to support the deployment of warships in any required area of the Central Mediterranean. However, during the Second World War this extensive coastline was also a weakness, as considerable resources had to be spent in defending such a large number of harbours, bases and shipyards.

Furthermore, from the end of the nineteenth century the Regia Marina had to face the problem of establishing naval bases and coast defences as far away as Somalia and Eritrea; also, the end of the war against Turkey in 1912 brought further territorial acquisitions in North Africa and in the Aegean which required the construction of port facilities and naval bases on the Libyan coast and in the Dodecanese Islands, and at the end of the First World War, Italian coastal territory increased again, to include the shoreline east of Venice as far

as Trieste and the whole Istrian peninsula. With the occupation of Albania in 1939, the length of coastline under Italian jurisdiction in the Mediterranean was well in excess of 10,000km (5,400nm).

In the Red Sea and Indian Ocean, after the occupation of Ethiopia the coastline under Italian jurisdiction was over 4,000km (2,100nm): however, the fact that this area was only under Italian control for a brief period, and its lesser strategic importance, meant that neither the naval bases, nor coastal defences in Africa Orientale Italiana (AOI – Italian East Africa) were as significant as those located in other areas.

Naval Bases

As early as a decade before the creation of the Kingdom of Italy, the Count of Cavour (appointed Minister of the Navy for a first term in

1850) had decided to transfer the Sardinian Navy's main base from Genoa to La Spezia. He assigned Col. Menabrea the task of studying the defences of the shore facilities previously planned in 1849 at the Le Grazie and Varignano inlets in the Gulf of La Spezia; the first projects were completed in 1852 (and were based on different designs, some of them dating as far back as the Napoleonic era), but it was not until 1858 that an Engineering Committee was appointed with the task of studying the matter in depth.

Finally, Major Domenico Chiodo of the Navy's Engineering Corps managed to get his plan approved, suggesting that a new dockyard be built in the area west of downtown La Spezia and east of the small town of San Vito. From then on, the construction of the new dockyard proceeded apace, until its formal inauguration on 28 August 1869: the final layout of the Arsenale of La Spezia – with two inner docks and several dry-docks – would spread over an area of 85 hectares, with 13km of roads.

The submarine *Alagi* during an overhaul in one of the dry-docks at La Spezia in mid-1942. (Author's collection)

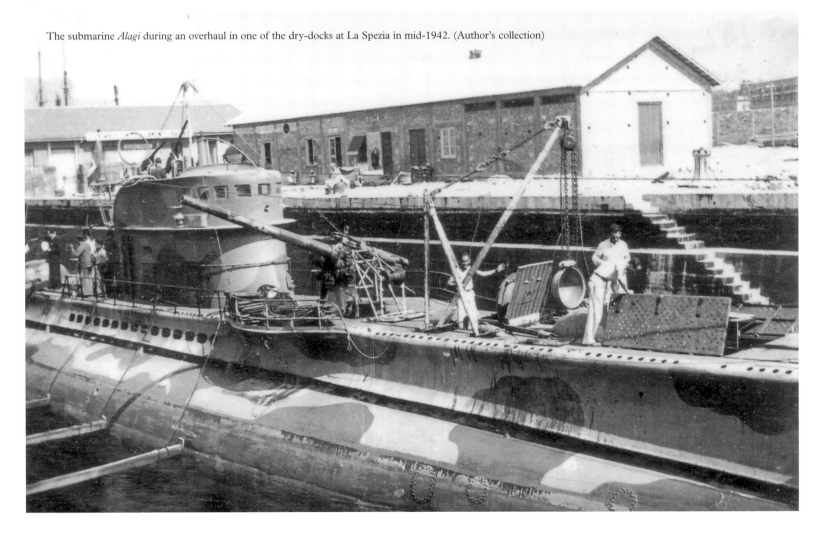

Although the Bourbon Navy maintained dockyards in Naples and Palermo (incorporated in the Italian Navy after 1861), it was decided to build a large new naval facility at Taranto, whose well-protected anchorage (Mar Grande, in the north-eastern part of the Ionian Gulf of Taranto) and inner harbour (Mar Piccolo) were particularly suitable for the construction of a new dockyard. Then-Captain Simone Pacoret di Saint-Bon drafted an initial plan for a new dockyard in 1866, but it was only in 1882 that the Italian Parliament passed legislation financing the massive works required for it. Actual building started in September 1883, and the project – again drawn up by the now General Chiodo – was put into effect under the direction of General Giovanni Cugini of the Army's Engineering Corps.

Of particular importance was the dredging of the Mar Piccolo, on the southern shore of which quays, workshops and dry docks were to be built. It was therefore necessary to widen and deepen the small channel between Mar Grande and Mar Piccolo, which was accomplished between 1884 and 1887; at the same time, a swing bridge (operated by hydraulic machinery) was built to connect the Old Town of Taranto with the new residential areas on the peninsula east of the Old Town and south of Mar Piccolo.

In June 1889 the Principe di Napoli dry-dock was completed and King Umberto I visited the new dockyard some two months later, on 21 August: this visit is considered by many historians as the dockyard's inauguration, although no formal ceremony was held either then or later. Building works in Taranto continued until the early twentieth century: in 1905 the Ferrati dry-dock (the largest in the dockyard) was begun, although it did not become fully operational until 1916, well after Italy's entry into the First World War.

Naval facilities were established in Ancona in 1862–5 and, after 1866, the Arsenale of Venice (whose oldest buildings dated back to the fourteenth century and had been used by the Austro-Hungarian Navy since 1820) became available as a base for the Regia Marina in the northern Adriatic. In the early 1900s, foreseeing the possible deterioration of diplomatic relations with Austria, plans were made to establish a smaller naval base at Brindisi, on the Adriatic coast south of Bari; in 1908, Adm. Giovanni Bettolo visited Brindisi and the Navy soon started building workshops and other facilities in the well-protected inlets there. By 1913, a considerable naval base had been built in Brindisi, whose importance would be greatly increased by the events of the First World War.

Victory against Austria in November 1918 led to territorial gains east of Trieste, with the whole Istrian peninsula falling under Italian control. The Austro-Hungarian Navy's large dockyard at Pola was virtually undamaged and soon began to be used by Regia Marina ships operating in the northern Adriatic

Over the years, Italian naval bases and dockyards have been classified in different ways but – in consideration of their importance in terms of workshops, availability of dry-docks and general technical efficiency – Regia Marina shore facilities can be grouped in four main categories:

Location of dockyards, naval bases and principal ports in Italy and North Africa.

• *1st class bases* – Dockyards with a great concentration of technical facilities (workshops, dry-docks etc.) and defences (shore batteries, anti-aircraft guns etc.), with wide availability of skilled manpower and where capital ships could be overhauled, repaired and modernised.

• *2nd class bases* – Smaller dockyards, with defences commensurate with smaller naval forces; in such bases supplies and ammunition were stored in smaller quantities than in 1st class bases, with fewer specialised workshops and less skilled manpower.

• *3rd class bases* – Installations that could accommodate small squadrons of escorts and

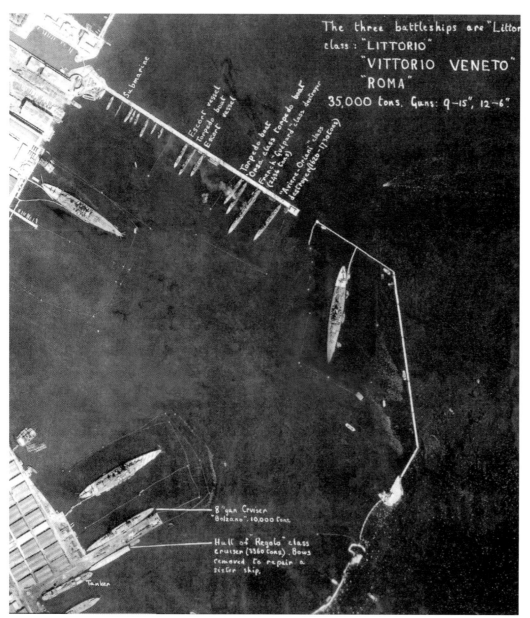

The three battleships are "Littorio class: "LITTORIO" "VITTORIO VENETO" "ROMA" 35,000 tons. Guns: 9–15", 12–6"

Submarine

Escort vessel
Torpedo boat
Escort vessel

Torpedo boat
Orsa class torpedo boat
French Galpard class destroyer (1380 tons)
'Aviere-Oriani' class destroyer (1620–1730 tons)

8"gun Cruiser "Bolzano". 10,000 tons.

Hull of "Regolo" class cruiser (3360 tons). Bows removed to repair a sister ship.

Tanker

Above: A smoke generator on a railway truck at La Spezia dockyard in autumn 1942. (E Bagnasco collection)

Left: All three *Littorio* class battleships as photographed by a RAF reconnaissance aircraft on 18 April 1943 in La Spezia's Darsena Duca degli Abruzzi. This is a very rare image as it is the only one known showing these three ships together. Photographic analysts also duly identified the heavy cruiser *Bolzano* and the 'Capitani Romani' class light cruiser *Caio Mario* (without her bow, which was used to repair her sister-ship *Attilio Regolo*) in the lower left-hand corner. (E Bagnasco collection)

Below: The high cliffs of the seacoast just west of the Gulf of La Spezia may be seen in this photograph of *MAS 424* and *426* dating from the early 1930s. (Fotocelere, Torino; Author's collection)

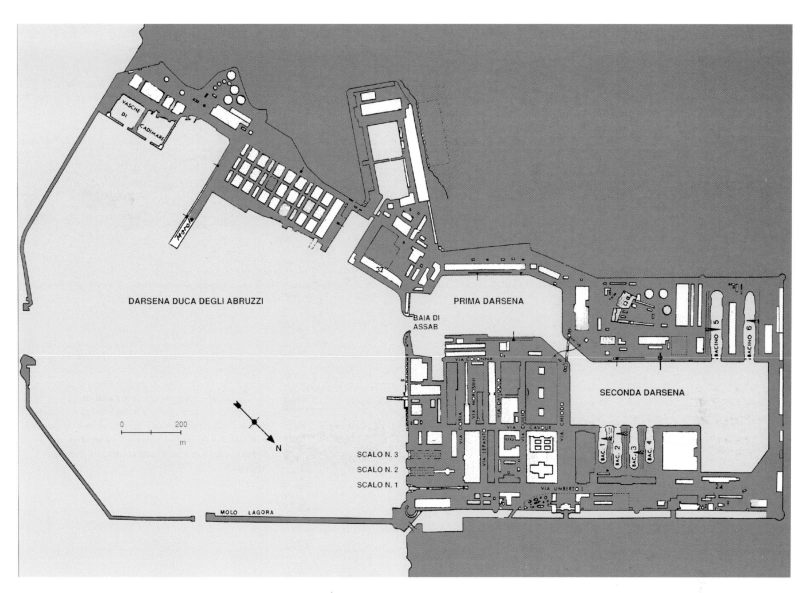

Plan of the La Spezia Dockyard. Areas in white show buildings and workshops destroyed or damaged by Allied air raids as of April 1945. (Courtesy *STORIA militare*)

The battleship *Cavour* in a floating dry-dock at Taranto in 1941, refloated after suffering torpedo damage in November 1940. (E Bagnasco collection)

coastal forces, with almost no workshops, no dry-docks and defences limited to anti-aircraft guns and machine guns.

• *Supply facilities* – ('Punto d'appoggio' in Italian), small ports and shore installations where the Navy operated replenishment facilities only, particularly for fuel and lubricants.

Another classification is more general, but equally precise: 1st class bases were often defined as 'permanent installations', while all other bases were defined as 'operational'. Permanent installations provided the highest possible security for naval forces, with heavy overhaul and repair facilities; operational bases were important in the forward deployment of naval forces and were thus of great help in achieving their strategic and tactical tasks.

In 1919, Italian naval bases were classified more simply than was to be the case in later years.

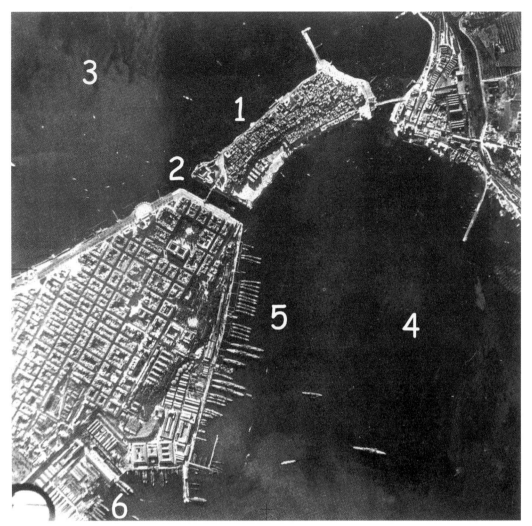

Above: Torpedo boats, destroyers and cruisers in Taranto's Mar Piccolo in the late 1930s. The light cruiser at upper left is either *Diaz* or *Cadorna*. (Author's collection)

Left: The Taranto dockyard in early November 1940, as photographed by a British reconnaissance aircraft. The Old Town lies on the island at top (1), separated from the New Town by the channel (2) between Mar Grande (3) and Mar Piccolo (4); the swing-bridge may be easily seen at the middle of the channel. Several destroyers and four cruisers are moored at the Banchina torpediniere (torpedo-boat quay) (5); dry-docks are in the bottom left corner (6). (From the Italian Navy's *Rivista Marittima*, November 2006)

• *1st class bases*: La Spezia, Naples, Taranto, Venice and Pola (all dockyards or 'Arsenali').
• *2nd class bases*: La Maddalena, Brindisi.
• *Supply facilities*: Messina.

The great building programmes of the Italian Navy between 1928 and 1940 had thus to consider the allocation of important financial resources for the upgrading of dockyards and naval bases. Estimates in the 1932/33 budget provided for the appropriation of about 350 million Lira, but the 1939/40 budget almost quadrupled this amount, with 1,147 million Lira for dockyard improvement and the construction of naval bases, i.e. about 42 per cent of the entire Navy budget. It should be noted that the 1938/39 estimates provided a great amount of money for overseas bases and to accelerate the improvement of facilities in the Mediterranean (Pantelleria, Leros, Tobruk and Tripoli) as well as in East Africa (Massawa, Assab and Chisimaio).

Between 1930 and 1940, the technical and operational capabilities of almost all Italian naval bases were greatly enhanced, in particular as regards the activities, services and workshops administered by the Engineering Corps ('Genio Navale'); so, it is of interest to examine in detail the improvements made to the various shore facilities. Very briefly, on 10 June 1940, Italian naval bases were classified as follows:

• *1st class bases*: La Spezia and Taranto (the two

principal dockyards of the Regia Marina).
• *2nd class bases*: Naples, La Maddalena (Northern Sardinia), Venice, Pola, Brindisi, Leros, Tobruk and Massawa.
• *3rd class bases*: Cagliari, Messina, Augusta, Trapani, Assab.
• *Supply facilities*: Portoferraio, Gaeta, Reggio Calabria, Palermo, Valona-Saseno (Albania), Ancona, Pantelleria, Tripoli, Bengazi, Rodi, Chisimaio.

It is interesting to note that very important ports such as Genoa, Livorno (Leghorn) and Trieste were not included in this list, but this is easily understood when considering their distance from the main supply routes to North Africa; furthermore, as will be seen later on, all of these ports were home to important privately-owned shipyards, which the navy considered differently.

This extensive system of dockyards and naval bases enhanced the operational capabilities of the Regia Marina: while during the First World War Italian naval bases could only support a war conducted mainly in the Tyrrhenian and Adriatic Seas, by 1940 they could quite easily face the challenges of a naval war fought in the whole Central Mediterranean, reaching into the Red Sea and the Indian Ocean. However, the classification above does not tell the whole story. For example, although Messina was officially a 3rd class base, it hosted important coastal defences protecting the straits between Sicily and the Italian mainland;

Trapani and Augusta were important supply and fuel depots (as well as having strong coastal fortifications), but had little in the way of workshops or dry docks; Palermo and Ancona hosted important private yards not directly owned by the Navy, and Pantelleria had significant shore defences but its harbour could accommodate only very small vessels (motor torpedo boats, submarine chasers etc.).

Here in more detail is the situation of Italy's dockyards and major naval bases on 10 June 1940:

• La Spezia – In 1930–4 the submarine quays and workshop had been modernised, the dry-docks were enlarged, the main one being lengthened from 151m to 201m; a new electric powerplant was built in a tunnel on the western side of the dockyard and new distilling plants, depots and workshops were built around the two inner basins. One of the most important works carried out in the second half of the 1930s was the construction of a new seaward dock south of the 'Arsenale', with long, modern quays fitted with fuel and water hoses, electric connections and other shore facilities, where a large number of heavy cruisers and capital ships could easily be moored.
• Taranto – As this dockyard was more modern than La Spezia's, no major works were carried out in the 1930s at the shore facilities of Mar Piccolo; however, several floating dry-docks were built or transferred from other areas, in order to

The light cruiser *Alberto di Giussano* in one of Taranto's dry-docks in the late 1930s. (Author's collection)

improve the repair and refit capabilities of the base. In 1937 a large new naval base on the northern shore of Mar Grande was begun, but its completion was halted by Italy's entry in the Second World War; this new facility was to have included a large dry-dock, 406m long and 51m wide, workshops, depots and a long underground tunnel connecting it with the dockyard. In mid-1940, the tunnel was 80 per cent complete and the excavation of the dry-dock was almost finished, but its inner stone cladding had not yet been put in place, and the construction of most of the surrounding buildings and workshops had not yet begun. It was not until June 2004 that a new naval base was opened there, with no dry-docks but with moorings and workshops for berthing and supporting a significant number of naval vessels.

- Naples – The dockyard was closed on 1 July 1923, but workshops and depots were maintained; a submarine support area was built between 1925 and 1932 at the Molo San Vincenzo (San Vincenzo Quay), and another, smaller submarine station was set up in the Vigliena area of the port in 1939–40.
- La Maddalena – Personnel training facilities, technical schools and workshops were improved and enlarged in the 1930s, and a new electric powerplant was built. The local submarine base

was improved to allow berthing and shore support for about ten boats.

- Venice – The very old dockyard was decommissioned at the end of the First World War but some new workshops and depots were built between 1923 and 1934, and the three dry-docks were handed over to a private company that modernised them in order to overhaul and repair the largest warships. In particular, the Principe di Piemonte dry-dock – 250m long – was the only one in the Adriatic that could accommodate the Italian '35,000-ton' battleships. During the war, the Venice dockyard was mostly used for repairs and refits of older destroyers, torpedo boats, submarines and auxiliaries.
- Pola – From the early 1920s, the large former KuK (Kaiserliche und Königliche) Marine dockyard was used as a minor naval base, hosting workshops, technical facilities and the Submarine School, along with a quite important submarine base.
- Brindisi – Technical workshops and shore facilities were enhanced in the years before the Second World War: the capabilities of the local submarine base, active since the First World War, were maintained.
- Leros, Tobruk and Massawa – These three bases were established after 1923 and over the years were equipped with workshops, a couple of

The destroyer *Corazziere* in dry-dock at Taranto dockyard on 3 February 1942 to repair her bow, damaged on 18 December 1941 in a collision with her sister-ship *Granatiere*. The other destroyer at left is *Grecale*. This official photograph is labelled 'Maricost – Taranto', this being the acronym for the local Direzione Costruzioni Navali (Naval Construction Directorate) that was in charge of *Corazziere*'s repairs. (A Asta collection).

The inner part ('Porto Vecchio') of the port of Genoa in mid-May 1938. The battleships *Cavour* and *Cesare* are moored at Calata Sanità; the destroyer *Scirocco* is steaming astern to position herself on *Cesare*'s starboard side. Cruisers and two torpedo boats are in the background. The photo was taken during a visit to the port by several Regia Marina ships, following the 'H Review' held in Naples in early May, at the time of Hitler's visit to Italy. (G Parodi collection)

floating dry-docks each, and a submarine station. At Tobruk, a large seawater distilling station was built inside a tunnel near the naval base.

• Cagliari – In 1938 workshops and depots began to be built, but their small size allowed only the support of small auxiliary ships and submarines during the Second World War.

• Messina – In 1933 the Regia Marina took over the management of a small dry-dock, establishing workshops, mooring quays and the headquarters of the Naval Engineering Corps in Sicily.

• Augusta – The well-protected Bay of Augusta was a forward-deployment anchorage for naval forces, but shore installations were limited to a submarine base (as at Trapani).

• Assab and Chisimaio – A small naval and submarine base had been planned for both of these ports in East Africa but on 10 June 1940 construction had not yet begun.

It must therefore be pointed out that the *Littorio* class battleships could use only three dry-docks in Italy: one in the 'zona bacini' of the port of Genoa, the Principe di Piemonte dock at Venice and the Ferrati dock in Taranto.

On Italy's entry into the war, the Regia Marina had almost 1.9 million tons of fuel in storage; the most important depots were at Taranto (602,000 tons), Naples (130,000 tons), Augusta (267,000 tons) and Palermo (140,000 tons). The construction of a large underground depot at Taranto (capable of holding over 300,000 tons) was begun in 1941, but work stopped in mid-1942. At the beginning of June 1940, other fuel supplies included 20,000 tons of gasoline, 7,000 tons of oil and 7,000 tons of lubricants.

Shipyards

As this book is intended as an introduction to the Italian navy of the Second World War, shipyards are dealt with succinctly, leaving out the many interdependencies between the technical departments of the Navy, the dockyards and private industry, which are described in more detail in several books listed in the Bibliography.

During the First World War, most Italian shipyards were already well established, ships being built by important private yards as Ansaldo and Odero (Genoa), Orlando (Leghorn) and Pattison (Naples). From the final decades of the nineteenth century until 1918, the dockyards of La Spezia and Venice launched quite a number of warships, among them some battleships and cruisers, but by the early 1920s naval shipbuilding was largely in the hands of private yards.

Genoa, its seaport and the surrounding area hosted some of Italy's most important shipyards: the Cantiere Ansaldo, established in 1886, is surely the best known and was soon involved in the Navy's development plans (from 1903 until 1912 Ansaldo was linked with the British company Armstrong Whitworth, owner of a gun factory in Pozzuoli, near Naples). In the early 1930s, Ansaldo bought part of the Odero shipyard's technical facilities, thus creating Italy's largest shipyard in Genoa's western suburb of Sestri Ponente.

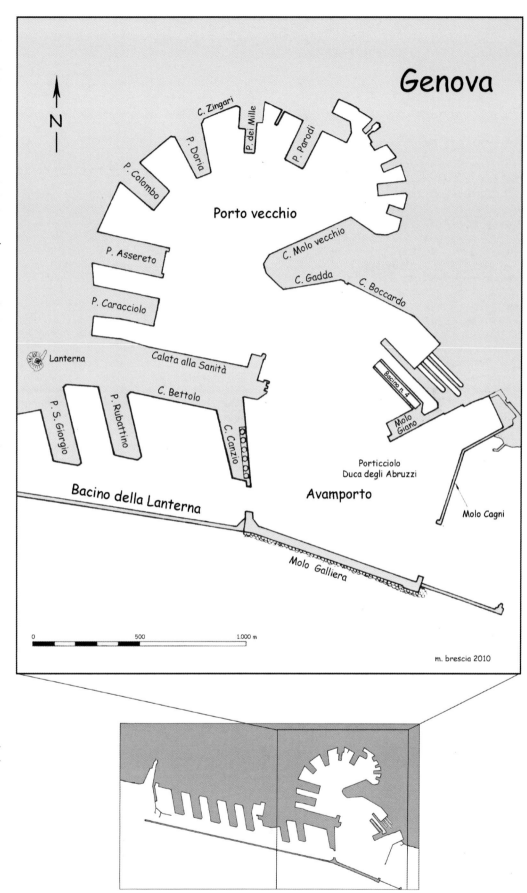

The Porto Vecchio area in the port of Genoa (top) and a general plan of the port as in 1940 (bottom), with the modern quays built to the west in the late 1930s. (Author's drawing, courtesy *STORIA militare*)

The destroyers *Saetta* (foreground) and *Fulmine* leaving the port of Naples in the late 1930s. (E Bagnasco collection)

A partial view of the port of Naples in summer 1943 in a British reconnaissance photograph. In the foreground, the hulk of the liner *Lombardia* of 20,006grt and – at the top – the damaged hulls of other merchant vessels. (IWM).

In 1906 the Muggiano shipyard, located on the east coast of the Gulf of La Spezia, joined with two private shipyards of Palermo and Ancona, giving rise to a new company named Cantieri Navali Riuniti that in 1925 incorporated the shipyard of Riva Trigoso, east of Genoa.

The Orlando shipyard at Leghorn, established in 1866, operated without signing agreements with other yards until 1929, when the OTO (Odero-Terni-Orlando) Corporation was established by gathering Orlando's activities together with those of the former Odero Yard in Sestri Ponente (Genoa), the Terni steelworks at Terni, the Vickers-Terni steelworks at La Spezia and the Muggiano shipyard, the Riva Trigoso yard of Cantieri Navali Riuniti being incorporated in a new holding named Cantieri Navali del Tirreno (while Ancona's and Palermo's yards maintained their former Cantieri Navali Riuniti ownership).

In 1931, the Pattison shipyard of Naples merged with the Bacini & Scali Partenopei

The destroyers of 8ª Squadriglia Cacciatorpediniere (8th Destroyer Flotilla) *Folgore*, *Lampo*, *Baleno* and *Fulmine* moored at buoys at Punta della Salute in Venice's Canale della Giudecca in the late 1930s. (Foto Baschetti, Venice; Author's collection)

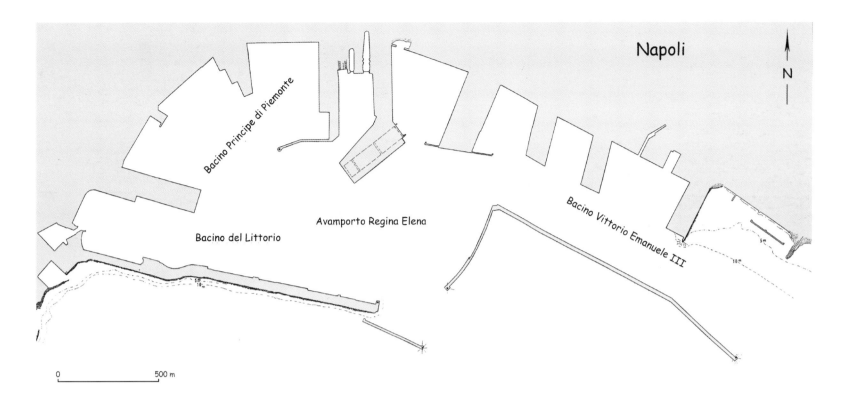

Plan of the port of Naples, from where many convoys bound for Libya departed during the Second World War. (Courtesy *STORIA militare*)

shipyard, forming the new Ansaldo-controlled corporation of Bacini & Scali Napoletani; this company, in 1939, gained financial and managerial autonomy, joining with the former naval shipyard of Castellammare nearby, and giving birth to the Naples-based company of Navalmeccanica.

At Taranto, the Tosi shipyard was established in 1914 and – until 1943 – built and launched a great number of submarines both for the Regia Marina and, during the 1930s, for foreign navies as well.

Since the second half of the nineteenth century, Trieste had been the location for strategically important factories and shipyards and after a few years its port became the most important in the Austro-Hungarian empire. In the early 1850s, the Austrian entrepreneur Georg Strudthoff established there the Fabbrica Macchine S. Andrea, for the production of steam engines, and – some time later – the San Marco shipyard. In 1857, Strudthoff founded at Muggia the Cantiere San

Palermo, 1 March 1943, late afternoon: the dry-dock in the port area flooded and partially destroyed after an Allied air raid. The destroyer *Geniere* (foreground) that was refitting in the dry-dock was seriously damaged by the bombs and, when the dry-dock's gate was destroyed, rapidly flooded, capsized to starboard, and sank. Just below the crane, the upturned motozattera (landing craft) *MZ 743* may be seen. (E Bagnasco collection)

The same dry-dock in late July 1943, with the half-sunk hulk of the destroyer *Geniere*. (US National Archives; A Albergoni collection)

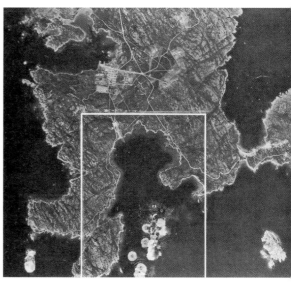

Left: The submarine *Veniero* entering the port of Cagliari on 16 April 1942, with a pirate flag flying from the top of the periscope. She was lost on 7 June 1942, midway between Sardinia and the Balearic Islands, during her next patrol when she was attacked and sunk with the loss of all of her crew by a Sunderland of 204 Squadron, RAF Coastal Command.
(F Petronio collection)

Above: The Porto Palma inlet in the Island of Caprera, west of La Maddalena naval base during the USAAF raid of 10 April 1943. Bombs in the white rectangle (overpainted on the original image) are exploding close to the heavy cruiser *Gorizia*, which was badly damaged. Two days later, with four boilers and two engines out of order, *Gorizia* would depart for La Spezia to be repaired and refitted.
(US National Archives; E Bagnasco collection)

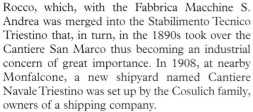

Left: *MAS 543, 546, 547, 548,* and *549* at Trapani in early 1940; all boats are painted in an experimental dull black overall livery, particularly suited for night operations. (Author's collection)

Rocco, which, with the Fabbrica Macchine S. Andrea was merged into the Stabilimento Tecnico Triestino that, in turn, in the 1890s took over the Cantiere San Marco thus becoming an industrial concern of great importance. In 1908, at nearby Monfalcone, a new shipyard named Cantiere Navale Triestino was set up by the Cosulich family, owners of a shipping company.

In September 1930 the Corporation of Cantieri Riuniti dell'Adriatico (CRDA) was established, with Admiral Umberto Cagni, the famous Arctic explorer, as President. Several shipyards were joined in a single company under the CRDA acronym: Cantiere San Marco, Cantiere San Rocco and Fabbrica Macchine S. Andrea of Trieste, the Cantiere Navale Triestino of Monfalcone and quite a number of smaller workshops and yards in Trieste as well as in Gorizia, Pola and Venice.

Last but not least, after the First World War (when the Istrian peninsula was annexed to Italy) the Danubius shipyard of Fiume passed into the control of the 'Orlando' corporation of Leghorn and, renamed Cantieri Navali del Quarnaro, fully resumed its activities in the field of naval construction.

The following list shows the main Italian shipyards that built most warships and submarines in service with the Regia Marina in 1940–5. The yards are listed following the Italian coastline counterclockwise from Genoa to Trieste, and each may be easily identified by the corresponding number on the map on page 33.

Cerusa – Genoa [1]
Corvettes: *Gabbiano* class

Ansaldo – Genoa (Sestri Ponente) [2]
Battleships: *Cesare, Littorio, Impero*

Cruisers: *Bolzano, Da Barbiano, Di Giussano, Colleoni, Montecuccoli, Eugenio di Savoia*
Destroyers: *Mirabello, Leone, Turbine* and 'Navigatori' classes
Torpedo boats: *Spica* and *Ariete* classes
Destroyer escorts: *Animoso* class
Corvettes: *Gabbiano* class

Odero (OTO since 1929) – Genoa (Sestri Ponente) [3]
Destroyers: *Sauro, Turbine*, 'Navigatori' and *Dardo* classes
Torpedo boats (ex-destroyers): *Pilo, Sirtori, La Masa* and 'Generali' classes

Cantieri del Tirreno – Riva Trigoso (Genoa) [4]
Destroyers: *Turbine*, 'Navigatori', *Dardo, Maestrale* and 'Soldati' classes
Torpedo boats: *Spica* class

Destroyer escorts: *Animoso* class

Dockyard – La Spezia [5]
Battleships: *Cavour, Doria*

OTO Muggiano – La Spezia [6]
Cruisers: *Zara, Diaz* and *Abruzzi*
Submarines: *Balilla, Calvi, Cappellini, Marconi, Bandiera, Argonauta, Sirena, Perla, Adua, Acciaio* and *Flutto* classes

Orlando (OTO since 1929) – Leghorn [7]
Cruisers: *Trento, Gorizia, Pola, Aosta, Attilio Regolo* and *Scipione Africano*
Destroyers: *Oriani* and 'Soldati' classes
Torpedo boats (ex-destroyers): *Palestro* and *Curtatone* classes
Corvettes: *Gabbiano* class

Pattison – Naples [8]
Destroyers: *Sella* class
Torpedo boats (ex-destroyers): *Pilo* class

Officine e Cantieri Partenopei – Naples [9]
Destroyers: *Folgore* class

Bacini e Scali Napoletani (Ansaldo Corp.) – Naples [10]
Destroyer escorts: *Orsa* class

Navalmeccanica – Castellammare di Stabia (Naples) [11]
Destroyer escorts: *Animoso* class
Corvettes: *Gabbiano* class

Royal Shipyard – Castellammare di Stabia (Naples) [12]
Battleship: *Duilio*
Cruisers: *Bande Nere* and *Giulio Germanico*

Cantieri Navali Riuniti – Palermo [13]
Cruiser: *Ulpio Traiano*
Destroyers: 'Soldati' class
Destroyer escorts: *Orsa* class

Tosi – Taranto [14]
Submarines: *Fieramosca, Micca, Archimede, Foca, Brin, Liuzzi,* 'R', *Mameli, Bragadin, Argonauta, Settembrini, Sirena, Adua, Acciaio* and *Flutto* classes

Cantieri Navali Riuniti – Ancona [15]
Cruiser: *Pompeo Magno*
Destroyers: 'Navigatori', *Maestrale* and 'Soldati' classes
Torpedo boats: *Spica* class

Breda – Porto Marghera (Venice) [16]
Corvettes: *Gabbiano* class

Cantieri Navali Triestini – Monfalcone [17]
Submarines: *Pisani* and *Bandiera* classes
Cantieri Riuniti dell'Adriatico – Monfalcone
Corvettes: *Gabbiano* class
Submarines: *Glauco, Marcello, Cagni, Squalo, Argonauta, Sirena, Perla, Adua, Argo, Acciaio* and *Flutto* classes

Cantieri Riuniti dell'Adriatico – Trieste [18]

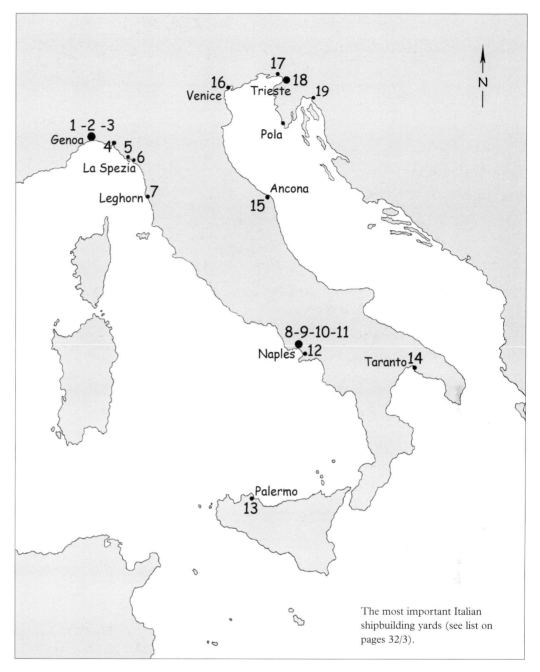

The most important Italian shipbuilding yards (see list on pages 32/3).

Battleships: *Vittorio Veneto* and *Roma*
Cruisers: *Trieste* (★), *Fiume* (★), *Cadorna, Attendolo, Garibaldi*
Destroyer escorts: *Animoso* class
Torpedo boats: *Ariete* class
Corvettes: *Gabbiano* class
(★) as Stabilimento Tecnico Triestino

Cantieri Navali del Quarnaro – Fiume [19]
Destroyers: *Sauro,* 'Navigatori' and *Folgore* classes
Torpedo boats: *Spica* and *Ariete* classes
Submarines: *Sirena* class

Coastal Defences

Italian seacoast fortifications were systematically enhanced from the late 1870s: after a first 'Fortifications Plan' in 1871, a second plan was approved in 1882, providing defences mostly on Italy's western coasts against a potential threat from France.

Although powerful batteries (armed with 13.5in and 12in guns) had been established at La Spezia, La Maddalena, Gaeta and Messina, Italy's entry into the First World War led to new fortifications being built on the Adriatic coast, the most important being the Batteria Amalfi at Venice (with a twin 15in/40 turret) and two batteries defending Brindisi's inlets, both armed with 15in/40 guns (batteries Fratelli Bandiera and Brin, but Battery Brin was not completed until 1922).

In the inter-war period, additional batteries were planned for the defence of the harbours of La Spezia and Augusta; according to plans dating from the mid-1930s Tobruk was to have been defended by thirteen 12in/42 guns and several 8in batteries were to have been built to defend the most important ports and naval bases, but despite such plans many coastal areas remained without up-to-date defences during the Second World War.

In the 1920s and early 1930s, coastal batteries were manned by the Italian Army, but in 1935 the Army's Reggimenti dell'Artiglieria da Costa were

The submarine *Flutto* – name-ship of her class – fitting out at Cantieri Riuniti dell'Adriatico (CRDA), Monfalcone, in early 1943. Some boats of this class were also built at OTO-Muggiano. (Author's collection)

The launch of the heavy cruiser *Bolzano* on 31 August 1932, at the Ansaldo Yard in Genoa. (Author's collection)

The destroyer *Folgore* going down the ways at Officine e Cantieri Partenopei at Naples, on 26 April 1931. (Author's collection)

The scout *Lanzerotto Malocello* on the ways at the
Ansaldo Yard at Genoa in January 1929. *Malocello*
was launched on 14 March 1929 and, like the rest
of the 'Navigatori' class ships, she was reclassified as
a destroyer on 5 September 1938. (Archivio Storico
Ansaldo; Author's collection)

A fine photograph of the Ansaldo Yard in Genoa,
probably taken in 1947–8 when the yard still
retained its wartime appearance. Note the tall
concrete pillars, still camouflaged, supporting a
large number of steel cables used – with the aid of
travelling hooks – to move steel plates and other
heavy pieces of equipment. (Author's collection)

The torpedo boat *Polluce* at Piraeus on 28 August 1942. (Photo A Fraccaroli)

forty-eight single-howitzer emplacements.
• 8in/50 guns – One battery (Luigi di Savoia) with two guns at Augusta.
• 8in/45 guns – One battery with four guns (Rubin de Cervin at La Maddalena) and another four-gun battery nearly completed at Taranto (Toscano).
• 7.4in/39 guns – Two two-gun batteries, one at Pola (Cappa) and one at Naples (Caracciolo).

In addition, other batteries – with 6.1in, 6in, 5.8in, 5.7in, 4.7in, 4in and 3.9in guns – defended the above areas as well as less important naval bases and ports both on the mainland and in the colonies.

For additional shore defence, the Regia Marina had in service several pontoons dating from the First World War, armed with 12in, 7.4in and 5.8in guns, as well as the old monitor *G.M. 194* (ex-*Faà di Bruno*) armed with a 15in/40 twin turret that was used for the defence of the port of Genoa and later of Savona.

On 10 June 1940 the Navy also manned several armed trains, a couple of which saw active service during the few weeks before the surrender of France. These Batterie Mobili Ferroviarie ('Mobile Railway Batteries') were operationally divided into two Groups, whose commands were located at Genoa and Palermo and with logistic facilities, respectively, at La Spezia and Taranto.

The Genoa Group operated four trains armed with 4.7in/45 guns, one with 6in/40 guns and one with 76mm/40 guns; The Palermo Group had four trains with 6in guns, one with 4in guns and one with 76mm guns. All trains were armed with 13.2mm machine guns, later replaced with 20mm cannon on a one-for-one basis.

From left to right, the colonial sloop *Eritrea* and the destroyers *Tigre* and *Pantera* at anchor at Massawa in 1938. (A Fraccaroli collection)

replaced by independent units of the Milizia Costiera; in 1938, the Milizia Costiera was renamed 'Milmart' (Milizia Artiglieria Marittima) and, under the direct control of the Navy, manned the shore batteries that defended Augusta, Brindisi, Cagliari, La Maddalena, La Spezia, Messina, Pantelleria, Pola, Taranto, Trapani and Venice.

Soon after Italy's entry into the Second World War, the first enemy action against the Italian mainland was a French naval bombardment of the industrial areas of Genoa and Savona on 14 June 1940. Genoa's harbour was defended by several medium-calibre coastal batteries and by some armed trains, but they were unable to drive off the enemy warships; nevertheless, the French destroyer *Albatros* was hit by a 6in shell from Batteria Mameli at Pegli (in the hills west of Genoa) that caused considerable damage.

The very heavy British naval bombardment of Genoa on 9 February 1941 prompted the Italian Army to build two 15in/40 batteries on the hills above the city, one east and one west of the centre; these two huge fortifications were completed in summer of 1942, but never had the chance to fire their guns in anger.

In July 1943, in the weeks before the invasion of Sicily and the beginning of the 'Italian campaign', the most important coastal batteries on the Italian mainland were the following:

• 15in/40 guns – Six batteries, all armed with a twin turret (Batteries Brin and Fratelli Bandiera at Brindisi, Amalfi at Venice, Opera A at Augusta and the two batteries at Genoa, located at Monte Moro [east] and Arenzano [west]).
• 12in/50 guns – Three batteries with six guns in total (Batteries Dandolo, Emo and San Marco, all at Venice).
• 12in/42 guns – Battery Cattaneo with three guns, at Taranto, not yet completed as of 8 September 1943.
• 12in/17 howitzers – Four batteries (each with four howitzers) located at La Spezia (Cascino and Cavour) and at La Maddalena (Pes di Villamarina and De Caroli).
• 11in/9 howitzers – Batteries on both sides of the Straits of Messina: in 1942 four batteries (with twenty-two howitzers) were operational, but on 10 June 1940 there were eight batteries with

The hull of the battleship *Impero* on Ansaldo's building ways at Genova Sestri Ponente in late October 1939, a few days before her launch on 15 November 1939. (Archivio Storico Ansaldo; Author's collection)

The corvettes *Pellicano* (left) and *Cormorano* under construction at the Cerusa Yard in Genoa, in 1942. (Author's collection)

A 6in/50 gun of Emmanuele Russo Battery at Syracuse, soon after the fall of the city to the Allies. (IWN NA 4602)

One of the 15in/40 guns of the Monte Moro Battery (west of Genoa) being moved, in late 1941, to the top of the hill where the battery was under construction. (E Bagnasco collection)

The coast defences of the Augusta-Syracuse area in July 1943. Note, just north of Syracuse, Opera A with a twin 15in/40 turret. (Courtesy *STORIA militare*)

• anti-ship battery
• anti-aircraft battery
• anti-ship & anti-aircraft battery

General plan showing the coast defences of the Island of Leros in the Dodecanese from an original Italian map of the early 1940s. (Ufficio Storico della Marina Militare)

The 15in/40 twin turret of Opera A at Capo Santa Panagia, on the coast south of Augusta. The turret was protected by a concrete roof; the magazines and auxiliary machinery were housed in hardened tunnels beneath the turret. (Ufficio Storico della Marina Militare)

Treno Armato (Armoured Train) 120/2/S during gunnery exercises near Deiva Marina (east of Genoa) in late summer of 1940. (Author's collection)

CHAPTER 3

Fleet Organisation and Operations

UNTIL 1933, THE POSTS of Minister of the Navy and Capo di Stato Maggiore della Marina (equivalent to the Chief of Naval Operations of the US Navy and to the British Commander-in-Chief Fleet) were kept separate, thus keeping operational and administrative command apart. In that year, the Navy's CinC – ranking as a Minister on the authority of Mussolini himself – was made an operational commander only, and the political leadership of the Navy was assumed by Mussolini who served as Navy Minister (as well as Minister of War and for Air) until 25 July 1943.

Thus, for the period covered by this book, the post of Ministro della Marina (Minister of the Navy) was held by Adm. Giuseppe Sirianni from 1929 to 1933, and by Mussolini from 1933 until July 1943; during the same period, five admirals were appointed Capo di Stato Maggiore della Marina, as listed below:

1927–31: Ammiraglio d'Armata Ernesto Burzagli
1931–4: Ammiraglio d'Armata Gino Ducci
1934–40: Ammiraglio d'Armata Domenico Cavagnari
1940–3: Ammiraglio d'Armata Arturo Riccardi
1943–6: Ammiraglio di Squadra Raffaele de Courten

Between 1919 and 1940, the 'Ufficio di Stato Maggiore' of the Regia Marina consisted of three main Departments: Intelligence, Naval Operations and Training, and a support organisation for mobilisation, coast defence and miscellaneous services; four additional Inspectorates (naval weapons and ammunition, underwater weapons, naval engineering and naval aviation) were established in 1938–9.

The Abyssinian war of 1935–6 had demonstrated the need for a centralised command structure, and in 1938 plans were drawn up to transform the 1st Naval Operations Section of the Naval Operations and Training Department into a full operational command to plan and direct all Italian naval activities in wartime. In May 1940, Mussolini – as supreme commander – determined to reform the Navy's top structure which, from that time, consisted of an operational central command (Supermarina) and various departments and inspectorates controlled by the reformed structure of the Stato Maggiore ('Maristat').

During the war, the top level of Supermarina included the Navy's Commander-in-Chief and his deputy, four Admirals assisting them, and a large staff of officers; other Admirals assigned to Supermarina were the chiefs of the Operations and Plans bureaux, and liaison officers assigned to Comando Supremo, i.e. the unified military high command.

Although Supermarina was generally speaking a well-organised and efficient command, in several

Battle of Punta Stilo, 9 July 1940: *Cesare* firing a salvo from her 12.6in guns, as seen from aboard *Cavour*. This picture must have been taken between 15.53 (when the two battleships opened fire) and 15.59, when *Cesare* was damaged by a 15in direct hit from HMS *Warspite*; soon after, the two ships would begin to disengage from the action. (Istituto Luce, Rome; Author's collection)

cases its operating procedures were rather cumbersome and complex, particularly when cooperating with the Regia Aeronautica: this often meant that orders issued reflected the situation some hours ago rather than as it was at the time. Also, because of the seniority of the naval officers at Supermarina, commanders at sea often failed to act on their own initiative, even though they may well have had a clearer grasp of the tactical situation than the commanders ashore in Rome.

Daily activity at Supermarina took place in a hardened operations room, with a large map of the Mediterranean on the wall where the positions of Italian and enemy ships were displayed. An Admiral (or Rear-Admiral) was always on duty there and, if necessary, could give orders directly to ships at sea or even order ships to sail from their ports or naval bases; when the situation was particularly serious (for instance, when large convoys were at sea, or when strong enemy forces were reported approaching the central Mediterranean), the Commander-in-Chief or his deputy went to the operations room. Until 31 January 1943 the operations room was located in the Navy Building (the Palazzo Marina) in Rome on the east bank of the Tiber; on 1 February 1943, Supermarina was moved to a well-protected location outside Rome, in Santa Rosa, where the Italian Navy's Command and Communications Centre is still located today.

The daily routine at Supermarina usually began at 08.00 (at the changing of the guard), when all the documents, messages and records related to the previous day had to have been processed and filed. Around 11.30 a meeting – with the deputy Commander-in-Chief as chairman – was held to discuss the actions and orders for the next 24 hours, and the decisions taken during this meeting (if not particularly

important and urgent) would go to the Commander-in-Chief for approval before the following morning.

As for operational, personnel and technical responsibilities in home, Mediterranean and colonial waters, since 1932 Dipartimenti or Comandi Militari Marittimi ('naval departments', each one with jurisdiction over specific coastal and sea areas), with lesser subordinate commands (Comandi Marina), became the standard in the

Fire damage aboard the battleship *Cesare*, after she was hit by a 15in shell from HMS *Warspite* that, hitting the Italian battleship on the starboard side, perforated a funnel and detonated on the port side. (E Bagnasco collection)

Navy's chain of command, and they were subdivided as follows:

The battleship HMS *Warspite* at Punta Stilo, with a salvo of Italian 12.6in rounds falling astern. The shots are probably from *Cesare* as it is not certain if *Cavour* fired against *Warspite* or against the other British battleships (*Malaya* and *Royal Sovereign*) astern of her. (Author's collection)

Home waters
Comando in Capo del Dipartimento dell'Alto Tirreno (La Spezia)
- Comando Marina Genova [Genoa]
- Comando Marina Livorno
- Comando Militare Marittimo of the Elba/Piombino Area

Comando in Capo del Dipartimento del Basso Tirreno (Naples)
- Comando Marina Gaeta
- Comando Marina Civitavecchia
- Comando Servizi Marina (Auxiliary services) Naples
- Comando Servizi Marina (Auxiliary services) Castellammare di Stabia

Comando Militare Marittimo in Sardegna [Sardinia] (La Maddalena)
- Comando Marina Porto Torres
- Comando Marina Olbia
- Comando Settore Militare Marittimo (Cagliari)

Comando Militare Marittimo in Sicilia (Messina)
- Comando Servizi Marina (Auxiliary services) Messina
- Comando Settore Militare Marittimo (Augusta /Siracusa)
- Comando Marina Catania
- Comando Marina Palermo
- Comando Settore Militare Marittimo (Trapani)
- Comando Marina Porto Empedocle
- Comando Marina Pantelleria

Comando in Capo del Dipartimento dello Ionio e del Basso Adriatico (Taranto)
- Comando Marina Crotone
- Comando Marina Gallipoli
- Comando Militare Marittimo (Brindisi)
- Comando Marina Bari
- Comando Marina Otranto
- Comando Marina Lagosta

Comando Militare Marittimo Autonomo Alto Adriatico (Venice)
- Comando Marina Ancona
- Comando Militare Marittimo (Pola)
- Comando Marina Zara
- Comando Marina Trieste
- Comando Militare Marittimo (Lussino)
- Comando Servizi Marina (Auxiliary services) Lussino
- Comando Marina Fiume

Foreign waters
Comando Militare Marittimo in Albania (Durazzo)
- Comando Marina Durazzo
- Comando Marina Valona/Saseno
- Comando Marina Porto Edda (Santi Quaranta)
- Comando Marina San Giovanni di Medua

Colonies
Comando Militare Marittimo Isole Italiane dell'Egeo (Rodi) [Rhodes]
- Comando Marina Lero
- Comando Marina Stampalia
- Comando Servizi Marina (Auxiliary services) Rodi

Comando Superiore Marina in Libia (Tripoli)
- Comando Marina Tripoli
- Comando Marina Bengazi
- Comando Settore Militare Marittimo (Tobruk)

Comando Superiore Marina in Africa Orientale Italiana (Massawa)
- Comando Marina Massaua
- Comando Marina Assab
- Comando Marina Chisimaio

From 1928, the Italian fleet was divided in to two Squadre (large naval groups), the 1ª Squadra based at La Spezia and the 2ª Squadra at Taranto. In 1935 it was planned to combine the two Squadre into a single fleet with a centralised operational command, and the Comando in Capo delle Forze Navali Riunite was established aboard the heavy cruiser *Pola*; nevertheless, there were still two Squadre when Italy declared war on Great Britain and France, and they were united for the first time at the battle of Punta Stilo on 9 July 1940. The submarine command (Squadra sommergibili) and other departmental and local naval commands remained independent throughout the war.

On 10 June 1940, the Regia Marina was therefore still divided into the 1ª Squadra and 2ª Squadra and the list that follows shows in detail the composition of the various battleship and cruiser divisions (Divisioni) and destroyer and torpedo boat flotillas (Squadriglie) on that date

---

Note:
Each battleship or cruiser division is followed by the accompanying destroyer flotillas.

1ª Squadra Navale
(CinC Adm. Campioni – *Cesare*)

5ª Divisione Navi da Battaglia
Cesare (Radm. Brivonesi), *Cavour*
7ª Squadriglia cacciatorpediniere
Freccia, Dardo, Saetta, Strale
8ª Squadriglia cacciatorpediniere
Folgore, Fulmine, Lampo, Baleno

9ª Divisione Navi da Battaglia
Littorio (Radm. Bergamini), *Veneto*
14ª Squadriglia cacciatorpediniere
Vivaldi, Da Noli, Pancaldo
15ª Squadriglia cacciatorpediniere
Pigafetta, Zeno, Da Mosto, Da Verazzano, Malocello

1ª Divisione incrociatori pesanti
Zara (Radm. Matteucci), *Gorizia, Fiume*
9ª Squadriglia cacciatorpediniere
Alfieri, Oriani, Carducci, Gioberti

4ª Divisione incrociatori leggeri
Da Barbiano (Radm. Marenco), *Cadorna, Di Giussano* (Radm. Da Zara), *Diaz*

8ª Divisione incrociatori leggeri
Duca degli Abruzzi (Radm. Legnani), *Garibaldi*
16ª Squadriglia cacciatorpediniere
Da Recco, Usodimare, Tarigo, Pessagno

Auxiliaries
Seaplane tender *Miraglia*; tankers *Isonzo, Po* and *Garda*; tugs *Atlante* and *Lipari*
24 seaplanes

2ª Squadra navale
(CinC Adm. Paladini – *Pola*)
Cruiser *Pola*
12ª Squadriglia cacciatorpediniere
Lanciere, Carabiniere, Corazziere, Ascari

2ª Divisione incrociatori pesanti
Trento (Radm. Cattaneo), *Bolzano, Trieste*
11ª Squadriglia cacciatorpediniere
Artigliere, Camicia Nera, Aviere, Geniere

7ª Divisione incrociatori leggeri
Eugenio di Savoia (Radm. Sansonetti), *Duca d'Aosta, Attendolo, Montecuccoli*
13ª Squadriglia cacciatorpediniere
Granatiere, Fuciliere, Bersagliere, Alpino

2ª Divisione incrociatori leggeri
Bande Nere (Radm. Casardi), *Colleoni*
10ª Squadriglia cacciatorpediniere
Maestrale, Libeccio, Grecale, Scirocco

Auxiliaries
Repair ship *Quarnaro*; water tankers *Volturno, Istria, Flegetonte* and *Mincio*; tanker *Cocito*; tugs *Ercole* and *Portoferraio*
20 seaplanes
One minesweeper flotilla at Taranto, Messina, Palermo and Augusta respectively.

Squadra Sommergibili
(Adm. Falangola)

1° Gruppo (La Spezia)
11ª Squadriglia sommergibili
Calvi, Finzi, Tazzoli, Fieramosca
12ª Squadriglia sommergibili
Cappellini, Faà di Bruno, Mocenigo, Veniero, Glauco, Otaria
13ª Squadriglia sommergibili
Berillo, Onice, Gemma
14ª Squadriglia sommergibili
Iride, Argo, Velella
15ª Squadriglia sommergibili
Gondar, Neghelli, Ascianghi, Scirè
16ª Squadriglia sommergibili
Micca, Foca
17ª Squadriglia sommergibili
H1, H2, H3, H4, H6, H8

2° Gruppo (Naples)
21ª Squadriglia sommergibili
Marcello, Nani, Dandolo, Provana
22ª Squadriglia sommergibili
Barbarigo, Emo, Morosini, Marconi, Da Vinci

3° Gruppo sommergibili (Messina)
31ª Squadriglia sommergibili
Pisani, Colonna, Bausan, Des Geneys
33ª Squadriglia sommergibili
Bandiera, Manara, Menotti, Santarosa
34ª Squadriglia sommergibili
Mameli, Capponi, Speri, Da Procida
35ª Squadriglia sommergibili
Durbo, Tembien, Beilul
37ª Squadriglia sommergibili
X2, X3

4° Gruppo sommergibili (Taranto)
40ª Squadriglia sommergibili
Balilla, Sciesa, Toti, Millelire
41ª Squadriglia sommergibili
Liuzzi, Bagnolini, Giuliani, Tarantini
42ª Squadriglia sommergibili
Brin
43ª Squadriglia sommergibili
Settimo, Settembrini
44ª Squadriglia sommergibili
Anfitrite
45ª Squadriglia sommergibili
Salpa, Serpente

46ª Squadriglia sommergibili
Dessié, Dagabur, Uarsciek, Uebi Scebeli
47ª Squadriglia sommergibili
Malachite, Rubino, Ambra
48ª Squadriglia sommergibili
Ondina
49ª Squadriglia sommergibili
Atropo, Zoea, Corridoni

5° Gruppo sommergibili (Cagliari)
71ª Squadriglia sommergibili
Alagi, Adua, Axum, Aradam
72ª Squadriglia sommergibili
Diaspro, Corallo, Turchese, Medusa

Local Naval Commands ('Forze Dipartimentali')
Settore Alto Tirreno
(CinC Adm. Savoia Aosta – La Spezia)
10ª Squadriglia torpediniere
Vega, Sagittario, Perseo, Sirio
16ª Squadriglia torpediniere
Monzambano, Curtatone, Castelfidardo, Calatafimi
1ª Flottiglia MAS
Turr plus twenty MAS (1ª, 5ª, 12ª, 13ª and 14ª Squadriglia)
Auxiliaries
Minelayers *Orlando, Gasperi, Crotone* and *Fasana*; transport *Matteucci*; gunboat *Rimini*; water tanker *Dalmazia*

Settore Basso Tirreno
(CinC Adm. Pini – Naples)
3ª Squadriglia torpediniere
Carini, La Masa, Prestinari, Cantore
4ª Squadriglia torpediniere
Procione, Orione, Orsa, Pegaso
Auxiliaries
Minelayers *Partenope* and *Buffoluto*; water tankers *Arno* and *Metauro*

Sardegna
(Radm. Sportiello – La Maddalena)
2ª Squadriglia torpediniere
Papa, Montanari, Cascino, Chinotto
9ª Squadriglia torpediniere
Cassiopea, Canopo, Cairoli, Mosto
4ª Squadriglia MAS
4 MAS
Auxiliaries
Minelayers *Durazzo, Pelagosa, Caralis, Deffenu, Mazara*

Sicilia
(Radm. Barone – Messina)
1ª Flottiglia torpediniere
13ª Squadriglia torpediniere
Circe, Clio, Calliope, Calipso
14ª Squadriglia torpediniere
Partenope, Polluce, Pleiadi, Pallade
2ª Flottiglia torpediniere
12ª Squadriglia torpediniere
Altair, Antares, Aldebaran, Andromeda
3ª Squadriglia torpediniere
Airone, Ariel, Aretusa, Alcione
2ª Flottiglia MAS
16 MAS (2ª, 9ª, 10ª, and 15ª Squadriglia)
Auxiliaries
Minelayers *Buccari, Scilla, Brioni* and *Adriatico*; submarine tenders *Volta* and *Pacinotti*; water tankers *Verde, Prometeo, Bormida* and *Brenta*

Settore Ionio e Basso Adriatico
(Adm. Pasetti – Taranto)
Light cruisers *Bari* and *Taranto*
2ª Squadriglia cacciatorpediniere
Espero, Borea, Zeffiro, Ostro
6ª Squadriglia torpediniere
Pilo, Stocco, Missori, Sirtori
Auxiliaries
Minelayers *Barletta, Vieste, Otranto* and *Gallipoli*; transports *Cherso* and
Lussino; water tankers/landing ships *Sesia, Garigliano* and *Tirso*

Brindisi
(Radm. Spalice – Brindisi)
Destroyers *Riboty* and *Mirabello*
7ª Squadriglia torpediniere
Bassini, Cosenz, Fabrizi, Medici
3ª Squadriglia MAS (3 vessels)
Auxiliaries
Gunboat *Cirene*

Settore Alto Adriatico
(Adm. Ferdinando di Savoia – Genova, Venice)
15ª Squadriglia torpediniere
Confienza, Solferino, San Martino, Palestro
Sail training ships *Colombo, Vespucci*
Auxiliaries
Minelayers *Albona, Laurana* and *Rovigno*

Pola
(Radm. Bobbiese)
Gunboat *Giovannini*
6ª Squadriglia MAS (4 vessels)
Auxiliaries
Minelayers *Azio, San Giorgio* and *San Giusto*; small tanker *Lete*; water
tankers *Scrivia* and *Verbano*

Settore Albania
(Adm. Turr – Durazzo)
Auxiliaries
Water tanker *Pagano*: minesweepers *Vigilante* and *Vedetta*

Settore Egeo
(Adm Biancheri – Rodi)
4ª Squadriglia cacciatorpediniere
Crispi, Sella
8ª Squadriglia torpediniere
Lupo, Lince, Lira, Libra
5° Gruppo sommergibili
51ª Squadriglia sommergibili
Narvalo, Squalo, Tricheco, Delfino
52ª Squadriglia sommergibili
Jalea, Iantina, Ametista, Zaffiro
3ª Flottiglia MAS
15 MAS (7ª, 11ª, 16ª and 22ª Squadriglia)
Auxiliaries
Minelayers *Lero* and *Legnano*; gunboats *Sonzini* and *Caboto*; tanker *Cerere*

Settore Libia
(Radm. Brivonesi – Bengazi)

Tripoli/Bengazi
11ª Squadriglia torpediniere
Cigno, Castore, Climene, Centauro
Auxiliaries
Minelayer *Monte Gargano*; gunboat *Alula*

Tobruk
Armoured cruiser *San Giorgio*
1ª Squadriglia cacciatorpediniere
Turbine, Aquilone, Euro, Nembo
6° Gruppo sommergibili
61ª Squadriglia sommergibili
Sirena, Argonauta, Fisalia, Smeraldo, Naiade
62ª Squadriglia sommergibili
Diamante, Topazio, Nereide, Galatea, Lafolè
Auxiliaries
Gunboats *Palmaiola, De Lutti, Grazioli Lante, Berta, Valoroso*; water tankers
Lina Campanella, Ticino and *Polifemo*

Settore Africa Orientale
(Radm. Balsamo)

Comando Superiore Navale
Colonial ship *Eritrea* (Capt. Zamboni)
3ª Squadriglia cacciatorpediniere
Nullo, Sauro, Manin, Battisti
5ª Squadriglia cacciatorpediniere
Pantera, Tigre, Leone
Flottiglia sommergibili
81ª Squadriglia sommergibili
Guglielmotti, Ferraris, Galvani, Galilei
2ª Squadriglia sommergibili
Perla, Macallé, Archimede, Torricelli

Massawa
Torpedo boats *Acerbi* and *Orsini*
21ª Squadriglia MAS (5 vessels)
Auxiliaries
Gunboats *Porto Corsini* and *Biglieri*; minelayer *Ostia*; water tankers *Sile,
Sebeto* and *Bacchiglione*

Settore Estremo Orientale
(Lt.Cdr. Galletti)
Minelayer *Lepanto*; gunboat *Carlotto*

Naviglio Ausiliario Autonomo
(Subordinate to the Navy's General Staff)

Yachts/Gunboats *Savoia, Aurora, Illiria*
Target ship *San Marco*
Hydrographic ships *Magnaghi* and *Cariddi*
Transports *Enrichetta, Tripoli, Vallelunga, Panigaglia, Asmara*
Hospital ship *Aquileia*
Cable ships *Città di Milano* and *Giasone*
Tankers *Tarvisio, Brennero, Urano, Bronte, Nettuno, Giove* and *Marte*
Gasoline tanker *Stige*
Tugs *Teseo, Titano, Ciclope, Marettimo, Luni, Egadi, Nereo, Marsigli* and
Montecristo

The two Squadre operated independently until 9 December 1940, when a unified Comando in Capo della Squadra Navale was established; on 12 January 1942 the two-Squadra system was re-instituted, but – by now – they were to operate as a single fleet called the Forze Navali ('Naval Forces'), under the command of the Admiral commanding the 1ª Squadra (Comandante in Capo delle Forze Navali, i.e. 'CinC, Naval Forces'), while the Admiral commanding the 2ª Squadra was second in command to the CinC, Naval Forces (these changes to the order of battle and command positions took place when Adm. Angelo Iachino was relieved of the command of the Forze Navali and replaced by Adm. Carlo Bergamini).

On 1 January 1943, the six battleships of the Regia Marina were reunited in the 1ª Squadra (Adm. Bergamini), and all of the cruisers in the 2ª Squadra (Adm. Iachino) but three months later – on 1 April – the subdivision of the

The cruiser *Bartolomeo Colleoni* off Cape Spada (north-western Crete) at the beginning of the encounter during which she was sunk by HMAS *Sydney* and by the destroyers accompanying the Australian cruiser. This photograph was taken from aboard the *Bande Nere* around 07.40 on 19 July 1940: notice that *Colleoni* is laying a smokescreen, while an 'over' – but well-grouped – salvo from *Sydney* is falling off *Colleoni's* starboard bow quarter. (Author's collection)

Italian fleet into two separate units was abolished again, the Comando in Capo Forze Navali da Battaglia ('CinC, Naval Battle Forces') under the command of Adm. Bergamini being created by Supermarina. Adm. Bergamini's flagship was the *Littorio*, as part of the 9ª Divisione Navi da Battaglia (Radm. Accoretti) along with *Vittorio Veneto* and *Roma*; the other three battleships (*Duilio*, *Doria* and *Cesare*) formed the 5ª Divisione Navi da Battaglia (Radm. Brenta, flying his flag on the *Duilio*).

After the Armistice and the loss of *Roma* (which had become Bergamini's flagship), most of the ships of the Regia Marina were concentrated at Malta, where the Comando Superiore delle Forze Navali was established under the two-star flag of Radm. Alberto Da Zara (Bergamini's second-in-command) who led the Italian fleet after the loss of *Roma* and the death of Adm. Bergamini himself.

During the war, other naval commands were established in order to conduct specific activities or to operate in specific areas in the Mediterranean or elsewhere. Among them, these were the most significant:

• On 1 September 1940 the Comando Gruppo Sommergibili Atlantico ('Betasom', Atlantic Submarine Command, Bordeaux) was established at Bordeaux. This was later renamed Comando Superiore Forze Subacquee in Atlantico; three submarines were based in Bordeaux in September, but no less than twenty-one boats were based there by November 1940 and twenty-seven in June 1941; war losses, and the general Italian military situation, led to a decrease in numbers from mid-1942 onwards, and by 8 September 1943 – only seven boats remained at Bordeaux.

• The Forza Navale Speciale (FNS, Special Naval Force) was created on 21 October 1940 with the task of conducting landing operations and, in particular, to plan and execute landings in Malta in

mid-1942; the FNS conducted landing operations at Cefalonia in May 1941, at Cattaro in July 1941 and in Corsica in November 1942, being disbanded a few months later, in January 1943.

• On 10 August 1941 the Ispettorato dei mezzi antisommergibili ('Mariantisom', i.e. 'Anti-submarine Warfare Command' was formed to co-ordinate various anti-submarine escort groups whose number was increased during the war: on 1 August 1943 these groups were based at Toulon, La Spezia, La Maddalena, Naples, Taranto, Brindisi, in Greece (Argostoli, Piraeus and Leros), Messina and Palermo. Smaller anti-submarine units (often formed with old or requisitioned trawlers) were based in Nice, Civitavecchia, Gaeta, Bastia, Crotone, Gallipoli, Spalato, Augusta and Trapani.

• The complex activities of Italian convoys bound for the Aegean and to North Africa required the

establishment of the Comando Difesa Traffico ('Maricotraf'), along with several specific branches:
- Comando Motonavi Veloci ('Mariconvo', i.e. 'Fast Merchant Vessels Command'), that began operating in Naples in March 1942;
- Comando Gruppo incrociatori Ausiliari e Navi Trasporto ('Maritrasporti'), with jurisdiction over auxiliary cruisers;
- Comando Superiore del Dragaggio ('Maridrag') co-ordinating the very large number of minesweeper groups scattered throughout home waters as well as in the Aegean and North Africa.

A specific command for both surface and underwater assault craft operations ('Generalmas') was established early in the war, and the actions of its surface and underwater craft will be dealt with in a separate chapter.

The battleship *Caio Duilio* in Taranto's Mar Grande on the morning of 12 November 1940, damaged and half sunk the night before by a British aerial torpedo launched by a Fairey Swordfish during the night attack of 11 November 1940. (E Bagnasco collection)

The Regia Marina at war 1940–5 – a brief chronology

1940

4–8 June
Italian submarines leave their bases for their assigned patrol areas (fifty-five in the Mediterranean, two in the Atlantic and four in the Red Sea/Indian Ocean).

10 June
Italian declaration of war against Great Britain and France; more than one-third of the Italian merchant fleet is caught by surprise in neutral ports and is consequently interned.

12 June
The light cruiser HMS *Calypso* is sunk west of Crete by the submarine *Bagnolini*.

14 June
Bombardment by French warships of industrial areas and factories in the Savona and Vado Ligure area; coastal batteries return fire, and the French squadron is attacked by the torpedo boat *Calatafimi*.

18 June
Urgent supplies are transported to Libya by the submarines *Zoea*, *Bragadin* and *Corridoni*.

25 June
The first Italian convoy bound for Libya leaves Naples (the liners *Esperia* and *Victoria* with troops and supplies, escorted by the ships of the 4ª Squadriglia Torpediniere).

28 June
British cruisers sink the destroyer *Espero*, ferrying supplies to Libya along with her two sister-ships, in the central Mediterranean.

3 July
The Royal Navy's Force H attacks French warships moored at Mers-el-Kebir. The battleship *Bretagne* is sunk, and *Dunkerque* and *Provence* are heavily damaged. The *Strasbourg* manages to leave Mers-el-Kebir bound for Toulon.

9 July
Battle of Punta Stilo between the Regia Marina and the Royal Navy off the eastern coast of Calabria; both fleets are at sea to provide distant escort for convoys. The *Cesare* is damaged and the Italian ships break contact.

10 July
The destroyer *Pancaldo* is sunk at Augusta by British torpedo bombers; she will later be refloated and rebuilt.

19 July
Off Cape Spada (western Crete) the light cruiser *Colleoni* is sunk by HMAS *Sydney* and accompanying destroyers.

15 August
The submarine *Delfino* torpedoes and sinks the small Greek cruiser *Helli* off the island of Tinos. Tension between Italy and Greece (still neutral) increases.

30 August / 6 September
British Operations 'Hats' and 'M.B.3' to reinforce the Mediterranean Fleet; five Italian battleships are at sea but, in part because of the very bad weather, no contact with enemy ships is established.

End of September/beginning of October
British Operations 'M.B.5' (23 September – 4 October) and 'M.B.6' (8–14 October) to supply Malta. Again, the Italian fleet does not make contact with the enemy. On the 12th, west of Malta, British cruisers sink the destroyer *Artigliere* and the torpedo boats *Airone* and *Ariel*.

30 October
First attack on Gibraltar by Italian human torpedoes ('SLC') ferried by the submarine *Sciré* has to be abandoned due to technical problems.

11–12 November
Torpedo bombers from HMS *Illustrious* attack the Italian battle fleet at Taranto. *Cavour* is heavily damaged and, although refloated and transferred to Trieste for rebuilding, will never return to service. *Littorio* and *Duilio* are also damaged and have to be beached to prevent them sinking.

27 November
Battle of Cape Teulada (south-western Sardinia): no significant results.

18 December
Naval bombardment (by *Montecuccoli*, *Eugenio di Savoia* and four destroyers) of Greek positions in the Lukova area in the north of Corfu.

This photograph – taken from on board the light cruiser *Garibaldi* at about 11.00 on 27 March 1941 – is perhaps the best known of those related to the ill-fated Operation 'Gaudo', and the last showing the three *Zara* class heavy cruisers, lost on the night of 28 March during the action south of Cape Matapan. *Fiume*, which had been camouflaged with an experimental scheme a few weeks before, is third from left and appears darker than the other ships (from left to right, *Zara*, *Pola* and *Duca degli Abruzzi*). (E Bagnasco collection)

A P. 200 mine is released from the stern of a cruiser during a minelaying mission. The P. 200 type was one of the most common and effective mines of the Second World War: with a weight of 1,100kg, it could be moored in more than 800m of water and could also be used in an anti-submarine role. (E Bagnasco collection)

1941

6–13 January
British Operation 'Excess' to resupply Malta from Gibraltar and Greece from Alexandria. Torpedo boat *Vega* is sunk in the Canale di Sicilia; Italian and German aircraft damage HMS *Warspite* and *Illustrious* and sink the cruiser HMS *Southampton*.

9 February
The British Force H (HMS *Malaya*, *Renown*, *Ark Royal*, *Sheffield* and accompanying destroyers) bombards Genoa. Three Italian battleships, three cruisers and several destroyers do not intercept the enemy ships on their way back to Gibraltar due to failures in communications and air reconnaissance.

26 March
First success of Italian surface assault craft: six 'barchini' (explosive motorboats) attack Suda Bay at Crete, seriously damaging the heavy cruiser HMS *York* and a tanker.

26–29 March
Italian Operation 'Gaudo' south of Crete, with the battleship *Vittorio Veneto*, eight cruisers and several destroyers involved. The naval action off Gaudo is inconclusive, but on the way back to Taranto the Italian squadron is attacked by British torpedo bombers that damage the *Vittorio Veneto* and stop the cruiser *Pola* dead in the water. The *Pola*, *Zara* and *Fiume* and the destroyers *Alfieri* and *Carducci* are sunk in the ensuing battle of Cape Matapan.

27 March
Pro-British *coup d'etat* in Yugoslavia.

31 March
South of Crete the submarine *Ambra* sinks the British cruiser HMS *Bonaventure* (the largest warship sunk by an Italian submarine in the Second World War).

6 April
Italy and Germany attack Yugoslavia; German troops invade Greece from the north.

8 April
The fall of Massawa marks the end of all Italian naval operations in the Red Sea.

16 April
Naval action off the Kerkennah Shoals (Tunisia). Loss of the destroyers *Tarigo* and *Baleno* and five merchant ships – HMS *Mohawk* is, in turn, sunk by *Tarigo*'s torpedoes.

17 April
Most ships of the Yugoslavian Navy are captured by the Regia Marina at Cattaro, Sebenico and in minor ports on the Dalmatian coast.

27–28 April
Fall of Athens to the Germans; Rommel's Afrika Korps captures the Egyptian stronghold of Sollum.

20 May
Invasion of Crete begins; the torpedo boats *Lupo* and *Sagittario* engage superior enemy naval forces north of the island.

24 May
The liner *Conte Rosso*, ferrying troops to North Africa, is torpedoed and sunk off Syracuse by HMS *Upholder*.

28 May
British troops leave Crete. The Royal Navy loses three cruisers and six destroyers during the evacuation.

22 June
German attack against the USSR; Italy and Romania also declare war.

21–27 July
Successful British Operation 'Substance' to resupply Malta from Gibraltar.

26 July
Attack by surface and underwater assault craft of the 'Xª Flottiglia MAS' against Malta. Most of the craft are destroyed and their crews captured or killed.

22–26 August
British Operation 'Mincemeat', against dams and industrial targets in Sardinia, to cover a minelaying operation off Leghorn. The battleships *Littorio* and *Vittorio Veneto* and eight cruisers are dispatched to intercept the British ships, but no contact is made.

18 September
Off Tripoli, HMS *Upholder* torpedoes and sinks the liners *Neptunia* and *Oceania*, ferrying troops to Libya.

21 September
First success of Italian human torpedoes against Gibraltar (three merchant ships damaged or sunk). *U-371* – the first of sixty-two German submarines sent into the Mediterranean – enters the Straits of Gibraltar eastbound.

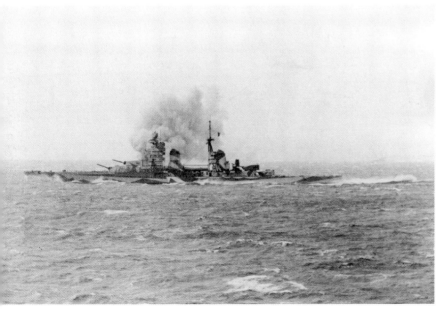

The heavy cruiser *Gorizia* firing her 8in guns on 22 March 1942, during the 'Seconda battaglia della Sirte'. The Italian cruisers accompanying *Littorio* (*Gorizia*, *Trento* and *Bande Nere*) fired on the British light cruisers *Cleopatra*, *Euryalus*, *Dido* and *Penelope*, but both sides failed to score any significant hits. (A Fraccaroli collection)

The cruiser *Bolzano* off Panarea, Aeolian Islands, on the afternoon of 13 August 1942. The *Bolzano* had been torpedoed late in the morning by the British submarine HMS *Unbroken* and, on fire and down by the bow, was grounded in 12m of water to prevent her sinking, but during the manoeuvre she listed dangerously 45° to port and was abandoned by her crew. Some time later, part of the crew reboarded the ship and managed to reduce the listing; the fire was only extinguished in the afternoon of 14 August. The camouflage of the destroyer on the right clearly identifies the ship as *Geniere*. (N Siracusano collection)

The naval base of La Spezia during an air raid by B-17 bombers of the 12th Bomber Command USAAF, flying from Algiers, at around 13.45 on 5 June 1943. The battleship at right is *Littorio* and, at the extreme right, the heavy cruiser *Bolzano* may be seen. The *Littorio* was not hit, but *Vittorio Veneto* was damaged and had to be moved to Genoa for repairs, getting back into service on 1 July. (E Bagnasco collection)

The battleship *Roma*, listing to starboard after having been hit by the second German PC 1400X glider bomb launched by German aircraft off Asinara Island, on 9 September 1943. Note that 'B' turret is gone, as it has been blown overboard by the explosion of the forward magazines below it. (P Solimano collection, via Società Capitani e Macchinisti Navali, Camogli [Genoa])

24 September/1 October

British Operation 'Halberd' to supply Malta from Gibraltar with nine merchant ships escorted by three battleships and one aircraft carrier. Poor reconnaissance prevents the battleships *Littorio* and *Vittorio Veneto* from intercepting the enemy formation, but the Regia Aeronautica attacks the British convoy sinking one freighter and damaging the battleship *Nelson*.

9 November

The 'Duisburg' convoy (named for a German merchant ship) is completely destroyed east of Sicily by 'Force K' (two cruisers and two destroyers) from Malta.

14 and 25 November

The German submarines *U-81* and *U-331* sink – respectively – HMS *Ark Royal* off Gibraltar and HMS *Barham* off Sollum.

7 December

Japanese attack on Pearl Harbor.

13 December

The light cruisers *Da Barbiano* and *Di Giussano*, with a deckload of petrol cans, are sunk off Cape Bon by three British and one Dutch destroyers.

15–18 December

HMS *Galatea* sunk by *U-557* off Alexandria (15 December). Italian Operation 'M. 42' (two convoys sent to Libya with urgent supplies); inconclusive First Battle of the Sirte between Italian warships and some British cruisers; the battleship *Vittorio Veneto* torpedoed and damaged in the Straits of Messina by HMS *Urge* (16–17 December). HMS *Neptune* and the destroyer HMS *Kandahar* sunk by Italian mines north of Tripoli, with HMS *Aurora* and HMS *Penelope* damaged.

19 December

Italian human torpedoes from the submarine *Sciré* enter the port of Alexandria and manage to seriously damage the British battleships HMS *Valiant* and HMS *Queen Elizabeth* and the tanker *Sagona*.

1942

3–6 January

Italian Operation 'M.43': a large convoy reaches Tripoli escorted by the battleship *Duilio* and several destroyers.

22–25 January

Italian Operation 'T. 18' similar to 'M.43'; the Italian convoy is escorted again by *Duilio*, along with cruisers and destroyers. Torpedo bombers from Malta sink the liner *Victoria* (13,000 grt), laden with troops.

11–16 February

British Operations 'MW.9/ME.10' to supply Malta. Convoy 'MW.9' loses two merchant ships to Axis aircraft and is forced to return to Alexandria.

21–24 February

Successful Italian Operation 'K.7': two convoys escorted by *Duilio*, three destroyers and almost twenty escort ships reach Libya without loss. British aircraft attacking the convoys from Malta are beaten off by Luftwaffe and Regia Aeronautica fighters escorting them.

22 March

Second Battle of the Sirte. The *Littorio*, two heavy cruisers, one light cruiser and ten destroyers engage at long range a squadron of British ships (four light cruisers and nine destroyers) escorting Convoy 'MW. 10' (four merchant ships). Slight

The battleship *Vittorio Veneto* at Malta, off the Grand Harbour on the morning of 11 September 1943, just arrived after the surrender of the Italian fleet. Note the two aerials of the EC 3/ter 'Gufo' radar over the anti-aircraft lookout station atop the conning tower. (Imperial War Museum)

damage suffered by ships on both sides, but the convoy is delayed and its four vessels will all be sunk. The destroyers *Lanciere* and *Scirocco* are lost in a gale in central Mediterranean on their way back to Taranto.

22 April

Four MAS are sent to the Black Sea by road through the Balkans.

11 May

Three British destroyers (*Jackal*, *Kipling* and *Lively*) are attacked and sunk by German aircraft while steaming towards Benghazi.

25 May

Again via road, four MAS are sent to the Russian front; they will operate on Lake Ladoga.

12–16 June

'Battaglia di mezzo giugno' (the Battle of Mid-June'). Two British convoys leave Gibraltar ('GM.4', six merchant ships) and Alexandria ('MW.11', eleven merchant ships) ferrying supplies to Malta. Convoy 'MW.11' is forced to return to Alexandria when the presence of *Vittorio Veneto* and *Littorio* east of Malta is discovered; HMS *Hermione* is sunk by *U-205*, and the heavy cruiser *Trento* is torpedoed by an aircraft and finally sunk by a British submarine. Convoy 'GM.4' is intercepted near Pantelleria by *Eugenio di Savoia* and *Montecuccoli*; four ships are sunk and only two reach Malta.

July

The projected invasion of Malta (Operation 'C.3') is postponed and will be finally cancelled in October.

14 July

Assault swimmers (Uomini 'Gamma' – 'nuotatori d'assalto') leave from a secret base near Algeciras, on the Spanish mainland, and attack merchant ships moored at Gibraltar sinking four of them totalling of 9,465 grt.

10–15 August

British Operation 'Pedestal' to resupply Malta from Gibraltar suffers co-ordinated attacks by Italian and German submarines, MTBs and aircraft; nine freighters out of thirteen are sunk in what is known as 'Battaglia di mezzo agosto' ('the Battle of mid-August'); aircraft carrier HMS *Eagle* is sunk by *U-73*, HMS *Cairo* by the submarine *Axum* and the cruiser HMS *Manchester* by MTBs *MS 16* and *MS 22* (the largest surface warship sunk by MTBs in the Second World War). The cruisers *Bolzano* and *Attendolo* torpedoed and heavily damaged by HMS *Unbroken* in the southern Tyrrhenian Sea. Despite this, the four British merchant ships that manage to reach Malta deliver vital supplies and ammunition for the island's population and garrison, allowing the British to plan new air and naval attacks from the island against Italian convoys bound for Northern Africa.

23 October

Gen. Montgomery's army attacks Axis positions at El Alamein.

8 November

Operation 'Torch'; Allied landings in Morocco and Algeria, British troops capture Mersa Matruh.

11–12 November

Allied landings at Bona and Bougie; most French territory is occupied by the Germans with the exception of Toulon and its surrounding area. Italian occupation of Corsica; Italo-German occupation of Tunisia.

27 November

German troops enter Toulon; most of the French ships in port are scuttled or sabotaged by their crews.

2 December

Naval action in the shallow waters near Banco Skerki, in the 'Canale di Sicilia'; four Italian merchant ships and one destroyer sunk.

6 December

The three modern battleships *Roma*, *Littorio* and *Vittorio Veneto* shift their homeport from Naples to La Spezia in an attempt to escape Allied bombing.

8 December

Axis occupation of Bizerte.

12 December

Human torpedoes and assault swimmers from the submarine *Ambra* attack Allied shipping in the port of Algiers; two steamers are damaged and two more (totalling of 8,667 grt) sunk.

In Sliema Creek (Marsamxsett) at the end of September 1943, a group of Italian submarines interned in Malta since mid-September. In the first row, from left to right: *Corridoni*, *Atropo*, *Bandiera*, *Settembrini*, *Onice*, *Galatea*, *Zoea*, *Bragadin*, *Brin*, *Jalea*, *Alagi*, *Menotti*, *Squalo*, *H.4* and *Nichelio*. All the Italian submarines interned in Malta had returned to Taranto by the end of October, soon after the Italian declaration of war against Germany (13 October 1943). (IWM)

1943

3 January
British 'Chariots' attack the port of Palermo, sinking the hull of the incomplete cruiser *Ulpio Traiano* and damaging a freighter.

23 January
British occupation of Tripoli and loss of Libya.

29 January
The British Eighth Army enters Tunisia.

February/March
High volume of convoy traffic between the ports of western Sicily and Tunisia, with torpedo boats and destroyers often employed as fast transports. Heavy losses due to Allied air superiority.

7 April
The British Eighth Army links up with the US Army in southern Tunisia; Axis land forces are surrounded in the northernmost part of Tunisia.

10 April
Heavy USAAF raid on La Maddalena and surrounding islands; the heavy cruiser *Trieste* capsizes and sinks. *Gorizia* is heavily damaged and will be towed later to La Spezia for repairs.

7 /13 May
Final phases of the occupation of Tunisia; Bizerte and Tunis are taken on the 7th and on the 13th all Axis military operations in Tunisia cease.

11 June
After heavy naval and air bombardment, the Italian garrison at Pantelleria surrenders; the Allies occupy the island.

10 July
Allied landings in Sicily (Operation 'Husky').

12 July
Fall of Syracuse.

The liners *Victoria*, *Marco Polo* and *Esperia* (from left to right) steaming towards Tripoli in the spring of 1941, as seen from on board an escorting torpedo boat. (E Bagnasco collection)

16 July
The carrier HMS *Indomitable* is damaged by a torpedo bomber and the cruiser HMS *Cleopatra* is torpedoed by the submarine *Alagi*, but both British ships manage to reach Malta.

17 July
High-speed engagement between the light cruiser *Scipione Africano* and British MTBs in the Straits of Messina. One MTB is sunk and another damaged.

23 July
US troops occupy Palermo.

The liner *Neptunia* sinking at 06.50 on 18 September 1941, after having been torpedoed east of Tripoli, at 04.15, by the British submarine *Upholder* that, in the same action, also sank *Neptunia*'s sister-ship *Oceania*. (A Rastelli collection)

25 July
Fall of the Fascist regime; Mussolini is deposed and arrested and the 'Maresciallo d'Italia' Pietro Badoglio is appointed Prime Minister.

31 July
The battleship *Littorio* is renamed *Italia* and the destroyers *Camicia Nera* and *Squadrista* are renamed *Artigliere* and *Corsaro* respectively.

6–8 August
Two attempts – both unsuccessful – by the cruisers of the 7ª and 8ª Divisione Navale to attack Allied naval and merchant ships in Palermo from La Spezia.

17 August
Fall of Messina; the Allied occupation of Sicily is completed.

3 September
Allied landings at Reggio Calabria. At Cassibile (near Syracuse) the so-called 'Armistizio breve' ('Short Armistice') concerning the military clauses of the Italian surrender is signed between Italy and the Allies.

8 September
The Armistice between Italy and the Allies is officially promulgated. As only the most senior officers have been informed of the impending negotiations, all operational commands, units and ships are taken by surprise. In the ensuing chaos, many Italian ships fall into German hands.

9 September
Allied landings at Salerno; in central and northern Italy, almost all Italian Army and Air Force units

The steamer *Caterina*, with a deckload of trucks and other supplies, sinking on the morning of 19 October 1941 on the route from Naples to Tripoli, after having been fatally damaged by a British torpedo bomber (photograph taken from the destroyer *Sebenico*). (Author's collection)

are overpowered and disarmed by the Germans. Sailing from ports and naval bases in northern Italy, almost all Italian ships able to make for ports under Allied control; ships overhauling or fitting out are abandoned or in several cases sabotaged by their crews. The battleship *Roma* is sunk north of Sardinia by German aircraft that attack her with the new PC 1400X glider bombs; *Italia* is also damaged. US and British ships arrive at Taranto (Operation 'Musket').

10–11 September
Most of the Italian battle fleet (*Vittorio Veneto*, *Italia*, *Doria* and *Duilio*), plus cruisers and destroyers, arrive at Malta; *Cesare* arrives on the 13th from Pola, after a brief stop at Taranto to refuel. The cruiser *Attilio Regolo*, three destroyers and three torpedo boats (with survivors of the *Roma* aboard) arrive in Port Mahon in the Balearics where they are interned (apart from two torpedo boats scuttled by their crew off the port's entrance).

12 September
Italian escort ships begin to operate on the Allied side.

14 September
The destroyers *Legionario* and *Oriani* leave Malta to ferry US troops and supplies to Ajaccio in Corsica.

23 September
Proclamation of the Repubblica Sociale Italiana (RSI) in northern Italy, with Mussolini as Head of State, claiming jurisdiction over all Italian territory

not occupied by the Allies. Relatively few naval personnel remaining in northern Italy join the Marina Nazionale Repubblicana, the former commander of the 'Xª Flottiglia MAS', Cdr. Junio Valerio Borghese, being one of the most notable exceptions.

29 September
Aboard the battleship HMS *Nelson*, moored at Malta, Marshal Badoglio and Gen. Eisenhower sign the 'Armistizio lungo' ('Long Armistice), that confirms and expands the clauses of the 'Short Armistice' signed early in September.

4 October
The first Italian vessels (three cruisers, two destroyers, escort ships, MTBs and VASs) leave Malta to return to Taranto.

13 October
The Kingdom of Italy declares war against Germany; the official co-belligerency with the Allies begins, and the Regia Marina begins its reorganisation in southern Italy. The Naval Infantry's Reggimento San Marco is reconstituted, as well as an underwater assault craft unit ('Mariassalto') that will operate during the rest of the war with the few human torpedoes still available in southern Italian bases.

18 October
The battleships *Vittorio Veneto* and *Italia* are transferred to the Great Bitter Lake in the Suez Canal area, where they will be interned until February 1947.

27 October
The cruisers *Duca degli Abruzzi* and *Duca d'Aosta* leave Taranto for Freetown, to be employed in patrols in mid-Atlantic area. The *Garibaldi* will join them later, and the three ships will return to Italy in April 1944.

16 November
Fall of Leros in the Dodecanese which by now is completely under German control.

2 December
German air raid on the port of Bari: eighteen Allied merchant ships (totalling over 71,000 grt) are sunk.

1944

22 January
Allied landings at Anzio; Kriegsmarine and RSI Navy MTBs and assault craft attack US and British vessels off the landing area.

February
Nine Italian submarines are sent in the Atlantic to operate as training boats for Allied anti-submarine vessels. On 15 November the *Settembrini* would be lost, and the remaining eight boats would return to Italy in summer 1945.

22 June
British 'Chariots' and Italian assault swimmers attack the Gulf of La Spezia, sinking the hulk of the heavy cruiser *Bolzano*.

1945

17 February
Heavy Allied air raids on Trieste. The abandoned hulks of the battleship *Conte di Cavour* and of the destroyer *Pigafetta* (by now the German *TA 44*) are sunk.

17 April
A surface attack motorboat ('barchino esplosivo') manned by a rating of the RSI Xᵃ MAS attacks and damages the French destroyer *Trombe* off the Ligurian coast.

19 April
Attack by 'Mariassalto' against the port of Genoa; the incomplete and abandoned aircraft carrier *Aquila* is damaged, but does not sink.

25–26 April
Uprisings in the most important cities in Northern Italy, under the guidance of the Comitato di Liberazione Nazionale.

27 April
Formal surrender of German forces in Italy.

8 May
In Berlin, the final capitulation of Germany is signed, thus ending the Second World War in Europe.

Convoy Operations

During the Second World War, the Regia Marina had among its principal tasks the protection of sea lanes and convoys from Italy to

The German freighter *Ankara* in 1942, as part of a convoy bound for Africa. (Author's collection)

the various overseas fronts, North Africa in particular. The Stato Maggiore Generale (General Staff), in meetings held between March and May 1940, initially seemed to rule out – in the event of a conflict against Great Britain – the possibility of supplying Libya continuously with merchant ships in large convoys: the risks that the freighters and their escorts would run were considered excessive and, moreover, there was the widespread belief that the war would be very short. During the early weeks of the war, supplying Libya was entrusted mainly to aircraft and submarines but as hostilities continued, organising regular convoy traffic became an urgent necessity.

The Regia Marina had been considering the issue of supplying Libya in the event of war since 1938: a study on this subject (D.G. 10/A2) was prepared by the Navy's General Staff and, once the needs of the Army and Air Force were known, the Navy identified the quantities of supplies that in its judgement had to be shipped to Libya during the first month of the war (about 180,000 men, 13,000 vehicles and 50,000 tonnes of ammunition and other supplies).

These estimates were largely rendered obsolete as the war progressed, especially given the long duration of the African campaign: however, the Regia Marina's study had already highlighted that

The M/S *Foscolo* moored at a quay – probably at Piraeus – on 6 September 1942. (Photo A Fraccaroli)

The steamer *Rosandra* unloading her cargo in 1942 in a Greek port, probably Corinth. (Author's collection)

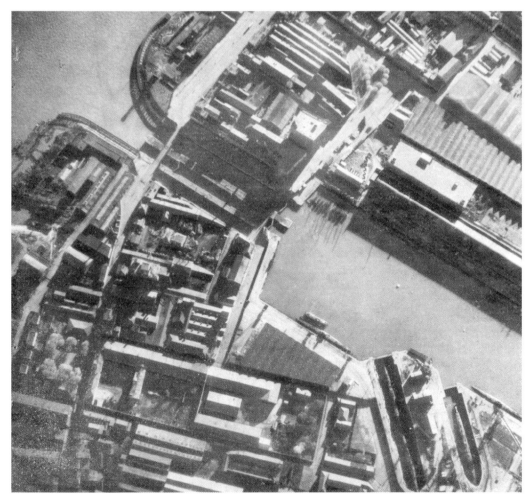

The *Spica* class torpedo boat *Polluce* sinking in the Central Mediterranean on 4 September 1942. She was hit and fatally damaged during a convoy escort mission from Piraeus to Tobruk. The convoy was composed of the steamers *Paderna*, *Sportivo* and *Bianchi* and escorted – besides the *Polluce* – by the torpedo boats *Lupo*, *Castore* and *Calliope*. (Author's collection)

the restricted capacity for loading and unloading in Italian and particularly North African ports would be the determining factor in the transport of supplies to North Africa.

In fact, the Libyan ports could only accommodate the following numbers of ships simultaneously:

• Tripoli: five freighters and four troopships.
• Benghazi: three freighters and two troopships (having had to abandon unloading operations in the harbour, this was reduced to just three ships in total).
• Tobruk: three freighters and two troopships.

During the war, these figures were further reduced: in mid-1941, for instance, because of enemy air raids, the capacity of the port of Tripoli had been reduced to a mere 50 per cent. For comparison, fourteen freighters could be loaded at the same time at Naples, five at Bari and five at Brindisi, and the Sicilian ports also had similar capacities.

Therefore, it would have been useless to organise convoys consisting of ten or more ships, as most of them would have been obliged to wait for long periods in harbour before unloading, thus remaining exposed to attack. In practice, therefore, the convoys were often very small, and many examples can be found of single merchant ships being sent to Libya escorted by two or three warships. This dispersion of the available assets, which in many cases did allow the convoys to evade enemy attack, did not help the continuity in the flow of supplies, as these were often redistributed up to Derna, Bardia, Ain el Gazala and Mersa Matruh in smaller coastal vessels that themselves had to be escorted.

Nevertheless, until the fall of the colony on 23 January 1943, 86 per cent of supplies (more than two million tons) and 90 per cent of the troops dispatched from Italy arrived safely in Libyan ports. As for traffic with Tunisia (from November 1942 to May 1943) more than 92 per cent of the men and about 70 per cent of the material reached their destination. However, there were times when losses were high, which had a considerable impact on the progress of the land campaigns.

In the early part of the war, Supermarina tried to organise convoys made up of the same ships: in particular, the liners *Oceania*, *Neptunia*, *Esperia*, *Marco Polo*, *Victoria* and *Conte Rosso* always operated together, although grouped differently, escorted by the 11ª Squadriglia cacciatorpediniere (*Aviere*) or by the 14ª (*Vivaldi*). In the second half of 1941, however, losses of merchant ships forced the abandonment of this policy, and likewise the escorts were provided by whatever warships were available. However, this meant that convoys were now made up of both naval and merchant crews inexperienced in convoy operations, resulting in misunderstandings and misinterpretations of the orders of the convoy commodores (Capi Scorta, i.e. the most senior officers at sea), slowness in carrying out manoeuvres (particularly on the part of the merchant ships) and ever-decreasing levels of training; from the end of 1941, these were perhaps the major operational constraints faced by the Italian forces employed in the 'Battaglia dei Convogli'.

Within Supermarina the Ufficio Traffico Oltremare ('Overseas Shipping Office') – initially headed by Capt. Emilio Ferreri – had been formed to manage convoy operations; this office worked along with the Comando Difesa Traffico ('Shipping Defence Command', organising convoy escorts in Italian coastal waters and in other areas with low enemy threat) and the RTSO (Rifornimento, Traffico, Spedizioni Oltremare – 'Overseas Supply and Shipping') Office of the Naval General Staff. The RTSO provided logistic shipping by selecting the merchant ships needed and indicating modifications to make them suitable for various forms of military transport (troops, tanks, fuel etc.). The direct responsibility for all convoy-related operations was, however, left entirely to Supermarina's Operations Room.

Before a convoy's departure, the Capo Scorta met with the merchant ships' captains and distributed their operational orders with details of the routes to be followed, communications, navigation and zigzagging techniques etc.

An aerial view of the lock connecting the Garonne River and the tidal basin where the Italian 'Betasom' submarine base was located. (Ufficio Storico della Marina Militare)

An armed guard of the Reggimento San Marco saluting the submarine *Da Vinci* entering the 'Betasom' lock on 31 October 1940, at the end of her first Atlantic mission. (E Bagnasco collection)

Communications proved to be a weak point in the convoys: the vast majority of freighters did not have the VHF radiotelephones installed aboard warships which could not be intercepted by the enemy beyond their 10–12 mile range. Therefore, radio communication was restricted to wireless telegraphy which required encryption, and since the merchant ships' radio operators were not trained to decipher naval signals, commodores fell back on visual signalling, using flags by day and lights by night. These, however, were open to errors of interpretation. Likewise, aircraft escorting the convoys relied on warning shots or dropping coloured flares to indicate the presence of submarines or, worse, the launching of torpedoes: the chaos that these rudimentary signals could cause in the convoy can well be imagined.

Aircraft escorts for convoys were almost always insufficient: from May 1941 until the end the year aircraft of the German X Fliegerkorps protected numerous convoys, but when the responsibility for air escorts returned exclusively to the Regia Aeronautica, its aircraft – whose pilots were not trained to fly over the open sea – were able only to operate in daylight, and often experiencing serious difficulties even in finding the convoys they had been assigned to. The situation for British aircraft, on the other hand, was entirely different. In many cases already equipped with radar, they were able to operate at night and in bad weather, and almost always faced no aerial opposition when attacking the convoys.

Depending on the number of escorts available, the convoys could assume different formations. In particular, when only two destroyers or torpedo boats were available, they were positioned – staggered by about 45° – about a mile ahead of the merchant ships. By increasing the number of escort ships, it was possible to position them all

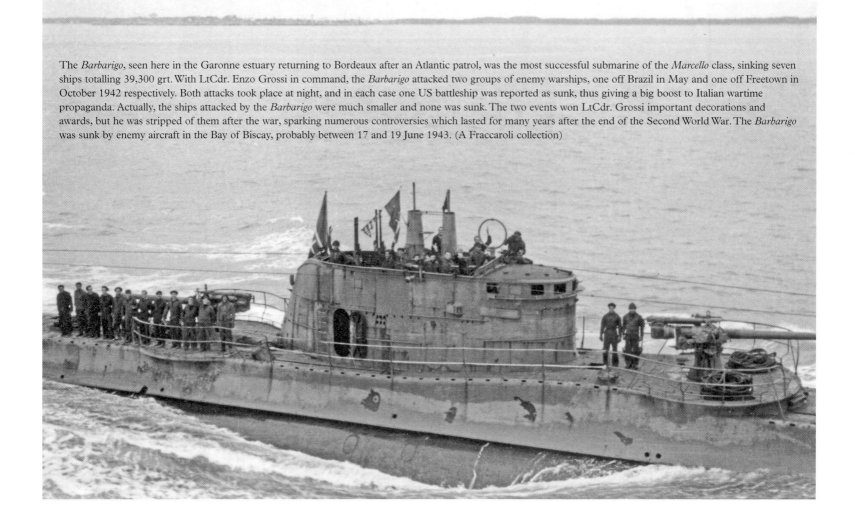

The *Barbarigo*, seen here in the Garonne estuary returning to Bordeaux after an Atlantic patrol, was the most successful submarine of the *Marcello* class, sinking seven ships totalling 39,300 grt. With LtCdr. Enzo Grossi in command, the *Barbarigo* attacked two groups of enemy warships, one off Brazil in May and one off Freetown in October 1942 respectively. Both attacks took place at night, and in each case one US battleship was reported as sunk, thus giving a big boost to Italian wartime propaganda. Actually, the ships attacked by the *Barbarigo* were much smaller and none was sunk. The two events won LtCdr. Grossi important decorations and awards, but he was stripped of them after the war, sparking numerous controversies which lasted for many years after the end of the Second World War. The *Barbarigo* was sunk by enemy aircraft in the Bay of Biscay, probably between 17 and 19 June 1943. (A Fraccaroli collection)

The submarine *Galvani*, along with other *Brin* class boats (*Archimede*, *Guglielmotti* and *Torricelli*) on 10 June 1940 was deployed in the Red Sea. The *Galvani* was sunk by British ships on 24 June 1940 at the entrance to the Gulf of Oman; the previous day, the *Torricelli* had been sunk in action in the Red Sea but managed to damage the British destroyer HMS *Khartoum* which sank after a fierce fire lasting several hours. Note, in this photograph dating back to early 1939, the 3.9in/43 gun located in its awkward position atop the conning tower, facing aft; later in the war, aboard the surviving boats, the gun was relocated on the main deck, forward of the conning tower. (E Bagnasco collection)

around the convoy to make enemy attacks as difficult as possible, especially those from submarines. Merchant ships in the convoys maintained line abreast or even several lines abreast of two or three ships each, but the inexperience of their captains in convoy navigation often led to 'chequerboard' formations that offered a greater number of targets to enemy submarines.

Frequently, especially at night, the ships in the largest convoys shifted from line abreast formation to the line ahead, as this was easier to maintain in darkness, although with smaller, two- or three-ship convoys the Capi Scorta sought to keep the ships in line abreast as this formation was easier to maintain with a small number of ships. Finally, direct or distant escort by cruiser divisions (once it was possible to organise it – i.e. until late 1941) occasionally prevented enemy naval formations attacking convoys.

Submarines in the Atlantic

As stated previously, the Comando Gruppo Sommergibili Atlantico (Atlantic Submarine Command) was established at Bordeaux, France on 1 September 1940. This was a direct consequence, following the treaty signed in Berlin by Italy and Germany on 22 May 1939, of the operational agreements between the Kriegsmarine and the Regia Marina to conduct a naval war against Great Britain that would include action against merchant shipping in the Atlantic.

The Regia Marina's choice for an independent submarine base on the French Atlantic coast (excluding of course ports and bases already being used by the Germans), fell on the river port of Bordeaux, located on the Garonne, about 50 miles upstream from its mouth on the Bay of Biscay, originating from the confluence of the Garonne and Dordogne in the wide estuary of the Gironde. From the letter 'B' (*Beta* in the naval phonetic alphabet and also the initial letter of 'Bordeaux')

the code name 'Betasom' – i.e. 'Bordeaux – Comando sommergibili' – was derived and it became both the official and the common term for the Italian Atlantic submarine base.

Repair, supply and command facilities were soon established on one of the tidal basins south of Bordeaux, as well as accommodation for the boats' crews; the requisitioned French liner *De Grasse* (18,435 grt) and the German passenger ship *Usaramo* (7,775 grt) were berthed on the Garonne river near the lock, to be used as tenders and barracks ships, with medical facilities and an infirmary for 24 patients aboard the *De Grasse*. Two hundred and twenty-five men of the Battaglione San Marco provided security for the base, and there were also German army units stationed in the surrounding area.

Rear Admiral Angelo Parona was the first CinC of 'Betasom', with Capt. Aldo Cocchia as Chief of Staff; Cocchia was replaced in April 1941 by Capt. Romolo Polacchini who, at the end of 1941, relieved Adm. Parona as CinC; on 2 December 1942 – upon his promotion to Rear Admiral – Polacchini was relieved by Capt. Enzo Grossi, who held the post until 8 September 1943, later choosing to collaborate with the Germans.

The first boat to arrive at 'Betasom' was the *Malaspina* on 4 September 1940, at the end of her first Atlantic patrol just four days after the establishment of the base. A few days later the *Barbarigo* also arrived, and before the end of September four more boats (*Dandolo*, *Marconi*, *Finzi* and *Bagnolini*) followed. By the end of October, there were eighteen Italian submarines at Bordeaux as in the meanwhile twelve more boats (*Emo*, *Tarantini*, *Torelli*, *Faà di Bruno*, *Otaria*, *Baracca*, *Giuliani*, *Glauco*, *Calvi*, *Tazzoli*, *Argo* and *Da Vinci*) had arrived. Before the end of the year, nine further boats reached Bordeaux: four in November (*Veniero*, *Nani*, *Cappellini* and *Morosini*) and five (*Marcello*, *Bianchi*, *Brin*, *Velella* and *Mocenigo*) in December. Almost all of the boats based in Bordeaux up to the end of 1940 were originally part of the Gruppi

sommergibili of La Spezia and Naples, and only four had come from Taranto.

In March 1941, the submarines *Guglielmotti*, *Archimede*, *Ferraris* and *Perla*, which had fled from Massawa in Italian East Africa after the evacuation of that base, arrived in Bordeaux; almost two years later on 20 February 1943 the *Cagni* also arrived in Bordeaux, after leaving La Maddalena on 6 October 1942 and thus having conducted an unbelievably long voyage (136 days) that brought her to patrol the western African coast before steaming northbound to Bordeaux.

Altogether, thirty-two Italian boats operated in the Atlantic between 1940 and 1943, of which sixteen were lost as shown in the following list:

1940: *Tarantini*, *Faà di Bruno* and *Nani*.
1941: *Marcello*, *Glauco*, *Bianchi*, *Baracca*, *Malaspina*, *Ferraris*, *Marconi*.
1942: *Calvi* and *Morosini*.
1943: *Archimede*, *Tazzoli*, *Da Vinci* and *Barbarigo*.

Of the sixteen remaining boats, on 8 September 1943 the *Cagni* was in the southern Indian Ocean, and made for the Allied port of Durban, South Africa; prior to that, other submarines had returned to the Mediterranean and only seven boats were in Bordeaux as of mid-1943: *Cappellini*, *Tazzoli*, *Giuliani*, *Barbarigo*, *Finzi*, *Bagnolini* and *Torelli*. All were scheduled to be converted into transport submarines to ferry strategic materials to and from the Far East and, in fact, three one-way transport missions were carried out successfully. *Tazzoli* and *Barbarigo* were sunk on their first missions, while *Cappellini*, *Giuliani* and *Torelli* managed to reach Singapore between July and August 1943; after the Armistice they were seized by the Japanese, and later handed over to the Kriegsmarine. The *Giuliani* was lost in 1944, while the *Cappellini* and *Torelli* came under Japanese control after May 1945 and were scrapped after the war. The two last transport boats – *Bagnolini* and *Finzi* – were being overhauled at Bordeaux when the Armistice was proclaimed, and were thus seized by the Germans.

Altogether, the thirty-two submarines of the Regia Marina operating in the Atlantic between 1940 and 1943 sank 101 Allied merchant ships totalling 568,573 grt; an additional four freighters (35,765 grt) were damaged. The most successful submarine was the *Da Vinci*, with sixteen ships totalling over 120,000 grt, and other boats sank from one to seven ships each; only four submarines (*Faà di Bruno*, *Glauco*, *Marcello* and *Velella*) sank no ships at all.

The Red Sea

The Red Sea and the eastern Indian Ocean were the most important of the Regia Marina's subsidiary theatres of operations in the Second World War, as the Italians had maintained a naval presence there since the end of the nineteenth century. On 10 June 1940 the first-line naval assets in the area consisted of six destroyers, eight submarines, four torpedo boats, the colonial sloop *Eritrea*, five MAS and other smaller vessels based at Massawa.

Three submarines (*Macallé*, *Torricelli* and *Galvani*) were lost and one captured (*Galilei*) by the end of June; some success was scored against British shipping in the Red Sea, but on 20 September 1940 the destroyer *Nullo* was lost in action with enemy ships. By early 1941 the British offensive against Italian Somaliland had begun, and Chisimaio was evacuated on 12 February; in early March, the four surviving submarines (*Perla*, *Ferraris*, *Archimede* and *Guglielmotti*) sailed for Bordeaux via the Cape of Good Hope and, between 1 and 4 April, the three *Leone* class destroyers, as well as the *Manin* and *Battisti*, were all lost. On 16 April 1941, the gun batteries on the Dahlahc Islands, off Massawa, surrendered and the Italian presence in East Africa swiftly came to an end: the Amba Alagi area fell on 27 May, Assab on 11 June and the last Italian stronghold, Gondar, fell on 27 November 1941.

The Black Sea

Following the Axis offensive against the USSR, between late April and May 1942 the first MAS of the Regia Marina began to arrive at Foros in the Crimea, soon followed by some 'CB'-type midget submarines and other surface assault craft. After the fall of Sevastopol, on 3 August 1942 *MAS 568* torpedoed and seriously damaged the Soviet cruiser *Molotov* but, as the Axis situation on the Eastern Front deteriorated, all Italian naval activity came to an end in May 1943, and the remaining MAS and 'CB' were handed over to the Kriegsmarine. Finally, it should be remembered that four MAS (*'526-'529*) were transferred to the Baltic to operate on Lake Ladoga in support of the Axis forces engaged in the siege of Leningrad between April and November 1942.

Four 'CB' type midget submarines at Sevastopol in July 1942, moored at one of the quays of the large Soviet naval base there that was now under Axis control. (E Bagnasco collection)

CHAPTER 4

Ships in Service 1940–5

Notes on technical data

Displacement is given in tons for standard/full load; for submarines figures for surfaced/submerged displacement are shown.

Dimensions in metres (m) are: length overall, length between perpendiculars, maximum beam and mean or maximum draught.

Machinery includes number of boilers and propeller shafts, the type of engines and horsepower (if needed, both under operational conditions and on trials)

Speed is expressed in knots and must be understood as maximum speed under operational conditions; other specific data – when indicated – is shown in brackets.

Endurance is shown in nautical miles (nm) and is related to various speeds where this information is available. Fuel capacity is indicated in tons.

Armour shows maximum thickness (in millimetres [mm]), in the named areas of the ship.

Armament includes guns, machine guns, depth-charge throwers (DCT), torpedo tubes (and mines, if carried) in wartime. For guns, total number of guns and calibre in inches is given,

Builders are shown by the following abbreviations:

A, Sp	Regio Arsenale, La Spezia
An	Ansaldo, Genoa
BSN	Bacini e Scali Napoletani, Naples
CCM	Regio Cantiere (Royal Naval Yard), Castellammare di Stabia
Cdt, RT	Cantieri del Tirreno, Riva Trigoso
CNR, A	Cantieri Navali Riuniti, Ancona
CNR, P	Cantieri Navali Riuniti, Palermo
CNQ	Cantiere Navale del Quarnaro, Fiume
CRDA, T	Cantieri Riuniti dell'Adriatico, Trieste
NM	Navalmeccanica, Castellammare di Stabia
OS	Odero, Genoa
OCP	Officine e Cantieri Partenopei, Naples
OTO, L	Odero-Terni-Orlando, Leghorn
OTO, M	Odero-Terni-Orlando, Muggiano (La Spezia)
OTO, S	Odero-Terni-Orlando, Genoa (Sestri)
STT	Stabilimento Tecnico Triestino, Trieste

followed in brackets by the number and type of mounts (i.e.: 2 x III means two triple turrets, 4 x II means four twin turrets or mounts etc.). For machine guns and cannon, calibre is given in millimetres (mm).

Complement is given as the total ship's company (with the number of officers in brackets).

Conte di Cavour in early 1916 a few months after commissioning. Note the small false bow wave to give the impression of greater speed. (Ufficio Storico della Marina Militare via Adm. G Vignati)

Cavour class

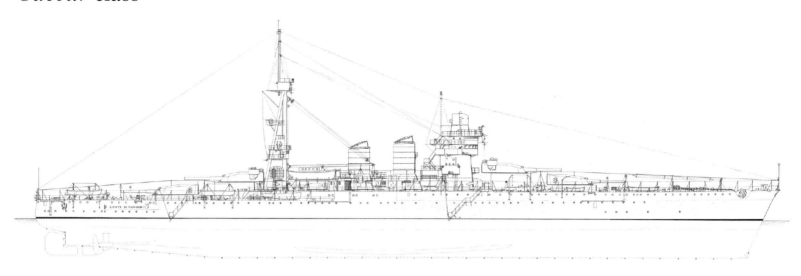

The *Conte di Cavour* in 1936, at the end of her major rebuilding in an original drawing from the Cantiere San Marco of Trieste. (Courtesy Gruppo di Cultura Navale, Bologna)

Displacement (tons): 26,140/29,100				
Dimensions (m): 186.4 overall, 168.9 pp, 28.6 max. beam, 10.4 max. draught.				
Machinery: 8 boilers and 2 turbines, 75,000hp (over 93,000hp on trials)				
Speed (kts): 26 (*Cavour* 28.0 and *Cesare* 28.2 on trials).				
Endurance (nm/kts): 5,200-5,400/18, 1,700/26: fuel 2,500 tons.				
Armour (mm): 250 (waterline); 135 (main deck); 260 (conning tower); 280 (main turrets); 120 (secondary turrets).				
Armament: Ten 12.6in/44 (2 x III, 2 x II); twelve 4.7in/50 (6 x II); eight 3.9in/47 AA (4 x II); eight 37mm/54 light AA guns (4 x II); sixteen 20mm/65 cannon (8 x II, *Cesare* from 1941).				
Complement: 1,260 (60)				

	Builders	Laid down	Launched	Completed
Conte di Cavour	A, Sp	10 Aug 1910	10 Aug 1911	1 Apr 1915
Sunk 23 Feb 1945; refloated and scrapped 1946-7.				
Giulio Cesare	CCM	24 Jun 1910	15 Oct 1911	14 May 1914
To USSR 1949 (*Novorossiisk*); sunk 29 Oct 1955.				

The first Italian dreadnought was the *Dante Alighieri*, launched in 1909 by the Royal Naval Yard of Castellammare di Stabia (Naples) and commissioned on 15 January 1913. Although Italy was quite late in commissioning all-big-gun ships (as already envisaged by the Italian naval engineer Vittorio Cuniberti in the 1903 edition of *Jane's Fighting Ships*) the *Dante Alighieri* incorporated many 'firsts' on her appearance on the international naval scene. She was the first Italian battleship, and one of the first in the world, armed with triple large-calibre (12in) turrets, and the first with some of her medium-calibre guns mounted in turrets; she was also the first Italian battleship with four screws.

The good performance of the *Dante Alighieri* prompted the Regia Marina to plan and build the three ships of the *Cavour* class (*Conte di Cavour, Giulio Cesare* and *Leonardo da Vinci*), laid down in 1910, launched in 1911 and commissioned between 1914 and 1916. As built, these ships displaced 24,300 tons full load and were armed with thirteen 12in/46 guns, three in triple turrets ('A', 'Q' and 'Y'), and two in twin superimposed turrets ('B' and 'X'); secondary armament was eighteen 4.7in/50 guns in casemates. The ships had a rather 'classical' appearance, with a long forecastle extending up to the barbette of 'X' turret, small superstructures, two tall funnels and two tripod masts. The Parsons geared turbines of the four-shaft plant received steam from twenty boilers (twenty-four aboard *Da Vinci*) and the maximum speed was 22 knots, with an endurance of 4,800nm at 10 knots.

Leonardo da Vinci was the only ship of the class lost during the war, sunk in an explosion at Taranto on 2 August 1916 that was blamed on sabotage; she was refloated in 1919 and despite initial plans to rebuild her with her midships turret removed, she was sold for scrap in March 1923.

The *Cavour* and *Cesare* remained in service in their original configuration until early 1933, the only structural change being the re-positioning of the fore mast in front of the forward funnel in the early 1920s. In October 1933 they were taken in hand by CRDA at Trieste and Cantieri del Tirreno at Genoa respectively, for a complete reconstruction based on the design drawn up in

the early 1930s, by Col. Francesco Rotundi of the Genio Navale (Naval Engineering Corps).

The fore part of the hull was completely rebuilt and lengthened, with a new raked 'oceanic' bow built around the former ram bow ; the stern remained almost unchanged, and a 'Pugliese' underwater protection system (based on two cylinders placed inside each side of the hull, designed to absorb the energy of underwater explosions by predetermined deformation) was fitted. A new 75,000hp powerplant (which in fact delivered more than 90,000hp on trials) was fitted, with eight boilers, two geared turbines and two shafts. Speed was thus increased to 26/27 knots. The superstructure was completely rebuilt, with a conning tower similar to that of the *Montecuccoli* class light cruisers, two funnels grouped amidships and a tripod mast aft of the funnels.

Because of the new arrangement of the propulsion plant, 'Q' turret amidships was removed, and the ten guns of the remaining four turrets were re-bored to 12.6in, the barrels' length in calibres decreasing correspondingly to 43.8. The development of new large-calibre guns would have been impossible (and uneconomic) in the short term, and the now re-bored guns could fire a heavier and more powerful projectile, although there was the problem of increased salvo dispersion. Secondary armament consisted of twelve 4.7in/50 guns in six fully-enclosed twin turrets and eight 3.9in/47 guns in four twin mounts.

Both ships took part in the Battle of Punta Stilo, during which *Cesare* was hit by a 15in shell from HMS *Warspite*: damage was not extensive, and after repairs lasting a few weeks she was back in service. *Cesare* took part in other surface actions and convoy operations until spring 1942, when she was placed in reserve at Taranto; later, her homeport shifted to Pola, where she served as a training ship and – after the Armistice – she was decommissioned at the Taranto Dockyard until the end of the war.

The *Cavour* was damaged by a torpedo during

the air attack on Taranto on the night of 11 November 1940: she was not beached in time and sank in shallow water, leaving only the superstructure visible the next morning. She was refloated after a long and expensive operation and at the end of 1941 she was able to proceed to Trieste, where she was scheduled to be repaired and modernised again: in particular, the project envisaged the replacement of the old 4.7in and 3.9in guns with new 5.3in dual-purpose guns and 65mm/64 AA guns. The repairs were finally suspended in June 1943 and, after the Armistice, the *Cavour* was captured by the Germans who began to dismantle her. She capsized and sank on 23 February 1945 after an Allied air raid on Trieste, and the hulk, which had been refloated soon after the end of the war, was scrapped in 1946.

The *Cesare* was transferred to the Soviet Union in 1949 as part of the war reparations paid by Italy and was renamed *Novorossiisk*; she sank on 29 October 1955, after hitting a German wartime mine while anchored just off Sevastopol. Her sinking was quite similar to that of *Cavour* at Taranto in November 1940: in both cases,

Giulio Cesare in 1940. Note the new bow, bridge tower and funnels. (E Bagnasco collection)

misguided rescue attempts combined with insufficient hull strength and internal subdivision led to the loss of the ships.

Conte di Cavour at Taranto, in late 1941, ready to sail to Trieste for repairs and partial rebuilding after the damage sustained during the British attack on Taranto on 11 November 1940. The *Cavour* has just been painted in an experimental 'Claudus' camouflage scheme for the transfer to Trieste; at this time similar schemes were also applied to *Cesare* and *Doria*. (E Bagnasco collection)

Conte di Cavour in Taranto's Mar Piccolo in 1938, as rebuilt between 1933 and 1937. (E Bagnasco collection)

Andrea Doria class

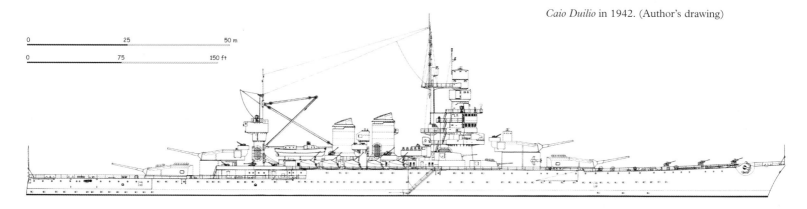

Caio Duilio in 1942. (Author's drawing)

Displacement (tons): *Doria* 25,924/28,200; *Duilio* 26,434 – 28,680
Dimensions (m): 186.9 overall, 168.9 pp, 28.03 max. beam, 10.3 max. draught
Machinery: 8 boilers and 2 turbines, 75,000hp (over 84,000hp on trials)
Speed (kts): 26 (*Doria* 26.9 and *Duilio* 27.0 on trials).
Endurance (nm/kts): 4,000/18, 1,800/25; fuel 2,530 tons.
Armour (mm): 250 (waterline); 135 (main deck); 260 (conning tower); 280 (main turrets); 120 (secondary turrets).
Armament: Ten 12.6in/44 (2 x III, 2 x II); twelve 5.3in/45 (4 x III); ten 3.5in/50 AA (10 x I); fifteen 37mm/54 light AA guns (various mounts); twelve 20mm/65 cannon (various mounts).
Complement: 1,520 (70)

	Builders	Laid down	Launched	Completed
Andrea Doria	A, Sp	24 Mar 1912	30 Mar 1913	13 Mar 1916
Removed from the list 1 Nov 1956; scrapped at La Spezia 1961.				
Caio Duilio	CCM	24 Feb 1912	24 Apr 1913	10 May 1915
Removed from the list 15 Sep 1956; scrapped at La Spezia 1958-9.				

The two *Andrea Doria* class battleships (*Andrea Doria* and *Caio Duilio*) were built to the plans drafted by Gen. Valsecchi of the Genio Navale, who based his work widely on Gen. Masdea's *Cavour* class. Minor changes were made in the disposition of the main armament ('A' and 'Y' turrets were closer to 'B' and 'X' turrets, and 'Q' turret was one deck lower because of the shorter forecastle), and in the secondary armament which was now sixteen casemated 6in/45 guns, while the funnels were taller, with the fore mast directly positioned forward of the fore funnel.

Basically, the *Doria*s were very similar to the *Cavour*s, and they were used in similar roles until 1932–3, when they were placed in reserve. The

success of the reconstruction of the *Cavour*s, together with renewed tension with France, led the Regia Marina to plan a similar reconstruction for the *Doria*s, in order to have six battleships available in 1940, when it was expected that the two modern '35,000-tonners', *Littorio* and *Vittorio Veneto*, would have been commissioned.

In spring 1937, the two battleships were taken in hand by Cantieri del Tirreno, Genoa (*Duilio*) and CRDA, Trieste (*Doria*) and these two yards slightly improved the plans and projects already carried out for the two *Cavour*s. The former bow structure was dismantled and a new raked bow – in this case with a slight sheer – was built, side and underwater protection (with 'Pugliese' cylinders)

was similar to that of the *Cavour*, and the ten 12in guns of the main armament were again re-bored to 12.6in. The propulsion plant was rebuilt with two screws, as for the *Cavour* class, but speed on trials was almost one knot less than that of *Cavour* and *Cesare*, although the maximum operational speed was about 26 knots for all four ships.

The reconstruction of the superstructure was more extensive than for the two *Cavour*s, and was firmly based on the design of the *Littorio* class battleships: the conical conning tower was topped by three co-axial fire control stations and there was no tripod aft of the two funnels, a stubby cylindrical structure supporting the secondary fire control station and the short mainmast.

The secondary armament consisted of twelve 5.3in/45 (135mm) guns in four triple turrets and ten 3.5in/50 (90mm) AA guns in stabilised single mounts; the 5.3in turrets were placed two on each side of the conning tower (the aft one being superimposed), and the 3.5in guns were mounted five on each side of the superstructure.

The *Duilio* was hit by a torpedo below the forward turrets during the attack on Taranto on 11 November 1940, but she was beached in time and rapidly refloated, returning to service in about six months.

Despite their inferiority to similar enemy ships, both battleships took part in several operations and engagements until early 1942: during the winter of 1941/42, the *Duilio* formed part of the escort for important convoys bound for North Africa. From mid-1942, the shortage of fuel meant both battleships' operations had to be restricted

Andrea Doria in 1940. (E Bagnasco collection)

and in September 1943 they sailed to Malta in accordance with terms of the Armistice. Later, they operated between Augusta, Syracuse and Taranto until the end of the war.

Doria and Duilio were the only battleships left to Italy by the peace treaty of 1947 and, equipped with wartime British radar, they operated alternately as the flagship of the new, smaller Marina Militare until 1953. Discarded in 1956, both were broken up at La Spezia between 1958 and 1961.

Andrea Doria at sea, in June 1942, with two 'Soldati' class destroyers. (E Bagnasco collection)

Andrea Doria at the CRDA yard, Trieste, in late 1937 at the start of her reconstruction. (Author's collection)

Andrea Doria being towed through Taranto's Canale Navigabile in late 1960 bound for La Spezia, where she would be completely broken up before the end of the following year. (E Bagnasco collection)

Caio Duilio during sea trials in late 1915. (Archivio Storico Ansaldo)

Andrea Doria at Pola in October 1940, at the completion of her reconstruction at CRDA, Trieste. (Foto Mioni, Trieste; Author's collection)

Littorio class

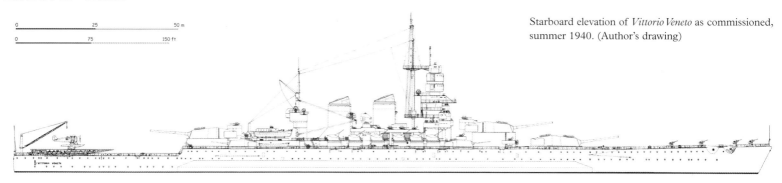

Starboard elevation of *Vittorio Veneto* as commissioned, summer 1940. (Author's drawing)

Displacement (tons): 41,377/41,650; *Littorio/Roma* 45,963/46,215			
Dimensions (m): 237.8 overall (*Roma* 240.1), 224.5 pp, 32.9 max. beam, 10.5 max. draught.			
Machinery: 8 boilers and 4 shaft-geared turbines, 130,000hp (134,000 / 139,000hp on trials)			
Speed (kts): 28–29 (31.2 / 31.4 on trials)			
Endurance (nm/kts): 4,580/16, 3,920/20; fuel 4,000 tons			
Armour (mm): 350 (waterline); 207 (main deck); 207 (conning tower); 350 (main turrets); 150 (secondary turrets)			

Armament: Nine 15in/50 (3 x III); twelve 6in/55 (4 x III); four 4.7in/40 illuminating (4 x I); twelve 3.5in/50 AA (12 x I); twenty 37mm/54 light AA guns (8 x II and 4 x I); twenty 20mm/65 cannon (10 x II: from 28 to 32 late in the war). One catapult, three Ro.43 floatplanes (from late 1942: one–two Ro.43 and one–two Re 2000 fighters)

Complement: 1,830–1,960 (80 + 30 flag staff)

	Builders	Laid down	Launched	Completed
Littorio	An	28 Oct 1934	22 Aug 1937	6 May 1940
(*Italia* from 25 Jul 1943)				
Removed from the list 1 Jun 1948; scrapped at La Spezia 1951–5.				
Vittorio Veneto	CRDA, T	28 Oct 1934	25 Jul 1937	28 Apr 1940
Removed from the list 1 Feb 1948; scrapped at La Spezia 1951–5.				
Impero	An	14 May 1938	15 Nov 1939	Not completed
Scrapped at Venice 1948–9				
Roma	CRDA, T	18 Sep 1938	9 Jun 1940	14 Jun 1942
Sunk by German guided bombs off Asinara Island on 9 Sep 1943.				

Littorio at sea in late summer 1940 with the typical early-war colour scheme (light grey on all vertical surfaces and dark grey on decks); note the wooden planking on the main deck aft. On the forecastle, the red and white diagonal recognition stripes applied soon after the Battle of Punta Stilo can easily be seen. (Istituto Luce, Author's collection)

The first studies for a new class of battleships complying with the provisions of the Washington Treaty of 1922 started in 1928, and the final design, drafted by Gen. Umberto Pugliese of the Genio Navale, was completed between 1933 and 1934 on behalf of the Comitato Progetti Navi of the Regia Marina's General Staff.

It was correctly decided that the design and construction of new 16in guns would be uneconomic and take too long, so a 15in, 50 calibre, gun was developed, partly based on the experience already gained with the 15in/40 guns built for the projected *Caracciolo* class battleships, later used aboard monitors, armed pontoons, in coastal batteries etc.

Gen. Pugliese's project was then passed on to CRDA, Trieste and to Ansaldo, Genoa who, in order to build one ship each, drew up the final plans for the new battleships. The hull lines were drawn up by CRDA, and the standard displacement was soon recalculated to 38,600 tons: by the time the ships were commissioned, standard displacement had risen to well in excess of 41,000 tons, with a full load displacement of over 45,700 tons for *Littorio* and *Vittorio Veneto* and 46,215 tons for *Roma*.

Armour protection was well balanced, with 350mm on the hull sides (based on an innovative 'two-layer' system of plates, one of 70mm thick

Vittorio Veneto during official speed trials off Genoa in spring 1940. The ship is completely fitted out and the new bow can easily be seen in this fine broadside image. (E Bagnasco collection)

and the other 280mm), 207mm for the main deck and 260mm on the conning tower; the main gun turrets were protected by 350mm of armour and a full Pugliese underwater protection system had been incorporated from the start, giving the *Littorio*s quite a good chance of surviving underwater damage, as they in fact did. Another innovative feature in the design was the presence of three rudders, one astern on the centreline and one on each side aft of the outer propellers, affording good handling in a seaway, either in normal conditions or when damaged.

The ten boilers in the original design were reduced to eight, powering four shaft-geared turbines, with an output of 130,000hp: a maximum speed of 28–29 knots was attained in wartime, this being considered more than enough under operational conditions, although all ships easily exceeded 31 knots during trials.

These ships had a long forecastle, extending as far as the barbette of 'C' turret and, on the main deck astern, a catapult and a crane were fitted: initially, three IMAM Ro 43 floatplanes were embarked but during summer 1943 a couple of Reggiane Re 2000 land fighters replaced two of the Ro 43, thus giving these ships a minimal air-defence capability. A long deckhouse was built between the barbettes of 'B' and 'C' turrets and, above the deckhouse, running fore to aft, the conning tower, the two funnels and a stub structure supporting the main mast were found. The funnel design was quite similar to that of the rebuilt *Cavour* and *Doria* classes, and of the *Garibaldi* class light cruisers.

The main armament consisted of three triple 15in turrets, two forward ('B' turret superimposed)

The launch of the battleship *Roma* at CRDA, Trieste, on 9 June 1940 – the day before Italy's entry into the Second World War. Note the new design of the bow, with less flared sides and a straight cutwater (fitted to *Littorio* and *Vittorio Veneto* after early sea trials). (F Petronio collection)

Roma, at the end of her fitting-out period, leaves Trieste bound for her homeport at Taranto, on 21 August 1942. The ship is now fully camouflaged: this photograph shows the ship's port side, and may be combined with that showing her starboard side pattern on page 212. (E Bagnasco collection)

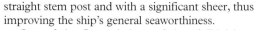

Littorio moored in Mar Grande at Taranto on 25 June 1942. Crewmen are manning the side as Mussolini is about to board the ship in order to present decorations after the successful outcome of the 'Battaglia di Mezzo Giugno', during which two convoys bound for Malta were attacked and seriously damaged by Italian naval forces. (E Bagnasco collection)

and one aft; the secondary armament consisted of four triple 6in turrets, one on each corner of the superstructure. Twelve 3.5in AA guns, six on each side, were fitted in gyrostabilised mounts, but the performance of these weapons was never completely satisfactory, because of the complexity of the stabilising machinery and the unreliability of the optical directors. The main fire directors were placed co-axially above the conning tower and, late in the war, one or two sets of the E.C. 3/ter 'Gufo' air and surface-search radar were fitted.

The first two ships, *Vittorio Veneto* and *Littorio*, were built by CRDA, Trieste and Ansaldo, Genoa respectively; during sea trials in early 1940, it was found that strong vibrations were produced in the fore part of the hull, with bow waves rising well over the forecastle even at moderate speeds. The cause of all this was identified in the shape of the hull sides and in the 'arched' design of the stem post, so a new bow structure – less flared and with a 'straight' stem post – was built over the old one, finally solving the problem. The pressure of war prevented this modification being made to the third ship of the class (*Impero*), while the fourth (*Roma*, commissioned in 1942) was built by CRDA with a bow of the modified design, incorporating the straight stem post and with a significant sheer, thus improving the ship's general seaworthiness.

One of the first missions of the 9ª Divisione Navi da Battaglia (9th Battleship Division) came when both *Littorio* and *Vittorio Veneto* put to sea in order to oppose the British Operation 'Hats' (late August/early September 1940); the *Littorio* was damaged by an aerial torpedo during the British attack on Taranto on 11 November 1940, returning to service in March 1941, while the *Vittorio Veneto* took part in the battle of Cape Teulada on 27th November. *Vittorio Veneto* herself was damaged during Operation 'Gaudo', the ill-fated sweep south of Crete which led to the night action of Cape Matapan between 28 and 29 March 1941. The *Littorio* was among the Italian ships at the First Battle of Sirte in December 1941 and at the Second Battle of Sirte in March 1942. By the end of 1942, after *Roma*'s commissioning the previous summer, the three battleships shifted their homeport to La Spezia, because Allied air superiority made Taranto and the other southern Italian ports too vulnerable.

Following the Armistice of 8 September 1943, the ships at La Spezia complied with the condition that Italian ships should make for a port under Allied control. While steaming to Malta the Italian ships that had left La Spezia were attacked off the island of Asinara (north-western coast of Sardinia) by Luftwaffe bombers that hit the *Roma* with two PC 1400X guided bombs, sinking her. The former *Littorio* (renamed *Italia* after 25 July 1943) and *Vittorio Veneto*, after short stays in Malta and Alexandria, were interned in the Great Bitter Lake area of the Suez Canal, getting back to Italy only on 9 February 1947. Great Britain and the United States, which were to have received one ship each as war reparations, gave them up, requiring the ships to be scrapped, and these two fine battleships, decommissioned in the first half of 1948, were later stricken and broken up at La Spezia between 1951 and 1955.

The incomplete hull of *Impero* was towed in May 1941 from Genoa to Brindisi, where it was expected to continue her fitting out. In January 1942, under her own power, the *Impero* sailed out of Brindisi bound for Venice in order to be definitely completed, shifting in November 1942 to the CRDA San Marco yard in Trieste. After the Armistice, the incomplete battleship fell into German hands and her breaking-up began, but at the end of the war her still-floating hull was sabotaged by the Germans soon before abandoning Trieste. Having been refloated in 1947, *Impero*'s hulk was towed to Venice, where her breaking up was completed between 1948 and 1949.

An impressive image of *Vittorio Veneto* entering the Canale Navigabile at Taranto on 1 April 1941, bound from Mar Grande to the dockyard in Mar Piccolo, having been damaged by a British aerial torpedo on 28 March, after the clash with the British off Gaudo. All the weapons of the *Littorio* class battleships may be seen in this image: the 15in guns of 'B' turret, the 6in guns of the forward starboard triple turret, the six starboard 3.5in AA guns, two illuminating 4.7in/40 guns on the side of the forecastle deck abreast the funnels and twin 37mm and 20mm cannon. (E Bagnasco collection)

Littorio on early sea trials at full speed off Genoa (on the Portofino/Punta Chiappa course) on 21 December 1939, some months before commissioning. Note the original bow and the incomplete bridge tower, with the armoured tube around which the main gun directors still have to be fitted. (M Cicogna collection)

Left: Fitting out at Trieste, the *Roma* is virtually complete in this late spring 1942 photograph. Note 'standard' camouflage, the red and white recognition stripes extending aft up to the forward 6in turrets, and the different shape of the main gun directors compared to those of *Littorio* and *Vittorio Veneto*. (Courtesy Museo Storico Navale, Venice)

Above: *Italia* (ex-*Littorio*) being broken up at La Spezia in 1952. View from the main deck, looking forward, with the 15in gun barrels of 'C' turret already cut up and the 6in and 3.5in guns removed. (E Bagnasco collection)

In the Great Bitter Lake area of the Suez Canal, *Vittorio Veneto* lies at anchor in 1945 during her long internment before her return to Italy, along with her sister-ship *Italia* (ex- *Littorio*), on 9 February 1947. (M Cicogna collection)

Aquila

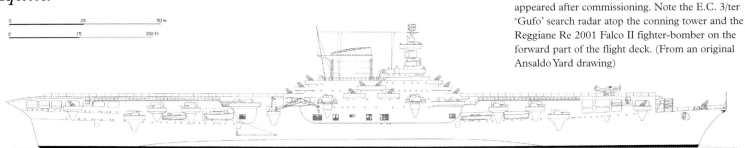

Starboard elevation of *Aquila* as she would have appeared after commissioning. Note the E.C. 3/ter 'Gufo' search radar atop the conning tower and the Reggiane Re 2001 Falco II fighter-bomber on the forward part of the flight deck. (From an original Ansaldo Yard drawing)

Displacement (tons): 23,350/27,800				
Dimensions (m): 231.4 overall, 211.6 pp, 25.2 max. beam, 7.4 max. draught. (flight deck: length 211.6m – max beam 25.2m)				
Machinery: 8 boilers and 4 shaft-geared turbines, 140,000hp				
Speed (kts): 30 (forecasted)				
Endurance (nm/kts): 5.500/18, 1,580/29; fuel 3,660 tons				
Armour (mm): 60–80 (ammunition storage and handling rooms and aviation fuel tanks)				
Armament: Eight 5.3in/45 AA (8 x I); twelve 2.55in/64 AA (12 x I); ten 12.6mm/44 AA (2 x III, 2 x II); 132 20mm/65 cannon (33 x IV) light				
Aircraft: 38 (max. 51) Re 2001 fighter-bombers; 2 catapults				
Complement: 1,420 (65) plus 245 (43) Air Group				

	Builders	Laid down	Launched	Completed
Aquila	An	–	25 Feb 1926	Conversion begun 1941 – not completed

Towed to La Spezia in 1949 and broken up 1952-4.

The creation of the Regia Aeronautica as an independent air force in 1923, and the exclusive control that it exercised from then on over all Italian military aviation, meant that the Regia Marina paid little attention to the development of aircraft carriers and unlike the British, US and Japanese navies never had its own independent naval air arm. Although there were a couple of feasibility studies, for example one in 1920 to convert the incomplete battleship *Caracciolo* into a flush-decked carrier, a plan in 1932 by Gen. Vian of the Genio Navale for a new-built 16,000-ton carrier and some further designs drawn up by another Genio Navale officer, Gen. Bonfiglietti,

nothing ever came of them, the Regia Marina concentrating on the modernisation of its old dreadnoughts and the construction of the *Littorio* class battleships. Therefore, on 10 June 1940 there were no aircraft carrier projects under way.

The course of the naval air war in the Mediterranean led to the revival of a 1935 plan to convert the liner *Roma* into an aircraft carrier, but the 30,816grt, 215.2m-long ship was not taken in hand by Ansaldo of Genoa (the same yard where she had been launched in 1926) until 9 July 1941. Work on the *Roma* (renamed *Aquila* in early 1942) proceeded quickly after that, the liner's superstructure being completely removed;

forward, the hull was rebuilt with a new elegantly-arched stem, and the stern was also partially modified. New machinery was fitted: the boilers and shaft-geared turbines came from the two light cruisers *Paolo Emilio* and *Cornelio Silla* of the 'Capitani Romani' class, the construction of which had been suspended in June 1940. With eight boilers and four shafts – and improved underwater lines – *Aquila*'s speed would have been in the 30-knot range, more than enough to operate with the Regia Marina's most modern ships and to conduct air operations safely in most weather conditions.

The flight deck extended 15m over the bow and was sponsored out 10m over the stern, causing *Aquila* to resemble the US carrier *Ranger* forward and most contemporary British carriers aft. A rather long and low island was built sponsored-out on the starboard side of the flight deck; atop the island, there was a multi-level conning tower forward and a single large raked funnel aft. Bilge keels were fitted on each side, to improve both stability and resistance to underwater damage. Anti-aircraft armament would have comprised eight 5.3in guns and twelve 2.55in (65mm) guns of a new design; a total of up to 132 20mm cannon in newly-designed quadruple mounts were to have been fitted around the sides of the flight deck. Two German-designed catapults were to have been fitted.

In April 1943, with the ship moored at her fitting-out quay in the port of Genoa, the *Aquila*'s machinery was satisfactorily tested for the first time. Machinery and speed trials at sea had been planned for September 1943, but on 22 June 1943 it was decided to discontinue the fitting-out of *Aquila* (whose hull and machinery were 99 per cent and 98 per cent complete respectively, with other components about 70 per cent complete) to give priority to much-needed escort ships.

The main problem with *Aquila*'s completion was her air group. This was to consist of thirty-eight Reggiane Re 2001 Falco II fighter-bombers, some of which had already been converted for carrier operations by the Reggiane factory with the addition of arrestor hooks and catapult couplings in the landing gear: unfortunately, folding wings were not provided in this modified version and this would have greatly hindered the aircraft's movement and storage aboard the carrier. Furthermore, the training of pilots and air crew had only begun in the summer of 1942, so the earliest she could have been ready for combat operations, had the Armistice not intervened, would have been mid-1945.

The *Aquila* was captured by the Germans in

The liner *Roma* in the late 1920s, soon after her completion. The vessel was then in service as a passenger ship of the Navigazione Generale Italiana line. (E Bagnasco collection)

Genoa on 9 September 1943, who began to dismantle her; on 16 June 1944 she was damaged in an Allied air raid and on 19 April 1945 she was attacked by an Italian human torpedo of the 'Mariassalto', suffering further damage. The hulk was then used a few days later, along with those of other ships, to block the inner anchorage of the port of Genoa, where she was found at the end of the war. She was towed to La Spezia in 1949 and broken up between 1952 and 1954.

A detail of the starboard side of *Aquila*'s island, covered with camouflage nets. Some 20mm cannon had been temporarily embarked to be used in case of air attack, but the final configuration of *Aquila*'s 20mm weapons should have included thirty-three quadruple mounts of a new design. This photograph was taken by the noted naval photographer Aldo Fraccaroli on 23 August 1943, when the ship's fitting-out had already been discontinued. (Photo A Fraccaroli)

Aquila had been attacked by an Italian-manned human torpedo on 19 April 1945 and damaged. Some days later, when German troops left Genoa at the end of the war in Italy, the ship was towed into a position blocking the passage between the inner basin of the port of Genoa and the new docks west of the Old Port to be scuttled. Luckily, the ship remained afloat and in early May she was moved to another mooring where she would no longer obstruct the movements of other ships in port. The last phase of this operation was accomplished, as shown in this photograph, by hand-warping the ship alongside the quay. (Imperial War Museum)

Augustus

Another conversion of a liner into an aircraft carrier, as for *Aquila* begun but not completed, was that of the *Augustus*, another passenger ship similar to *Roma* and also launched in 1926 but with diesel machinery. It was decided to retain the diesel engines, so the new ship (renamed *Falco* initially, and then *Sparviero*) would have been only able to operate as an escort carrier, with a maximum speed of 18 knots. The conversion of *Augustus* (30,418grt, more than 200m long) started in October 1942, but the work was stopped in early 1943 when only the superstructure had been dismantled. On 5 October 1944, she was sunk by the Germans to block the eastern entrance of the port of Genoa; refloated in 1947, the *Sparviero* was immediately broken up.

Trento class

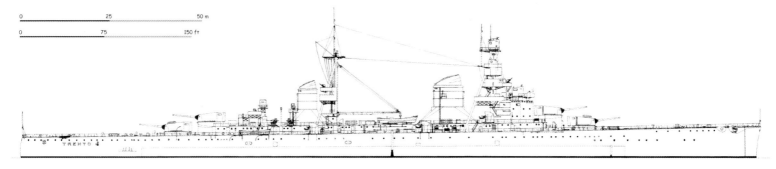

Starboard elevation of *Trento* in her last wartime configuration (spring 1942), before her sinking. (Author's drawing)

Displacement (tons): 10,500/ *Trento* 13,358, *Trieste* 13,530

Dimensions (m): 196.6 overall, 20.6 max. beam, 6.8 max. draught

Machinery: 12 boilers and 4 shaft-geared turbines, 150,000hp

Speed (kts): 31 (35.6 on trials at 11,250 tons about displ.)

Endurance (nm/kts): 4,160/16, 1,010/35; fuel 2,120-2,250 tons.

Armour (mm): 70 (waterline); 50 (main deck); 70 (conning tower); 70 (main turrets)

Armament: Eight 8in/50 (4 x II); sixteen 4.7in/47 (8 x I), reduced to twelve in 1937; eight 37mm/54 light AA guns (II x 4); eight 13.2mm MG (4 x II) replaced by eight 20mm light AA guns (8 x I) in 1942; eight 21in torpedo tubes (4 x II): one fixed bow catapult, 2 Ro.43 floatplanes.

Complement: 781 (25)

	Builders	Laid down	Launched	Completed
Trento	OTO, L	8 Feb 1925	4 Oct 1927	3 Apr 1929

Sunk on 15 June 1942 in the Ionian Sea by the British submarine HMS *Umbra*.

	Builders	Laid down	Launched	Completed
Trieste	STT	22 Jun 1925	26 Oct 1926	21 Dec 1928

Sunk by a USAAF air raid on 10 April 1943 at Palau (La Maddalena); hulk refloated in 1950 and sold to Spain; broken up at El Ferrol in 1956-9.

'C' and 'D' turrets of *Trento* trained to starboard in a 1936 photograph. The twin guns of the main armament of the two *Trentos*, like those of the other Italian heavy cruisers and of most light cruisers, suffered from being mounted in a single cradle, with detrimental effects on performance. (N Siracusano collection)

Studies for the first Italian 'treaty' cruisers started soon after the end of the Washington Conference of 1921–2 which for this type of warship set the maximum displacement at 10,000 tons and the maximum calibre of the main armament at 8in. As with all first-generation treaty cruisers, these restrictions meant that in order to get a main battery of eight 8in guns and stay within the displacement limit, armour protection had to be sacrificed. The Italian and French navies, in particular, took this even further with the *Trento*s and the *Duquense* class, fitting powerful machinery allowing speeds in excess of 30 knots, all at the cost of armour protection which was reduced to a scale suitable only for smaller and less heavily-armed ships.

The heavy cruiser *Trento* soon after commissioning. Note that two more legs have already been added to the original tripod mast; the secondary armament was originally composed of eight twin 4.7in/47 dual-purpose guns. (Fotocelere, Torino; Author's collection)

Trento and *Trieste* moored at the Stazione Marittima quay in the port of Genoa in late May 1938. Both cruisers, along with most Italian warships of the 1ª Squadra and 2ª Squadra, visited Genoa between 14 and 30 May 1938, after the successful 'H Review', held in the Gulf of Naples on 5 May during Hitler's state visit. The liner at right is the *Conte di Savoia*; the battleships *Cesare* and *Cavour* may be seen in the far background. (Author's collection)

The design of the *Trento* class, drawn up in 1923 by Gen. Filippo Bonfiglietti of the Genio Navale, envisaged two big ships armed with eight 8in guns in four twin turrets – two fore and two aft, with 'B' and 'C' turrets superimposed – on a long flush-decked hull with, for the first time on Italian ships, a bulbous bow. A rather stubby tripod mast, supporting the main fire directors, was built around the conning tower forward of the fore funnel, and a taller tripod main mast was fitted ahead of the after funnel. When the ships were commissioned, secondary armament consisted of eight twin dual-purpose 4.7in gun mounts, four 40mm/39 light AA guns and eight 12.7mm (later 13.2mm) MG in twin mounts. Eight fixed 21in torpedo tubes were fitted four on each side – athwartships on the lower deck, two between the funnels and two astern of the after funnel.

The main fault in the main armament of the *Trento* class (as well for all the heavy cruisers that followed, most light cruisers and many classes of destroyer) was that the twin guns were mounted close together in a single cradle, which caused the shells to interfere with one another's trajectories in

Trento at sea in late 1940. Note that the cap on the forward funnel, added early that year, is already painted light grey (as are all other vertical surfaces) in order to make the ship less conspicuous. A Ro.43 seaplane is positioned forward, showing what was at best an awkward arrangement of the bow catapult. (A Fraccaroli collection)

flight which, coupled with excessive muzzle velocities and inconsistent performance of the propellant charges, caused excessive salvo dispersion, a problem which plagued the Regia Marina's gunnery throughout the war.

The two ships, named *Trento* and *Trieste* to honour the two most important cities reunited with Italy at the end of the First World War, were laid down in 1925 and commissioned in December 1928 (*Trieste*) and April 1929 (*Trento*). They were also the first ships in Italian service to be fitted with a fixed catapult on the forecastle: this arrangement, which had already been tested aboard the cruiser *Ancona* (the former German *Graudenz*) in the second half of the 1920s, did not prove particularly effective as an aircraft parked on the catapult restricted the firing arcs of the forward turrets and was prone to wave damage even at moderate speeds.

At the end of 1929, the tripod masts had two extra legs added in an attempt to reduce the serious vibration that affected the main directors at speeds over 25 knots; later, the two aft 4.7in/47 mounts were disembarked, four 37mm/54 twin light anti-aircraft guns being fitted in their place, two on each side; during the war, the 13.2mm MG were replaced by 20mm cannon on a one-for-one basis. In early 1940, an obvious modification from the aesthetic point of view occurred when the two funnels each received a prominent cap that greatly enhanced the look of these two sleek ships.

Trento and *Trieste* took part in the battles of Punta Stilo, Cape Teulada and Matapan; on 21 November 1941 *Trieste* was torpedoed by the British submarine HMS *Utmost* but managed to reach Messina from where she was later towed to La Spezia for repairs. *Trento* (despite the faults in her main armament described above), heavily

damaged the destroyer HMS *Kingston* with a single hit at the Second Battle of Sirte in March 1942; she was torpedoed and sunk in the Ionian Sea by the submarine HMS *Umbra* on the morning of 15 June 1942, after having been stopped dead in the water, three hours before, by a torpedo launched from a British torpedo bomber.

Trieste shifted her homeport to La Maddalena in December 1942; she was sunk in a USAAF air raid on 10 April 1943, while she was moored at a buoy in the Mezzo Schifo bay (Palau, on the north-western coast of Sardinia just in front of La Maddalena island). The capsized hull of *Trieste* was refloated in 1950 and, as her machinery was still in good order, he was sold to Spain to be rebuilt as an aircraft carrier; these plans were later abandoned and *Trieste*'s hulk was broken up at El Ferrol in 1956–9.

Trento at Messina in April 1942, painted in a camouflage pattern with 'standard' colours (light grey, dark grey and greyish white) whose scheme was suggested by the noted naval painter Rudolf Claudus. (E Bagnasco collection)

The camouflaged *Trieste*, about at 07.50 on 13 August 1942 in the southern Tyrrhenian Sea. Along with *Gorizia* and *Bolzano*, she was part of 3ª Divisione Navale (Admiral Angelo Parona) bound for Messina along with eight destroyers; at 08.08 *Bolzano* was torpedoed and seriously damaged, north-west of Panarea (Aeolian Islands) by the British submarine HMS *Unbroken*. (E Bagnasco collection)

Above: An amidships detail of *Trieste*'s starboard side in the late 1930s. The Ro.43 seaplane is parked on the bow catapult and its crane can be seen between its tail and the guns of 'A' turret. Note the fore funnel in its original configuration and on the side of the hull at the extreme left, below the tripod mainmast, the two circular openings of a pair of fixed torpedo tubes. (E Bagnasco collection)

Left: The capsized *Trieste* in 1950 at the La Spezia Dockyard, following her refloating from the bottom of the Mezzo Schifo bay (Palau), where she had been sunk by a USAAF air raid on 10 April 1943. (E Bagnasco collection)

Below: The hulk of *Trieste* under tow off Cartagena by the Dutch tug *Thames* on 3 September 1951, having been sold to the Spanish Navy which planned to rebuild her as an aircraft carrier. Despite these ambitious plans, the former *Trieste* was later broken up at El Ferrol between 1956 and 1959. (E Bagnasco collection)

Zara class

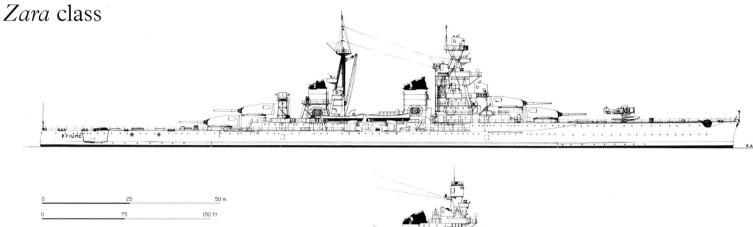

Starboard elevation of *Fiume* at the time of her loss in March 1941 (top); detail of *Pola*'s tower (bottom). (Line drawing by the late E Andò)

Displacement (tons): *Fiume* and *Zara* 11,508-11,870/ *Fiume* 14,168, *Zara* 14,530

Dimensions (m): 192.8 overall, 20.6 max. beam, 7.2 max. draught

Machinery: 8 boilers and 2 shaft-geared turbines, 95,000hp (more than 110,000hp on trials)

Speed (kts): 30-31 (max 35.2 on trials at about 11,000 tons displ.).

Endurance (nm/kts): 4,480-5,400/16, 1,150-1,900/31; fuel 2,300-2,400 tons.

Armour (mm): 150 (waterline); 70 (main deck); 150 (conning tower and main turrets)

Armament: Eight 8in/53 (4 x II); sixteen 4.7in/47 (8 x II) - from 1937-8 twelve 4.7in/47 (6 x II); eight 37mm/54 light AA guns (II x 4); two 4.7in/15 illuminating howitzers (I x 2) - [twelve 37mm/54 (6 x II) aboard *Gorizia* from 1942]; eight 13.2mm MG (4 x II); one fixed bow catapult, 2 Ro.43 floatplanes.

Complement: 841 (31)

	Builders	Laid down	Launched	Completed
Fiume	STT	22 Feb 1929	27 Apr 1930	23 Nov 1931
Sunk by gunfire of British battleships south of Cape Matapan on 28 Mar 1941.				
Gorizia	OTO, L	17 Mar 1930	28 Dec 1930	23 Dec 1931
Captured by the Germans at La Spezia on 9 Sep 1943; found half-sunk and partially dismantled at the end of the war: broken up in 1947.				
Pola	OTO, L	17 Mar 1931	5 Dec 1931	21 Dec 1932
Torpedoed and sunk by destroyers HMS *Jervis* and HMS *Nubian* at dawn, 29 Mar 1941 south of Cape Matapan, after having been stopped dead in the water in the evening of 28 March by a torpedo launched by a FAA torpedo bomber.				
Zara	OTO, M	4 Jul 1929	27 Apr 1930	20 Oct 1931
Heavily damaged by gunfire of British battleships south of Cape Matapan on 28 Mar 1941, she was scuttled by her crew at 00.30 on 29 Mar 1941 by blowing up the forward ammunition magazine.				

Even while *Trento* and *Trieste* were still on the building ways, doubts about the effectiveness of their scanty protection were being voiced and, at the end of 1928, studies for a new class of four more balanced heavy cruisers were almost complete. The new ships exceeded the standard displacement limits set by the Washington treaty by almost 2,000 tons, but this allowed them to embark the same armament as the *Trento* class, with an armour belt 150mm thick; reduced power (95,000hp and two shafts) saved on boiler and turbine weights, but this did not prevent a more than acceptable speed of 30–31 knots under operational conditions being maintained.

In order to further reduce weight and improve seakeeping, the *Zara* class ships had a long forecastle extending to the base of the tower; all were equipped with the new 8in/53 guns (Ansaldo

models 1927 or 1929) that although still in a single cradle like the guns of the *Trento*s, had a higher rate of fire and were generally more reliable.

The secondary armament was the same as on *Trento* and *Trieste* and, similarly, at the end of the 1930s the two after twin 4.7in mounts were replaced by four 37mm/54 twin light anti-aircraft guns; a catapult was fitted forward on the forecastle and up to three Ro.43 floatplanes could be embarked, two of them being stored in a small hangar below the forecastle.

The four cruisers were named after smaller cities which Italy had acquired after 1918 and were laid down between 1929 and 1931: *Fiume* was built by the Stabilimento Tecnico Triestino at Trieste, *Gorizia* and *Pola* by OTO at Leghorn and *Zara* by OTO at La Spezia. *Fiume* and *Zara* were very similar, but *Gorizia* had a taller forward

funnel, with a wider base; *Pola*, built as a flagship, had a larger bridge structure of a different design which extended aft and faired into the forward funnel.

On trials, all ships exceeded 33–34 knots with more than 118,000hp, but their operational speed was in the range of 31–32 knots when commissioned, and a knot less in wartime; the eight boilers were located in five compartments and the ships' weights were more rationally apportioned than in the two *Trento*s, with hull and machinery reduced by 7 per cent and 9.3 per cent respectively; at the same time, the armour weight percentage increased from 8.7 per cent to a much

A detail of *Fiume*'s forecastle in late 1930, during fitting-out at the Stabilimento Tecnico Triestino, Trieste. Note the temporary coverings over the barbettes (as the 8in turrets still have to be fitted), and the bow catapult. The two white rectangles on the forecastle deck, aft of the catapult, are the sliding doors of the hangar, which housed two Ro.43 seaplanes. (Author's collection)

more effective 24.8 per cent.

Pola, *Zara* and *Fiume* underwent no major modifications before all three were lost in the night action of Matapan on 28 March 1941, receiving no major changes or refits in wartime; it was planned to replace the twin 13.2mm MG aboard *Gorizia* with 20mm cannon, but this was not possible as on 8 September 1943 she was still in dockyard hands at La Spezia (having been damaged at Golfo Palma [island of Caprera, near La Maddalena] on 10 April 1943 – see *Trieste*), and the repairs were far from complete. *Gorizia* was found abandoned, partially dismantled and half-sunk at La Spezia at the end of the war; later refloated, her hulk was broken up in 1947.

The four *Zara* class ships were surely the best Italian heavy cruisers, and the exceptional

conditions of the loss of *Zara* and *Fiume* at Matapan (wrecked by 15in shells fired at almost point-blank range) do not allow a fair judgment of their robustness to be made; at the Battle of Capo Teulada, *Pola* hit the cruiser HMS *Berwick* with two 8in shells, knocking out one of her 8in turrets; in the brief gunfire action of the First Battle of Sirte, in December 1941, *Gorizia* damaged the destroyer HMS *Kipling* with a near miss.

Right: *Fiume* during sea trials in late summer 1931. The directors and main and secondary armament have already been fitted, but the 8in gun turrets are painted with an anti-rust primer and still have to receive their final light grey livery. (Author's collection)

Fiume at Trieste during fitting-out in 1931; the forward main turrets and all the twin 4.7in/47 guns are in place, but the aft 8in turrets still have to be fitted. (E Bagnasco collection)

Fiume at high speed, with the crew manning the side, in the late 1930s; the two twin 4.7in twin mounts on 01 level aft have already been removed, and four twin 37mm/54 anti-aircraft guns (two on each side) have replaced them. (E Bagnasco collection)

Below: A detail of *Gorizia*'s port side amidships, shortly before the Second World War; the tower was generally similar to that of *Fiume* and *Pola*, but the funnel was taller and with a wider base. Note the flared indentation in the hull side below the tower and the fore 8in gun turrets, intended to give a somewhat wider arc of fire to the two twin 4.7in mounts located forward on the main deck (the starboard one is visible on the extreme right of this photograph). (Istituto Luce, Rome)

Left: *Gorizia* 'taking it green' in the Ionian Sea in the afternoon of 1 September 1940, when the Italian battleships and cruisers dispatched to oppose the British Operation 'Hats' were making for their homeports without having been able to engage the enemy convoy in the morning. The awkward, and in weather such as this dangerous, position of the Ro 43 floatplane is obvious here. (E Leproni collection)

Above: Moored at Messina in early March 1942, *Gorizia* shows her newly-applied camouflage scheme, which may be considered a transitional pattern from the early war 'Claudus' schemes to the 'standard' schemes applied to most Italian ships from mid-1942 onwards. Part of the crew is drawn up on the quay for some sort of parade or ceremony.
G Vaccaro collection)

A detail of *Pola*'s port side amidships in the late 1930s, with 'A' and 'B' turrets, the tower faired into the fore funnel and the port 4.7in/15 illuminating howitzer on a platform on 01 level just aft of 'B' turret. *Pola* was the only cruiser of the *Zara* class without the curved indentation in the hull sides at the aft end of the forecastle. (Istituto Luce, Rome)

Below: An impressive starboard bow view of *Pola*, shown here leaving Genoa on 30 May 1938. Note the Ro 43 seaplane on the catapult and the paravane chains on both sides of the bow. (G Parodi collection)

Zara at sea in the early 1930s, soon after commissioning. (E Bagnasco collection)

The tower and fore funnel of *Zara* in the mid-1930s. Note the ladders connecting the various levels of the tower and the rarely-seen detail of the backs of the secondary directors; the insides of the shields of the 4.7in twin mounts were painted dark blue. In left foreground are the two barrels of a twin 37mm/54 light AA gun aboard the ship from where this photograph was taken. (A Fraccaroli collection)

Zara on 30 May 1938; this photograph was taken when many ships of the 1ª Squadra and 2ª Squadra left Genoa at the end of a visit after the 'H Review' on 5 May. (G Parodi collection)

Bolzano

Displacement (tons): 11,065/13,885
Dimensions (m): 196.9 overall, 20.6 max. beam, 6.8 max. draught
Machinery: 10 boilers and 4 shaft-geared turbines, 150,000hp
Speed (kts): 33 (36.8 on trials at 11,022 tons about displ.)
Endurance (nm/kts): 4,432/16, 915/35; fuel 2,260 tons
Armour (mm): 70 (waterline); 50 (main deck); 100 (conning tower); 80 (main turrets)
Armament: Eight 8in/53 (4 x II); sixteen 4.7/47 (II x 8) - from 1937 twelve 4.7in/47 (6 x II) and eight 37mm/54 light AA guns (4 x II x 4); eight 13.2mm MG (4 x II) - from 1942 eight 20mm light AA guns (8 x I); eight 21in torpedo tubes (4 x II): one trainable catapult amidships, 2/3 Ro.43 floatplanes. Minelaying capacity (111 tons)
Complement: 788 (28)

	Builders	Laid down	Launched	Completed
Bolzano	An	11 Jun 1930	31 Aug 1932	19 Aug 1933

Captured by the Germans on 9 Sep 1943 at La Spezia; sunk by a British 'Chariot' on 21 Jun 1944 at La Spezia, refloated and broken up after the war.

Above: *Bolzano* at Venice, about 1935. Note that the seaplane on the catapult is a CANT 25AR, as the Ro 43 – that would become standard in wartime – was introduced some time later; the secondary directors still have to be embarked, their position being shown by the inverted cone-shaped structure in the upper part of the tower, forward of the funnel. (Museo Storico Navale, Venice, via E Bagnasco)

Right: *Bolzano* off Panarea after being torpedoed, on fire and stranded in shallow water; note the list to port and the smoke from the fire in the tower and fore funnel area. (Author's collection)

With hindsight, the construction of the *Bolzano* does not appear fully justified, at least in relation to her characteristics: the original programme of the Regia Marina in fact initially envisaged six heavy cruisers (the two *Trento*s and the four *Zara*s), and a seventh unit was planned only when it became clear that *Pola* would operate as a flagship until the commissioning of the rebuilt battleships *Cesare* and *Cavour*. This would have allowed two 'Cruiser Divisions' of three ships each to be deployed, and it was said that *Bolzano* – albeit built when the *Zara*s were in the final stages of fitting out – should be more similar to the *Trento*s to enable them to operate together more efficiently.

On the contrary, it appears that *Bolzano* was built because of powerful lobbying on behalf of the Ansaldo yard (that had been left out of the heavy cruiser building programme until then) and the continuing belief in parts of the Regia Marina high command that speed was a more important factor than protection and robustness.

It was therefore decided to improve the design of the *Trento*s, adopting the type of forecastle found in the *Zara*s; at the same time, *Bolzano* embarked the improved 8in/53 guns of the four previous ships and the catapult was fitted amidships between the funnels. The secondary armament of eight (later reduced to six) twin 4.7in guns and lighter AA guns was quite similar to that of the four *Zara*s and – from a distance – *Bolzano* resembled the *Pola*, with the bridge structure, of a less complex design, faired into the fore funnel.

Speed was again a feature of the utmost importance and the machinery – with ten boilers and four shafts – delivered 150,000hp for a maximum speed of 33 knots. With protection reduced to 70mm at the waterline and 50mm on the main deck, a speed of only two knots higher than that of the *Zara*s did not compensate for the general weakness of the ship which only a short time after her commissioning began to be called 'un errore splendidamente riuscito', i.e. 'an error beautifully executed', given the attention lavished on her design.

Being part of the 3ª Divisione Incrociatori, *Bolzano* fought in the most important naval engagements of the first part of the war; at Punta Stilo she was hit by three 6in shells that slightly

Bolzano, camouflaged in 'standard' colours and with the bow and stern painted greyish-white, at La Spezia in June 1942, at the end of extensive repairs following the damage sustained after being torpedoed by the British submarine *Triumph* on 26 August 1941. (E Bagnasco collection)

damaged her steering gear and an 8in gun turret which was able to keep firing. In March 1941 she took part in the action off Gaudo with *Trento* and *Trieste* and, on 26 August 1941, she was torpedoed and damaged by HMS *Triumph* north of the Straits of Messina; repairs in Genoa lasted until June 1942.

On 13 August 1942, again in the Southern Tyrrhenian Sea North of Messina, *Bolzano* was torpedoed by the British submarine HMS *Unbroken* (that, firing four torpedoes, also damaged the light cruiser *Attendolo*). The ship was heavily damaged, a fire broke out and it was decided to flood the forward ammunition magazines; the bow-heavy *Bolzano* was then beached on a sand bank off the Aeolian island of Panarea. She was refloated in September and towed to La Spezia for permanent repairs. Plans to convert her into an 'aircraft launching' ship were drawn up but by early 1943 all work on the cruiser had ceased.

Bolzano was abandoned on 9 September 1943, and the Germans later began to dismantle her; on the evening of 21 June 1944 she was damaged and sunk in shallow waters by a British 'Chariot' in the Gulf of La Spezia, where she was found partially-submerged at the end of the war. Refloated upside-down, *Bolzano* was quickly broken up just after the war.

Above: In this impressive image, actually one of the best showing an Italian naval ship in the pre-war years, *Bolzano* is moored in the Gulf of La Spezia on 10 March 1938. (Photo A Fraccaroli)

'Condottieri' class – *Da Barbiano* group

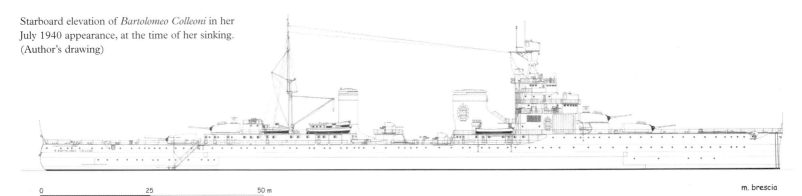

Starboard elevation of *Bartolomeo Colleoni* in her
July 1940 appearance, at the time of her sinking.
(Author's drawing)

| 0 | 25 | 50 m |
| 0 | 75 | 150 ft |

m. brescia

Displacement (tons): 5,200/7,800-8,050

Dimensions (m): 169.3 overall, 15.6 max. beam, 5.9 max. draught

Machinery: 6 boilers and 2 shaft-geared turbines, 95,000hp

Speed (kts): 31-32 (38-42 on trials with 101,200-123,000hp)

Endurance (nm/kts): 3,800/18, 970/36; fuel 1,290 tons

Armour (mm): 24-18 (waterline); 20 (main deck); 40 (conning tower); 23 (main turrets)

Armament: Eight 6in/53 (4 x II); six 4.7in/47 (3 x II); eight 20mm cannon (8 x I); eight 13.2mm MG (4 x II); four 21in torpedo tubes (2 x II): one fixed bow catapult, 2 Ro.43 floatplanes. Minelaying capacity (111 mines)

Complement: 521 (21)

	Builders	Laid down	Launched	Completed
Alberico da Barbiano	An	16 Apr 1928	23 Aug 1930	9 Jun 1931
Sunk off Cape Bon on 13 Dec 1941 by British destroyers *Legion*, *Maori* and *Sikh* and by the Dutch destroyer *Isaac Sweers*.				
Alberto di Giussano	An	29 Mar 1928	27 Apr 1930	5 Feb 1931
As *Da Barbiano*.				
Bartolomeo Colleoni	An.	21 Jun 1928	21 Dec 1930	10 Feb 1932
Sunk off Cape Spada (western coast of Crete) by HMAS Sydney and the British destroyers *Hero*, *Havock*, *Hasty*, *Hyperion* and *Ilex*.				
Giovanni delle Bande Nere	CCM	31 Oct 1928	27 Apr 1930	Apr 1932
Torpedoed and sunk off Stromboli (Aeolian Islands) on 1 Apr 1942 by the submarine HMS *Urge*.				

These four light cruisers, designed by Gen. Giuseppe Vian of the Genio Navale with the help of Gen. Giuseppe Rota, were initially designated 'grandi esploratori' (i.e. 'large scouts') and were intended to oppose the large destroyers armed with 5.1in and 5.4in guns built by the French Navy since 1922. For this purpose, the four *Da Barbiano* group ships had a standard displacement of about 5,200 tons and were armed with four twin 6in/53 turrets, three twin 4.7in/47 gun mounts and two twin 21in torpedo tubes; as all the emphasis was on speed, they had very little protection and were on the whole rather fragile. Furthermore, the desire for maximum speed had left them with a very high length to width ratio (10.7), making them bad seaboats in rough weather.

The bow was rather straight – the 'Condottieri' class were the last major Italian warships to have a vestigial ram bow and the forecastle extending to the base of the tower (that also housed the hangar for two seaplanes); the catapult was mounted on the bow, as in the *Trento* and *Zara* classes, and this awkward arrangement severely limited aircraft operations in even moderate weather, never mind in action. The three Ansaldo-built ships were very

Alberto di Giussano on speed trials off Genoa on 19 September 1930, some months before commissioning. In light condition, without directors and secondary armament, the 'Condottieris' reached speeds well in excess of 40 knots. In wartime, the realistic top speed was 31–32 knots. (Archivio Storico Ansaldo)

Alberico da Barbiano at Venice on 18 July 1934. The full weapon outfit of these ships may be seen in this fine view: the four 6in/53 twin turrets, the three twin 4.7in/47 gun mounts amidships and the canvas-covered port torpedo tubes. Note the identification markings (probably three red and one white triangles) atop 'D' turret: this was not a standard practice, and it is likely that such markings were temporarily applied as air-identification aids during some sort of fleet exercise. (Foto Baschetti, Venice; Author's collection)

similar, and the differences between them were very hard to spot; on the other hand the Castellammare-built *Giovanni delle Bande Nere* could easily be distinguished from the other ships by her funnels, whose prominent horizontal piping – on four levels – was very distinctive and visible even at moderate distances, and by an extra enclosed bridge atop the tower. In general *Bande Nere*'s construction was not up to the same standard as that of *Da Barbiano*, *Di Giussano* and *Colleoni*, and she never enjoyed a particularly good reputation.

The machinery arrangement (six boilers and two geared turbines) was based – fore to aft – on two boiler rooms, with two boilers each, followed by the starboard engine room, then a boiler room with boilers Nos 5 and 6 and then the port engine room. This affected the design of the funnels, with the fore funnel rather large and of a distinctive shape and the aft funnel cylindrical, vertical and with no rake. Although on trials, with more than 100,000/110,000hp, astonishing speeds of more than 40 knots were reached, operational speeds were considerably lower and in wartime were in the range of 31/32 knots at full load displacement.

The three 4.7in twin mounts and the torpedo tubes were grouped amidships and, some time after they were commissioned, single 20mm cannon were embarked; at the same time, in the early 1930s, in order to lighten the ship and improve transverse stability the tripod mast had

two legs removed, becoming a pole mast, while the lower hull was strengthened to avoid damage and leaks at high speeds. These modifications improved seakeeping, but the seaworthiness and general robustness of the 'Condottieri' class light cruisers remained questionable throughout their service lives.

In fact, all four were war losses. *Colleoni* was badly damaged off Cape Spada (western coast of Crete) on 19 July 1940 by only three direct hits from HMAS *Sydney*, and was later torpedoed and

sunk by the Australian cruiser's accompanying destroyers. *Da Barbiano* and *Di Giussano*, during a supply mission to North Africa loaded with barrels of gasoline, were wrecked and sunk by torpedoes and gunfire from three British and one Dutch destroyers off Cape Bon on 13 December 1941. *Bande Nere* had a somewhat longer wartime career: torpedoed on 1 April 1942 in the southern Tyrrhenian Sea by the British submarine HMS *Urge*, she broke in two and sank rapidly with heavy loss of life.

Alberto di Giussano at Messina in late summer 1941: this is one of the last known images of this ship, later sunk off Cape Bon on 13 December 1941 when bound for North Africa with a cargo of gasoline. Note the Ro 43 seaplane on the bow catapult and the funnels completely painted light grey, with no black caps, to make the ship less conspicuous. (Gruppo ANMI Savona)

Colleoni at Taranto in 1936. She is steaming at low speed from Mar Piccolo to Mar Grande, and this photograph was taken from the east bank of the short channel between the new and old town of Taranto, close to the turntable bridge. The seaplane on the catapult is a CANT 25 AR. (Foto De Siati, Taranto; Author's collection)

Giovanni delle Bande Nere leaving the port of Genoa on 30 May 1938. This photograph, taken a few minutes later than the one below (of *Colleoni*), makes it possible to identify the differences between the *Bande Nere* and the other three Ansaldo-built 'Condottieris' (*Da Barbiano*, *di Giussano* and *Colleoni*). In particular, notice the horizontal pipework on the sides of the funnel sides and the extra platform on top of the tower. (G Parodi collection)

A striking image of *Da Barbiano*'s forward turrets and main director, taken from the forecastle. The 'single cradle' arrangement of the 6in guns can clearly be seen: this feature, intended to save weight, adversely affected the performance of many Italian medium-calibre guns. (Author's collection)

Colleoni leaving Genoa on 30 May 1938. (G Parodi collection)

The six light cruisers of the two groups of the 'Condottieri' class moored inside the Molo Galliera in the port of Genoa, in late May 1938. From left to right: *Bande Nere*, *Colleoni*, *Di Giussano*, *Cadorna*, *Diaz* and *Da Barbiano*. In the left foreground, the yacht *Elettra*, then owned by the noted scientist Guglielmo Marconi and aboard which he conducted many scientific experiments. (G Parodi collection)

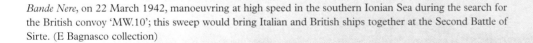

Bande Nere, on 22 March 1942, manoeuvring at high speed in the southern Ionian Sea during the search for the British convoy 'MW.10'; this sweep would bring Italian and British ships together at the Second Battle of Sirte. (E Bagnasco collection)

'Condottieri' class – *Cadorna* group

Displacement (tons): 5,316/7,935
Dimensions (m): 169.3 overall, 15.5 max. beam, 5.5 max. draught
Machinery: 6 boilers and 2 shaft-geared turbines, 95,000hp
Speed (kts): 31–32 (38–40 on trials with 110,000–120,000hp)
Endurance (nm/kts): 3,000/16, 900–995/36; fuel 1,150–1,180 tons
Armour (mm): 24–18 (waterline); 20 (main deck); 40 (conning tower); 23 (main turrets)
Armament: Eight 6in/53 (4 x II); six 4.7in/47 (3 x II); eight 20mm cannon (8 x I); eight 13.2mm MG (4 x II); four 21in torpedo tubes (2 x II): one fixed catapult, 2 Ro.43 floatplanes. Minelaying capacity (94 mines)
Complement: 521 (21)

	Builders	Laid down	Launched	Completed
Luigi Cadorna	CRDA, T	19 Sep 1930	30 Sep 1931	11 Aug 1933
Stricken on 1 May 1951 and broken up 1953-4.				
Armando Diaz	OTO, M	28 Jul 1930	10 Jul 1932	29 Apr 1933
Torpedoed and sunk off the Kerkennah Islands by the submarine HMS *Upright*.				

When the four *Da Barbiano* light cruisers were still on the building ways, it was decided to build two similar ships incorporating some improvements; they were named after Italy's two most important generals of the First World War, the names of the four previous ships having honoured Italian military leaders of the Middle Ages and of the Renaissance.

Hull form and dimensions remained unchanged but – in order to improve seakeeping and stability – the height of the tower was reduced by eliminating the aircraft hangar. At the same time, the catapult was shifted aft of the second funnel, on 01 level: the catapult was again fixed, offset 23° to starboard, but its position was far more sensible and allowed the launch of aircraft, which were stowed on the same level, even in moderately heavy weather conditions, as well as freeing the arcs of fire of the forward 6in turrets.

They had a tripod main mast, and the disposition of the twin 4.7in/47 gun mounts and of the torpedo tubes resembled that of the four *Da Barbiano*s; the machinery arrangement followed that of the previous ships, and similarly their speed did not exceed 31–32 knots at full load displacement in wartime. *Diaz* and *Cadorna* were built with a troop transport capability: 15 officers and 320 men could be berthed in the crew quarters on the main deck forward and in other spaces below the catapult deck aft of the second funnel.

Both ships took part in the action off Punta Stilo and in convoy escort operations in the winter of 1940/41; during one of these missions *Diaz* was torpedoed and sunk by a British submarine on 25 February 1941. *Cadorna* made some troop transport runs to North Africa for the rest of 1941 but from January 1942 she shifted her homeport to Pola, where she was employed as a training ship by the local naval schools; after the Armistice, *Cadorna* took part only in personnel transport operations and she was one of the four cruisers left to Italy by the peace treaty. Old and worn out, *Cadorna* remained in Taranto for stationary duties until 1950; stricken in 1951, she was broken up in 1953–4.

The light cruiser *Luigi Cadorna* entering the Mar Grande at Taranto in the late 1930s. Two IMAM Ro.43 floatplanes rest on the 01 level aft of the second funnel; the fixed catapult, angled 23° to starboard, may be seen in this view taken from the west side of the channel connecting Mar Grande to Mar Piccolo. (Author's collection)

Diaz during a visit to Australia in October 1934; the ship was commanded by then-Captain Angelo Iachino and during the cruise called in at Melbourne, Sydney and other ports in the area. (A Asta collection)

Diaz at La Spezia, in the late 1930s. (A Fraccaroli collection)

The old and worn-out *Cadorna* at Taranto in 1947. She was one of the four cruisers left to Italy by the peace treaty, but because of her poor material condition she never went to sea after the end of the war. She remained moored at Taranto Dockyard for stationary duties until 1950, and was broken up a few years later. (Photo A Fraccaroli)

Montecuccoli class – first and second group

Montecuccoli during speed trials in the Gulf of Genoa in spring 1935, shortly before commissioning. In one of the runs, at a 'light' displacement of 7,020 tons and 126,099hp, she reached a top speed of 38.72 knots. In service, however, the maximum speed the four ships of the class could make was 33–34 knots. (Biblioteca 'A Maj', Bergamo via M Piovano)

Displacement (tons): 7,550/8,995

Dimensions (m): 182.2 overall, 16.5 max. beam, 6.0 max. draught

Machinery: 6 boilers and 2 shaft-geared turbines, 106,000hp

Speed (kts): 33-34 (38.7 on trials with 126,000hp).

Endurance (nm/kts): 4,200/18, 1,150/35; fuel 1,150-1,300 tons

Armour (mm): 60-25 (waterline); 30-20 (main deck); 100 (conning tower); 70 (main turrets)

Armament: Eight 6in/53 (4 x II); six 4.7in/47 (3 x II); eight 37mm/54 light AA guns (4 x II); eight 13.2mm MG (4 x II); (*Montecuccoli*: eight 20mm/70 cannon [8 x I] from 1943); four 21in torpedo tubes (2 x II): one turntable catapult, 2 Ro.43 floatplanes. Minelaying capacity (112 mines - 146 from 1941)

Complement: 648 (38)

	Builders	Laid down	Launched	Completed
Raimondo Montecuccoli	An	1 Oct 1931	2 Aug 1934	30 Jun 1935
Stricken on 1 June 1964 and broken up at La Spezia in 1972.				
Muzio Attendolo	CRDA, T	10 Apr 1933	9 Sep 1934	7 Aug 1935
Sunk in a USAAF air raid on Naples on 4 December 1942; refloated in 1949 and broken up.				

The extreme characteristics of the *Da Barbiano* and *Cadorna* class light cruisers led the Comitato Progetti Navi ('Maricominav') to plan more balanced ships, whose design, drawn up by General Umberto Pugliese of the Genio Navale, was passed to the Ansaldo yard, Genoa, in October 1930 for implementation.

Standard displacement was of the order of 6,900 tons, and full load displacement just below 9,000 tons; the two ships – named *Raimondo*

Montecuccoli and *Muzio Attendolo* (after two famous Italian military leaders of the seventeenth century and the Middle Ages respectively) – were about 10m longer than the previous 'Condottieris' and maximum armour thickness was increased to 60mm on the waterline. Their general appearance was undeniably more elegant than that of the previous ships and, along with the ships of the second group, may be considered the best-looking Italian cruisers of the period. The most interesting feature of General Pugliese's design was the new, simpler circular bridge tower, well suited to accommodating both the admiral's and the navigating bridge as well as providing increased protection to the wheelhouse and its hydraulic pipes. Main and secondary armament was quite similar to that of the previous light cruisers, with four twin 6in/53 turrets (two fore and two aft) and three twin 4.7in/47 dual purpose gun mounts. *Montecuccoli* and *Attendolo* were completed with four twin 37mm/54 light AA guns and, later in the war, the twin 13.2mm MG originally fitted were replaced with 20mm/70 cannon. The two twin 21in torpedo tubes, located one on each side on the main deck, abaft the forecastle, were

An unbelievably clear view of *Montecuccoli*, shown here off Leghorn probably in early 1937, before her Far Eastern cruise. The distinctive features of the *Montecuccoli* class light cruisers may be seen: conical bridge tower, widely spaced funnels, tripod main mast and aeronautical arrangements between the funnels. (Foto Miniati, Leghorn; Author's collection)

A wonderful view of *Raimondo Montecuccoli*, shown here at the mouth of the Yangtze River in mid-September 1937. *Montecuccoli* visited Shanghai and other Far East ports, leaving La Spezia on 30 August 1937; in late December she was in Australian waters, returning to Shanghai in early 1938. After calls in Yokohama and Shanghai once more, *Montecuccoli* returned to Italy, arriving at Naples on 7 December 1938. (Author's collection)

disembarked from *Montecuccoli* in 1944.

These two light cruisers were fast (33–34 knots in wartime and more than 38 knots on trials), sufficiently protected and all in all fairly good seaboats, even though their transverse stability could never be considered their best feature; the two raked, widely spaced funnels greatly contributed to the general elegance of these ships, and between them – on 01 level of the deckhouse aft of the forecastle – a turntable catapult was fitted; two Ro.43 seaplanes could be transported, usually stored on cradles on 01 level when not in use. *Montecuccoli* and *Attendolo* were fitted with mine rails and, as commissioned, could carry 112 mines; in 1941 mine capacity was increased to 146 weapons, and along with other cruisers and destroyers, both ships took part in numerous minelaying missions in the waters between Sicily and Tunisia.

Three views of *Montecuccoli* showing various details. From left to right: the bridge tower seen from the port side, topped by the main director; a stern-on view, with the stern anchor hawsepipe and the exhausts of the stern smoke generators; a photograph taken from the platform abaft the second funnel, showing a twin 37mm/54 light anti-aircraft gun, the twin 4.7in/47 mount on the aft section at 01 level and the starboard mine rails. In wartime, the four *Montecuccoli* class light cruisers could carry up to 146 mines. (from left to right: Author's collection; E Bagnasco collection; M. Cicogna collection)

Attendolo at sea, in late 1941/early 1942. She was painted with this 'Claudus' scheme between July 1941 and July 1942; thereafter, she reverted to a 'standard' scheme with shades of light and dark grey. See also photo on page 207. (E Bagnasco collection)

A detail of *Montecuccoli* as a training ship for midshipmen, here moored in Genoa in the late 1950s. Note 'A' turret, the twin 40mm/56 Bofors mount atop 'B' barbette, the new bridge, the American-built Bofors directors and the SPS-6 air-search radar on a sponson in front of the new, enlarged mainmast. (Author's collection)

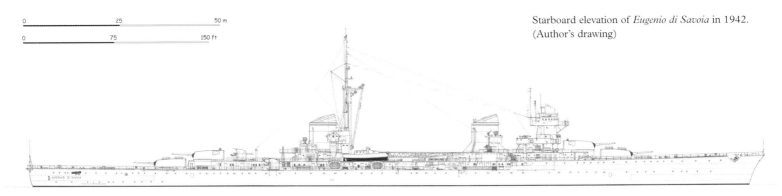

Starboard elevation of *Eugenio di Savoia* in 1942. (Author's drawing)

Displacement (tons): *Aosta* 8,450, *Eugenio* 8,750; *Aosta* 10,540, *Eugenio* 10,843

Dimensions (m): 186.9 overall, 17.5 max. beam, 6.5 max. draught

Machinery: 6 boilers and 2 shaft-geared turbines, 110,000hp

Speed (kts): 33–34 (37.3 on trials with 121,000/128,000hp)

Endurance (nm/kts): 3,900/14, 890/36; fuel 1,680 tons

Armour (mm): 70–35 (waterline); 35–20 (main deck); 100 (conning tower); 90 (main turrets)

Armament: Eight 6in/53 (4 x II); six 4.7in/47 (3 x II); eight 37mm/54 light AA guns (4 x II); eight 13.2mm MG (4 x II); (ten 20mm/70 cannon [10 x I] from 1943); six 21in torpedo tubes (2 x III): one turntable catapult, 2 Ro.43 floatplanes. Minelaying capacity (112 mines – 146 from 1941)

Complement: 694 (42)

	Builders	Laid down	Launched	Completed
Eugenio di Savoia	An	6 Jul 1933	16 Mar 1935	16 Jan 1936

Stricken on 26 June 1951 and transferred to Greece 1 July 1951. Renamed *Helli*, discarded in 1964 and later broken up at Piraeus.

| **Emanuele Filiberto Duca d'Aosta** | OTO, L | 29 Oct 1932 | 22 Apr 1934 | 13 Jul 1935 |

Stricken on 12 February 1949 and transferred to USSR (as *Z.15*) at Odessa 2 March 1949. Renamed *Kerch*, discarded and broken up in 1959.

By the end of 1931, the Regia Marina decided to build two more *Montecuccoli* class light cruisers, and the design of these two ships incorporated some improvements in protection (now 70mm maximum on the waterline, with 22.8 per cent of displacement now assigned to armour as opposed to 19.6 per cent for *Montecuccoli* and *Attendolo*), and for the machinery (whose output was increased to 110,000hp). The Ansaldo-built *Eugenio di Savoia* had Yarrow boilers and Belluzzo type turbines, while the OTO Leghorn-built *Emanuele Filiberto Duca d'Aosta* had Thornycroft boilers and Parsons turbines. Armament, fittings, aviation equipment and minelaying arrangements repeated those of *Montecuccoli* and *Attendolo*, the only difference being the torpedo tubes, twins on the first two ships and triples on the third and fourth units of the class.

Aosta and *Eugenio* were quite similar to *Montecuccoli* and *Attendolo*, and had a similar bridge tower, but could easily be distinguished from the two previous ships because of an extra enclosed bridge atop the tower, to increase their flagship accommodation. In 1943, a lattice mast was built between the tower and the fore funnel, but only *Eugenio* was fitted with an EC 3/ter 'Gufo' search radar. *Aosta* never received her planned German Fu.Mo 21/39 'De.Te' radar, as at the Armistice of 8 September 1943 her refit was still far from complete.

The two light cruisers were named after Prince Eugenio of Savoia (1663–1736), the noted general who fought at Vienna during the Turkish siege of 1683 and commanded the Habsburg armies in many campaigns against the Turks, and the Duke of Aosta, commander of the Italian Third Army during the First World War, who had died in July 1931, only a year before the cruiser's keel-laying ceremony.

During the war, the four light cruisers of the *Montecuccoli* class often operated together, forming the famous 7ª Divisione Navale: all fought at the battles of Punta Stilo (July 1940) and Pantelleria in June 1942, and – minus *Attendolo* – took part in August 1943, along with the cruisers of the 8ª Divisione Navale, in the abortive missions against enemy shipping in southern Tyrrhenian waters,

A detail of the aft twin 4.7in/47 mount and 'C' turret of *Attendolo*, in late 1942, looking aft. Note the compass on the platform atop the short lattice mast in the foreground and the mine rails on the main deck. (M Cicogna collection)

following the Allied landings in Sicily in July.

Montecuccoli, *Attendolo*, *Eugenio* and *Aosta* also variously operated as convoy escorts and on minelaying missions in 1941–2; they also took part in shore bombardments during the Greek campaign. *Aosta* was a lucky ship, and was never damaged in wartime, while *Eugenio* was hit by bombs in Naples in December 1942 and was damaged by a German mine off Calabria in February 1944. *Attendolo* was sunk in a USAAF air raid on Naples on 4 December 1942, where she was undergoing repairs following the torpedo damage suffered on the previous 13 August (see

also *Bolzano*). She listed to starboard and sank at her moorings in the inner port; during the same attack, *Montecuccoli* was badly damaged by a bomb that hit her near the fore funnel and she had to be towed to Genoa, where her repairs lasted until July 1943.

After the war, *Attendolo* was refloated; it was planned to rebuild her as an anti-aircraft cruiser, but the idea was soon abandoned and the hulk was broken up in 1949–50. *Montecuccoli*, one of the four cruisers left to Italy by the peace treaty, began service as a training ship for the Naval Academy in 1949; five years later she was specifically rebuilt for

this new role, disembarking 'B' turret and being fitted with a new bridge, enlarged forecastle and four twin 40mm/56 Bofors guns. *Montecuccoli* left active service in May 1964 and – after some years in reserve – was broken up at La Spezia in 1972.

Duca d'Aosta was allotted to the USSR as war reparations in 1949, and – as *Kerch* – served until 1959, when she was broken up. Similarly, *Eugenio di Savoia* went to Greece in 1951 (after repairing the February 1944 mine damage): renamed *Helli* in Greek service, she was discarded in 1964 and later broken up at Piraeus.

Eugenio di Savoia in early 1938. *Montecuccoli* is moored on the starboard side of *Eugenio*, and it is thus possible to point out the two main differences between *Eugenio* and *Aosta* and the first two ships of the *Montecuccoli* class (*Montecuccoli* and *Attendolo*). Note, in fact, the different bridge towers (that of *Eugenio* had an enclosed platform in its lower part and an extra enclosed bridge on the top), and *Eugenio*'s larger after funnel. (N. Siracusano collection)

Left: An IMAM Ro.43 seaplane being launched from the amidships turntable catapult of *Aosta* in late 1941. (M. Cicogna collection)

Right: *Eugenio di Savoia* being launched at the Ansaldo yard, Genoa, on 16 January 1936. (Author's collection)

Below: A striking detail of *Eugenio*'s starboard side amidships in summer 1940, showing the bridge tower, the fore funnel and the Ro.43 seaplane on the catapult. (E Bagnasco collection)

Garibaldi class

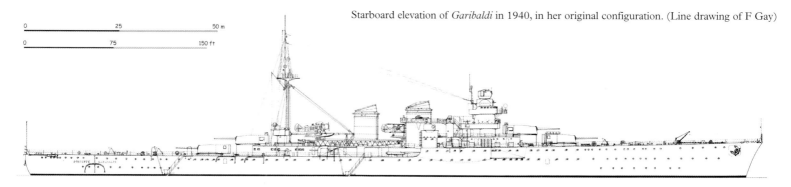

Starboard elevation of *Garibaldi* in 1940, in her original configuration. (Line drawing of F Gay)

Displacement (tons): *Garibaldi* 9,195, *Abruzzi* 9,592/ *Garibaldi* 11,528, *Abruzzi* 11,542

Dimensions (m): 187.05 overall, 18.9 max. beam, 6.8 max. draught

Machinery: 8 boilers and 2 shaft-geared turbines, 100,000hp

Speed (kts): 31 (33/34 on trials)

Endurance (nm/kts): 5,360/14, 2,400/28, 1,650/31; fuel 1,650 tons

Armour (mm): 30 (waterline) + 100 (inner belt); 40 (main deck); 140 (conning tower); 135 (main turrets)

Armament: Ten 6in/55 (2 x III, 2 x II); eight 4.7in/47 (4 x II); eight 37mm/54 light AA guns (4 x II); eight 13.2mm MG (4 x II); (ten 20mm/70 cannon [10 x I] from 1942-3); six 21in torpedo tubes (2 x III, removed after 1944 and replaced by two 4.7in/47 [2 x I]): two turntable catapults, up to 4 Ro.43 floatplanes. Minelaying capacity (120 mines)

Complement: 850 (42)

	Builders	Laid down	Launched	Completed
Luigi di Savoia Duca degli Abruzzi	OTO, M	28 Dec 1933	21 Apr 1936	1 Dec 1937
Stricken on 1 April 1961 and broken up in 1965.				
Giuseppe Garibaldi	CRDA, T	1 Dec 1933	21 Apr 1936	20 Dec 1937
Rebuilt as a guided missile cruiser, 1954-61; Stricken on 20 February 1971 and broken up at La Spezia, 1978-9.				

The building of the six French light cruisers of the *La Galissonière* class prompted the Regia Marina to further strengthen its cruiser force even more and, when building of the two *Aosta*s had just begun, planning for two new, improved ships was initiated. The two new ships were designed to be able to outperform the French light cruisers and even to fight on equal terms against 8in cruisers: it was thus necessary to mount new 6in guns and improve protection, reducing maximum speed to 31 knots at the same time.

The two ships were allotted one each to OTO, Muggiano (La Spezia) and to CRDA Trieste's yard: laid down in December 1933, both were launched on 21 April 1936 and commissioned in December 1937; their names honoured Luigi Amedeo di Savoia, Duca degli Abruzzi, leader of expeditions in Africa and to the North Pole and CinC of the joint Allied naval forces in the early part of the First World War, and the famous general and patriot Giuseppe Garibaldi, hero of Italian independence in the nineteenth century.

The design of the two ships differed from that

Abruzzi in 1938, soon after commissioning. Note the sleek hull lines, the bridge tower very similar to that of *Duca d'Aosta* and *Eugenio di Savoia*, the close-set funnels and the port catapult. From a distance, *Garibaldi* and *Abruzzi* could easily be confused with the *Cavour* and *Doria* class battleships. Both *Abruzzi* and *Garibaldi* were launched on the same date – 21 April, known as the 'Natale di Roma' – the day in 753 BC by convention celebrated as the date on which Rome was founded. Many Italian ships of the 1920s and 1930s were laid down, launched or commissioned on important anniversaries in Italian history or on dates closely linked to events of the Fascist regime (the battleships *Littorio* and *Vittorio Veneto*, for instance, were both laid down on 28 October 1934, the twelfth anniversary of Mussolini's 'March on Rome'). (E Bagnasco collection)

Abruzzi at La Spezia on 4 July 1942, at the end of a long refit to repair torpedo damage sustained in November 1941. The camouflage on the port side is quite similar to that on the starboard side (see photo on page 211). (E Bagnasco collection)

of the earlier light cruiser classes in the very prolonged forecastle and quarterdeck, the two funnels quite close together and the tall pole main mast, lacking the two 'legs' of all previous Italian cruisers. Protection was of the 'composite' type, with a 30mm external decapping armour plate, and a stronger inner 100mm vertical plate; the armoured citadel was rather short (protecting the central part of the hull from the fore to the after ammunition magazines), but strongly built, with main deck protection 40mm thick.

Eight boilers produced 100,000hp, giving *Garibaldi* and *Abruzzi* a top speed of 31 knots; on trials, however, with a displacement 1,300 tons lighter and more than 104,000hp, the *Garibaldi* reached the speed of 33.62 knots. Displacing only 8,635 tons and with almost 104,000hp the *Abruzzi* made 34.78 knots on trials, but such performances (and that of *Abruzzi* in particular) were impossible under service conditions, and a more realistic speed of 31 knots may nonetheless be deemed excellent considering the conditions in which Italian battleships and cruisers actually operated.

The ten 6in/55 guns of the main armament

Giuseppe Garibaldi at Taranto, in May 1942. In November 1941 the *Garibaldi* had been painted with this 'Claudus' scheme that was even more complex on the port side, with green panels and greyish white simulating a large bow wave. Later in 1943, *Garibaldi* was painted in a 'standard' scheme with the usual shades of light and dark grey. (E Bagnasco collection)

Abruzzi at Taranto on 29 April 1944. The flagship of 8ª Divisione Navale (Adm. Biancheri), she was returning from Freetown via Gibraltar where she had stopped for a short refit. The German 'De.Te' radar is still on the lattice mast; notice that the catapults and the Ro 43 seaplanes had been disembarked previously, as they would have been of no use on operations in the Atlantic. (E Bagnasco collection)

were divided into two triple turrets ('A' and 'D', similar to those fitted as secondary armament in the *Littorio* class) and two twin turrets ('B' and 'C', superimposed); each gun was mounted on an independent cradle and could fire 5–6 rounds per minute as the new design of loading trays, chain rammers and other equipment, incorporated in an oscillating loading arm, allowed the guns to be reloaded at elevations up to 20°. The layout of the turrets, the cylindrical bridge tower very similar to that of *Aosta* and *Eugenio*, the close-set funnels and the long, sleek lines of the hull reinforced their resemblance to the *Cavour* and *Doria* class battleships; the secondary armament consisted of four twin 4.7in/47 dual-purpose guns and, in 1942/43, the four twin 13.2mm MG originally fitted were replaced by ten single 20mm cannon. Two triple 21in torpedo tubes were found amidships on the main deck between the funnels, but in 1944 they were replaced by two single 4.7in guns, one on each side.

For the first time aboard Italian cruisers, two turntable catapults were embarked, one on each side of the aft funnel on 01 level; up to four Ro.43 seaplanes could be carried, and a couple could be partially protected in two small hangars abreast the fore funnel. Both *Garibaldi* and *Abruzzi* could transport and lay up to 120 mines in wartime. In August 1943 the *Abruzzi* was fitted with a stub lattice mast abaft the conning tower with a German Fu.Mo 21/39 'De.Te' radar on top; in 1944, a British Type 286 navigational radar was fitted aboard both ships.

During the war, the *Garibaldi* and *Abruzzi* (forming the 8ª Divisione Navale) engaged enemy ships only once, at Punta Stilo, in July 1940; they took part also in other operations but – as a general rule – they were somehow 'spared' as they were Regia Marina's most modern and thus precious cruisers and, in particular, they were never used for minelaying or fast transport duties, even if the robustness of these ships allowed them to withstand severe damage. On 28 July 1941,

Garibaldi, while on the way back from a convoy escort mission, was torpedoed west the Island of Marettimo (off Trapani) by the British submarine *Upholder*; in spite of the more than 700 tons of water that flooded the forward part of the ship, she managed to reach Palermo and then Naples, where she was repaired in two months. On 22 November 1941, the *Abruzzi* had her stern and rudder badly damaged in the Ionian Sea by a torpedo from a British torpedo bomber and, as her rudder was jammed to starboard, she had to be towed to La Spezia for permanent repairs.

After the Armistice, both *Garibaldi* and *Abruzzi* went to Malta, but at the beginning of October 1943 they were back in Taranto again. Between November 1943 and April 1944, the *Abruzzi* (initially with *Aosta* and then *Garibaldi*), were based at Freetown (Sierra Leone), taking part in patrols against German raiders and merchant ships trying to force the Allied naval blockade in mid-Atlantic. After the peace treaty of 1947, the two ships were the only major ships of any value left to Italy and were often based in Taranto and La Spezia in the early 1950s. Refitted with new radars and 40mm/56 Bofors guns, the *Abruzzi* was discarded in 1961 and later scrapped; the *Garibaldi* was rebuilt between 1954 and 1961 as the first Italian guided missile cruiser (and the first guided missile cruiser of a Western-European Navy as well), and served – often as flagship of the Squadra Navale – until 1971, when she was discarded and transferred to the reserve. Later decommissioned, she was broken up at La Spezia in 1978–9.

When returned to service after her conversion, *Garibaldi* had a new multi-level tower, enlarged superstructure, a new square stern, a single funnel and new 135mm/45 and 76mm guns of Italian origin. A twin US Mark 4 launcher for Terrier missiles was fitted aft of the funnel and, astern of the Terrier launcher, four vertical launch tubes for Polaris ballistic missiles were embarked. Although no Italian nuclear deterrent ever came about, due

to financial and, mainly, political reasons, in her day *Garibaldi* was still one of the most advanced warships in Europe.

The 1939 naval programme had envisaged two ships (with a possible third) of an improved *Garibaldi* type. These cruisers would have had the same dimensions and main armament of the *Garibaldi*s, but with the new 3.5in guns, four on each side, fitted in gyrostabilised mounts. Different arrangements were studied for their machinery, a 'traditional' one with eight boilers and two shaft-geared turbines for 115,000hp, and at least two more including auxiliary diesel engines (as for the Ansaldo-designed cruiser *Kirov* for the USSR), to improve endurance at cruising speed. With the entry of Italy into the Second World War, Adm. Cavagnari – then CinC of the Regia Marina and Under-secretary of the Navy – postponed these studies indefinitely and the work was later abandoned. The first ship would have been named after Costanzo Ciano, a naval hero in motor torpedo boats in the First World War and later a minister in Mussolini's government, but no details are known of the names suggested for the second and third ships.

Right: *Garibaldi* in 1966, in her final configuration as a guided missile cruiser after her major reconstruction in 1954–61. All the new features of the completely rebuilt ship may be seen; from left to right: the square stern (that improved seakeeping because of the weight of the missile installations astern), the four vertical tubes for Polaris, the twin launcher for Terrier surface-to-air missiles, the SPG-51 radar directors for the missiles, the Italian-built 'Argos 5000' air-search radar, the single funnel, four 76mm/62 OTO Allargato type dual-purpose guns, the new multi-level tower with lattice mast supporting the 3D SPS-39 radar and the twin 135mm/45 DP guns on the forecastle. The *Garibaldi* was decommissioned on 20 February 1971 and scrapped at La Spezia in 1978-1979. (Author's collection)

Right: *Abruzzi* was decommissioned in 1961, but in 1962 she played the part of the British battleship in the movie *HMS Valiant*, an Italian/British production directed by Roy Ward Baker, starring John Mills and Ettore Manni. The movie was distributed in Italy with the title *L'affondamento della Valiant* and is a balanced account of the Italian human torpedo attack on Alexandria of 18 December 1941. To play the role of *HMS Valiant*, the *Abruzzi* was painted with this entirely fictional camouflage scheme, which she retained after shooting ended; indeed, when she was towed to the breaker's yard in 1965, *Abruzzi* was still painted in this way. (E Bagnasco collection)

'Capitani Romani' class

Starboard elevation of *Attilio Regolo* in 1943. (From an original OTO, Leghorn Yard drawing – courtesy Gruppo di Cultura Navale, Bologna)

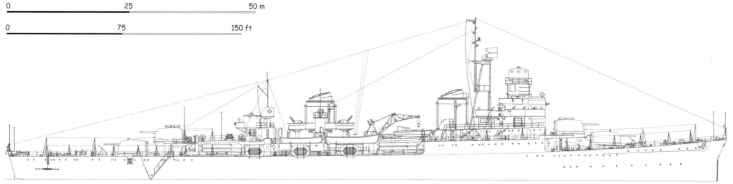

| 0 | 25 | 50 m |
| 0 | 75 | 150 ft |

Displacement (tons): 3,084/5,420

Dimensions (m): 142.9 overall, 14.4 max. beam, 4.06 max. draught

Machinery: 4 boilers and 2 shaft-geared turbines, 110,000hp

Speed (kts): 37/38 (39/40 on trials)

Endurance (nm/kts): 4,300/17, 2,950/25; fuel 1,400 tons

Armament: Eight 5.3in/45 (4 x II); eight 37mm/54 light AA guns (8 x I); eight 20mm/70 cannon (8 x I); eight 21in torpedo tubes (2 x IV); two depth charge throwers; minelaying capacity (max 130 mines)

Complement: 420 (22)

	Builders	Laid down	Launched	Completed
Attilio Regolo	OTO, L	28 Sep 1939	28 Aug 1940	15 May 1942
To France 1 August 1948; renamed *Chateaurenault*; discarded in 1962 and broken up at La Spezia in 1970.				
Giulio Germanico	NM	3 Apr 1939	26 Jul 1941	––
Rebuilt in 1953-6 and commissioned by the Marina Militare Italiana as *San Marco*; stricken 1 February 1972.				
Pompeo Magno	CNR, A	23 Sep 1939	24 Aug 1941	24 Jun 1943
Allotted to France but retained by the Italian Navy; rebuilt 1953-6 and recommissioned as *San Giorgio*; stricken 1 June 1982.				
Scipione Africano	OTO, L	28 Sep 1939	12 Jan 1941	23 Apr 1943
To France 9 August 1948; renamed *Guichen*; discarded in 1961 and broken up.				

Ships not completed and hulks broken up 1942-5 or post-war (see also text):

Caio Mario, Claudio Tiberio	OTO, L
Claudio Druso, Vipsanio Agrippa	Cdt, RT
Cornelio Silla, Paolo Emilio	An
Ottaviano Augusto	CNR, A
Ulpio Traiano	CNR, P

The final design work for a new class of 'oceanic scouts' (so-called in order to differentiate them from the previous 'Navigatori' class, which were still classed as 'light scouts'), began in 1935–6 and was carried out by Generals Ignazio Alfano and Umberto Pugliese of the Genio Navale.

Repeating a pattern that had been established earlier during the 1930s, this new class of ships was intended as a response to similar French construction programmes and, in this specific case, to the six large and fast destroyers of the *Le Fantasque* class (speed 37 knots, armed with five 5.4in guns) and to the subsequent similar, and even larger, destroyers of the *Mogador* class.

Twelve ships were originally planned (which undoubtedly would have been quite useful in the naval war in the Mediterranean, if all of them had been built and commissioned by 1940), all named after Roman military generals or emperors: thus they were generally known as the 'Capitani Romani' or the *Attilio Regolo* class, from the name of the first ship to be commissioned in May 1942. The main contractor for this class was the OTO Yard of Leghorn, that partially based the project on its own design of the destroyer *Tashkent*, built in 1937–9 for the Soviet Navy: this was a fast (44.5 knots on trials, with 110,000hp) and large (2,700 tons standard displacement) ship, and many of her features were incorporated in the design of the 'Capitani Romanis'. Four ships of the class, including *Attilio Regolo*, were built by OTO in Leghorn; the other eight ships were allocated to Ansaldo, Cantieri Navali Riuniti – Ancona and Cantieri del Tirreno – Riva Trigoso (all with two

The Soviet scout *Tashkent* at Leghorn, near the completion of her fitting-out (late 1938/early 1939). This ship was built quite quickly: laid down on 11 January 1937, she was launched on 21 November 1938 from the Morosini building ways of OTO Leghorn's yard and officially commissioned into Soviet service at Odessa on 6 May 1939. OTO based the plans of the new 'Capitani Romani' class on the design of this fast and heavily armed scout (or large destroyer) which was to have been followed by twelve sister-ships built in the USSR; the outbreak of war on the Eastern Front meant that these were never built. Note that the *Tashkent* had her name painted on both bows, a very unusual location for the name of a warship. (E Zelikov collection)

Attilio Regolo in late 1942. When commissioned (in May 1942), the ship had a similar camouflage pattern, sporting also light green panels that were discontinued when this scheme was painted in September 1942. Note the pole mast, later replaced by a tripod. (A Fraccaroli collection)

ships each), and one ship each to be built by the Palermo Yard of Cantieri Navali Riuniti and by Navalmeccanica, Castellammare di Stabia.

The *Tashkent*'s design was slightly enlarged (standard displacement of 3,084 tons – 5,420 tons full load), and the hull was now flush-decked with a large deckhouse incorporating the barbettes of 'B' and 'C' turrets, partially flush with the hull sides below the conning tower and the fore funnel. Great importance was given to speed and the powerplant was quite similar to that of the *Tashkent*, developing speeds in excess of 40 knots on trials and of more than 37 knots under operational conditions.

In many respects, the 'Capitani Romani' represented the final evolution of the 'super-destroyers' of the 1930s era, and they may be considered very large ships of this category, rather than small light cruisers: in effect, they had no protection, but the main armament (new 135mm [5.3in] guns 45 calibres long, in twin turrets built by Ansaldo and OTO) made the 'Capitani Romani' effective opponents for any foreign ships of similar size and characteristics. It was originally planned to embark a secondary armament of six

65mm/64 dual-purpose guns (of Ansaldo-Terni design) but, as this weapon never progressed beyond the prototype stage, eight Breda 37mm/54 model 1939 light AA guns were fitted instead. The torpedo armament was powerful, with eight 21in torpedo tubes grouped in two quadruple mounts on the centreline; mine rails allowed the ships of this class to transport and lay 114 'P 200' mines, or 130 smaller 'Bollo' type weapons.

The wartime careers of the only three ships to be commissioned (*Attilio Regolo*, *Pompeo Magno* and *Scipione Africano*) were rather limited. On 8 November 1942 the *Regolo* was torpedoed while steaming from Trapani bound for Palermo by the British submarine *Unruffled*, losing her bow; she was towed to La Spezia, where the bow was replaced by that of her uncompleted sister-ship *Caio Mario*. On the night of 17 July 1943, *Scipione* clashed with four British torpedo boats in the Straits of Messina, sinking *MTB 316* and damaging two others, and the whole action was conducted by *Scipione* at 37 knots, well in excess of the enemy boats' speed; during the days of the Armistice, *Scipione* had the unenviable task of escorting the corvette *Baionetta*, with the King and

the Royal Family aboard, fleeing from Pescara and Ortona to Brindisi, in Allied-controlled Southern Italy.

The *Regolo* left La Spezia on 9 September, along with other Spezia-based ships, bound for Bona and then Malta, but remained in the area of Asinara Island (north-western Sardinia) to rescue survivors of the battleship *Roma* after her sinking; along with some destroyers and torpedo boats she then made for Port Mahon in the Balearic Islands, where she was interned until January 1945, when she returned to Taranto.

The machinery of the Ansaldo-built *Cornelio Silla* and *Paolo Emilio* was fitted aboard the aircraft carrier *Aquila*; the incomplete hull of *Cornelio Silla* was used by the Germans to block the eastern approaches of the port of Genoa and, refloated after the war, was not broken up until 1954. The *Paolo Emilio*, which was in a less advanced stage of construction, was broken up directly on the building ways in 1941–2. *Caio Mario*, *Claudio Druso*, *Claudio Tiberio*, *Ottaviano Augusto* and *Vipsanio Agrippa* were never completed and their incomplete hulls were removed from the building ways during the war, or scrapped in 1946–7; the

Pompeo Magno off Ancona in July 1943. As with *Scipione* in the previous photograph, the EC 3/ter 'Gufo' radar still has to be installed on the tripod mast. (A Molinari collection)

Ulpio Traiano, whose fitting out had just begun, was sunk in Palermo by British 'Chariots' on 1 March 1943 and after being refloated in 1946–7 was later broken up.

Scipione, *Regolo* and *Pompeo* were allotted to France as war reparations, although only the first two actually saw service with the Marine Nationale: modernised and fitted with French weapons and electronics, they were renamed *Guichen* and *Chateaurenault* and served until 1961 and 1962 respectively.

The *Pompeo Magno* was stripped of much equipment and machinery by the French Navy, but remained in Italian hands and the renewed Marina Militare Italiana rebuilt her as a destroyer leader at the Genoese yard of the Cantieri del Tirreno between 1953 and 1955: recommissioned as *San Giorgio*, now she embarked three twin US-built 5in/38 twin turrets, 40mm/56 Bofors guns and Italian and US electronics. Similarly, the *Giulio Germanico* was refloated at Castellammare di Stabia after the war, and rebuilt like the *San Giorgio* between 1953 and 1956; renamed *San Marco* she served until February 1972, when she was decommissioned and later broken up.

The *San Giorgio* was modernised again in 1963–5: the machinery was now of the CODAG (combined diesel and gas) type, with diesel engines for cruising and gas turbines for high-speed dashes: the maximum output of the new machinery was now 31,800hp only, but this nevertheless allowed *San Giorgio* to steam at 28 knots and 240rpm. The rebuilt *San Giorgio* retained only two 5in/38 twin turrets, but three 76mm/62 OTO 'Allargato' guns and the funnels of more modern design meant the ship still had a sleek and aggressive look. Employed mostly as a training ship for the senior classes of the Accademia Navale, the *San Giorgio* was stricken after a very long career in June 1982, and immediately broken up.

A detail of *Pompeo Magno*'s bridge tower and mast at La Spezia, on 16 June 1946. Note the single Breda 37mm/54 AA gun on the platform in foreground. Although fitted with a tripod mast, *Pompeo* did not receive the EC 3/ter 'Gufo' radar found aboard *Scipione* and *Regolo*; the ship is still painted with the late war 'Allied' scheme (dark grey hull and light grey superstructure). (Photo A Fraccaroli)

Chateaurenault (the former *Attilio Regolo*) at Toulon, on 21 October 1954 soon after rebuilding (like *Guichen*, ex-*Scipione Africano*) at Forges et Cantieres de la Méditerranée, La Seyne (near Toulon). Note enlarged deckhouses, the degaussing cable, three German twin 105mm SKC/33 AA guns and French 57mm guns and electronics. *Guichen* and *Chateaurenault*, when rebuilt, were fitted with four triple 21.65in torpedo tubes located in an unusual position on the main deck, forward of the superstructure. (Marius Bar)

San Marco in her final configuration with CODAG machinery (note the new funnels), two twin 5in/38 mounts and three 76mm Allargato guns; the forward anti-submarine mortar has been retained. After the reconstruction of 1963–5, the former *Pompeo Magno* also served as a training ship for the senior classes of the Accademia Navale and was stricken and broken up in 1982, more than forty years after her launch: a significant accomplishment for a ship built in wartime. (Italian Navy; Author's collection)

Chateaurenault at La Spezia on 28 May 1970. The ship had arrived from Toulon some time before and was completely broken up before the end of the year. (Photo G Ghiglione)

San Giorgio and *San Marco*

The armoured cruiser *San Marco* on 18 August 1910, soon after commissioning. Note four funnels in pairs and the very low conning tower and superstructure. When commissioned, *San Giorgio* and *San Marco* had taller funnels, but they were lowered during the first refit of both ships. (A Fraccaroli collection)

The armoured cruiser *San Giorgio* was built between 1905 and 1910 by the Royal Yard, Castellammare di Stabia, and was considered a well-designed and strongly-built ship at the time of her commissioning: with a displacement of more than 11,600 tons full load, her 18,000hp machinery originally allowed a speed in excess of 23 knots, and the main armament of two twin 10in/54 turrets (plus four 7.48in twin turrets) made the *San Giorgio* and her sister-ship *San Marco* quite successful vessels in their category.

The *San Giorgio* took part in the Italo-Turkish war of 1911–12 and served in the Adriatic during the First World War. In the mid-1930s, it was decided to convert her into a training ship: at La Spezia Dockyard, six boilers out of the original fourteen were disembarked, and the remaining eight were modified in order to burn oil instead of coal, thus reducing speed to 16–17 knots. The original four funnels were combined in two single funnels of more modern design and, after disembarking the old secondary 76mm guns, four twin 4.7in/47 dual-purpose mounts were fitted on the 01 level, abreast the funnels.

After being used briefly as a training ship between 1938 and 1939, the *San Giorgio* was dispatched to Tobruk in early May 1940, in order to operate as a floating battery, moored in Tobruk harbour; a fifth 4.7in/47 twin mount was fitted on the forecastle, and 20mm cannon and 13.2mm MG were embarked as well. While operating in Tobruk, *San Giorgio* was in effect a floating fort that greatly contributed to the harbour's AA defence: crewmen manning the guns were protected by sandbags to give some splinter protection and, before the fall of Tobruk on 22 January 1941, the old cruiser took an active part in more than 100 anti-aircraft actions, destroying several enemy aircraft.

In view of the impending first British capture of Tobruk, the *San Giorgio*'s crew scuttled the ship on the morning of 22 January 1941 by exploding demolition charges in the magazines, but the ship was not completely submerged in the shallow waters of the harbour. The hulk of *San Giorgio* was refloated in 1952, but sank whilst on tow to Italy, where it was planned to break her up.

San Giorgio's sister-ship, *San Marco*, after serving as an armoured cruiser until the late 1920s, was converted in 1931–5 into a radio-controlled target ship. She could effectively manoeuvre without a crew controlled by her mother-ship (the torpedo boat *Audace*) and, when needed, the few men aboard could find shelter in an armoured area inside the hull. Some imaginative uses were considered for *San Marco* at the beginning of the Second World War (among them, that of 'fire-ship' to block Malta's Grand Harbour), but in 1941 she was back in service as a radio-controlled target ship. On 9 September 1943, the *San Marco* was seized by the Germans at La Spezia; at the end of the war she was found half-sunk at the Banchina Scali of the dockyard and, after refloating, she was broken up.

San Giorgio in Tobruk harbour in late 1940, employed as a floating battery. Note the twin 4.7in/47 mount on the forecastle, its base protected by sandbags like a land artillery position. The ship was painted in a light sandy brown to camouflage her against the desert background. Note the buoys of the anti-torpedo net in foreground: after *San Giorgio* was scuttled, more than thirty aerial torpedoes were found caught in the nets, proof of their effectiveness. (F Bargoni collection)

Ex-German and Austro-Hungarian cruisers

At the end of the First World War, Italy received a number of Austro-Hungarian and German ships as war prizes, and several of them served with the Regia Marina for a considerable period.

In particular, three German light cruisers were allotted to Italy:

• *Graudenz* (Laid down in 1911 at Kaiserliche Werft, Kiel, commissioned on 25 October 1913 – 6,300 tons full load, length 142.7m, seven 5.9in/45 single guns).
• *Strassburg* (Laid down in 1910 at Kaiserliche Werft, Wilhelmshaven, commissioned on 9 October 1912 – 5,993 tons full load, length 138.7m, seven 5.9in/45 single guns);
• *Pillau* (originally laid down in 1912 at Schicau Yard, Elbing, for the Russian Navy; commissioned on 14 December 1914 – 5,305 tons full load, length 135.3m, eight 5.9in/45 single guns).

These three German cruisers – all armed, as built, with 4.1in guns later replaced by 5.9in weapons – were handed over to the Regia Marina at Cherbourg on 20 July 1920 and, after rather long overhauls, were placed in service (renamed – respectively – *Ancona*, *Taranto* and *Bari*) because of their good material condition, fair protection and excellent main armament, which made them quite useful to the Regia Marina in the 1920s.

The *Ancona* was commissioned on 6 May 1925: during the overhaul her boilers had been partially modified, six being now oil-burning and six modified to burn either coal or oil. In 1928–9 *Ancona* was overhauled again in La Spezia Dockyard and a fixed bow catapult was fitted on the forecastle (requiring a new lengthened,

'clipper' stem): this allowed important tests to be carried out as completion of the first bow-catapult equipped cruisers (the two ships of the *Trento* class and the light cruisers of the first batch of the 'Condottieri' class) was by now imminent. After serving in second-line duties until the mid-1930s, *Ancona* was decommissioned in 1937 as she was still useful as a source of spare parts for the other two German-built cruisers (*Taranto* and *Bari*) then in service, and broken up before the end of the decade.

The cruiser *Taranto*, commissioned into Regia Marina service on 2 June 1925, was initially classed as a 'scout' and only in 1929 as a 'light cruiser'; she was employed overseas, mostly in East African waters, in 1926 and again in 1935–6 and, at the end of 1936, was overhauled and put back to service without the two forward boilers. This made the fore funnel useless, and *Taranto* now had only three funnels; speed decreased from 27 to 20–21 knots, but range, crew accommodation and living spaces were thus increased and improved.

In the Second World War *Taranto* was of limited value, and she was employed only in some mine laying missions and bombardments of the Yugoslavian coastline; along with *Bari* she was later attached to the Forza Navale Speciale that, in late 1940 – early 1941, was being assembled to take part in amphibious operations on the Greek coast and in the projected invasion of Malta (scheduled for late spring 1942). In December 1942 *Taranto* was decommissioned at La Spezia, and the crew scuttled her while moored at a quay on 9 September 1943; her hulk was used by the Germans to block one of the entrances to the Gulf of La Spezia, near the western end of the outer

breakwater. Raised in 1946, she was immediately broken up.

The *Bari* was commissioned some time earlier than *Ancona* and *Taranto*, on 21 January 1924, being initially listed among the scouts and classed a light cruiser in 1929. In 1934 she was modernised at Taranto: six coal-burning boilers were eliminated – thus reducing power from 28,000 to 21,000hp and top speed to 24 knots – and the fore funnel was also eliminated, leaving *Bari* with only two funnels. With crew quarters and endurance greatly enhanced, she operated in the Red Sea until 1937, returning to Italy afterwards.

In 1940 *Bari* became flagship of the Forza Navale Speciale, taking part in the landings at Kefallonia and in shore bombardments on the Greek coast, as well as in convoy escort missions from Italy to Greek ports. In 1942, along with *Taranto*, she was based at Leghorn where the landing force for the projected Malta invasion was being assembled; the Malta landings did not come about, and *Bari* later supported the Italian landings in Corsica, being placed in reserve in January 1943 at Leghorn, where it had been planned to convert her, in spite of her age, into an anti-aircraft cruiser. However, such rebuilding would have required an extensive technical effort, and the works were never begun; moreover, on 28 June 1943 *Bari* was heavily damaged in a USAAF air raid. She sank in the shallow waters of the port of Leghorn and, a few days later, she rolled over to port remaining half-sunk until the end of the war. Refloated in 1948, the hulk was towed to a breakers' yard and completely dismantled by the end of the year.

The cruiser *Ancona* (the ex-German *Graudenz*) at La Spezia in the early 1930s, after her 1928–9 refit during which a 'clipper' bow was fitted to support an experimental fixed catapult located on the forecastle. The white shadow in the upper right-hand corner is on the original photograph, an image taken by a photographer of the famous Studio Pucci, active at La Spezia in the 1920s and 1930s. (Author's collection)

Cruisers built for Siam

In 1938 the Kingdom of Siam ordered two small cruisers from CRDA, Trieste (standard displacement 4,300 tons, three twin 6in turrets, 153.8m long) partly inspired by the design of the *Montecuccoli* class: the two Siamese cruisers would have been smaller, single funnelled and lightly protected, and three boilers and two shaft-geared turbines, with an output of 40,000–45,000hp would have allowed only a rather low 28 knots. The construction of the two ships, named *Taksin* and *Naresuan*, continued under Siamese control until December 1941, when both were requisitioned by the Regia Marina and renamed *Etna* and *Vesuvio* respectively, from the names of Italy's most notable volcanoes. Their design and features were altered according to the new role envisaged for the two ships, now designated 'anti-aircraft cruisers': the bridge tower was to have been larger, surrounded by platforms on three levels and flush with the funnel's sides. It was decided to embark three twin 5.3in/45 turrets of the same type found aboard the 'Capitani Romani' class; the catapult was no longer needed, being replaced by a deckhouse abaft the funnel, and modifications were planned in order to operate *Etna* and *Vesuvio* as fast transports. In fact – had they been commissioned – *Etna* and *Vesuvio* would have been able to transport 1,000 fully-equipped soldiers, plus 450m³ of ammunition and provisions in four small centreline holds, three abaft the funnel and one

The hulks of *Vesuvio* (left) and *Etna* on 16 October 1947 in the Zaule Inlet near Trieste, where they had been towed by the Germans in 1944. A few months later they were broken up. (Photo A Fraccaroli)

on the quarterdeck, aft of 'C' turret.

It was also planned to fit new 65mm/64 AA guns (ten single mounts), but studies that dragged on too long for the final draft, released by 'Comitato Progetti Navi' only in May 1942 and the unavailability of the 65mm guns and of other equipment resulted in time-consuming delays in the building of the two cruisers: as for many other major Italian ships whose construction was then underway, all fitting-out aboard *Etna* and *Vesuvio* (which had been launched on 28 May 1942 and 6

August 1941 respectively) was discontinued in June 1943.

After 8 September 1943, the two ex-Siamese cruisers were seized by the Germans who began to dismantle them; at the beginning of 1944 both ships were towed inside the Vallone di Muggia (more precisely in the Zaule Inlet) near Trieste in shallow waters, where they were found half-sunk at the end of the war. Refloated post-war, the incomplete hulks of *Etna* and *Vesuvio* were broken up locally in the early 1950s.

French cruisers seized at Toulon

The scuttling of the French fleet at Toulon of 27 November 1942 allowed the Axis powers to take over many ships even if, in most cases, they had been badly damaged and needed long overhauls to become operational again. In part, this was not the case with the two light cruisers *Jean de Vienne* and *La Galissonière* (of the *La Galissonière* or '7,600 tonnes' class), both dry-docked in Toulon the day the French fleet was scuttled. The dry docks were flooded and the two cruisers, whose kingstons and seawater intakes had been deliberately opened, sank almost upright, resting on the dry docks' keelblocks with the water up to main deck level. Only one of *La Galissonière*'s propeller shafts was bent, and the two vessels, apart from some flooding and sabotaged rangefinders and directors, did not suffer particularly serious damage.

Both *Jean de Vienne* and *La Galissonière* were refloated between February and May 1943 and – as agreements between Germany and Italy assigned the two ships to the Regia Marina – they were temporarily renamed *FR 11* and *FR 12* respectively. They remained in Toulon to be overhauled, but the lack of spare parts and the protests of dockyard workers (who were of course strongly opposed to getting the ships into Regia Marina service) prevented the rapid repair of the two vessels, whose recommissioning was planned no earlier than 1944 for the *Jean de Vienne* and 1945 for the *La Galissonière*.

After the Armistice of 8 September, the two vessels – whose characteristics (displacement 10,200 tons, 97,000hp, speed 31 knots, length 179.5m and main armament three triple 6in/55 turrets) made them quite effective ships, very similar to the cruisers of the *Garibaldi* class – were abandoned by the Regia Marina and taken over by

the Kriegsmarine. The *Jean de Vienne* was sunk at Toulon on 24 November 1943 during an air raid, and similar was the fate of *La Galissonière*, sunk on 18 August 1944 in a USAAF air raid while moored at Lazaret Bay, in Toulon harbour. The hulks of the two cruisers were finally broken up in 1948 (*Jean de Vienne*) and in 1955–6 (*La Galissonière*).

The cruisers *FR 12* (ex-*La Galissonière*) at left, and *FR 11* (ex-*Jean de Vienne*) at Toulon in spring 1943. The ships had already been refloated, and having been seized by the Regia Marina, they were scheduled to be commissioned into Italian service in 1944–5. (A Fraccaroli collection)

Old destroyers

Augusto Riboty at Venice in November 1942, camouflaged in a standard dark grey and light grey pattern. Both *Riboty* and *Mirabello* were named after admirals of the late nineteenth century. (E Bagnasco collection)

The oldest destroyers in Regia Marina service during the Second World War were the *Carlo Mirabello* and *Augusto Riboty*, both built by Ansaldo, Genoa in 1914–17 and originally classed as scouts like the previous similar – but smaller – ships of the *Poerio* class. A third ship in the class, *Carlo Alberto Racchia*, was lost to a mine in the Black Sea off Odessa, on 21 July 1920.

Although originally planned as 5,000-ton ships, the *Mirabello*s had a full load displacement of just over 2,300 tons, but were quite powerfully armed for their time (eight single 4in/45 guns, two 40mm/39 light AA guns and two twin 17.7in torpedo tubes. A single 6in/40 gun on the forecastle, fitted in 1917–18, was disembarked in 1919, being replaced by the former 4in gun, as it proved to be too heavy and the stress of firing was too much for the bow structures of these ships.

The *Mirabello* was lost to a mine north of Kefallonia on 30 April 1941, in its original configuration with eight 4in guns; later in the war, two 4in guns were removed from *Riboty* in 1942 and two more in 1943, leaving her with four single 4in/45, six 20mm/70 cannon and the torpedo tubes (which were disembarked in 1944). During the war, *Riboty* was almost always employed in second-line duties but nevertheless she served

A view of *Leone* during speed trials off Genoa in spring 1924. *Leone* was commissioned on 1 July 1924; *Tigre* and *Pantera* followed her a few months later, being commissioned on 10 and 28 October respectively. (Archivio Storico Ansaldo)

Tigre on 23 February 1938. This is one of the last photographs of this ship as a scout, as on 5 September 1938 the three *Leone* class (along with *Mirabello* and *Riboty*, and the twelve 'Navigatoris') were reclassified as destroyers, with identification letters painted on the bows and at the stern. These were 'LE' for *Leone*, 'PA' for *Pantera* and 'TI' for *Tigre*. (Photo A Fraccaroli)

throughout the war as an escort ship either in the southern Adriatic Sea, in the Aegean and on the North African routes. Along with other vessels, she was to have been transferred to the USSR as war reparations, but because of her poor material condition the Soviet Navy rejected her and the Italian Navy discarded her in May 1950; after having been employed as an accommodation ship at Taranto for a few years, *Riboty* was finally broken up in the mid-1950s.

Before the end of the First World War the Regia Marina ordered five new ships from Ansaldo, Genoa, that were to have been enlarged versions of the *Mirabello*s (2,648 tons full load, length 113.4m versus 103.7m for the *Mirabello*s). Economic

problems and steel shortages in the Ansaldo yard during the war meant that only three ships (*Leone*, *Tigre* and *Pantera*) could be laid down, instead of five, and not until 1921–2: they were armed with four 4.7in/45 twin guns and two twin torpedo tubes (initially for 17.7in, and later for larger 21in weapons). Their machinery (four boilers and two turbines), with 42,000hp, allowed them to achieve a speed of 29 knots, and they were often employed as flotilla leaders in the 1920s and early 1930s.

The three *Leone*s (originally referred to as 'light scouts', but reclassified as destroyers in September 1938) were homeported in Massawa, Eritrea in early 1939, thus forming the 5th Destroyer Flotilla (5ª Squadriglia Cacciatorpediniere); at the time of

their East African assignment they were already worn out, and their twin Canet-Schneider-Armstrong 4.7in/45 gun mounts (designed and built in 1918–19) were obsolete, as well as their other weapons and fittings.

Their operations were seriously affected by lack of fuel and spare parts in Italian East Africa, and after some sweeps in the Red Sea that did not result in any encounters with enemy shipping, they remained inactive until late March 1941, shortly before the fall of Massawa. It was then decided to employ the three ships in two separate missions, at the end of which they were to have been scuttled by their crews. During the first mission, a bold but abortive plan to attack the

In April 1940 the *Francesco Nicotera* and *Bettino Ricasoli* were sold to Sweden, being renamed *Psilander* and *Puke* (shown in the photograph). Both were decommissioned in 1947. (Swedish Navy, Author's collection)

Francesco Crispi, camouflaged, at Venice in summer 1942. (E Bagnasco collection)

seaport of Suez, *Leone* ran aground on an uncharted rock and was scuttled in the Red Sea on 1 April 1941. The second sortie was planned against Port Sudan, but the Italian ships were attacked by British aircraft that sank the destroyers *Sauro* and *Manin*; as had been previously planned, *Tigre* and *Pantera* made for the coast of neutral Saudi Arabia where they were scuttled by their crews 15 miles south of Gedda. When the men of both ships were already safely ashore, the British destroyer HMS *Kingston* arrived on the scene, firing several 4.7in rounds into the wrecks of the two Italian destroyers and further damaging *Pantera* with a torpedo hit.

The '1,200-ton' destroyers of the *Palestro* and *Curtatone* classes of 1917–24 (reclassified as torpedo boats in 1938) did not prove particularly

successful, so in the early 1920s the Regia Marina asked the Pattison yard of Naples to design and build a class of four new and larger destroyers, which were, however, considered 'experimental' in various respects.

Between 1922 and 1927, the four *Sella* class (*Quintino Sella*, *Francesco Crispi*, *Giovanni Nicotera* and *Bettino Ricasoli* – all named after Italian statesmen of the late nineteenth century) were laid down and commissioned. For the first time, Italian destroyers were to be armed with 4.7in guns, initially a single mount on the forecastle (replaced by a twin mount in 1929), and a twin mount atop a small deckhouse abaft the two twin 21in torpedo tubes. The output of the machinery (more than 35,000hp) gave very good results on trials, when all ships exceeded 38 knots, but in wartime,

because of the rather worn-out boilers and turbines, as well as of weight increases due to hull strengthening and to the forward twin mount, the *Sella*s were unable to make more than 31 knots. At the same time, they had a limited endurance and their transverse stability, combined with an excessively low freeboard, was at best questionable.

The *Nicotera* and *Ricasoli* (along with the torpedo boats *Astore* and *Spica*) were sold to Sweden on 1 April 1940 and, renamed *Psilander* and *Puke*, served with the Swedish Navy until 1947. In June 1940, *Sella* and *Crispi* were stationed in the Dodecanese, where they remained for most of the war until the Armistice; their most notable operation was in March 1941, when they transported the surface assault craft to Suda Bay, Crete, which seriously damaged the heavy cruiser HMS *York* and a tanker. The *Sella* was sunk by the German motor torpedo boat *S 54* in the Adriatic Sea on 11 September 1943, while *Crispi*, captured by the Germans at Piraeus after 9 September 1943, served for some time with the Kriegsmarine in the Aegean and was sunk by enemy aircraft near Crete on 8 March 1944. Later refloated, *Crispi* was towed to Piraeus and was finally sunk during an Allied air raid in October 1944.

While the construction of the *Sella* class was still underway, four similar destroyers were ordered by the Regia Marina: accordingly, they were about 10 per cent larger (length 90.7m and displacement 1,650 tons full load, versus 85m and 1,480 tons for the *Sella*), with greater freeboard, increased beam and endurance raised to over 2,000 miles at 16 knots. With three boilers, two shafts and 36,000hp, these ships had a maximum speed of 30 knots in wartime, although on trials with more than 40,000hp they easily exceeded 37 knots in light condition.

Between 1924 and 1927 two of these new ships (*Nazario Sauro* and *Cesare Battisti*) were built by Odero, Genova and two (*Daniele Manin* and *Francesco Nullo*) by Cantieri Navali del Quarnaro,

Quintino Sella in early 1943, probably in the Aegean, photographed from aboard a MAS of the third series of the '500' type. (Author's collection)

Nazario Sauro leading a group of torpedo boats (with *Abba* and *Dezza* immediately astern of her), entering Taranto's Mar Piccolo in the mid-1930s. (N Siracusano collection)

Fiume. They were named after Italian patriots, who had fallen either during the 'Risorgimento' or during the First World War. Their seaworthiness was not an improvement on the *Sella* class, partly because two twin 4.7in gun mounts were embarked from the start and in 1933 a large cylindrical fire director was fitted atop the bridge, increasing topweight; torpedo armament was also increased, the *Sauro*s having two triple 21in torpedo tubes.

On 10 June 1940, the four *Sauro*s formed the 3rd Destroyer Flotilla (3ª Squadriglia Cacciatorpediniere) at Massawa, and, as with the three *Leone*s, did not see much action. The *Nullo*, after grounding on a reef, was sunk on 21 October 1940 by HMS *Kimberley*; *Sauro* and the *Manin* were sunk by British aircraft on 3 April 1941 during the aborted operation against Port Sudan that saw the scuttling of *Tigre* and *Pantera*, and the *Battisti* which, because of engine trouble, had not been included in the squadron bound for Port Sudan, was scuttled on the same day by her crew off the Saudi Arabian coast.

Eight more destroyers, representing the final evolution of the *Sella* and *Sauro* classes, were included in the naval programmes of 1923/24 and 1924/25 (four ships each). These were the destroyers of the *Turbine* class, all with wind names, planned by the Odero yard, laid down in 1925 and commissioned between August 1927

(*Turbine*) and June 1928 (*Ostro*). Four ships were built by Ansaldo, Genoa (*Borea*, *Espero*, *Ostro* and *Zeffiro*) and two each by Odero, Genoa (*Aquilone* and *Turbine*) and by Cantieri del Tirreno, Riva Trigoso (*Euro* and *Nembo*).

The gun and torpedo armament of the *Turbine* class was the same as the previous *Sauro* class, but the *Turbine*s were 3m longer, with a full load displacement of 1,780 tons. With 40,000hp (more than 45,000hp on trials), their maximum speed was 31 knots, and endurance was now about 2,700 miles at 16 knots. Nevertheless, again seaworthiness was not their best feature, being further decreased when in the early 1930s a new cylindrical director was fitted atop the bridge.

In 1930–2, four similar ships (the *Tinaztepe* and *Kocatepe* classes, of two ships each) were built for the Turkish Navy and the eight *Turbine*s took part in the naval operations of the Spanish Civil War; in August 1937 *Ostro* and *Turbine* torpedoed and sank two merchant ships during clandestine night actions.

By the end of summer 1940, six ships in the class had already been lost: four sunk in North African ports by British aircraft (*Borea* bombed at Benghazi, *Nembo*, *Ostro* and *Zeffiro* torpedoed in the harbour of Tobruk), one (*Aquilone*) mined off Benghazi and *Espero*, sunk by British cruisers in the central Mediterranean on 28 June 1940, thus

Euro at sea, on convoy escort duty, in April/May 1941. (A, Fraccaroli collection)

holding the unpleasant distinction of being the first Italian destroyer lost in the Second World War. The *Euro* was sunk at Parteni Bay (Leros in the Dodecanese) during a German air raid on 1 October 1943, and *Turbine* was captured by the Germans at Piraeus on 9 September 1943, being pressed in Kriegsmarine service before the end of October. Renamed *TA 14*, she operated in the Aegean and was damaged at Portolago (Leros) by British commandos on 18 June 1944; the ex-*Turbine* finally met her end when she was sunk during an Allied air raid on 15 September 1944, at Salamina, where she was undergoing repairs to the damage sustained at Leros.

The *Turbine* entering Mar Piccolo at Taranto in the late 1930s. (Author's collection)

Turbine, camouflaged, moored at Piraeus on 3 September 1942. Note that the tip of the bow is still painted in greyish white. (Photo A Fraccaroli)

'Navigatori' class

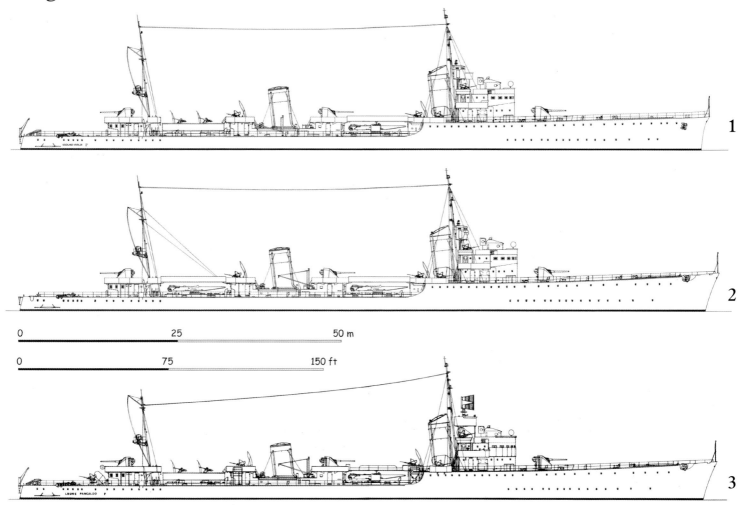

Starboard view of three 'Navigatori' class destroyers after the major modifications of 1939–40.

1) *Vivaldi*, prototype (1939): notice different shape of the stem, less sheer forward and hawsepipes at the bows.

2) *Zeno*, 1940: typical 'Navigatori' class layout after modifications, with 'clipper' stem, enhanced sheer and two torpedo tubes. Hawse and hawsehole fitted directly on the deck-edge.

3) *Pancaldo*, early 1943: two Breda 37mm/54 guns have replaced the after torpedo tubes; notice the 'Gufo' radar and extra 20mm cannon. (Author's drawing)

General Giuseppe Rota of the Genio Navale began designing a new class of 'light scouts' in early 1924, partly basing their design on the idea that they should be able to compete with the large French destroyers of the *Jaguar* class. In effect, in the mid-1920s the most important navies had already started studies that would have resulted in the commissioning in the 1930s of several classes of 'super-destroyers' that in many aspects prefigured the characteristics of the larger and more advanced destroyers built in the Second World War on the basis of wartime experience.

Although twenty-four ships had originally been planned, only twelve were included in the 1926/27 naval construction programme and, with a standard displacement of more than 2,000 tons, they were 107.2m long and heavily armed with three twin 4.7in/50 gun mounts. All were named after famous Italian navigators of the thirteenth, fourteenth and fifteenth centuries, hence being known as the 'Navigatori' class; they were built between 1927 and 1931, the first ship to be laid down being *Antoniotto Usodimare* (on 1 June

Ugolino Vivaldi leaving Taranto's Mar Piccolo in 1933–4. (Foto De Siati; Author's collection)

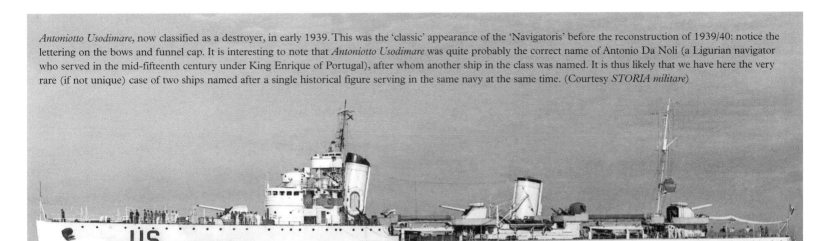

Antoniotto Usodimare, now classified as a destroyer, in early 1939. This was the 'classic' appearance of the 'Navigatoris' before the reconstruction of 1939/40: notice the lettering on the bows and funnel cap. It is interesting to note that *Antoniotto Usodimare* was quite probably the correct name of Antonio Da Noli (a Ligurian navigator who served in the mid-fifteenth century under King Enrique of Portugal), after whom another ship in the class was named. It is thus likely that we have here the very rare (if not unique) case of two ships named after a single historical figure serving in the same navy at the same time. (Courtesy *STORIA militare*)

1927) and the last to be commissioned was the *Antonio Pigafetta* (on 1 May 1931). Four ships were allotted to Cantieri Navali del Quarnaro (Fiume) and two ships each to Cantieri del Tirreno – Riva Trigoso, Cantieri Navali Riuniti – Ancona, Ansaldo – Genoa and Odero – Genoa (this last yard also drew up the final design of the entire class).

As originally built, the 'Navigatoris' had an almost vertical stem, a long forecastle and a three-level bridge structure; the two funnels, of elliptical section and elegantly raked back, were widely spaced as the machinery – four boilers and two shaft-geared turbines – had alternating boiler and engine rooms, in order to reduce the chance that a single lucky hit could stop the ship, damaging either all the boilers or both engines. The machinery's 55,000hp allowed speed in the range of 35 knots, but on trials – with an output of more than 65,000hp – speeds in excess of 40 knots were reached, *Pigafetta* being the fastest in the class achieving 41.6 knots with 65,915hp.

On the other hand, general seaworthiness (and transverse stability in particular) proved to be grossly inadequate from the very beginning, and, besides other minor changes, it was deemed necessary to reduce topweight by reducing the bridge structure, removing its lower level (that originally housed some electrical shops and magazines), and relocating the remaining bridge structure in the same location. Moreover, the two lateral 'legs' of the tripod mast were eliminated and the fuel tanks above the waterline were suppressed: this latter measure reduced fuel capacity by more than 100 tons and therefore their maximum range even at moderate speeds. *Da Mosto* and *Pigafetta* were so modified when their building was still underway, while the other ten ships were overhauled between 1930 and 1931, shortly after commissioning; in 1932 a small cap was added atop the fore funnel.

The 'Navigatoris' were all almost identical, the only minor differences being found in small details such as the position of the boat-handling cranes abreast the aft funnel or the design of the enclosed crow's nest at the base of the fore mast, atop the bridge. Only *Da Recco* could be easily told apart from the other eleven vessels as, having been completed as a flotilla leader, her aft deckhouse was considerably larger than that of her sister-ships.

In September 1938 the 'Navigatoris' were classed as destroyers, but at the same time worn-out machinery and poor seakeeping (further reduced because of topweight added in the meantime in the form of further 13.2mm MGs, triple torpedo tubes on some ships etc.) made it necessary to plan a new and even more radical

---

(Data as of 1940, after the second major rebuild)

Displacement (tons): 2,125/2,888

Dimensions (m): 110.0 overall (*Vivaldi* 107.2), 11.15 max. beam, 4.50 max. draught

Machinery: 4 boilers and 2 shaft-geared turbines, 55,000hp

Speed (kts): 28 (38/41 on trials); *Da Recco* and *Usodimare* 32–33

Endurance (nm/kts): 5,000/18, 1,200/28; fuel 560 tons

Armament: Six 4.7in/50 (3 x II); two 37mm/54 light AA guns (2 x I); seven/nine 20mm/70 light AA guns (7/9 x I); four/six 21in torpedo tubes (2 x II/III), later two/three 21in torpedo tubes (1 x II/III); minelaying capacity (max 104 mines from 1941)

Complement: 230 (15)

	Builders	Laid down	Launched	Completed
Alvise Da Mosto	CNQ	22 Aug 1928	1 Jul 1929	15 Mar 1931
Sunk by British warships 75nm N/W of Tripoli on 1 Dec 1941.				
Antonio Da Noli	Cdt, RT	25 Jul 1927	21 May 1929	15 Mar 1931
Mined in the Bonifacio Straits (northern Sardinia) on 9 Sep 1943.				
Nicoloso Da Recco	CNR, A	14 Dec 1927	5 Jan 1930	20 May 1930
Decommissioned on 15 Jul 1954 and broken up.				
Giovanni Da Verazzano	CNQ	17 Aug 1927	15 Dec 1928	25 Sep 1930
Torpedoed and sunk south of Lampedusa by HMS *Unbending* on 19 Oct 1942.				
Lanzerotto Malocello	An	30 Aug 1927	14 Mar 1929	18 Jan 1930
Mined off Cape Bon (Tunisia) on 24 Mar 1943, during a troop transport mission.				
Leone Pancaldo	Cdt, RT	7 Jul 1927	5 Feb 1929	30 Nov 1929
Bombed and sunk by US aircraft off Cape Bon (Tunisia), during a troop transport mission.				
Emanuele Pessagno	CNR, A	9 Oct 1927	12 Aug 1929	10 Mar 1930
Torpedoed and sunk off Benghazi by HMS *Turbulent* on 29 May 1942.				
Antonio Pigafetta	CNQ	29 Dec 1928	10 Nov 1929	1 May 1931
Captured by the Germans at Fiume on 9 Sep 1943. Incorporated into the Kriegsmarine (as *TA 44*); sunk at Trieste in an Allied air raid on 17 Feb 1945; hulk refloated and broken up in 1947.				
Luca Tarigo	An	30 Aug 1927	9 Dec 1928	16 Nov 1929
Sunk off the Kerkennah Shoals by British destroyers led by HMS *Mohawk* on 16 Apr 1941.				
Antoniotto Usodimare	OS	1 Jun 1927	12 May 1929	21 Nov 1929
Mistakenly sunk by the Italian submarine *Alagi* on 8 Jun 1942 in the 'Canale di Sicilia'.				
Ugolino Vivaldi	OS	16 May 1927	9 Jan 1929	6 Mar 1930
Scuttled by her crew west of Asinara Island (northern Sardinia) on 10 Sep 1943, after having been damaged the previous day by German shore batteries on the southern coast of Corsica.				
Nicolò Zeno	CNQ	5 Jun 1927	12 Aug 1928	27 May 1930
Scuttled by her crew at La Spezia on 9 Sep 1943. Hulk refloated and broken up in 1948.				

rebuilding of these ships, in order to correct their poor seaworthiness once and for all. The first ship to be modified, between October 1938 and February 1939, was the *Vivaldi*: a new 'clipper' stem and new bows were fitted, thus increasing the sheer of the forecastle; the beam between the forward twin mount and the aft torpedo tubes was increased by about 1m by adding a new side plating, and the newly-obtained space was used as fuel tanks which greatly enhanced endurance.

The rebuilding of *Vivaldi* served as a prototype for the other nine ships in the class that were fitted with a more arched (and elegant) stem and an even more evident sheer; these modifications probably made the nine rebuilt 'Navigatoris' (*Da Mosto, Da Noli, Da Verazzano, Malocello, Pancaldo, Pessagno, Pigafetta, Tarigo* and *Zeno*) the most beautiful and 'aggressive' Italian ships of the period; the outbreak of war prevented the similar rebuilding of *Da Recco* and *Usodimare*. But most importantly, the 250-ton increase in displacement along with the greater beam that reduced speed to 28 knots, although initially criticised, made the rebuilt 'Navigatoris' really seaworthy ships that performed at their best during the long and demanding convoy-escort missions on the North African routes and may thus be considered among the best ships of the Regia Marina in the Second World War.

The 'Navigatoris' had very intense wartime

A wonderful starboard bow view of *Leone Pancaldo* in the Gulf of La Spezia in April 1940, immediately after her time in dockyard hands that saw her fitted with new bows and increased beam. The *Pancaldo* was in refit from after 2 January 1940 until 31 March 1940; between 1939 and 1940 seven more 'Navigatori' class destroyers (*Vivaldi, Da Noli, Pessagno, Zeno, Pigafetta, Da Mosto* and *Da Verazzano*) were similarly rebuilt at La Spezia; two more ships (*Malocello* and *Tarigo*) were taken in hand by OTO, Leghorn, while *Da Recco* and *Usodimare* were never modernised. (Courtesy *STORIA militare*)

careers, and only a few highlights can be given here. The *Vivaldi*, for instance, sank the submarine HMS *Oswald* on 1 August 1940 in the Gulf of Taranto, and on 16 April 1941 *Tarigo* torpedoed and sank HMS *Mohawk* off Kerkennah Shoals being, in turn, sunk herself by torpedoes launched almost simultaneously by the British destroyer. The *Vivaldi* was damaged at Pantelleria on 15 June 1942 and *Da Recco* in the Canale di Sicilia on 2 December 1942, but both survived because of their robustness. The *Pancaldo* was torpedoed in shallow waters by British aircraft in Augusta harbour on 10 July 1940; later refloated, she was back in service in November 1942 only to be sunk in April 1943 off Cape Bon. In wartime, the aft torpedo tubes were often replaced by two Breda

Two dramatic views of *Da Verazzano* in 1941, taken from another 'Navigatori' class destroyer. (A Fraccaroli collection)

37mm/54 light anti-aircraft guns; in 1942–3 *Pancaldo* and *Da Recco* were fitted with an E.C. 3/ter 'Gufo' air and surface search radar, and *Malocello* with a German Fu.Mo 21/39 'De.Te' set.

Seven ships were lost during convoy-escort and transport missions before September 1943; *Da* *Noli* and *Vivaldi* were lost in northern Sardinian waters in the days immediately following the Armistice and *Pigafetta* was captured by the Germans at Fiume; renamed *TA 44*, she was sunk at Trieste in an Allied air raid in February 1945. As *Zeno* was scuttled by her crew at La Spezia on 9 September 1943, at the end of the war only the *Da Recco* survived of the entire class: employed after war in stationary duties at Taranto, she was decommissioned on 15 July 1954, stricken on 30 July and immediately broken up.

Nicoloso Da Recco off La Spezia, in summer 1942, with her first 'standard' camouflage scheme. *Da Recco* and *Usodimare* were the only 'Navigatoris' not to be modified with new stem, bows and increased beam, so their maximum speed remained in the range of 32–33 knots, at the expense of endurance (3,800 miles at 18 knots instead of the 5,000 miles at 18 knots of the rebuilt ships). (E Bagnasco collection)

Malocello moored at La Goulette on 20 March 1943, at the end of a troop transport mission to Tunisia. Atop the bridge, the 'bedspring' aerial of the German FuMo 21/39 G 'De.Te' radar can be clearly seen. (Photo U Schreier; E Bagnasco collection)

The refloated hulk of *Nicolò Zeno*, minus her bow, in one of the dry-docks of the La Spezia Dockyard in 1948, after having been refloated and shortly before being towed to the breakers' yard. (E Bagnasco collection)

Freccia/*Folgore* class

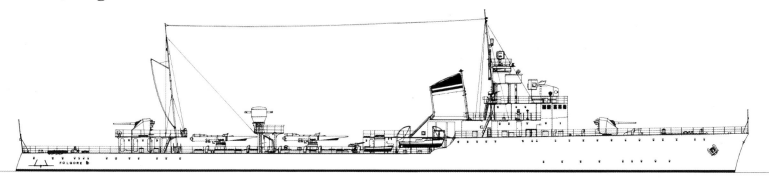

Folgore as she appeared in the mid-1930s. (Author's drawing)

When the *Turbine*s were just commissioning and the 'Navigatoris' were still on the building ways the Regia Marina decided to build eight new destroyers, partly based on the design of the *Turbine*: the best and most promising proposal was submitted by the OTO yard of Genoa, for destroyers slightly (2m) longer than the *Turbine*s, with increased displacement (more than 2,000 tons full load) and armed with two Ansaldo-designed 4.7in/50 twin mounts, of the same 1926 model fitted aboard the 'Navigatoris'.

The most striking aesthetic feature was the adoption of a single, large funnel that grouped the three boiler uptakes (a solution also adopted, a few years later, by the British and US navies and later still by the Japanese), in order to reduce the clutter of the superstructure and increase the firing arcs of AA guns; the new destroyers had a rather large bridge and were armed with two triple 21in torpedo tubes; the secondary fire director was located atop a small deckhouse on the main deck, between the torpedo tubes.

It was soon decided to fit 'arched' stem posts, but the first and second ship of the first series (*Dardo* and *Strale*) kept straight stems throughout their careers as their construction was already too advanced for the change to be made. During sea trials, very high speeds were reached – as usual for Italian warships of the period: the fastest in the class was the *Freccia*, which made 39.43 knots with more than 46,000hp in light condition but, as always, under operational conditions 30 knots was the practical maximum.

Very soon, it was clear that again transverse stability and general seaworthiness were questionable, if not totally insufficient, and soon after commissioning weights had to be reduced in the upper superstructure by disembarking two 'legs' of the tripod masts (from all ships) and the searchlights from most ships in both series. Bilge keels were enlarged and 90 tons of ballast fitted, but these measures (the ballast particularly) further reduced the operational speed of these destroyers. In fact *Dardo*, because of continuing poor stability, actually capsized in the port of Palermo on 23 September 1941 while under tow at very light displacement whilst undergoing maintenance.

Four similar ships (the *Hydra* class) were built by Orlando, Leghorn in 1930–2 for the Greek navy, but they were all armed with single 4.7in guns, demonstrating other navies' lack of confidence in Italian twin single-cradle medium gun mounts.

In 1938–9, starting with the ships of the second series, the anchor hawse pipes were relocated to the forecastle's stringer from their original position lower on the bows; at the same time, the ships of the first series (the *Freccia*s) were fitted with a funnel cap similar to that which the second series (the *Folgore*s) had had since their commissioning. In 1943, the last two surviving ships (*Freccia* and *Dardo*) had their aft triple torpedo tubes replaced by a gun tub for two Breda 37mm/54 light AA guns.

In the late 1930s and in the first months of the war, the speed of these destroyers allowed them to sail as escorts only for the slower battleships (*Cesare* and *Cavour*), but their reduced endurance and frequent machinery breakdowns made it necessary to transfer them to convoy-escort duties by late 1940. Six ships of the class were lost between 1941 and early 1943 on North African routes, with *Lampo* heavily damaged and stranded on Kerkennah Shoals on 16 April 1941 after an

---

(Data as of 1940)

Displacement (tons): 1,520/2,200 (1st series); 1,540/2,100 (2nd series)

Dimensions (m): 95.9 overall, 9.75 max. beam, 4.3 max. draught. (96.2m - 9.3m - 4.5m 2nd series)

Machinery: 3 boilers and 2 shaft-geared turbines, 44,000hp

Speed (kts): 30 (38/39 on trials)

Endurance (nm/kts): 4,600/12, 2,000/20, 680/32; fuel 640 tons; 2nd series 3,600/12, 600/32; fuel 530 tons.

Armament: Four 4.7in/50 (2 x II); six/eleven 20mm/65 cannon (6/11 x I); six 21in torpedo tubes (2 x III): *Freccia* and *Dardo* in 1943: two 37mm/54 light AA guns (2 x I) and three 21in torpedo tubes (1 x III)

Complement: 165 (6)

	Builders	Laid down	Launched	Completed
1st series (*Freccia*)				
Dardo	OTO, S	23 Jan 1929	6 Sep 1930	26 Jan 1932
Captured by the Germans at Genoa on 9 Sep 1943; *TA 31* from 17 Jun 1944; stricken 20 Oct 1944; scuttled at Genoa on 24 Apr 1945; hulk refloated and broken up in 1946.				
Freccia	Cdt, RT	29 Feb 1929	3 Aug 1930	2 Oct 1931
Sunk during an air raid at Genoa on 8 Aug 1943; hulk refloated in 1949 and broken up.				
Saetta	Cdt, RT	27 May 1929	17 Jan 1932	10 May 1932
Mined and sunk in the 'Canale di Sicilia' on 3 Feb 1942 during a convoy-escort mission.				
Strale	OTO, S	20 Feb 1929	26 Mar 1931	6 Feb 1932
Ran aground off Cape Bon (Tunisia) on 21 Jun 1942; constructive total loss.				
2nd series (*Folgore*)				
Baleno	CNQ	1 May 1930	22 Mar 1931	15 Jun 1932
Ran aground on 16 Apr 1941 on Kerkennah Shoals; sunk on 17 Apr.				
Folgore	OCP	30 Jan 1930	26 Apr 1931	1 Jul 1932
Sunk on 2 Dec 1941 during an action with British warships in the 'Canale di Sicilia'.				
Fulmine	CNQ	1 Apr 1929	2 Aug 1931	4 Sep 1932
Sunk on 9 Nov 1941 in the Ionian Sea during a convoy-escort mission.				
Lampo	OCP	30 Jan 1930	26 Jul 1931	13 Aug 1932
Stranded on the Kerkennah Shoals on 16 Apr 1941; recovered in August 1941, repaired and recommissioned on 18 May 1942; sunk on 30 Apr 1943 by enemy aircraft off the coast of Tunisia during a transport mission,				

Lampo on trials off Naples in late summer 1932, soon after commissioning. Note that the shields for the twin Ansaldo 1926 4.7in/50 gun mounts and the rangefinder atop the small deckhouse between the torpedo tubes have yet to be fitted. (Author's collection)

action with British destroyers. She was refloated in August 1941, repaired and recommissioned in May 1942 but was finally lost to aircraft on 30 April 1943 during an ammunition-transport run to Tunisia.

The *Freccia* was sunk in the port of Genoa during an air raid on 8 August 1943, and the hulk was refloated and broken up after war. The *Dardo* (almost fully repaired after her capsizing in September 1941) was captured at Genoa by the Kriegsmarine on 9 September 1943 and recommissioned into German service as *TA 31* in

June 1944, after a long overhaul; because of her poor material condition, she was stricken later that year (on 20 October) and scuttled in the port of Genoa a few days before the end of the war.

Baleno at sea, mid-1930s. This was the typical layout of the *Folgore* series in the class, with funnel cap and curved stem post (fitted also on *Freccia* and *Saetta*). The *Fulmine* and *Baleno* (built by Cantieri Navali del Quarnaro, Fiume) were the only ships of the *Freccia*/*Folgore* class with a rounded front to their superstructure: the other six ships all had an angular front, as may be clearly seen in several images of *Freccia*, *Dardo*, *Saetta*, *Strale*, *Folgore* and *Lampo*. (E Bagnasco collection)

From left to right: *Fulmine*, *Baleno*, *Lampo*, *Folgore* and *Freccia* moored at Messina on 24 May 1935, celebrating the 20th anniversary of Italy's entry into the First World War. The rounded bridges of *Fulmine* and *Baleno* may be easily compared with the angled ones of the other ships. (N Siracusano collection)

Fulmine in the late 1930s, leaving the Gulf of La Spezia, in a heavily retouched photograph by Studio Pucci, a well-known photography company working in La Spezia from the late nineteenth century until the 1930s. It appears that *Fulmine* was photographed moored at a quay, as shown by the ensign hoisted at the stern, the lack of any wake and – conclusively – by the canvas cover over the funnel uptake only fitted when the ship was at rest. The ship's image was then 'transferred' onto a background showing the outer Gulf of La Spezia, adding small bow waves to simulate low speed. An excellent example of retouching, at a time when digital image manipulation techniques were still far in the future. (Author's collection)

Baleno just before the Battle of Punta Stilo, on the morning of 9 July 1940. (E Bagnasco collection)

Fulmine dry-docked at Taranto, in late summer 1941. (E Bagnasco collection)

Dardo soon after capsizing in the port of Palermo on 23 September 1941. The poor stability of the *Freccia/Folgore* class ships, combined with the very light displacement of the *Dardo* while she was being overhauled, caused the capsizing of the ship while under tow in the port, as she was shifting her berth; forty men were lost in the disaster. (E Bagnasco collection)

A detail of *Folgore*'s bridge and funnel at Piraeus, on 23 August 1942. (Photo A Fraccaroli)

Folgore moored stern-on at Piraeus in August 1942. Note the depth charge rail and the smoke generator in the left foreground; the funnel of the camouflaged torpedo boat *Lince* can be seen above the stern awning. (Photo A Fraccaroli)

The hulk of *TA 31*, the former destroyer *Dardo*, was scuttled by the Germans on 24 April 1945 and, as shown in this photograph, was found half-submerged, with her bow out of the water, in the Zona bacini ('Drydock area') of the port of Genoa by the Allied troops that occupied the city. (A Rastelli collection)

Maestrale and *Oriani* classes

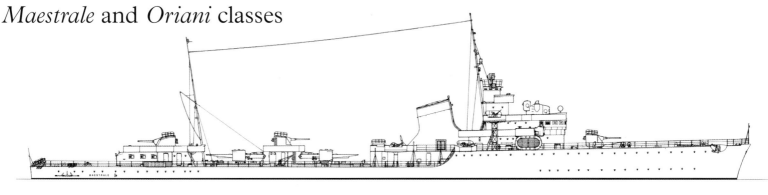

The *Maestrale* in 1942, with one twin 4.7in/50 gun on the aft deckhouse and two single 4.7in guns, one on the forecastle and one atop the small deckhouse between the torpedo tubes. Note the light plates armour below the bridge windows and the 20mm/65 cannon on the upper level of the bridge, at the rear end of the forecastle and abaft the funnel. (Author's drawing)

The eight destroyers of the *Freccia/Folgore* class were the final evolution of the Italian destroyers designed and built in the 1920s, and their design could not be further improved. Therefore a plan for four new destroyers, included in the 1930/31 naval programme, was drafted by Col. Giulio Truccone of the Genio Navale, on behalf of the Comitato Progetti Navi, with two ships to be built by Cantieri Navali Riuniti – Ancona, and two by Cantieri del Tirreno – Riva Trigoso.

Although initially described as the '*Freccia* migliorato' ('Improved *Freccia*') type, these four destroyers were in fact completely new ships: 10m longer than the *Freccia*s, with a full load displacement of 2,400 tons and armed with two twin 4.7in/50 Model OTO 1931 guns of a new design. Their appearance was sleeker and more modern, with well-proportioned superstructure, a single large funnel of elliptical section elegantly raked back, arched stem post and a small deckhouse between the two triple 21in torpedo tubes. While the eight previous destroyers had been named either after kinetic-energy weapons (the *Freccia*s, all the names of which were various Italian forms of the words for arrow or dart) or after synonyms for 'lightning' (the *Folgore*s), the four new destroyers bore the names of the winds coming from the intermediate quadrants of the compass, known to be particularly strong in Mediterranean weather: *Maestrale* (north-west wind), *Libeccio* (south-west wind), *Scirocco* (south-east wind) and *Grecale* (north-east wind).

Machinery layout was what by now had become the standard type, with the three boilers followed by the two engine rooms aft of them: power output was in the range of 44,000hp, allowing sustained speeds of more than 31 knots in wartime. Finally, stability was no longer a problem (as weights were quite rationally apportioned and the metacentric height allowed decent seaworthiness) and the *Maestrale*s – as well as the other destroyers that followed them in Regia Marina service – were sufficiently good seaboats in most weather conditions. The loss of *Scirocco* (along with *Lanciere* of the 'Soldati' class on the same occasion) in March 1942, during a storm of exceptional severity in the southern Ionian Sea, should not be considered as a consequence of bad seaworthiness, because she experienced a complete machinery breakdown that left her dead in the water: in a short time, enormous waves capsized *Scirocco* and she sank with heavy loss of life. The *Maestrale*s were structurally sound and well-built, and could withstand severe damage: as a matter of fact, *Maestrale* and *Libeccio* lost their bows – and *Grecale* her stern – to mines and collisions, but all of them survived and, once repaired, returned to service.

In wartime, 20mm/65 cannon replaced the previous 13.2mm AA MG, and the two 4.7in/15 illuminating howitzers originally fitted were also disembarked. The *Maestrale*s benefited from some other armament changes during the war: in 1942 a single 4.7in/50 gun was installed atop the amidships deckhouse and in order to save weight the forward twin 4.7in gun was replaced by another single mount; in 1943, the aft triple 21in torpedo tubes were replaced by two Breda 37mm/54 light anti-aircraft guns. The *Grecale* survived the war and served for several years with the Marina Militare, initially converted into a fast anti-submarine frigate and later rebuilt as a command ship, serving in this role until May 1964, when she was finally stricken and later broken up.

(Data as of 1940)
Displacement (tons): 1,700–1,750/2,400–2,450

Dimensions (m): 106.7 overall, 10.2 max. beam, 4.3 max. draught. (4.8 *Oriani* class)

Machinery: 3 boilers and 2 shaft-geared turbines, 44,000hp (48,000hp *Oriani* class)

Speed (kts): 32–33 (38/39 on trials)

Endurance (nm/kts): 2,600–2,800/18, 900/32 (690/33 *Oriani* class)

Armament: Four 4.7in/50 (2 x II); ten 20mm/65 cannon (4 x II, 2 x I – 1942-3); six 21in torpedo tubes (2 x III); *Maestrale* and *Oriani* 1943: two 37mm/54 light AA guns (2 x I); three 21in torpedo tubes (1 x III); two depth charge throwers

Complement: 173 (7)

	Builders	Laid down	Launched	Completed
Maestrale class				
Grecale	CNR, A	25 Sep 1931	17 Jun 1934	15 Nov 1934
Stricken on 1 Jul 1965 and broken up.				
Libeccio	Cdt, RT	29 Sep 1931	4 Jul 1934	23 Nov 1934
Torpedoed and sunk on 9 Nov 1941 in the Ionian Sea by HMS *Upholder*.				
Maestrale	CNR, A	25 Sep 1931	15 Apr 1934	29 Sep 1934
Sabotaged on 9 Sep 1943; found partially dismantled and half sunk in the port of Genoa at the end of the war; refloated and broken up.				
Scirocco	Cdt, RT	29 Sep 1931	22 Apr 1934	21 Oct 1934
Sunk in a gale in the Southern Ionian Sea on 23 Mar 1942.				
Oriani class				
Vittorio Alfieri	OTO, L	4 Apr 1936	20 Dec 1936	1 Dec 1937
Sunk on 28 Mar 1941 off Cape Matapan by British battleships.				
Giosuè Carducci	OTO, L	5 Feb 1936	28 Oct 1936	1 Nov 1937
Sunk on 28 Mar 1941 off Cape Matapan by British battleships.				
Vincenzo Gioberti	OTO, L	2 Jan 1936	19 Sep 1936	27 Oct 1937
Torpedoed and sunk on 9 Aug 1943 off La Spezia by HMS *Simoon*.				
Alfredo Oriani	OTO, L	28 Oct 1935	30 Jul 1936	15 Jul 1937
Discarded on 16 Jul 1948; to France on 8 Aug 1948 and renamed *D'Estaing*; stricken and broken up in 1954.				

Four more destroyers, basically a repeat-*Maestrale* class, were built between 1936 and 1937 by OTO, Leghorn. The four new ships shared their armament and characteristics (with a few minor changes), and were named after poets and men of letters of the nineteenth century, becoming unofficially known as the 'Poeti', or *Oriani* class from the name of the first ship commissioned.

The machinery's 48,000hp gave a top speed of 33 knots (one knot more than the *Maestrale*s), and the *Oriani*s were also fitted with two depth-charge throwers; *Alfieri* and *Carducci* were lost early in the war (during the night action of Cape Matapan), while *Gioberti* – sunk on 9 August 1943 off La Spezia by the submarine HMS *Simoon* – was the last destroyer lost by the Regia Marina, of a total of over forty-three ships of this type sunk between June 1940 and September 1943.

In 1943, *Oriani* disembarked the aft torpedo tubes and mast, replacing them with a tub for two Breda 37mm/54 light anti-aircraft guns; during the same refit, a German Fu.Mo 21/39 'De.Te' radar was fitted atop the bridge. The *Oriani* was thus the only ship in the class to survive the war, and in 1948 she was transferred to France as reparations; renamed *D'Estaing* she never saw active service, being stricken and broken up in 1954.

Maestrale during early sea trials, soon after commissioning, in October 1934. (G Parodi collection)

Scirocco at high speed in the Tyrrhenian Sea on 10 April 1935, in a photograph taken at 15.00 that day from an aircraft of the 141st Reconnaissance Squadron (141ᵃ Squadriglia da Ricognizione) of the Regia Aeronautica. Note the two 4.7in/15 illuminating howitzers abaft the funnel; these weapons were removed from all the ships of the class at the beginning of the Second World War, being replaced with 13.2mm MGs and later with 20mm/65 cannon. (Author's collection)

Carducci in the Canale Navigabile at Taranto, heading for the Dockyard in Mar Piccolo, in 1938–9. (A Asta collection)

Carducci in 1939. Both *Carducci* and *Alfieri* were lost at Matapan in this configuration, with no camouflage and their original armament. (E Bagnasco collection)

As commissioned, the four *Maestrale*s were considered part of the light scout force of the Regia Marina and as such did not have identification letters painted on the bows and on the stern as did destroyers and torpedo boats, The class were grouped in the 10ª Squadriglia Esploratori, which in the late 1930s became the 10ª Squadriglia Cacciatorpediniere, when the *Maestrale*s were finally classed as destroyers. This photograph shows the four ships of the 10ª Squadriglia Esploratori in 1935–6 at Venice, with two 'Condottieri' class light cruisers in the distance. As scouts, they were visually identified by funnel bands, with the flotilla leader (*Maestrale*) having no bands and *Scirocco*, *Grecale* and *Libeccio* one, two and three bands respectively. (A Asta collection)

Libeccio, minus her stern, is towed into the port of Palermo in mid-April 1941. The *Libeccio* collided with M/S *Esperia*, during a convoy escort mission from Naples to Tripoli, on the night of 14 April; the merchant ship managed to steam back to Naples under her own power, but *Libeccio* remained dead in the water and had to be towed to Palermo by the torpedo boat *Orione*. After a brief refit in Naples, *Libeccio* was towed to Genoa where the repairs were completed by the end of August. ((G Vaccaro collection))

Libeccio was lost on the morning of 9 November 1941, torpedoed and sunk by the submarine HMS *Upholder* (Cdr. Wanklyn) in the southern Ionian Sea, east of Sicily. She was one of the escort ships of the 'Duisburg' convoy, attacked and destroyed by Malta's Force K on the night of 8/9 November; after having been torpedoed, *Libeccio* was taken in tow by the destroyer *Euro*, but leaks and hull damage caused her sinking – as shown in the photograph – at 11.18, in position 36°50'N – 18°10'W. (E Bagnasco collection)

Destroyers of the 10th and 14th Flotillas (10ª and 14ª Squadriglia Cacciatorpediniere) leaving the port of Palermo late in the afternoon of 14 June 1942. The ships were about to join the cruisers of 7ª Divisione Incrociatori despatched to intercept the British 'Harpoon' convoy, eastbound from Gibraltar to Malta. In the foreground, the *Oriani* with a 'standard' camouflage pattern; at left – above *Oriani*'s bow – the destroyer *Vivaldi* in an experimental overall dark grey scheme and, in the right background, the destroyer *Ascari* ('Soldati' class) in her 'Claudus' dazzle pattern. In the distance on the right, in the outer harbour, two more 'Navigatori' class destroyers – *Zeno* and *Malocello* – can be just made out.
(A Barilli collection)

'Soldati' class

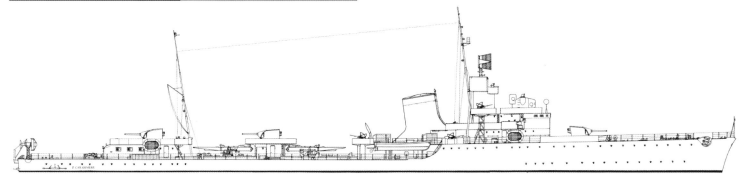

Starboard elevation of *Carabiniere* in 1943, with a single 4.7in/45 gun amidships and EC 3/ter 'Gufo' search radar. (Author's drawing).

As part of the 1936/37 naval programme it was decided to build a new class of twelve destroyers which apart from some minor improvements were to be very similar to the *Oriani*s, then fitting out at the OTO Yard in Leghorn.

The major differences between the new ships and the *Oriani* were found in the improved arrangements of internal spaces, in the slightly larger amidships deckhouse (designed from the outset to mount an additional single 4.7in gun mount) and fitting of 20mm cannon instead of the 13.2mm MG originally fitted on the *Oriani* and *Maestrale* classes. All this led to an increase in displacement of about 100 tons, and it was thus necessary to raise the total machinery power output to 50,000hp in order to maintain the same maximum speed of the *Oriani*s, i.e. 34–35 knots in service and 38 knots on trials.

It was decided to name these ships after soldiers belonging to corps or specialised units of the Italian Armed Forces: they were thus known as the 'Soldati' ('Soldiers') class, repeating in most cases the same names of the destroyers of the first 'Soldato' class of 1905–7, that served in the First

In May 1939, in the port of Leghorn, the twelve destroyers of the 'Soldati' class assembled for the ceremony known as 'Consegna della Bandiera di Combattimento' ('Delivery of the Battle Flag'). The Bandiera di Combattimento is a naval flag that, typically, is donated to a ship by a veterans' association, by a City Council, by the heirs of the recipient of a naval decoration or by some outstanding government official; this flag is hoisted only 'in the presence of the enemy', when action is imminent. For the ceremony involving the 'Soldati' class ships, the 'Battle Flag' was donated by officials of the Fascist Party to the *Camicia Nera*, and to the other eleven destroyers by representatives of Veteran Soldiers' Associations. (Author's collection)

World War and were phased out in the 1920s.

Six ships were built by OTO, Leghorn, and two each by Cantieri del Tirreno (Riva Trigoso) and by the Ancona and Palermo yards of Cantieri Navali Riuniti. The main difference in appearance was found in the funnel: bigger and less flared for the OTO-built ships (thus resembling the funnel of the four *Oriani*s), with the funnel of the destroyers built by the other yards being smaller and more raked and thus quite similar to that of the four *Maestrale*s.

The *Carabiniere* was initially fitted with the fifth, single 4.7in gun mount amidships, and in 1941–2 *Ascari, Camicia Nera, Corazziere, Geniere* and *Lanciere* were also fitted with it; the gun replaced a single 4.7in/15 illuminating howitzer, the range of which could not be compared with that of the single and twin 4.7in guns. During the war, the number of 20mm cannon was increased, additional single and twin mounts being installed.

Although it had initially been decided that twelve more 'Soldatis' were to have been built under the 1938/39 naval programme, they were never laid down due to Italy's entry into the Second World War, and it was not until August 1940 that five new destroyers were authorised to replace early war losses, with two additional ships being ordered in summer 1941. These seven ships (of which five were commissioned) are generally known as the second series of the 'Soldati' class – five being built by OTO, Leghorn and two by Cantieri Navali Riuniti, Ancona – and were essentially a repeat of those of the first series: apart from *Velite*, they were all built with the fifth single 4.7in gun amidships, and the power output was reduced to 44,000hp in order to reduce the complexity of the machinery and thus its maintenance load. The second series 'Soldatis'

Displacement (tons): 1,830–1,850/2,450–2,550	
Dimensions (m): 106.7 overall, 10.1–10.3 max. beam, 4.3 max. draught	
Machinery: 3 boilers and 2 shaft-geared turbines, 50,000hp (2nd series 44,000hp)	
Speed (kts): 1st series 34–45 (39–40 on trials), 2nd series 32–33 (34–36 on trials)	
Endurance (nm/kts): 1st series 2,340/14, 682/34; 2nd series 2,500/14, 885/32; fuel 506/514 tons	
Armament: Four/five 4.7in/50 (2 x II/2 x II and I x 1 - 1 x II and 2 x I); eight/twelve 20mm/65 cannon (1942-3, twin and single mounts); six 21in torpedo tubes (2 x III); *Fuciliere, Carabiniere, Granatiere* and *Legionario* 1943: two 37mm/54 light AA guns (2 x I) and three 21in torpedo tubes (1 x III); two depth charge throwers	
Complement: 215 (13)	

	Builders	Laid down	Launched	Completed
1st series				
Alpino	CNR, A	2 May 1937	2 Sep 1938	24 Apr 1939
Sunk at La Spezia on 19 Apr 1943 during an air raid. Refloated and broken up 1948.				
Artigliere	OTO, L	15 Feb 1937	19 Dec 1937	4 Nov 1938
Sunk on 12 Oct 1940 by HMS *York* after being damaged the previous night by HMS *Ajax*.				
Ascari	OTO, L	11 Dec 1937	21 Jul 1938	6 May 1939
Mined and sunk in the Canale di Sicilia on 24 Mar 1943.				
Aviere	OTO, L	16 Jan 1937	19 Sep 1937	21 Aug 1938
Torpedoed and sunk by British submarine HMS *Splendid* off Bizerte on 17 Dec 1942.				
Bersagliere	CNR, P	21 Apr 1937	3 Jul 1938	1 Apr 1939
Sunk at Palermo on 7 Jan 1943 during an air raid. Broken up in 1948-53.				
Camicia Nera	OTO, L	21 Jan 1937	8 Aug 1937	30 Apr 1938
Renamed *Artigliere* on 30 Jul 1943. Stricken 14 Dec 1948; to USSR as *Z.12* at Odessa, 23 Jan 1949. In Soviet service she was named *Neulovimyi, Bezposhchadnyi, Lovkiy, CL-58* and *KWN-II*; stricken Feb 1960.				
Carabiniere	Cdt, RT	1 Feb 1937	23 Aug 1938	20 Dec 1938
Stricken 18 Jan 1965; broken up in 1978 at La Spezia.				
Corazziere	OTO, L	7 Oct 1937	22 May 1938	4 Mar 1939
Sabotaged on 9 Sep 1943 at Genoa; hull partially dismantled by the Germans and finally broken up in 1953.				
Fuciliere	CNR, A	2 May 1937	31 Jul 1938	10 Jan 1939
Stricken 10 Jan 1950; to USSR as *Z.20* at Odessa, 31 Jan 1950. In Soviet service she was named *Nastoitchivyi, Byedovyi, Legkyi* and *CL-57*; stricken 21 Jan 1960.				
Geniere	OTO, L	26 Aug 1937	27 Feb 1938	15 Dec 1938
Sunk at Palermo on 1 Mar 1943 while dry-docking; refloated in 1944 and broken up at Taranto.				
Granatiere	CNR, P	5 Apr 1937	24 Apr 1938	1 Feb 1939
Stricken on 1 Jul 1958 and broken up.				
Lanciere	Cdt, RT	1 Feb 1937	18 Dec 1938	25 Mar 1939
Sunk in a gale in the Southern Ionian Sea on 23 Mar 1942.				
2nd series				
Bombardiere	CNR, A	7 Oct 1940	22 Mar 1942	15 Jul 1942
Torpedoed and sunk off the island of Marettimo (Trapani) by the British submarine HMS *United*.				
Carrista	OTO, L	11 Sep 1941	—	—
Bow fitted to *Carabinere* after she was torpedoed in 1942; stern fitted to *Velite* in 1943; hulk broken up by the Germans on the building ways after 9 Sep 1943.				
Corsaro	OTO, L	23 Jan 1941	16 Nov 1941	16 May 1942
Mined and sunk off Bizerte on 9 Jan 1943.				
Legionario	OTO, L	21 Oct 1940	16 Apr 1941	1 Mar 1942
Stricken 9 Aug 1948 and renamed *L.6*. To France at Toulon on 15 Aug 1948; renamed *Duchauffault* and discarded 1954.				
Mitragliere	CNR, A	7 Oct 1940	28 Sep 1941	1 Feb 1942
Stricken 14 Jul 1948 and renamed *M.2*. To France at Toulon on 15 Jul 1948; renamed *Jurien de La Gravière* and discarded 1956.				
Squadrista	OTO, L	1 Sep 1941	12 Sep 1942	—
Captured by the Germans on 9 Sep 1943 at Leghorn, when 96 per cent complete; renamed *TA 33* and towed to Genoa; sunk on 4 Sep 1944 during an Allied air raid shortly before commissioning into Kriegsmarine service.				
Velite	OTO, L	19 Apr 1941	31 Aug 1941	31 Aug 1942
Stricken 18 Jul 1948 and renamed *V.3*. To France at Toulon on 24 Jul 1948; renamed *Duperré* and discarded 1951.				

Stern view of *Aviere* in early 1941; notice the paravanes and minesweeping gear on the fantail and the secondary fire control position, co-axial with the main mast. This was found only aboard *Aviere, Carabiniere* and *Legionario* of the second series of the class; by the end of 1942 it was disembarked as it proved cumbersome and virtually useless under most operational conditions. (Photo A Fraccaroli)

A fine pre-war image of *Artigliere*, moored beside three other 'Soldati' class destroyers; notice the wider funnel, typical of the OTO-built ships. (Author's collection)

Lanciere foundered on 23 March 1942 in the same gale in which *Scirocco* was lost, but rather than to poor seaworthiness her loss must be ascribed to poor machinery maintenance (that caused major boiler and engine breakdowns) and to the weakness of the boiler and engine room skylights, that were torn out by the waves, with the consequent flooding of the hull spaces beneath them.

Nine ships were war losses, and *Corazziere* was sabotaged on 8 September 1943 by her crew at Genoa, where she was overhauling; in 1948–50 two ships (*Artigliere* [ex-*Camicia Nera*] and *Fuciliere*) went to the USSR and three (*Legionario*, *Mitragliere* and *Velite*) to France as reparations, with the Soviet ships being broken up in 1960 and the French ships discarded earlier, between 1951 and 1956.

The peace treaty thus left to Italy only two 'Soldati' class destroyers: *Granatiere* (in 1950–2) and *Carabiniere* (in 1953–5) were rebuilt similar to *Grecale* as fast anti-submarine frigates which served with the Marina Militare for several years, becoming a significant link between the 'old' and the 'new' Italian Navy. The *Granatiere* was stricken in 1958 and immediately broken up; from 1960 to 1964 *Carabiniere* enjoyed a 'third life' as an auxiliary ship for trials of new weapons and sensors and she was employed to test the new OTO 76mm/62 'Allargato' dual-purpose gun in the early 1960s. Discarded in 1964, her hulk was later employed at the Varignano inlet, in the Gulf of La Spezia, as a target for exercises of the 'Incursori' ('Special Forces') of the Marina Militare. Finally, the former *Carabiniere* foundered off La Spezia in March 1978, while she was being towed to Ortona to be broken up; hastily run aground on a sandbank to prevent her loss, the hulk was later towed to a local breakers' yard and dismantled.

were thus a couple of knots slower than those of the first series, and they suffered from some shortcomings arising from their hasty wartime construction, not always carried out with materials of the highest quality.

In 1942–3 *Fuciliere*, *Carabiniere*, *Granatiere* and *Legionario* traded their aft triple torpedo tubes for a gun tub for two single Breda 37mm/54 light anti-aircraft guns; *Legionario* herself, in spring 1942, was fitted with a German 'De.Te' radar atop the bridge, becoming the first Italian destroyer to be fitted with a radar. Later in 1943 *Carabiniere*,

Fuciliere and *Velite* embarked an Italian-built EC 3/ter 'Gufo' search radar in the same position.

The 'Soldatis' were the most uniform group of Italian destroyers in the Second World War and fought in almost all naval battles in the Mediterranean, also serving extensively, until September 1943, in the highly demanding convoy-escort and transport missions on the North African routes. Fair seaboats, they could withstand severe damage and several of them lost their bows or sterns to mines, torpedoes and collisions but survived and returned to service after repairs. The

Another fine image, showing the destroyer *Ascari* at high speed while laying a smokescreen during convoy escort duty in autumn 1940. (Author's collection)

On the right, *Carabiniere* at Messina in March 1942, with a temporary bow fitted after she lost her original bow when torpedoed by the submarine HMS *P 36* south of Cape Spartivento. In April 1942 *Carabiniere* left Messina under her own power and arrived at Leghorn on 11 April, where at the OTO yard she was fitted with the bow of the *Carrista* (second series), then under construction. On the left, *Geniere* with an experimental camouflage pattern, dark grey overall with bow and stern painted light grey. (N. Siracusano collection)

On 9 September 1943 *Carabiniere* picked up 112 survivors from the battleship *Roma* and, along with other Italian ships, sailed to Port Mahon, Menorca, where she was interned by the Spanish. This photograph, taken in autumn 1943, shows *Carabiniere* (with *Mitragliere* on her starboard side) with local boats passing by, probably during a religious ceremony. The Italian ships remained in Port Mahon for sixteen months, leaving on 15 January 1945 and arriving at Taranto on the 23rd, after a brief stop at Algiers. (P Solimano collection, via Società Capitanile Macchinisti Navale, Camogli [Genoa])

A very clear port-bow view of *Granatiere* as commissioned; notice that the 20mm cannon on the platforms in the upper superstructure still have to be fitted, as well as the 4.7in/15 illuminating howitzer atop the amidships deckhouse. (Author's collection)

Corsaro at Leghorn in late spring 1942, with fitting-out completed. Note the unusual position of her identification letters, very far forward on the bow and the shape of the superstructure atop the bridge, modified as it was planned to fit a 'Gufo' radar but which she never received before she was mined and sunk a few months later, on 9 January 1943, 38nm off Bizerta. (E Bagnasco collection)

Mitragliere fitting out at Ancona in January 1942. She was the first ship of the second series to be commissioned, on 1 February 1942; notice the provisional splinter camouflage scheme, applied by the yard, that was soon replaced by an official Regia Marina 'standard' scheme. (E Bagnasco collection)

Velite soon after commissioning, in early September 1942. (E Bagnasco collection)

Granatiere at Taranto in 1948–9, leading the destroyer *Grecale* and the torpedo boat *Orsa*. After a major overhaul in 1946, *Granatiere* joined the 1ᵃ Squadriglia Cacciatorpediniere, where the only three modern destroyers left to Italy by the peace treaty (the others being *Carabiniere* and *Grecale*) were grouped. Note the single 4.7in gun on the forecastle that replaced the twin mount to save weight on some of the ships fitted with the amidships 4.7in single gun. (Foto De Pace, Taranto; Author's collection)

Carabiniere off Rapallo (west of Genoa) on 22 April 1957. The new features of *Carabiniere* as a fast ASW frigate can clearly be seen: the new 'British-style' enclosed bridge, the enlarged forecastle extending abaft the funnel, twin 40mm/56 Bofors, and a tripod mast with AN/SPS-6 air-search radar. By the mid-1950s, all Italian destroyers and torpedo boats had replaced the two-letter identification code on the bows and at the stern with standard NATO pennant numbers in the 'D' and 'F' series. (Photo E Bagnasco)

Projected and war prize destroyers

'Comandanti' class

In 1941, Gen. Carlo Sigismondi and Col. Giuseppe Malagoli of the 'Genio Navale' began working on the design of a new class of destroyers that in characteristics and performance could be considered the final Italian destroyer design in the Second World War.

Although generally resembling the 'Soldati' class in their layout, the new destroyers, with a full load displacement of over 3,000 tons, would have introduced interesting new features such as new underwater hull lines, a straight stem post, a bow knuckle, 5.3in guns 45 calibres long in single mounts and a bridge of more modern and rational design. A 'Gufo' radar would have been mounted atop the bridge, and the 60,000hp of their newly-designed machinery (still based on three boilers and two shaft geared turbines) would have allowed a top speed of 35 knots and a fair endurance in the range of 3,300nm at 20 knots, with 740 tons of fuel.

It was decided to name the ships after commanding officers fallen in wartime and decorated with the Medaglia d'Oro al Valor Militare (Italy's highest military decoration) so even while they were being designed they were officially known as the 'Comandanti' class. Early plans envisaged two series of eight ships each, the first being ordered on 27 September 1941, and a third series of eight additional ships was soon added; in April 1943, the contract for four ships of the third series assigned to Ansaldo, Genoa, was replaced by an order for eight torpedo boats of the new *Ariete* class.

Only the first two ships ordered at CRDA, Trieste (*Comandante Botti* and *Comandante Ruta*) were actually laid down in August 1943, but what little had been built by 9 September 1943 was rapidly dismantled in the months which followed; steel plate and other materials allotted to CRDA as well as to Cantieri del Tirreno – Riva Trigoso and OTO – Livorno, were abandoned after the Armistice and in some cases requisitioned by the Germans to be used for other projects.

One of the ships of the first series (most likely the *Comandante Esposito*) would have had machinery of different design, with four boilers and alternated engine rooms, and as a consequence two funnels, thus resembling the ten modified vessels of the 'Navigatori' class.

Ex-Yugoslav destroyers

When the Axis powers occupied the Kingdom of Yugoslavia in April 1941, several warships of the former Yugoslav Navy were seized by the Regia Marina in Cattaro (Kotor) and Split. Three destroyers were found in reasonable condition and were pressed into Italian service.

The *Dubrovnik* was a large British-built destroyer (more than 2,800 tons displacement at full load, 113.2m long), launched in 1941 by Yarrow, Scotstoun, armed with four 5.5in/56 single guns and six 21in torpedo tubes in two triple mounts. After being seized in Cattaro, in spring 1941 the *Dubrovnik* was renamed *Premuda* and transferred to La Spezia to be overhauled and

fitted with 20mm/65 cannon replacing the original British 40mm weapons. The *Premuda* was commissioned in January 1942 and was the most important and effective Italian war prize vessel of the Second World War. She took part in the naval battle of Pantelleria on 15 June 1942 but, in July 1943, a very serious machinery breakdown made it necessary to transfer the ship to Genoa for a major boiler and engine overhaul; *Premuda* was captured by the Germans on 9 September 1943 and, her repairs having been completed, she was renamed *TA 32* and fitted with a 'De.Te' radar and new quadruple 20mm Flak Vierling cannon. The ex-*Premuda* was scuttled in Genoa in April 1945; the hulk was refloated in 1950 and immediately broken up.

Two French-designed destroyers, the *Ljubljana* and *Beograd*, were also seized and taken into service by the Regia Marina as *Lubiana* and *Sebenico* respectively (a third ship in the class, the *Zagreb*, was sabotaged and completely destroyed at Cattaro on 17 April 1941, just before the Italian occupation of the dockyard). With a displacement of 1,800 tons at full load, their main armament was four single 4.7in/46 guns and two 21.6in triple torpedo tubes; in Italian service they were fitted with Italian-made 20mm/65 cannon.

The *Sebenico*, built in 1936–9 at the Atcliers & Chantiers de la Loire, Nantes, was commissioned very soon, in August 1941, and served extensively with the Regia Marina during the Second World War: up to 8 September 1943, she took part in more than 100 convoy-escort missions on the

The builder's models of the projected 'Comandanti' class destroyers. Top: the ships of the first series would have been armed with four 5.3in/45 single mounts, with their bridge structure resembling that of the *Oriani* and 'Soldati' class. Bottom: it was decided to fit ships of the second and third series with five 5.3in guns; at the same time the bridge design was more squared, with four quadruple 37mm guns of a new design abreast it, on the forecastle below the bridge wings; the 'Comandanti' would have embarked a 'Gufo' radar above the main fire control position. As with the 'Soldati' class, it would have been possible to tell apart the OTO-built ships from vessels built by other yards by comparing the funnel shape: wider on OTO ships, smaller and more raked for ships of other yards, as in the case of the ships in this image. (E Bagnasco collection)

North African and Aegean routes. Seized by the Germans in Venice on 9 September 1943, she was renamed *TA 43* and was scuttled at Trieste on 1 May 1945; the hulk was broken up in 1947.

When the Sebenico (Sibenik) Dockyard fell into Italian hands in April 1941, *Ljubljana* was undergoing major repairs following her stranding and partial sinking, just off the port, in January 1941. She was first towed to Cattaro and then to Fiume, where her repairs were completed; commissioned into Italian service in November 1942 as *Lubiana*, she stranded on 1 April 1943 on the Tunisian coast near Ras el Ahmar and was immediately declared a constructive total loss.

A fourth Yugoslav destroyer, the *Split*, was seized on the building ways at the Jadranska Yard, Split; she was to have been an enlarged version of the previous *Beograd* class ships, and the Regia Marina, after renaming her *Spalato*, continued her construction. However, she was far from complete in late August 1943; the hull was recaptured by Yugoslavia at the end of the war and *Split*, fitted with new British and US weapons and sensors, was completed to a renewed design in 1958, serving until 1980.

Ex-French destroyers

Following the scuttling of the French Fleet at Toulon on 27 November 1942 and the German occupation of the dockyard, several Marine Nationale destroyers were seized – in some cases undamaged or in acceptable condition – and transferred to the Regia Marina as part of an agreement between the Italian and German navies.

The large destroyer *Lion* of the *Guepard* class (3,100 tons full load, 130.2m, five single 5.4in guns), in dry dock at the time of the German occupation of Toulon, was recommissioned into Italian service in January 1943, and in April proceeded under her own power to La Spezia, where she disembarked one triple torpedo mount and the light AA guns of French origin. Renamed *FR 21*, she was considered rather old and worn out and it was intended to employ her as a fast transport vessel. Scuttled on 9 September 1943, her hulk was refloated and broken up in 1950. *Lion*'s sister-ship *Valmy* became the Italian *FR 24* but, found half-sunk in Toulon although almost undamaged, was refloated only in July 1943 and towed to Savona, where she remained, partially dismantled, until April 1945; *FR 24* was scrapped locally shortly after the end of the war.

Two *Jaguar* class destroyers, *Panthère* and *Tigre*, (built 1922–6, 3,050 tons, four single 5.1in/40 guns) were seized undamaged at Toulon:

Sebenico (the ex-Yugoslav *Beograd*) in spring 1943. (E Bagnasco collection)

between March and April 1943 they became the Italian *FR 22* and *FR 23* respectively but, as in the case of *Lion*, their general condition allowed only their use as fast personnel and supply ships. *FR 22* was sabotaged at La Spezia immediately after the Armistice and broken up after the war; *FR 23*, returned to the French Navy at Bizerte on 28 October 1943, was phased out by the Marine Nationale in 1950.

The smaller destroyer *Trombe* of the *Bourrasque* class (2,040 tons full load, 105.7m, four single 5.1in/40 guns) found undamaged at Toulon, became *FR 31* and arrived at La Spezia in February 1943; on 2 May 1943, while bound to Taranto, she ran aground in shallow water off the port and had to be dry-docked for repairs. On 28 October 1943 she was returned to the French Navy at Bizerta, but the Italian connections of *Trombe* still remained, as she was attacked by a RSI surface assault craft on 17 April 1945, off the Ligurian coast. Severely damaged, she was not repaired, being broken up in summer 1945.

Finally, ten modern *torpilleurs d'escadre* of the *Le Hardi* class (2,570 tons, 117m, three twin 5.1in/40 guns) were fitting out at Toulon in November 1942, and six (*Le Siroco*, *L'Adroit*, *Lansquenet*, *Le Bison*, *Le Foudroyant* and *Le Hardi*) were seized by the Italian Navy, becoming *FR32–37*. The *FR 32*, *34* and *37* were found sabotaged and half sunk at Genoa at the end of the war, while *FR 33*, *35* and *36* never left Toulon and the hulks were captured by the Germans, who scrapped them, after the Armistice of 9 September 1943.

FR 21 (the ex-French *Lion*) at La Spezia in spring 1943. The forward triple torpedo tubes have already been landed, as it had been intended to employ the *FR 21*, like other ex-French destroyers, as fast troop-transports fitted to ferry over 400 fully equipped soldiers. (E Bagnasco collection)

Older torpedo boats

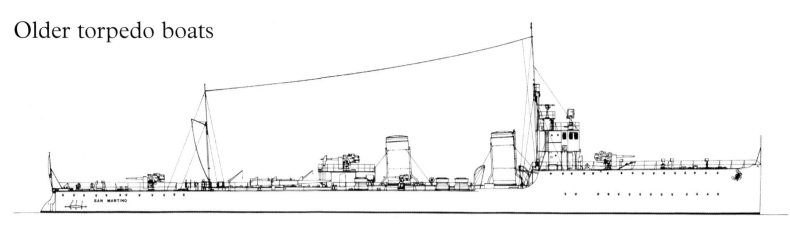

0	15	30 m
0	50	100 ft

The destroyer *San Martino* as commissioned, 1922. (Author's drawing)

On 10 June 1940, the Italian Navy had sixty-nine torpedo boats in service, but this apparently powerful force of ships was in fact quite unbalanced: the thirty ships of the *Spica* class, the four larger and more modern *Orsa* class ships (actually a sort of small destroyer escort) and the single, small submarine chaser *Albatros* – all built in the mid-1930s – were accompanied by more than thirty older vessels, all dating back to the First World War.

In fact, all the older torpedo boats were former destroyers built between 1913 and 1924 that could only be regarded as of limited combat value at best, and were unable to operate with more modern ships. Nevertheless, all of these vessels served through the whole war in the Mediterranean in the exhausting and arduous role of convoy escort (in which most of them were lost), but six survived the war and served until the early 1950s on second-line duties.

On 1 October 1929, all the former 'three-stacker' destroyers (cacciatorpediniere) of the *Pilo*, *Sirtori*, *La Masa* and *Cantore* classes – plus the single *Audace* – were reclassified as torpedo boats

(torpediniere); nine years later, on 1 October 1938, it was the turn of the eight larger and more modern 'two-stackers' of the *Palestro* and *Curtatone* classes to be so reclassified.

The *Audace* had been launched by Yarrow, Glasgow in 1913 as the Japanese *Kawakaze*, but she was acquired by the Italian Navy in July 1916 and she was commissioned on 1 March 1917. With a full load displacement of 1,364 tons and 87.6m long, in 1940–2 she was armed with three single 4in/35 guns, two 40mm light AA guns and two twin 17.7in torpedo tubes; in 1943, one 4in gun

Giuseppe Cesare Abba entering Taranto's Mar Piccolo in the early 1930s; note *MAS 400* and a similar craft partially hidden by the funnels. (A Fraccaroli collection)

A wartime view of *Abba*, camouflaged, at Messina in late 1942. (A Fraccaroli collection)

and the two 40mm light AA guns were disembarked and replaced with five single 20mm/65 cannon. After being employed in 1938–9 as control ship for the radio-controlled target ship *San Marco*, the *Audace* served as a convoy escort during the war, mostly in the Aegean, and also on the North African routes. Seized by the Germans after 8 September 1943 and renamed *TA 20*, she

served intensively – also as a minelayer – until she was sunk on 2 November 1944 by the British destroyers HMS *Wheatland* and *Avonvale* off the island of Pago, on the Dalmatian coast.

The seven *Pilo* class (*Giuseppe Cesare Abba*, *Giuseppe Dezza*, *Giuseppe Missori*, *Rosolino Pilo*, *Simone Schiaffino*, *Fratelli Cairoli* and *Antonio Mosto* – an eighth ship, the *Ippolito Nievo*, had been

stricken in 1938) were built as destroyers by the Odero Yard, Genoa, in 1913–16. Smaller than the *Audace* (displacement 900 tons full load and 73m long) they were quite powerfully armed when first commissioned (five 4in/35 guns and two twin 17.7in torpedo tubes), but in 1941–3 the number of 4in guns was reduced to two or three, and five (or, in some cases, six) 20mm/65 cannon were

Giacinto Carini, as a fast minesweeper, in 1950. She was one of the five 'three-stacker' torpedo boats that survived the Second World War and served with the Marina Militare well after the mid-1950s. (Photo A Fraccaroli)

The torpedo boat *Generale Achille Papa*, along with the *Chinotto* and other similar ships, in the late 1930s. (Author's collection)

Stocco, sunk at Corfu on 24 September 1943 by German aircraft.

By the later years of the First World War, the Odero Yard in Genoa was the leader in 'three-stacker' building, and in 1916–19 eight more ships of the *La Masa* class followed: one (*Benedetto Cairoli*) was lost in a collision in April 1918, and the other seven ships (*Angelo Bassini*, *Giacinto Carini*, *Enrico Cosenz*, *Nicola Fabrizi*, *Giuseppe La Farina*, *Giuseppe La Masa* and *Giacomo Medici*) served in the Second World War as torpedo boats. The main difference between the *La Masa* class and the previous ships was their main armament, now based on four 4in/45 and two 76mm/40 guns, with the usual twin 17.7in torpedo tubes. The 76mm guns were disembarked at the beginning of the Second World War, and several 20mm/65 cannon were fitted in late 1941/early 1942: by late 1942, the *La Masa* and *Carini* had a single 4in/45 gun, four 20mm/65 and one triple 21in torpedo tube, plus the usual twin 17.7in torpedo tubes. The *Carini* and *Fabrizi* survived the war, being employed as minesweepers and later as training hulks at La Maddalena (Sardinia) shortly before being stricken and broken up in 1957–8.

The last 'three-stackers' were built by Odero in 1919–22, well after the end of the First World War: it is likely that these six ships (the *Cantore* class – *Generale Antonio Cantore*, *Generale Antonino Cascino*, *Generale Antonio Chinotto*, *Generale Carlo Montanari*, *Generale Achille Papa* and *Generale Marcello Prestinari*) were ordered and built merely

fitted. Three ships (*Cairoli*, *Dezza* [as the German *TA 35*] and *Schiaffino*) were lost to mines in wartime. The *Missori* was seized by the Germans, and – recommissioned into Kriegsmarine service as *TA 22* – was broken up at the end of the war. The *Pilo*, *Abba* and *Mosto* remained in service with the Marina Militare after the war, being stricken and broken up between 1954 and 1958.

In 1916–17, the same Odero Yard built four 'improved *Pilo*' ships: this was the *Sirtori* class (*Giovanni Acerbi*, *Vincenzo Giordano Orsini*, *Giuseppe Sirtori* and *Francesco Stocco*) that – with the same dimensions as the *Pilo*s and similar power output and speed (16,000hp and 33 knots) – was armed with six 4in/35, later (1920) replaced by 4in/45 weapons. Wartime armament modifications were the same as for the *Pilo* class and all were lost during the war, the last one being

The destroyer *Solferino*, and at least two more ships of the *Palestro* class, at Messina in the mid-1930s. (N Siracusano collection)

to provide employment in the yard, and were thus already rather outdated when they were commissioned in 1921–2. Practically repeats of the *La Masa*s, they were armed with only three 4in guns, and had limited minelaying capabilities, being able to transport and lay only six mines. All were lost during the war (five ships by September 1943, while *Papa*, seized by the Germans and renamed *TA 17*, was deliberately sunk on 15 April 1944 to block the small port of Oneglia, on the Western Ligurian coast near the border with France). On 30 July 1941 *Papa* herself sank the British submarine *Cachalot* off Benghazi, which was lost with all hands.

In 1917, the Orlando Yard in Leghorn laid down four destroyers of a new design which – partially based on the *Indomito* class (from which the *Pilo*s derived) – had a full load displacement of 1,200 tons and were 80.4m long; machinery was four boilers and two turbines that with an output of 22,000hp gave a speed of 33 knots (largely reduced in wartime by wear and tear on components). This was the *Palestro* class

(*Confienza*, *Palestro*, *San Martino* and *Solferino*), armed with four single 4in/45 and two single 76mm/40 guns, as in the *La Masa* class; the most notable difference was the number of funnels (two, originally of the same height, with the fore funnel heightened in 1930), and in the longer forecastle. *Confienza* and *Palestro* had been lost by late 1940, while *San Martino* and *Solferino* were seized by the Germans after 8 September 1943; the Kriegsmarine greatly increased the AA armament of these two ships, fitting single 37mm and quadruple 20mm (Vierling) cannon. Both ships were lost in the Aegean in October 1944.

The four ships of the *Curtatone* class (*Calatafimi*, *Castelfidardo*, *Curtatone* and *Monzambano*) were all built by Orlando, Leghorn in 1920–4 and were largely based on the four previous *Palestro*s. However, the *Curtatone* were longer (84.6m) and armed with two twin, single-cradle 4in/45 guns of a new design; for the first time in Italian destroyers, the rudder was not found externally, abaft the transom, being now fitted in the classic (and more effective) position

below the stern, at the aft end of the keel. On 12 June 1940, two days after Italy's entry into the war, the *Calatafimi*, while on escort duty off Genoa, attacked a strong French naval squadron bombarding the nearby coast and, although scoring no hits on the enemy ships, disrupted their attack. The *Curtatone* was mined and sunk off Piraeus on 20 May 1941; *Calatafimi* and *Castelfidardo* – seized by the Germans after the Armistice – were lost in summer 1944 off Samos (*Calatafimi*) and at Iraklion (*Castelfidardo*). The *Monzambano* survived the war but, because of her poor material condition, was discarded in 1948 and broken up in 1951.

As for names, apart from *Audace* ('daring'), all the 'three-stackers' were named after patriots and heroes of the three Italian Wars of Independence (*Pilo*, *Sirtori* and *La Masa* classes) or generals of the First World War I (*Cantore* class). The 'two-stackers' of the *Palestro* and *Curtatone* classes bore the names of famous battles of the Wars of Independence and of the Italian 'Risorgimento'.

A clear view of *Monzambano*'s port side, showing her distinctive camouflage, at Piraeus on 22 July 1942. (Photo A Fraccaroli)

Spica class

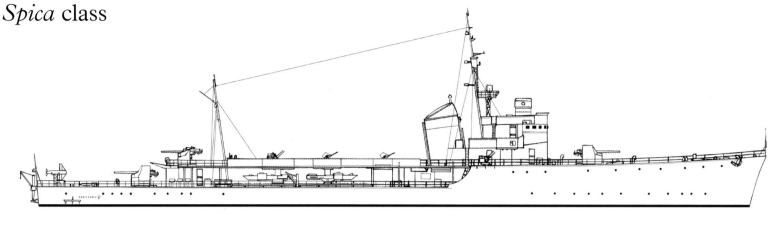

The torpedo boat *Sagittario* in 1942, with eight 20mm/65 cannon (three twins and two singles) and twin torpedo tubes on the centreline. On several *Spica* class boats, the shield of No 2 gun (atop the aft deckhouse) was cut down in order to reduce topweight. (Author's drawing)

These modern torpedo boats were designed in 1930–2 by General Gustavo Bozzoni of the Genio Navale, on behalf of the Regia Marina's Comitato Progetti Navi, but the origin of this class can be traced back more to political reasons than to real operational needs. The London Naval Treaty of 1930 allowed the building of any number of small warships of 600 tons standard displacement, and the Italian Navy used this opportunity to counter the programmes of the French Navy that was already building the similar escort vessels of the *La Melpomène* class, armed with three 3.9in guns and four 17.7in torpedo tubes. At the same time, the worn-out 'PN' class torpedo boats built during the First World War were being phased out and the reclassification of the 'three-stacker' destroyers described above only went some way towards keeping up the numbers of the torpedo boat fleet.

The two prototypes (*Spica* and *Astore*) were completed in 1935 by the Bacini e Scali Napoletani yard of Naples and, despite not being particularly good seaboats, they were fast (almost 35 knots) and well-armed, with three 3.9in/47 guns and four 17.7in torpedo tubes (one twin mount and two singles). Later, in April 1940, both *Spica* and *Astore* were sold to Sweden, along with the destroyers *Nicotera* and *Ricasoli*, and served with that Navy as *Romulus* and *Remus* until 1958. Six further ships, known as the *Climene* group, were laid down in 1934 and commissioned in 1936: their hull was 1m longer (81.4m instead of 80.4m) and standard displacement rose to 654 tons; the armament was the same as the two prototypes, but the four torpedo tubes were all single mount, two on each side on the main deck.

While the *Climene*s were being built by CNR, Ancona and Cantieri del Tirreno, Riva Trigoso, the Cantieri del Quarnaro, Fiume and Ansaldo at Genoa laid down four further *Spica* class torpedo boats: this was the *Perseo* series, which were quite similar to those of the previous ships: displacement 642 tons, and length increased by a few inches. Finally, in 1936, it was decided to produce sixteen additional ships (the *Alcione* group), all commissioned in 1938, whose building contracts were shared between Ansaldo (eight ships), and Cantieri del Quarnaro, Fiume and Bacini e Scali Napoletani, Naples (four vessels) each. The four Fiume-built ships (*Lira*, *Libra*, *Lince* and *Lupo*) were commissioned with four single torpedo tubes, but all the other ships in this series had two twin 17.7in torpedo tubes fitted on the centreline, thus allowing them to use all of their torpedoes at the same time against the same target. By 1941, however, all the remaining ships in the class had disembarked their single torpedo tubes and replaced them with twin mounts. The names of the thirty-two ships built in this class were all referred to stars, gods, heroes and characters of Greek and Roman mythology.

During speed trials, with a 710–730 tons displacement, all ships exceeded 34 knots but, when fully equipped (and even more so in wartime), with additional weapons and fuel tanks topped their speed decreased to no more than 28–29 knots in 1942, when their full load displacement exceeded 1,200 tons. The design of the single-funnelled *Spica*s was particularly elegant and, from a great distance, they resembled the most modern destroyers of the *Maestrale*, *Oriani* and 'Soldati' classes. Nevertheless, as already mentioned, their seakeeping was not good, and strong vibrations were experienced all over the hull in head seas; with swells on the stern quarters steering was quite difficult, as the *Spica* tended to yaw and lurch in these conditions, and the crew quarters were small, crowded and with few amenities, thus allowing only limited endurance and reduced efficiency under wartime conditions.

In 1939, the original twin 13.2mm MG began to be replaced with 20mm/65 cannon, and in 1942 the surviving vessels shipped from six to ten weapons of this kind. Although originally conceived as a sort of small destroyer, the *Spica*s

---

Prototypes – 1933/35
Spica, Astore (BSN)

Climene group – 1934/1937 [A]
Castore, Centauro, Cigno, Climene (CNR, A)
Canopo, Cassiopea (Cdt, RT)

Perseo group – 1934/1936 [B]
Perseo, Sagittario, Sirio, Vega (CNQ)
Aldebaran, Altair, Andromeda, Antares (An)

Alcione group – 1936/1938 [C]
Alcione, Airone, Aretusa, Ariel, Clio, Calliope, Calipso, Circe (An)
Libra, Lince, Lira, Lupo (CNQ)
Pallade, Partenope, Pleiadi, Polluce (BSN)

Displacement (tons):	[A] 652/1,010; [B] 642/1,000; [C] 679/975 (data as of 1940, in 1942 standard displacement was 1,200 tons)
Dimensions (m):	81.4 overall, 8.2 max. beam, 3.05 max. draught [A], overall length 81.95 [B] and 81.4 [C]
Machinery:	2 boilers and 2 shaft-geared turbines, 19,000hp (20,000/22,000hp on trials)
Speed (kts):	32 (34–35 on trials), 26–29 in 1942
Endurance (nm/kts):	700/30, 1,750–1,900/15; fuel 190/205 tons
Armament:	Three 3.9in/47 (3 x I); six-eight 13.2mm MG (3-4 x II); 1941-3 six-ten 20mm/65 cannon (3 x II, 4 x I x 4); four 17.7in torpedo tubes (see text for details); two-four depth-charge throwers; minelaying capacity (up to 20 mines)
Complement:	116-119 (6-9)

mostly operated as escort and ASW ships in wartime so, starting in 1941, they began to be fitted with single-barrel depth charge mortars and adequate supplies of depth charges; at the same time, the *Spica*s were among the first Italian vessels equipped with German-built sonars and later with similar Italian-built sets. During the war, *Spica* class ships sank five British submarines (*Grampus*, *Triton*, *Union*, *Tempest* and *P.38*) and the Greek *Proteus*. In May 1941, in two separate engagements, *Sagittario* and *Lupo* distinguished themselves in naval actions off Crete, when they fought against greatly superior enemy naval forces, consisting of several cruisers and destroyers, while escorting small ships transporting men and ammunition to Crete.

Before 8 September 1943, eleven *Spica* class torpedo boats were lost in surface actions in the central Mediterranean; twelve more were mined, sunk by aircraft, torpedoed or stranded, but none of the seven surviving ships were seized by the Germans after the Armistice. These seven vessels (*Aretusa*, *Calliope*, *Cassiopea*, *Clio*, *Libra*, *Sagittario* and *Sirio*) were refitted in 1950–3 and served as ASW ships until the end of decade; the *Sagittario* was the last *Spica* class torpedo boat in commission with the Marina Militare, operating as a MTB support ship until 1964, when she was stricken and broken up.

The torpedo boat *Spica*, name-ship of the class, somewhere in the Dodecanese in the late 1930s. (Author's collection)

The torpedo boat *Aretusa* on the building ways of Ansaldo, Genoa in early 1938, some time before her launch on 8 February. (Courtesy Archivio Storico Ansaldo)

Left: *Altair* running trials off Genoa in late 1936; she was commissioned on 23 December that year. Note the single torpedo tubes, as originally fitted on all *Perseo* series torpedo boats. (Courtesy Archivio Storico Ansaldo)

Below: In the night of 21/22 May 1941 the torpedo boat *Lupo*, while escorting a convoy consisting of small craft ferrying troops and supplies to Crete, clashed with a greatly superior British naval force (two cruisers and four destroyers). In the ensuing battle, the small craft were all sunk by the British ships, but *Lupo* boldly fought on; her CO, Capitano di corvetta (LtCdr) Francesco Mimbelli, was later awarded the Medaglia d'Oro al Valor Militare, Italy's highest decoration. The *Lupo* is seen here in a Greek port, a few days after the action, showing shell damage at her extreme bow; notice the hammocks and blankets drying on the forecastle railings. (A Fraccaroli collection)

Lupo in Taranto's Mar Piccolo on 3 June 1941, bound for the dockyard to be refitted and repaired. In fact, on her starboard side, shell holes and other damage sustained during the action of 21/22 May can be seen. Note the single 17.7in torpedo tubes, red and white recognition stripes (both on the forecastle and the quarterdeck), and the black funnel cap. (E Bagnasco collection)

A clean and very detailed port-side view of *Cassiopea* at sea, in early 1941. (G Parodi collection)

A stern view of the *Spica* class torpedo boat *Libra*, at Piraeus, on 21 April 1942. (Photo A Fraccaroli)

Circe at Tobruk, on the morning of 3 November 1942. Smoke in the background comes from fires following an air raid that took place on 2 November, during which the auxiliary cruiser *Brioni* (*D.13*) had also been damaged. *Circe* was returning to Tobruk after escorting vessels trying to tow the merchant ship *Zara*, damaged by an aerial torpedo on 2 November; in spite of all efforts, the *Zara*, loaded with valuable cans of gasoline, sank while under tow. (E Bagnasco collection)

Cassiopea and four other *Spica* class vessels leaving Taranto's Mar Piccolo in 1948–9. Note the twin 17.7in torpedo tubes fitted in 1942; her appearance is still the same as the post-1943 war period, with hull painted dark grey and superstructure light grey. (Foto De Pace, Taranto; Author's collection)

Ariete class

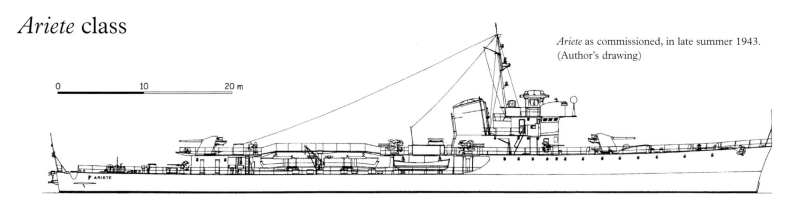

Ariete as commissioned, in late summer 1943. (Author's drawing)

In 1936–7 the Ansaldo Yard designed a new class of torpedo boats as a private venture, and in the years that followed the project was offered to the Regia Marina as well as Romania, Spain, Thailand and Sweden, but to no avail.

These ships were intended as improved *Alcione* series vessels, representing the final evolution of the *Spica* design; the new ships were bigger (1,130 tons displacement at full load, 83.5m long and 8.6m wide); only two 3.9in/47 guns in single mounts were carried but there were six torpedo tubes in two triple mounts.

In 1941, at last, in order to replace early war losses (and foreseeing the increased need for escort ships on North African routes), the Regia Marina ordered the first six ships at Ansaldo (*Ariete*, *Arturo*, *Auriga*, *Dragone*, *Eridano* and *Rigel*), and they were thus known as the *Ariete* class from the name of the first ship laid down (15 July 1942) and launched (6 March 1943). In fact, *Ariete* was the only ship of the class commissioned by the Italian Navy (on 5 August 1943) as all her sister-ships were still on the building ways on 8 September; ten additional ships had been laid down in 1942, six (*Alabarda*, *Daga*, *Gladio*, *Lancia*, *Pugnale* and *Spada*) at CRDA, Trieste and four (*Balestra*, *Fionda*, *Spica* and *Stella Polare*) at the Cantieri Navali del Quarnaro, Fiume, but all (plus the other five built at Ansaldo) were seized after the Italian Armistice by the Germans, who completed all of them (less *Balestra* and *Fionda*) between late 1943 and mid-1944. They were renamed in the 'TA' series, and were all lost before the end of the war, either by air attack, mines or during surface actions in the Adriatic, Aegean or Tyrrhenian Sea

Ariete served with the Regia Marina during the co-belligerency period (fitted with ten additional single 20mm/65 cannon); the ships in German service similarly embarked single 20mm and 37mm cannon, and some of them also had quad 20mm mounts (Vierling). Under the terms of the 1947 Peace Treaty, *Ariete* was transferred to the Yugoslavian Navy, serving as *Durmitor* until she was scrapped in 1963. *Fionda* and *Balestra* were seized by Yugoslavian forces at Fiume at the end of the war but *Fionda* was found submerged and heavily damaged so she was immediately broken up. *Balestra* was in fair condition on the building ways, and she was completed by the Yugoslavian Navy serving as *Ucka* from 1950 until 1968.

The sixteen *Ariete* class torpedo boats were originally named either after stars or after various types of weapons, swords, cutlasses and daggers.

Ariete (the only ship in the class commissioned into Italian service) at Taranto in 1944. Note the triple torpedo tubes and the absence of a mainmast, provided for in the original design but not fitted aboard *Ariete* or any of the other ships in the class commissioned by the Kriegsmarine. (E Bagnasco collection)

The German *TA 38* (the former Italian *Spada*) in the Adriatic in 1944; notice the degaussing cable running along the ship's side and the quad 20mm cannon abaft the funnel. *TA 38* was lost in the Aegean in an air attack in October 1944. (Author's collection)

Pegaso and *Ciclone* classes

Inboard profile of the *Pegaso* class, from an original design plan of the Bacini e Scali Napoletani Yard. (Courtesy Gruppo di Cultura Navale, Bologna)

Fortunale as commissioned in August 1942. (Line drawing by G Barbieri; courtesy Gruppo di Cultura Navale, Bologna)

0   10   20 m

The last series of the *Spica* class were still on the building ways when their designer General Bozzoni was asked by the Italian Navy to design a new class of torpedo boats that would be an enlarged version of the *Spica*s, with improved anti-submarine capability and thus more suited to operate as convoy escorts. These were the four ships of the *Pegaso* class (*Orsa, Orione, Pegaso* and *Procione*), the first two built in 1936-8 by Cantieri Navali Riuniti, Palermo, and the second pair by Bacini e Scali Napoletani, Naples.

The *Pegaso*s were larger than the *Spica*s (full load displacement 1,630 tons in 1940 and 1,750 tons in 1943, with increased AA and anti-submarine armament), with an overall length of 89.5m; the output of the machinery (two boilers and two geared turbines) was 16,000hp (17,000–18,000 on trials), less than that of the *Spica*s, granting a maximum speed of 28 knots on trials (25–26 knots under operational conditions), more than sufficient for the roles then envisaged for these ships. The general layout of the *Pegaso*s was similar to that of the *Spica* class, the main differences being the long deckhouse extending

from the aft end of the forecastle to the stern, and in the bow knuckle to improve seakeeping, a feature rarely seen on Italian ships. The combination of these characteristics prompted the Regia Marina to rate the *Pegaso* class as 'avvisi scorta' (i.e. 'escort ships') instead of 'torpediniere' ('torpedo boats') and, in most of their wartime and post-war service they were actually employed as small destroyer escorts.

Two single 3.9in/47 guns were fitted, one on the forecastle and one at the aft end of the deckhouse, and two twin 17.7in torpedo tubes

The *Pegaso* at sea in 1939. (E Bagnasco collection)

A stern view of *Pegaso* on 24 December 1941, taken at Piraeus; notice the small stern crane to handle the minesweeping paravanes. (Photo A Fraccaroli)

Details of *Pegaso*'s deckhouse and main deck looking aft; note the twin 20mm/65 cannon and the six single-barrelled depth-charge mortars. (A Fraccaroli collection)

were located on the main deck amidships. Anti-aircraft and anti-submarine armament were both increased in wartime: in 1942–3 eleven single 20mm/65 cannon and four depth-charge throwers and two depth-charge rails were fitted aboard all four ships.

One of the most interesting features found in the design of the *Pegaso* class was the provision for sonar from the start; *Orsa* had been fitted with an experimental set in 1938, but the three other ships received Italian-built sonar only after Italy's entry into the war. In 1943, *Orsa* and *Orione* disembarked the main mast aft, in order to improve the arcs of fire of the augmented AA battery; the four ships were very active in the Mediterranean war and it is almost certain that *Orsa* sank the famous British submarine HMS *Upholder* in April 1942.

Pegaso was scuttled by her crew on 11 September 1943 off Pollensa (Mallorca, Balearic Islands), to avoid internment in Spain following the Armistice. Two days earlier, *Procione* (the only ship in the class to be fitted with radar, a German Fu.Mo 24/40 'De.Te') had been scuttled in the La Spezia Dockyard to avoid being seized by the Germans; she was refloated in 1947 and broken up few years later.

Orsa, on the other hand, was interned in Spain until January 1945, while *Orione* reached Malta

after 8 September and fought on the Allied side until 1945; both ships remained with Italy by the 1947 treaty and thus served with the Marina Militare until discarded in 1964–5. Previously, in 1953–5, *Orsa* and *Orione* had been extensively refitted, returning to service as fast anti-submarine escorts, being used as target-towing vessels towards the end of their careers in the early 1960s.

In late summer 1940 the Regia Marina decided to build further ships of the *Pegaso* type, as such vessels were badly needed for escort work on the North African routes; all were laid down in the second half of 1941 (apart from *Indomito* and *Intrepido* which were laid down in January 1942) and fifteen were commissioned between 21 May 1942 (*Ciclone* – name-ship of the class) and 24 July 1943 (*Ghibli*); the sixteenth ship in the class (*Intrepido*) was completed in January 1944 by the Kriegsmarine, only to be sunk in the Tyrrhenian Sea on 15 June that year by US MTBs.

The *Ciclone* class escorts were built in groups of four by four different yards: Navalmeccanica, Castellammare di Stabia (*Aliseo*, *Ghibli*, *Groppo* and *Monsone*), Ansaldo, Genoa (*Animoso*, *Ardente*, *Ardimentoso* and *Ardito*), CRDA, Trieste (*Ciclone*, *Fortunale*, *Tifone* and *Uragano*) and Cantieri del Tirreno, Riva Trigoso (*Impavido*, *Impetuoso*, *Indomito* and *Intrepido*). They were repeat-*Orsa*s with improved seakeeping features (beam

increased to 9.9m, instead of 9.5m as for the *Orsa*s, this bringing full load displacement up to 1,800 tons) and provisions for a third single 3.9in/47 gun, actually fitted only aboard *Ghibli*, *Impavido*, *Impetuoso*, *Indomito* and *Monsone* on top of the deckhouse amidships, but later disembarked. The four *Pegaso*s all bore names of constellations, and the *Ciclone*s were named after winds and other meteorological events, as well as after adjectives indicating qualities of strength and courage.

Being built in wartime, the *Ciclone*s suffered from their hasty construction and also from poor-quality materials: some ships were not able to steam at the maximum speed of 25–26 knots called for in the contracts and their endurance was quite inferior to that of the *Pegaso*s (2,800 nm instead of 4,000 at 14 knots, and 1,400 nm instead of 2,000 at 25 knots).

Ardente, *Ciclone*, *Groppo*, *Monsone*, *Tifone* and *Uragano* were all lost in action before 9 September 1943; *Ardito*, *Impavido* and *Intrepido* were seized by the Germans after the Armistice and, renamed *TA 25*, *TA 23* and *TA 26* respectively, were all lost between April and June 1944. *Ghibli* was scuttled by her crew at La Spezia on 9 September 1943, and two days later *Impetuoso* and *Pegaso* were scuttled off Pollensa in the Balearic Islands, to avoid internment in Spain; the remaining five ships, after serving with the co-belligerent Regia Marina until the end of the war, went to the USSR and Yugoslavia as reparations. *Aliseo* and *Indomito* went to the Yugoslav Navy and, as *Biokovo* and *Triglav*, remained in commission until 1963 (*Biokovo*) and 1965 (*Triglav*). *Animoso*, *Ardimentoso* and *Fortunale* were allotted to the USSR and, with various names and acronyms assigned over the years, were employed in second-line duties until the late 1950s.

Procione moored at Piraeus on 3 September 1942, with the torpedo boat *Solferino* on her starboard side. (Photo A Fraccaroli)

Ciclone during speed trials off Trieste in early spring 1942. She was commissioned on 21 May 1942. (E Bagnasco collection)

Gabbiano class

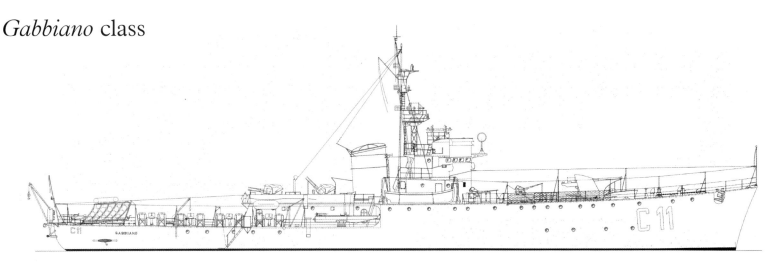

Starboard elevation of the corvette *Gabbiano* as built, from an original drawing by the Ansaldo Yard. (Courtesy Gruppo di Cultura Navale, Bologna)

In 1931–4, the Cantieri Navali Riuniti, Palermo, built the submarine chaser *Albatros*, a 500-ton full load vessel classified as a 'cacciasommergibili' (submarine chaser). The ship was commissioned with an experimental sonar, but her unsatisfactory characteristics and performance soon made her obsolete; for example her steam propulsion plant was difficult to use and maintain, and her armament soon proved outdated and inadequate. Employed in second-line duties after 10 June 1940, *Albatros* was sunk off Messina, on 27 September 1941 by the British submarine HMS *Upright*.

Following further studies in the late 1930s for a diesel-engined submarine chaser displacing 400 tons full load, the need for reliable and well-armed anti-submarine escorts prompted the Regia Marina to plan, soon after Italy's entry into the war, a large class of anti-submarine corvettes, designed by Gen. Leonardo Fea of the Genio Navale, basing the underwater hull lines of the new vessels on those of the *Azio* class minelayers of the 1920s.

Between 1942 and 1943, orders for sixty corvettes of the *Gabbiano* class (from the name of the first ship to be commissioned, on 3 October 1942) were placed with several Italian yards, as detailed below:

• Cerusa, Genoa-Voltri (part of the Ansaldo Corporation): *Gabbiano, Procellaria, Cormorano, Pellicano.*
• Ansaldo, Genoa: *Cicogna, Folaga, Ibis, Gru, Tuffetto, Marangone, Strolaga, Ardea.*
• OTO, Leghorn: *Antilope, Gazzella Camoscio, Capriolo, Alce, Renna, Daino, Cervo, Stambecco.*
• Navalmeccanica, Castellammare di Stabia: *Ape, Vespa, Lucciola, Grillo, Cicala, Calabrone, Cavalletta, Libellula, Crisalide, Farfalla, Maggiolino, Cocciniglia.*
• Breda, Venice: *Scimitarra, Baionetta, Colubrina, Spingarda, Carabina, Bombarda, Scure, Clava, Zagaglia.*
• CRDA, Monfalcone: *Artemide, Persefone, Euterpe, Minerva, Urania, Berenice, Egeria, Melpomene, Tersicore, Euridice.*
• CRDA, Trieste: *Driade, Danaide, Pomona, Flora, Sfinge, Chimera, Sibilla, Fenice.*

The ships built at Genoa were named after birds, those built at Leghorn after animals, those built at Castellammare after insects, the Breda-built ships after edged weapons or firearms, and the ships laid down by CRDA all bore the names of mythological creatures and characters.

The *Gabbiano*s – among the most successful ships built in Italy during the war – were efficient and well-built ships, 63.1m long overall, single-funnelled with a long forecastle and small superstructure, armed with a single 3.9in/47 gun forward, up to seven 20mm/65, two single 17.7in torpedo tubes (not all ships had these) and a powerful anti-submarine armament. All the ships were fitted with eight single-barrel depth-charge mortars, four on each side on the main deck, plus two large 'Gatteschi'-type multi-level depth charge rails astern; full load displacement exceeded 700 tons as commissioned. Two 3,500hp diesel engines gave a speed around 18 knots, and they were also initially fitted with two 150hp electric motors (later disembarked) for silent submarine-hunting at 5 knots.

There were only minor differences between the ships built at the various yards, the most obvious being the different arrangement of portholes and slight variations in bridge design: all were strongly built and generally well suited to escort work. Their powerful ASW armament and sonar equipment meant they scored several successes against enemy submarines: in the space of a few months, *Gabbiano* and *Cicogna* co-operated in the sinking of the British submarines HMS *Sahib* and *Thunderbolt*, and HMS *Saracen* was sunk by *Folaga* and *Minerva*: other submarines were damaged.

By September 1943, twenty-nine *Gabbiano* class corvettes had been commissioned by the Regia Marina and three (*Cicogna, Gazzella* and *Procellaria*) had already been lost. As of 8 September 1943, the Germans sank one and captured six of the remaining twenty-six ships, and completed almost all of the other vessels, still

Launch of the corvette *Marangone* at the Ansaldo Yard, Genoa, on 15 March 1943. She was still incomplete on 8 September 1943 and, having been seized by the Germans, she was commissioned into the Kriegsmarine on 16 August 1944 at Genoa, but was sunk the same day in an Allied air raid. (Courtesy Archivio Storico Ansaldo)

on the building ways or at various stages of fitting out. Several of these (classified by the Kriegsmarine as *U-boot jager* ['Uj'], i.e. 'submarine chaser', and armed with 37mm and quad 20mm cannon) were lost before April 1945.

The 1947 treaty luckily allowed Italy to keep the nineteen remaining *Gabbiano* class corvettes in commission, and – between 1951 and 1953 – three further ships of the class entered Marina Militare service: the *Bombarda* (refloated at Venice and rebuilt) and the *Crisalide* and *Farfalla*, captured by the Germans but never finished, which the Marina Militare completed to a design incorporating several technical improvements.

In the post-war years, the *Gabbiano*s were modernised to various designs, but all embarked new twin 40mm/56 Bofors guns and many were fitted with a US-produced 'Hedgehog' ASW mortar forward. These ships were one of the most homogeneous classes of the Marina Militare in the 1950s, being employed in anti-submarine and training duties, as well as for fishery protection and other auxiliary roles. By the mid-1960s they began to be decommissioned, but several were still serving ten years later. The *Ape* was the last *Gabbiano* in commission, employed during her last years of service as a Special Forces ('Incursori') support ship, and was not stricken until 31 July 1981.

Above: *Minerva* in summer 1943 at Genoa; notice the Gatteschi-type depth-charge rails aft, with two Carley life rafts on top. (A Fraccaroli collection)

The CRDA-built *Gabbiano* class *Sfinge* in April 1943, during sea trials before commissioning. This image was taken by photographers of the famed Trieste-based Studio Mioni, one of the best sources for photographs of ships built in that area in the 1930s and 1940s.
(F Petronio Collection)

The corvette *Chimera* at sea in summer 1943. (E Bagnasco collection)

Chimera at La Spezia in July 1971 with bow catapult but no twin Bofors or Hedgehog on the forecastle. Note the enlarged deckhouse forward of the bridge, probably for drone recovery and maintenance. (Photo G Ghiglione)

Ape at La Spezia on 16 September 1971, by now fully modified to operate as a support ship for the Gruppo Subacquei Incursori, based in Varignano inlet in the Gulf of La Spezia. The *Ape* was the last *Gabbiano* class vessel to be decommissioned almost ten years later, in July 1981. (Photo G Ghiglione)

Old, miscellaneous and war prize escort ships

The ex-Yugoslavian torpedo boat *T 6* was commissioned by the Regia Marina, keeping the same number. She was the former Austro-Hungarian *93 F*, commissioned by the newly-established Yugoslav Navy soon after the end of the First World War. (E Bagnasco collection)

Other escort vessels served with the Regia Marina in the Second World War, although several of them were old and outdated or, as in the case of the ex-French corvettes commissioned into Italian service in 1943, played no significant role in naval operations.

The old torpedo boat *Insidioso*, a former *Indomito* class destroyer of the First World War which had been decommissioned in 1938, was recommissioned in 1941 with reduced machinery and armament; used in second-line duties until 8 September 1943, she was seized by the Kriegsmarine and, as *TA 21*, was employed in the Adriatic until her loss on 5 November 1944, during an air raid off the Western coast of Istria.

In 1920–2 six *cannoniere di scorta* ('escort gunboats') of the *Bafile* class were built by Pattison, Naples; these were small vessels displacing less than 300 tons at full load, with steam machinery (speed 18/20 knots), armed with two single 4in/35 guns and two 17.7in torpedo tubes. As of 10 June 1940, only *Ernesto Giovannini*

survived, and was employed throughout the war as a coastal escort ship; very old and worn out, the *Giovannini* was stricken in 1946 and broken up in 1950.

Following the Axis invasion of Yugoslavia, in April 1941 several Yugoslav vessels were captured in ports on the Dalmatian coast: among them were six ex-Austro-Hungarian torpedo boats built in 1912–15 which were hastily commissioned into Regia Marina service. These old vessels were two former 'T' class and four former 'F' class torpedo boats of the KuK Marine, that – in Yugoslavian service – were named *T 1* and *T 3* ('T' class) and *T 5*, *T 6*, *T 7* and *T 8* ('F' class): the only difference was the number of funnels, two for the 'Ts' and one for the 'Fs', the original lettering in the two classes indicating the ships built at Trieste ('T') and at Fiume ('F'). In Italian service, these six torpedo boats had no names assigned and maintained their Yugoslavian designations. Displacing more than 330 tons at full load and 57.5m long, they were extensively refurbished in

Italian yards after their capture, but their old age and obsolescence made them fit only for coastal and second-line duties, in spite of the new armament later embarked (two single 76mm guns added to the original four 17.7in torpedo tubes). *T 1* and *T 5* were returned to Yugoslavia in December 1943, *T 6* and *T 8* were lost in the days following the Armistice of 8 September 1943, *T 3* and *T 7* were captured by the Germans and were both lost in the Adriatic before the end of the war.

The Regia Marina obtained two French *Elan/Chamois* class corvettes, captured by the Germans at Bizerte (Tunisia) on 8 December 1942. Transferred to La Spezia, by January 1943 they had been pressed into Italian service with their original armament (one single 3.9in/66 gun, seven 13.2mm MG and four trainable depth charge throwers: they were the former French *La Batailleuse* and *Commandant Rivière*, renamed *FR 51* and *FR 52* respectively. After 8 September 1943, both were scuttled at La Spezia, but they were later raised by the Germans and served with

The ex-French corvette *FR 51* (former *La Batailleuse*), at La Spezia in June 1942. Captured by the Germans at Genoa on 9 September 1943, she was redesignated *SG 23* and was scuttled while still at Genoa on 24 April 1945, shortly before the Germans left Genoa at the end of the war. (E Bagnasco collection)

The colonial sloop *Eritrea* in summer 1937, shortly after commissioning (28 June 1937). (E Bagnasco collection)

the Kriegsmarine in the Northern Tyrrhenian sea until their loss. Three additional ships of this class (*Chamois*, *La Curieuse* and *L'Impetueuse*), scuttled at Toulon in November 1942, were raised by the Regia Marina by the end of the year and renamed *FR 53*, *54* and *55*. Still refitting at Toulon when the Armistice was declared, they were taken over by the Germans but never entered Kriegsmarine service.

Among the lesser escort vessels of the Italian Navy, only two were classed as *avviso*, i.e. 'despatch vessel', comparable to the sloops and frigates of the Royal Navy. The colonial sloop *Eritrea* was built between 1935 and 1937 by the Regio Cantiere of Castellammare di Stabia (Naples), her design being inspired by the contemporary French *avisos coloniaux* of the *Bougainville* class. Displacing over 3,100 tons at full load, she was armed with two twin 4.7in/45 guns, two 40mm/39 light AA guns and two twin 13.2mm MG; until early 1941 she was fitted to lay mines, but the catapult for a Ro.43 seaplane provided for in the original design was never mounted.

Since 1938, the *Eritrea* had been based in Massawa, Italian East Africa: operating as flagship of the Commander of Italian naval forces in that area, she took part in some minelaying missions before leaving on 19 February shortly before the capitulation of the colony, bound for Japan; on 22 March she arrived at Kobe, and in summer 1943 she was sent to Singapore to serve as a submarine tender for the Italian boats arriving there from Bordeaux. At the Armistice, *Eritrea* managed to escape, arriving at Colombo (Ceylon) before the end of September 1943. She got back to Taranto in October 1944, but in 1945–6 she operated with the Allies in the Indian Ocean once more; one year later, she was handed over to France as reparations and, commissioned by the Marine Nationale as *Francis Garnier*, she served for several more years under the French flag, often in Indochinese waters, until her retirement in 1966, when she was stricken and broken up.

In 1937, Major Franco Spinelli of the 'Genio Navale' designed the *Diana*, a large, fast and sleek vessel that was to have been Mussolini's State Yacht. The *Diana* was a very elegant ship, 113.8m long, displacing almost 2,700 tons at full load, beautifully designed and luxuriously furnished, with 31,000hp machinery allowing speeds in excess of 28 knots. Commissioned on 12 November 1940, *Diana* was soon employed as a fast transport, being able to ferry over 300 tons of supplies and ammunition as well as 100 fully equipped soldiers; although fitted to carry more than 80 mines, she never took part in minelaying missions and her main armament consisting of two old 4in/35 single guns argued against employing her in convoy escort duties. Nevertheless, on 25 July 1941, she supported the unfortunate attack of the Xª Flottiglia MAS against Malta, transporting – and recovering – some barchini (i.e. 'MTM' surface assault craft). The *Diana* was lost on 29 June 1942 off the Gulf of Bomba (Libyan coast), torpedoed by the British submarine HMS *Thrasher* while ferrying troops to Tobruk.

The state yacht *Diana* in spring 1942. She was camouflaged at Taranto in late 1941 with the same scheme on both sides; initially the colours were those of the contemporary 'fishbone' experimental scheme applied in that period to some major Regia Marina surface vessels (dark grey and yellow-green). Later, maintaining the same pattern, the colours were changed to the usual light and dark grey of the 'standard' schemes of 1942 onwards. (E Bagnasco collection)

MAS, MTBs and VAS

MAS 527 of the second series of the '500' class, at high speed with another similar craft on Lake Ladoga, circa 1942. (A Fraccaroli collection)

The first Italian fast craft defined as 'MAS'('Motoscafo anti sommergibili', i.e. anti-submarine motorboat) were built during the First World War, the initial project being devised by Eng. Attilio Bisio of SVAN (Società Veneziana Automobili Nautiche) in 1915. Initially armed with a single small-calibre gun and some depth charges, the 'MAS' were at first employed in anti-submarine duties; nevertheless, it was soon decided to embark two drop collar torpedo launchers and – thus fitted with two torpedoes – Italian 'MAS' scored some very important successes against KuK ships during the First World War, sinking the battleship *Wien* in Trieste harbour (December 1917) and the modern dreadnought *Szent Istvàn* off Premuda on 10 June 1918. The sinking of the 22,000-ton *Szent Istvàn* was the greatest success achieved by motor torpedo boats between 1914 and 1918.

At the same time, before the end of the war and just after it, the Regia Marina experimentally built some larger 'MAS' specifically for anti-submarine warfare (in part derived from the US-built Elco boats, as well as the Royal Navy's 40-ton motor boats), and new smaller 'MAS' of the 'velocissimo' ('very fast') type, but these never achieved their expected performance because of faulty engines and their hull form.

The building of an improved design of 'MAS' began in 1924 and, fitted with new 740hp gasoline engines, such vessels were able to sustain speeds in excess of 40 knots. Later boats (*MAS 430* and *432–436*) had even better speed and general performance and, in 1932, the experimental Baglietto-built *MAS 431*, with a 'stepped' hull and 1,500hp machinery, reached 43 knots.

This new underwater hull form was clearly inspired by that of the British Coastal Motor Boats (C.M.B.) of the First World War, and was the starting point for the new series-built 'MAS' of the '500' class. They had a Baglietto-designed 'two

step' hull to improve lifting and longitudinal stability at high speed: this feature, coupled with the new and powerful Isotta Fraschini 'Asso 1000' engines, resulted in fast and reliable craft, 17m long and 4.7m wide, displacing 26–27 tons (later boats were 29.4 tons).

The first series of twenty-five boats (*MAS 501–525*) of 1936–7, was followed by a second, similar series of another twenty-five boats (*MAS 526–550*) with length increased to 18m; fourteen more boats (the third series, *MAS 551–564*) were built between 1940 and 1941 and the last boats of the fourth series (eleven craft, *MAS 565–575*, some built of steel instead of wood) followed in late 1941.

Main armament consisted of two 17.7in torpedoes; late in the war, some 'MAS' of the '500' class were also fitted with up to three 20mm/65 cannon, and up to ten depth charges. All these craft were, in effect, large fast sporting motorboats adapted for naval use, and their limited seakeeping characteristics soon became apparent, particularly in the often rough seas of the Canale di Sicilia. Nevertheless the 'MAS' of the '500' class were operated continuously by the Regia Marina until September 1943, and several were later seized by the Kriegsmarine or incorporated in the small RSI Navy (or 'MNR – Marina Nazionale Repubblicana').

MAS 538 at Piraeus on 27 February 1942; notice the depth-charge rack at the stern. (Photo A Fraccaroli)

MAS 533 at high speed with other '500' class 'MAS' boats off the Ligurian coast soon before Italy's entry into the Second World War, Note the dark grey overall painting scheme, replaced early in the war by light grey on all vertical surfaces. (Author's collection)

Four '500' class 'MAS' of the 17ª Squadriglia MAS at Pantelleria, in May 1942. (Author's collection)

The chance for Regia Marina to commission true Motor Torpedo Boats became a reality in April 1941, when six Yugoslavian MTBs, built in Germany by Lürssen in 1937–8, were captured at Cattaro. These were big and powerful vessels – 28m long, displacing 62 tons and armed with two French-built 550mm torpedo tubes – whose design derived from the German 'S 2' class Schnellboote, already in service with the Kriegsmarine. In Yugoslavian service, these boats had been named *Orjen*, *Velebit*, *Dinara*, *Triglav*, *Suvodor* and *Rudnik* but the Regia Marina renamed them *MAS 3D–8D*, 'D' standing for

'Dalmatia', where the vessels had been seized. Before recommissioning in Regia Marina service the six boats were refurbished, and the first four replaced their 40mm Bofors and 15mm MG with single Breda 20mm cannon; they formed the 24ª Squadriglia MAS and were dispatched to the Aegean, where they served until September 1943. Meanwhile, the Regia Marina laid down further vessels based on these ex-Yugoslavian boats, which were termed 'MS' (Motosiluranti – Motor Torpedo Boats), to distinguish them from the smaller 'MAS'. Therefore, *MAS 3D–8D* were renamed *MS 41–46* in 1942, to fit into the series

of similar Italian-built vessels. *MS 45* was scuttled by her crew after the Armistice, and the other five boats were seized by the Kriegsmarine. One (*MS 41*) was transferred to the RSI Navy and was lost off Porto Corsini in September 1944; the other boats were all destroyed at Salonika one month later.

In late spring 1941 the CRDA, Monfalcone Yard drew up a design for the hasty production of MTBs based on vessels seized in Yugoslavia; very few changes were carried out, the most important being the replacement of the German diesel engines with three Isotta Fraschini 'Asso 1000' gasoline engines that had proven to be reliable in prolonged service. All these vessels (known as 'CRDA 60t' type, because of their displacement) were armed with two 20mm/65 cannon and two 21in torpedo tubes; top speed exceeded 30 knots, with a power output of 3,300hp. They were built in two series, all by CRDA: the first group (*MS 11–16*, *21–26* and *31–36*) in 1941–2, and the second group (*MS 51–56*, *61–66* and *71–76*) in 1942–3. The main difference between the two groups were their torpedo tubes: partially open or 'a cucchiaio' ('spoon shaped') in the first series, and fully enclosed (with a hatch forward) for the second series; the boats of the second series also had a higher gunwale forward, therefore more closely resembling German 'Schnellboote'.

The first engagement in which CRDA-built MTBs were involved was the action against the British 'Pedestal' convoy in mid-August 1942. Along with several 'MAS' and some German 'Schnellboote', six Italian MTBs were patrolling in the Canale di Sicilia midway between Cape Bon and the Island of Pantelleria; on the night of 12/13 August, *MS 16* (some sources state it could possibly have been *MS 22*) torpedoed and sank the British cruiser HMS *Manchester*, and the *MS 31* sank the 9,000 grt British transport *Glenorchy*. With the sinking of *Manchester*, the Regia Marina scored a success similar to that of *MAS 21* in the First World War, as the British cruiser was the

MAS 3D (ex-Yugoslavian *Orjen*) camouflaged, at sea in 1942. (A Fraccaroli collection)

MS 15 (top) and *MS 53* (bottom) show the differences between the two series of MTBs built by CRDA, Monfalcone to the plans of the German *S 2* class vessels of the Yugoslavian Navy. The vessels of the second series had fully enclosed torpedo tubes and higher freeboard forward. (E Bagnasco collection)

largest surface warship sunk by an MTB between 1939 and 1945.

Between 1942 and 1943 a dozen of the CRDA-built MTBs were lost, often during battles with similar US and British craft, and several others were seized by the Germans after the Armistice, with some being later recommissioned into the RSI Navy. After the war, the Marina Militare kept some MTBs in service, initially classed as 'Motovedette' (police harbour craft), as the peace treaty did not allow Italy to operate MTBs and other fast attack craft but, finally, four boats – *MS 24, 31, 54* and *55* – were radically rebuilt in the late 1950s, serving extensively for twenty more years as *MS 472, 473, 474* and *481*.

In summer 1941 the Baglietto yard of Varazze designed a new class of 'Vedette antisommergibili' ('VAS', i.e. 'small submarine chaser'), whose design was also derived from the captured Yugoslav MTBs. They were intended for coastal and harbour patrols, and the first thirty vessels (built by Baglietto and by other minor yards between the end of 1941 and the early months of 1942) could carry up to fifteen 104kg depth charges, although their small size (length 28m and displacement 68 tons) meant they could not be fitted with sonar. Several 'VAS' also embarked two 17.7in torpedoes, for use against submerged submarines: of reasonable speed (20/21 knots), they were also employed as coastal convoy escorts

and in 1942 orders for an additional eighteen vessels were placed, only fifteen of which were completed before the Armistice.

In early 1942, the need for more small anti-submarine craft prompted Ansaldo to develop the project of a larger 'VAS', 34.1m long and displacing 94.5 tons full load (the 'Ansaldo 90 t' type); twelve vessels (*VAS 301–312*) were ordered, only six being completed before 8 September 1943. These six, as well as the other six still fitting out, were seized by the Kriegsmarine, and some of them were later employed by the RSI Navy; all twelve boats were lost before the end of the war. The gun and torpedo armament of the 'Ansaldo 90t' 'VAS' (whose seakeeping characteristics were fairly good) was the same as the Baglietto vessels, and their larger dimensions allowed them to carry an impressive anti-submarine armament of up to thirty depth charges.

The Regia Marina also operated some old 'MAS', as well as various types of experimental boat, during the Second World War. Five Baglietto (SVAN) type '12 t' 'MAS' of First World War vintage (*MAS 204, 206, 210, 213* and *216*) formed part of the Italian naval forces in the Red Sea as of 10 June 1940; before the fall of Italian East Africa, on 8 April 1941, *MAS 213* torpedoed and severely damaged the British light cruiser HMS *Capetown*. Other old 'MAS' were mostly employed in training and second-line duties: *MAS 423, 426* and *430* of the 'Velocissimo SVAN 13 t' type, the single *MAS 431* of the 'Baglietto 1931' type, the four diesel-engined 'Velocissimo SVAN 14t' boats (*MAS 432–434* and *437*), and the single experimental, Baglietto-built *MAS 424*, whose powerful 1,500hp machinery was not accompanied by acceptable seakeeping or the expected performance.

Between 1936 and 1939 the C.S.M.A. Yard of Marina di Pisa built the *Stefano Turr*, a large diesel-engined gunboat 32m long displacing 68.5 tons at full load. Her dimensions and characteristics, had further similar vessels been built, would have accorded the Regia Marina the distinction of having been some ten years ahead of the times in patrol gunboat design, but the all-aluminium structure of the *Turr*, as well as continuous and unresolved engine trouble, soon meant she was laid up at La Spezia (in July 1941), where she was broken soon after the end of the war.

Two experimental diesel-engined 'MAS' (*MAS 451–452*), based on '500' class hulls, were built by Baglietto, Varazze in 1938 but since their engines proved unsuccessful – they were later fitted with gasoline engines similar to those of the other '500' class vessels. They were assigned to Xª Flottiglia MAS and both were lost during the attack on Malta on the night of 25/26 July 1941.

Finally, two small Yugoslavian torpedo motorboats built by Thornycroft in 1926–7 (*Uskok* and *Cetnik*) were seized by the Regia Marina in April 1941 and commissioned into Italian service as *MAS 1D* and *MAS 2D*. Displacing 15 tons and 18m long, because of their old age and poor material condition they were only used for patrol and second-line duties; *1D* was lost in April 1942 when the rivets in her hull plating failed, while *2D* survived the war to be broken up in the early 1950s.

The Baglietto-built *VAS 204* at Trapani in autumn 1942, with a large number of depth charges on deck. (E Bagnasco collection)

Submarines

Enrico Toti in 1940. (Author's drawing)

On 10 June 1940 the Regia Marina had 115 submarines in commission, making the Italian submarine force one of the largest in the world: only the Soviet Navy had a larger number of boats (about 160), but they were divided between four different operational areas – the Black, Baltic and Arctic Seas and the Far East – and many of them were small boats for coastal operations only.

Balilla, on the surface, soon after commissioning (21 July 1928); notice the 4.7in/35 gun in the recess forward of the conning tower. She was laid up on 28 April 1941, and was used as a floating oil depot (*GR 247*) for the remainder of the war. (Author's collection)

Goffredo Mameli (*Mameli* class) in Taranto's Mar Grande in the mid-1930s. Note the destroyer *Bettino Ricasoli* (sold to Sweden shortly before Italy's entry into the Second World War) in the left background. The *Mameli* originally was to have been named *Masaniello*. Of the four ships in the class (*Mameli*, *Capponi*, *Da Procida* and *Speri*), only one, the *Pier Capponi*, was a war loss, torpedoed and sunk by the British submarine HMS *Rorqual* south of Stromboli on 31 March 1943. The other three boats, fully refitted after the Armistice, served as targets for the training of Allied anti-submarine forces in the Gulf of Mexico in 1944–5, all being decommissioned on 1 February 1948. (N Siracusano collection)

On that day, eighty-four Italian submarines were operational, twenty-nine were undergoing refits and two were fitting out; seven submarines were small boats built in the First World War, thirty-nine were 'oceanic' boats displacing between 950 and 1,750 tons, and sixty-nine were smaller 'coastal' boats ('di piccola o media crociera'), displacing between 650 and 950 tons.

In general, the Italian submarines commissioned in the 1930s (most of which were less than ten years old at the outbreak of war) were well built and reasonably habitable; they were fair seaboats and their machinery performed well in most conditions. This was, therefore, a fleet of significant size, although their performance, some technical features and above all the operational criteria set for them by the high command were disadvantages.

The Regia Marina's submarines still operated as they had done during the First World War, when they had been largely confined to the restricted waters of the Adriatic, and therefore the boats built post-war were designed for the type of 'static' operations that had been common then. Briefly, each boat was assigned a small 'zona d'agguato' ('attack area') where, without leaving its strict boundaries, she had to stay submerged during daylight hours, surfacing only at night to recharge the batteries and attack targets passing through the area. The 'zone d'agguato' were sited near enemy bases or in restricted waters where enemy ships could be more easily spotted and attacked. However, since the First World War, other navies (in particular the Kriegsmarine) had developed more 'dynamic' rules of engagement for their submarines, with more active search and attack procedures and had built submarines with characteristics suited to them (i.e. greater surface speed, faster diving times etc.).

In 1918 the Regia Marina had fifty-six submarines in commission (plus several midget boats); in the early 1920s the older boats were stricken and new boats came into service in several building programmes. In the first phase of new construction, between 1925 and 1929, several small classes of submarines with different characteristics were built, as prototypes for future series building programmes.

There were two basic designs for the new boats, based on the work of Eng. Cavallini and Eng. Bernardis of the Genio Navale. The 'Cavallini' boats had a 'partial double-hull', with the double bottoms (or diving tanks) mounted as a 'saddle'

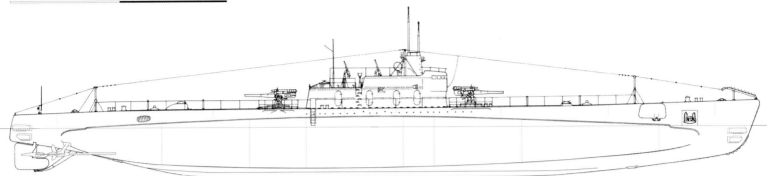

Enrico Tazzoli in 1940; later, the conning tower was significantly reduced in size to make the boat less conspicuous in Atlantic operations. (Adaptation from a plate by R Maggi; courtesy *STORIA militare*)

over the pressure hull. The four *Mameli* class submarines were built to this design and they were well-built boats, operationally safe, handy and good seaboats both surfaced and submerged.

The 'Bernardis' boats had a single pressure hull with the diving tanks inside: the four *Pisani* class were built according to this design, but their stability was so poor that side blisters had to be fitted later. Along with medium-sized boats, the Ansaldo San Giorgio Yard designed and built – as a private venture – the four *Balilla* class, large 'double-hulled' boats with great endurance, soon classed as 'oceanici' ('oceanic') as they were intended for long-range missions in distant waters. Three more 'Bernardis' boats were built in the same period: the single and rather unsatisfactory *Fieramosca* (whose original design envisaged facilities for a small seaplane) and the two minelayer submarines of the *Bragadin* class, all in all similarly unsatisfactory and with poor seakeeping and diving characteristics. It must be pointed out that the 'Ansaldo' arrangement (actually drafted by the technical departments of Ansaldo, OTO and CRDA) consisted of a 'full double hull', with diving tanks surrounding most of the pressure hull: it was adopted for a small number of boats (i.e. the *Balilla*, *Argo* and *Calvi* classes of the late 1920s / early 1930s) and was seen again only in the *Flutto* class submarines of 1941–3.

After this first experimental building phase, the Regia Marina began to order small series of boats with improved features and performance but, strangely, the less successful 'Bernardis' type was chosen. In 1928, the four *Bandiera* class boats – directly derived from the *Pisani* – were laid down, soon followed by the similar but improved *Squalo* class submarines. At the same time, Eng. Bernardis drafted the design of a small submarine with a surface displacement of 600 tons, and this design appeared in 1929/30 as the seven *Argonauta* class boats, commissioned three years later. This smaller design finally proved successful, and was repeated well into the Second World War (the *Sirena*, *Perla*, *Adua* and *Acciaio* classes), for a total of fifty-nine submarines, known collectively as the '600' class.

Only two more 'Cavallini' type submarines (the *Settembrini* class) were built in 1928, but this time the result was below expectations, and the *Settembrini*s may be considered generally inferior

Ettore Fieramosca at sea in December 1940; a few months later (April 1941) she was decommissioned, stricken and broken up. Laid down in 1926, the *Fieramosca* was initially intended as a cruiser-submarine, armed with an 8in gun and able to accommodate a small seaplane, but when commissioned she was armed with only a single 4.7in/45 gun and had no aviation facilities. Too large, the *Fieramosca* conducted only two war patrols during which she sank no enemy ships. (E. Bagnasco collection)

Leaving Taranto's Mar Piccolo through the Canale Navigabile in 1937, *Ciro Menotti* of the *Bandiera* class shows the new large and higher bow fitted to these four boats in the mid-1930s to improve seakeeping. Of this class, only *Santorre Santarosa* was a war loss, scuttled off Tripoli on 20 January 1943 after running aground following torpedo damage by the British torpedo boat *MTB 260*. *Bandiera*, *Manara* and *Menotti* survived the war and were broken up in 1947–8. (Author's collection)

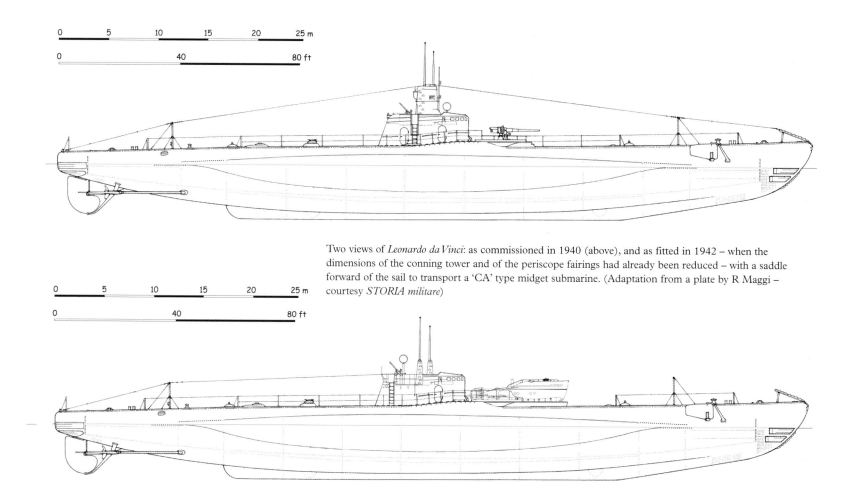

Two views of *Leonardo da Vinci*: as commissioned in 1940 (above), and as fitted in 1942 – when the dimensions of the conning tower and of the periscope fairings had already been reduced – with a saddle forward of the sail to transport a 'CA' type midget submarine. (Adaptation from a plate by R Maggi – courtesy *STORIA militare*)

when compared with the *Mameli*s. At the same time, in the early 1930s, other large boats were laid down: the four oceanic *Archimede* class (of the 'Cavallini' type) and the two *Otaria*s ('Bernardis' type); the *Otaria*s had originally been ordered by the Portuguese Navy, but were acquired by the Regia Marina before their launch and they proved so well built that they became the starting point for the later classes of Italian long-range submarines.

In the mid-1930s, the three large submarines of

the *Calvi* class followed: with a full double hull, their design was descended from that of the *Balilla*. These early oceanic boats were good vessels overall, with fairly good seakeeping, armament and crew accommodation, but they dived too slowly, being too large and not as manoeuvrable as expected. In 1931, another minelayer submarine was laid down: the large *Micca* ('Cavallini' type). Although quite successful, she was so expensive that she was the

only one built. The design for another, slightly smaller minelayer of the 'Cavallini' type was underway, later resulting in the three submarines of the *Foca* class.

In the mid-1930s, increasing military commitments and the deterioration of the international situation prompted an increase in the pace of naval construction and in submarine building in particular. Between 1935 and 1940, no less than eight classes of submarines were laid down: six were of oceanic boats (*Brin*, *Marconi*, *Marcello*, *Liuzzi*, *Cagni* and *Foca* [minelayers]) and two of coastal boats (the *Perla* and *Adua* series of the '600' class); two additional medium-displacement, long-range boats (*Argo* class), originally ordered by Portugal, had been built in 1931 by CRDA, Trieste. Again, all these submarines were reasonable vessels, but in wartime their design would prevent them from employing more active tactics that had been originally envisaged for them.

All of this became evident in the early months of the war and in spite of modernisations, modifications and general improvements, many technical problems would not be solved until the few modern boats designed and built in wartime entered service. Moreover, some submarines were not good seaboats when sailing surfaced in rough seas, and some classes (*Brin* and *Liuzzi* in particular) built in the mid-1930s were subject to frequent breakdowns because of the sub-standard quality of materials employed for their building, as a result of Mussolini's attempt to achieve autarky.

The modified bow structure – with the bulbous 'nose' typical of many Italian submarines of that era – is clearly noticeable in this fine port-side view of *Filippo Corridoni*, dating from the mid-1930s. The two minelayer submarines of this class (the other one was the *Marcantonio Bragadin*) had a bow 'nose' fitted shortly after their commissioning; in wartime, only the *Bragadin* made a single minelaying mission, after which both submarines were employed mostly for supply missions to North Africa and during a refit in 1943 the bow 'noses' were removed and the conning towers reduced in size, in an attempt to improve underwater performance. (A Fraccaroli collection)

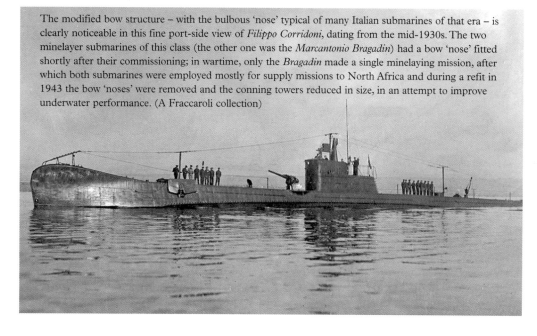

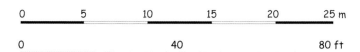

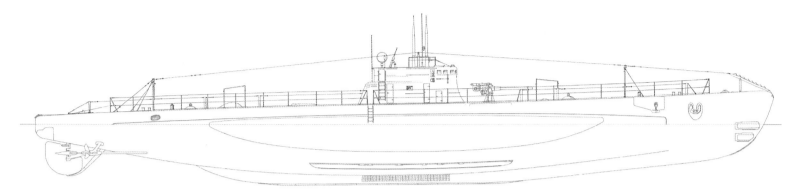

Perla, of the '600' class, as commissioned in 1936. (Courtesy Gruppo di Cultura Navale, Bologna)

In June 1940, Comando Supremo directed the Regia Marina to act 'defensively' with the surface fleet but more aggressively with the submarine force: when war was declared on 10 June, fifty-five boats (almost half the entire force) sailed for their patrol areas. According to the regulations then in force, the boats were to conduct 'static' patrols, with warships as their priority targets, although two boats were sent into the Atlantic to attack Allied merchant shipping. The boats of this 'first wave' returned to their bases after a few days having achieved little, and after that the number of boats on patrol in the Mediterranean at any one time never exceeded twenty to thirty.

During the first month of the war, submarine losses were particularly high (ten boats), because of two combined factors: the boats' tactics – always stationed just off enemy naval bases, with orders to remain in the area regardless – which made them easy targets for enemy ships, and the excellent training of British anti-submarine vessels and crews (as well as the modern anti-submarine equipment fitted aboard them – sonar etc.). Moreover, after 10 June 1940 British merchant shipping was quickly shifted to the Cape route around Africa, so the only targets left for the Italian submarines in the Mediterranean were fast and manoeuvrable warships, and capable escort vessels as well. However, after this first month, losses fell to an average of ten boats every six months, for three main reasons:

• Fewer submarines at sea at any one time.
• Crews had gained experience in dealing with enemy ASW tactics.
• Technical improvements to older boats, plus the entry into service of new boats reflecting wartime experience.

As an example of the last point, the original diving time of about 60 seconds was reduced to no more than 30/45 seconds by increasing the dimensions of the crash dive tanks and the diameters of their air and water valves. On some new-construction boats more powerful diesel engines were fitted, thus allowing greater surface speed; at the same time, much of the internal equipment and machinery was mounted on 'elastic' frames, reducing noise and vibrations. The visibility on the surface of all submarines was greatly reduced by reducing the size of their conning towers, and by eliminating the periscopes' external fairings; single 13.2mm MG were replaced by twin weapons of the same (but still insufficient) calibre: only some *Tritone* class boats embarked 20mm cannon. Electrically-powered torpedoes were introduced from mid-1942, but they were only available in small numbers; electromechanical fire-control computers began to be fitted early in the war and if the Armistice had not been signed they would have been replaced with more efficient German-produced types.

During the war the older and less capable boats (the *Ettore Fieramosca*, the 'X' class, the *Pisani*s and the *Balilla*s) were gradually reduced to the reserve or even stricken, and it was decided to build medium-sized submarines ('di media crociera'), able to dive in 30 seconds and with much higher surface speed: the design of these boats derived directly from the successful '600' and *Argo* classes and led to the laying down of the *Acciaio* and *Flutto* classes, very good vessels indeed but only commissioned in small numbers, with the building of several boats suspended because of the Armistice of 8 September 1943.

The Regia Marina also built some classes of midget submarines: the 'CA' and 'CB' types of 1941/42 were intended for coastal use and ambushes against enemy shipping, and later in the war (1943) the slightly larger 'CM' and 'CC' types followed, but none of these more capable boats saw service before the Armistice. At the same time, large transport submarines (the 'R' class) were laid down but only the first two boats – *Romolo* and *Remo* – were commissioned.

Some enemy submarines were seized and commissioned into Italian service; two French-built ex-Yugoslavian boats (*Ostvenik* and *Smeli*)

The conning tower of the *Luigi Settembrini*, with other boats in the background, in 1936–7. Both *Settembrini* and her sister-ship *Settimo* were 'Cavallini' type submarines whose design derived from the earlier vessels of the *Mameli* class. Note the lettering 'SB' (originally painted in red): for a period in the mid-1930s most Italian submarines had such lettering on the sides of the conning tower, whose purpose, as in the case of destroyers and torpedo boats, was the identification of the boat by name. *Settembrini*, while operating as a training boat in the Atlantic with the co-belligerent Regia Marina, was sunk in the Atlantic on 15 November 1944 in a collision with the destroyer escort USS *Frament* (DE-677). (N Siracusano collection)

The submarine *Otaria* as built, in 1936–7. Both *Glauco* class boats (*Glauco* and *Otaria*) operated in the Atlantic – with *Glauco* sunk west of Gibraltar by HMS *Wishart* on 27 June 1941 – from the Italian submarine base of Bordeaux, between September 1940 and summer 1941. *Otaria* was later assigned to the submarine school at Pola, and was also employed as a training boat at Taranto after the Armistice of 8 September 1943. (E Bagnasco collection)

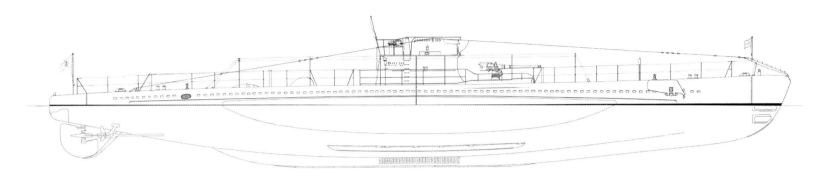

| 0 | 5 | 10 | 15 | 20 | 25 m |
| 0 | | 40 | | | 80 ft |

Platino (of the last series [*Acciaio*] of the '600' class) in 1942. (Courtesy Gruppo di Cultura Navale, Bologna)

Galilei at Taranto in the late 1930s: notice that the boat's name on the starboard bow is incorrectly spelled 'Galileo'. Both *Galilei* and *Ferraris* displaced 1,259 tons submerged, with a partial double-hull of the 'Cavallini' type. The *Ferraris* was sunk in the Atlantic on 25 October 1941, and the *Galilei* was seized by the British off Aden on 16 June 1940, after an engagement with British ships and aircraft. Two additional boats in the class (*Archimede* and *Torricelli*) were handed over to the Spanish Nationalist Navy in April 1937, serving until 1959. As a matter of political expediency, in order to keep the foreign transfer as secret as possible, the names of *Archimede* and *Torricelli* were repeated on two later submarines of the *Brin* class. (E Bagnasco collection)

became the *Francesco Rismondo* and *Antonio Bajamonti*, while a third vessel (the British-built *Hrabri*) was soon broken up, in 1941. In November 1942, several French submarines were also seized, but only one – the former *Foque* of the *Saphir* class – was recommissioned into the Italian Navy, as *FR.111*. In 1943, to replace several 'oceanic' boats then being converted to transport submarines, the Kriegsmarine transferred nine Type VIIC U-boats to the Regia Marina. Handed

Built by Tosi, Taranto between 1931 and 1935, the large *Pietro Micca* was a one-of-a-kind minelaying submarine but she carried out only two minelaying missions off Alexandria in the summer of 1940. From then on, *Micca* was always employed as a transport submarine to ferry supplies to Libya – as in this photograph showing her at Taranto on 30 January 1942, returning from a run to North Africa. The *Micca* – one of the last Italian boats lost before the Armistice – was sunk off Santa Maria di Leuca, in the Otranto area, by the British submarine HMS *Simoon*, on 29 July 1943. (E Bagnasco collection)

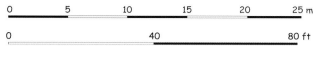

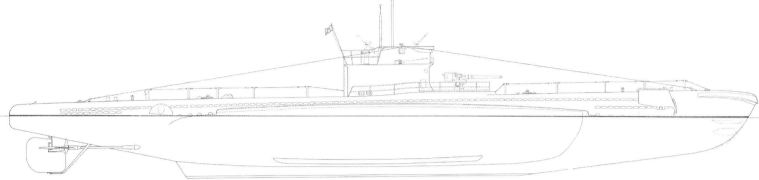

Tritone of the *Flutto* class, as commissioned in October 1942. This submarine had a very short life, as a few months later – on 19 January 1943 – she was sunk off Bougie by gunfire from the British destroyer *Antelope* and the Canadian corvette *Port Arthur*. (Courtesy Gruppo di Cultura Navale, Bologna)

over in Danzig in summer 1943, they were reincorporated into the German Navy soon after the Armistice.

Italian submarines' weaponry was generally good and reliable: their torpedoes were accurate and efficient although their pre-heated compressed air propulsion system was not as good as the electric motors of later torpedoes, that left no wake. The 3.9in, 4in and 4.7in deck guns of Italian submarines were excellent weapons; however, the standard anti-aircraft armament of

13.2mm MGs proved to be inadequate against increasingly fast enemy aircraft but, as mentioned earlier, only boats built late in the war were equipped with 20mm cannon.

During the war, Italian submarine operations were concentrated mostly in the Mediterranean and in the Atlantic; the few boats stationed in the Red Sea at the beginning of the war had scant opportunity to attack enemy ships and after the fall of Italian East Africa the four surviving submarines reached Bordeaux after a long and

eventful circumnavigation of Africa. In the two main theatres, the boats operated under different directives and instructions. Between 1940 and 1943, thirty-two boats served in the Atlantic, mostly targeting Allied merchant shipping. Their radius of operations gradually increased, reaching the east coast of the United States in 1942 and as far as the Indian Ocean by 1943. In general, the Italian 'oceanic' submarines were deployed to areas of 'limited traffic', off the main convoy routes where ships sailing alone could be easily

Bordeaux, 29 September 1940: the *Finzi* entering the lock connecting the Garonne River with the basin where the Italian submarine base ('Betasom') was located. The large dimensions of the three *Calvi* class boats (*Calvi*, *Finzi* and *Tazzoli* – entirely double-hulled and displacing over 2,000 tons submerged) made these submarines very suitable for operations in the Atlantic, where *Calvi* and *Tazzoli* were lost between 1942 and 1943. The *Finzi*, which had been refitted as a transport boat, was seized by the Germans after the Armistice of 9 September 1943 and was scuttled at Bordeaux on 25 August 1944, shortly before Allied troops arrived in the area. (E Bagnasco collection)

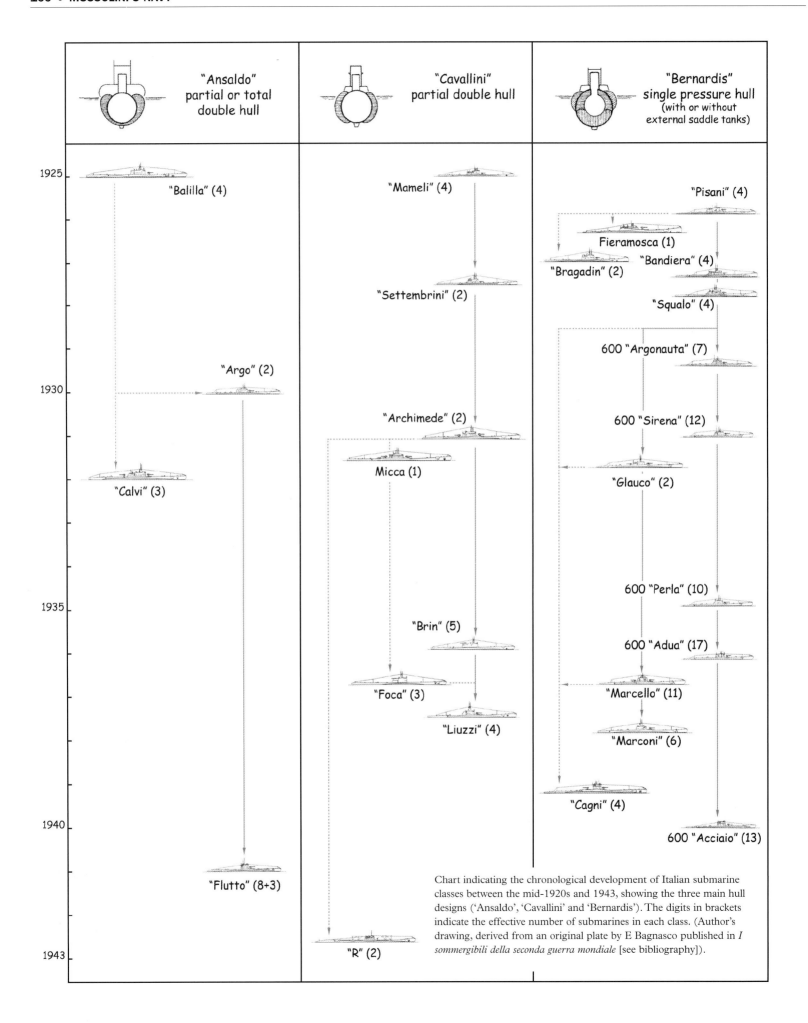

"Ansaldo"
partial or total
double hull

"Cavallini"
partial double hull

"Bernardis"
single pressure hull
(with or without
external saddle tanks)

1925

"Balilla" (4)

"Mameli" (4)

"Pisani" (4)

Fieramosca (1)

"Bragadin" (2)

"Bandiera" (4)

"Settembrini" (2)

"Squalo" (4)

600 "Argonauta" (7)

"Argo" (2)

1930

"Archimede" (2)

600 "Sirena" (12)

Micca (1)

"Calvi" (3)

"Glauco" (2)

600 "Perla" (10)

1935

"Brin" (5)

600 "Adua" (17)

"Foca" (3)

"Marcello" (11)

"Liuzzi" (4)

"Marconi" (6)

"Cagni" (4)

1940

600 "Acciaio" (13)

"Flutto" (8+3)

Chart indicating the chronological development of Italian submarine
classes between the mid-1920s and 1943, showing the three main hull
designs ('Ansaldo', 'Cavallini' and 'Bernardis'). The digits in brackets
indicate the effective number of submarines in each class. (Author's
drawing, derived from an original plate by E Bagnasco published in *I
sommergibili della seconda guerra mondiale* [see bibliography]).

1943

"R" (2)

The *Zoea* in spring 1938, soon after commissioning. The three large *Foca* class submarine minelayers (*Atropo*, *Foca* and *Zoea*) were partially double-hulled boats of the 'Cavallini' type, fitted with a central compartment holding 20 mines to be laid vertically and with two mine-launching tubes astern, capable of holding eight weapons each. In addition, the *Foca*s were armed with the usual six 21in bow torpedo tubes. *Foca* was lost off Haifa in October 1940, probably after running into a British minefield; the *Atropo* and *Zoea* spent most of the war on transport missions, being discarded and broken up in 1947. (E Bagnasco collection)

located and attacked, operations for which the Italian boats' powerful gun armament, good endurance and habitability suited them.

Thirty-two Italian boats saw service in the Atlantic from 1940 until 1943, being used mostly against Allied merchant shipping; their range of action was gradually increased, extending to the American coastline in 1942 and even to the Indian Ocean in 1943. As a general rule, the Italian 'oceanic' submarines were dispatched to 'limited traffic' areas, where isolated ships could be easily tracked and attacked if considering the boats' excellent guns, good endurance and fair habitability. They were rarely deployed against Allied convoys in the 'hot' areas of the North Atlantic, as they would have been easy prey for British and American escort ships because of their huge size, lack of speed and slow diving times. In 1943 the last Italian submarines stationed in the Atlantic, because of their large size, began to be converted into transport submarines to ferry valuable strategic materials to and from the Far East.

In the Mediterranean, the Italian submarines' deployment and tactics changed several times: beginning with the rigid and 'static' attack areas assigned to them early in the war, wider patrol areas were assigned from late 1940 onwards; in 1941, more 'dynamic' patrol lines ('sbarramenti mobili') became common practice and, a year later Regia Marina submarines began to be employed in mass actions when important British convoys were at sea. The number of boats on patrol at any one time decreased after the first few months of the war, but several were kept at short notice to sail to areas where enemy activity had been detected. Attempts were made to change their tactics from attacking submerged during the day to attacking at night on the surface, but the threat of air attack in the restricted waters of the Mediterranean made this a risky business. As well as being employed on offensive patrols and defensive deployments off the Italian coast, submarines frequently ferried fuel and supplies to North Africa when the surface convoys could not meet all of the demand. The large minelaying boats were used for this, as the unreliability of the mines they were supposed to lay meant that they had little else to do.

A few submarines were converted to transport underwater assault craft or other Special Forces, but the best results of the whole war were scored when Regia Marina boats operated in mass attacks against British convoys during the 'Mezzo giugno' and 'Mezzo agosto' operations in June and August 1942. The last of these took place in autumn 1942, when Italian and German submarines tried to oppose the Allied landings in North Africa but the results did not live up to expectations and losses were very high. It should be pointed out that the German U-boats sent to the Mediterranean in late autumn 1941 also suffered heavy losses, as indeed did British boats, proving how dangerous a theatre for submarines the Mediterranean was. After the Armistice of September 1943, the thirty-eight surviving submarines operated with the co-belligerent Regia Marina on the Allied side and, by April 1945, two more boats had been lost.

In fact, during the Second World War the Italian submarine arm did not obtain the results that might have been hoped for, given the large number of boats in service at the beginning of the war, and the money spent to build them and train their crews. The reason for this lack of results – in spite of the valour and sacrifice of their crews (more than 3,000 Italian submariners were killed in action) – was the outdated tactics developed in the inter-war period, which resulted in the limited technical and operational characteristics of the Italian boats described above; the modifications made on board most vessels during the war were only a partial solution to their many deficiencies, particularly the submarines built before 1940.

If these older boats could have been replaced by a large number of modern submarines, designed and built in accordance with genuine wartime requirements, the problem could have been solved, but the lack of shipyards, the shortage of raw materials (often assigned to more urgent projects) and the fact that the course of the war turned against Italy, meant that building a large number of submarines was impossible after 10 June 1940.

Only a few Italian shipyards had the specialised equipment and skilled manpower to build submarines: so, with a few exceptions, all Regia Marina submarines built from the 1920s until 1943 were laid down and launched by three main yards: Tosi at Taranto, Cantiere Navale Triestino (later CRDA) at Monfalcone and the Odero Terni (later OTO) yard at Muggiano, near La Spezia.

Submarine names were initially chosen from those of military commanders of the Renaissance and patriots of the 'Risorgimento'; these were followed by submarines named after fishes and other sea-creatures and in the mid/late-1930s some honoured heroes of the First World War. After 1940, boats were named after minerals or gemstones and once again after sea creatures.

A 21in torpedo being loaded aboard *Atropo* in summer 1941. (Authors collection)

Coastal and oceanic submarines

Balilla class – four boats
(Odero Terni, La Spezia, 1925–28/29)
Balilla, Domenico Millelire, Antonio Sciesa, Enrico Toti
Displ. 1,450/1,904 tons; length 86.75m; six 21in TT, one 4.7in/45 gun

Mameli class – four boats
(Tosi, Taranto, 1925–28/29)
Pier Capponi, Giovanni Da Procida, Goffredo Mameli, Tito Speri
Displ. 830/1,010 tons; length 64.6m; six 21in TT, one 4.7in/35 gun

Pisani class – four boats
(Cantiere Navale Triestino, Monfalcone, 1925–9)
Giovanni Bausan, Marcantonio Colonna, Des Geneys, Vittor Pisani
Displ. 880/1,058 tons; length 68.2m, six 21in TT, one 4.7in/35 gun

Fieramosca class – one boat
(Tosi, Taranto, 1926–31)
Ettore Fieramosca
Displ. 1,556/1,987 tons; length 84m; eight 21in TT, one 4.7in/45 gun

Bandiera class – four boats
(Cantiere Navale Triestino, Monfalcone – Odero Terni, La Spezia, 1928/30)
Fratelli Bandiera, Luciano Manara, Ciro Menotti, Santorre Santarosa
Displ. 993/1,153 tons; length 69.8m; eight 21in TT, one 4.7in/35 gun

Squalo class – four boats
(CRDA, Monfalcone, 1928–30/31)
Squalo, Narvalo, Delfino, Tricheco
Displ. 933/1,142 tons; length 69.8m; eight 21in TT, one 4.7in/35 gun

Bragadin class – two boats
(Tosi, Taranto, 1927/31)
Marcantonio Bragadin, Filippo Corridoni
Displ. 981/1,167 tons; length 68m; six 21in TT, one 4.7in/35 gun

'600' class (*Argonauta* series) – seven boats
(CRDA, Monfalcone – Tosi, Taranto – Odero Terni, La Spezia, 1929–32/33)
Argonauta, Fisalia, Medusa, Serpente, Salpa, Jantina, Jalea
Displ. 650/810 tons; length 61.5m; six 21in TT, one 4.7in/35 gun

Settembrini class – two boats
(Tosi, Taranto, 1928/32)
Luigi Settembrini, Ruggero Settimo
Displ. 953/1,153 tons; length 69.1m; eight 21in TT, one 4.7in/35 gun

'600 ' class (*Sirena* series) – twelve boats
(CRDA, Monfalcone – Tosi, Taranto – Cantieri del Quarnaro, Fiume – OTO, La Spezia – 1931–33/34)
Sirena, Naiade, Nereide, Anfitrite, Galatea, Ondina, Diamante, Smeraldo, Rubino, Topazio, Ametista, Zaffiro
Displ. 679/860 tons; length 60.2m; six 21in TT, one 3.9in/47 gun

Archimede class – two boats
(Tosi, Taranto, 1931–34/35)
Ferraris, Galilei
Displ. 985/1,259 tons; length 70.5m; eight 21in TT, one 3.9in/43 gun

Glauco class – two boats
(CRDA, Monfalcone, 1932/35)
Glauco, Otaria
Displ. 1,055/1,325 tons; length 73.0m; eight 21in TT, two 4.7in/47 guns

Micca class – one boat
(Tosi, Taranto, 1931/35)
Pietro Micca
Displ. 1,570/1,970 tons; length 90.3m; six 21in TT, one 4.7in/45 gun, twenty mines

Calvi class – three boats
(OTO, La Spezia, 1932–35/36)
Pietro Calvi, Giuseppe Finzi, Enrico Tazzoli
Displ. 1,550/2,060 tons; length 84.3m; eight 21in TT, two 4.7in/45 guns

'600' class (*Perla* series) – ten boats
(CRDA, Monfalcone – OTO, La Spezia, 1935/36)
Perla, Gemma, Berillo, Diaspro, Turchese, Corallo, Ambra, Onice, Iride, Malachite
Displ. 696/860 tons; length 60.2m; six 21in TT, one 3.9in/47 gun

'600' class (*Adua* series) – seventeen boats
(CRDA, Monfalcone – OTO, La Spezia – Tosi, Taranto, 1936/37)
Adua, Axum, Aradam, Alagi, Macallè, Gondar, Neghelli, Ascianghi, Scirè, Durbo, Tembien, Dagabur, Dessiè, Uarsciek, Uebi Scebeli, Beilul, Lafolè
Displ. 680/866 tons; length 60.2m; six 21in TT, one 3.9in/47 gun

Foca class – three boats
(Tosi, Taranto, 1936–37/1939)
Foca, Zoea, Atropo
Displ. 1,318/1,659 tons; length 62.8m; six 21in TT, one 3.9in/43 gun, twenty mines

Argo class – two boats
(CRDA, Monfalcone, 1931/37)
Argo, Velella
Displ. 794/1,018 tons; length 63.1m; six 21in TT, one 3.9in/47 gun

Marcello class – eleven boats
(CRDA, Monfalcone – OTO, La Spezia, 1937–38/39)
Mocenigo, Dandolo, Veniero, Provana, Marcello, Nani, Barbarigo, Emo, Morosini, Cappellini, Faà di Bruno
Displ. 1,060/1,317 tons; length 83.0m; eight 21in TT, two 3.9in/47 guns

Brin class – five boats
(Tosi, Taranto, 1936–38/39)
Brin, Galvani, Guglielmotti, Archimede, Torricelli
Displ. 1,016/1,266 tons; length 72.4m; eight 21in TT, one 3.9in/43 gun

Liuzzi class – four boats
(Tosi, Taranto, 1938/39–40)
Console Generale Liuzzi, Reginaldo Giuliani, Alpino Bagnolini, Capitano Tarantini
Displ. 1,166/1,510 tons; length 76.1m; eight 21in TT, one 3.9in/47 gun

Marconi class – six boats
(CRDA, Monfalcone – OTO, La Spezia, 1938/39–1940)
Guglielmo Marconi, Leonardo Da Vinci, Michele Bianchi, Luigi Torelli, Alessandro Malaspina, Maggiore Baracca
Displ. 1,195/1,490 tons; length 76.5m; eight 21in TT, one 3.9in/47 gun

Cagni class – four boats
(CRDA, Monfalcone, 1939/41)
Ammiraglio Cagni, Ammiraglio Caracciolo, Ammiraglio Millo, Ammiraglio Saint Bon
Displ. 1,708/2,190 tons; length 87.9m; fourteen 17.7in TT, two 3.9in/47 guns

'600' class (*Acciaio* series) – thirteen boats
(OTO, La Spezia – CRDA, Monfalcone – Tosi, Taranto, 1940–41/42)
Acciaio, Cobalto, Nichelio, Platino, Alabastro, Asteria, Avorio, Giada, Granito, Porfido, Argento, Bronzo, Volframio
Displ. 715/870 tons; length 60.2m; six/eight 21in TT, one 3.9in/47 gun

Flutto class – eight + three boats
(CRDA, Monfalcone – OTO, La Spezia, 1941/42–42/43)
Flutto, Gorgo, Nautilo, Marea, Tritone, Vortice, Murena, Sparide (*Grongo, Litio* and *Sodio* launched but not commissioned)
Displ. 945/1,113 tons; length 63.1m/64.1m; six 21in TT, one 3.9in/47 gun

'R' class – two + ten boats
(Tosi, Taranto, 1942/43)
Romolo, Remo
Displ. 2,210/2,606 tons; length 70.7m; two 20mm/70 cannon

Midget submarines

'CA' class – four boats
(Caproni, Taliedo, 1938–43)
CA 1 / 4
Displ. 36/45 tons; length 15m; two 17.7in torpedoes in external cradles

'CB' class – twelve boats (plus twelve commissioned by the Marina Nazionale Repubblicana in 1944)
(Caproni, Taliedo, 1939–45)
CB 1 / 12
Displ. 13.5/16.4 tons; length 10m; two 17.7in torpedoes in external cradles

'CM' class (three submarines, only one commissioned by the Marina Nazionale Repubblicana)
(CRDA, Monfalcone)
CM 1
Displ. 92/114 tons; length 32.9m; two 17.7in TT

Old, war prize and transferred submarines

'X' class – two boats
(Ansaldo, 1917–18)
X.2, X.3
Displ. 403/468 tons; length 42.6m; two 17.7in torpedoes in external cradles, one 76mm/30 gun
(Used as training boats since 1936; discarded in September 1940)

'H' class – five boats
(Canadian-built – 1916–18)
H.1, 2, 4, 6 and *8*
Displ. 365/474 tons; length 45.8m; four 17.7in TT, one 76mm/30 gun
(Used as training boats 1940–5; *H.1* and *H.6* were war losses, all other boats were scrapped in 1948)

Antonio Bajamonti and *Francesco Rismondo* (former Yugoslavian *Smeli* and *Ostvenik*)
(French-built, 1927/29)
Displ. 665/822 tons; length 66.5m; six 21.6in TT, one 3.9in/35 gun
(Mostly employed for training, both lost in 1943)

FR.111 (former French *Phoque*, of the *Requin* class)
(Brest Arsenal, 1923/27)
Displ. 1,150/1,441 tons; length 78.2m; ten 21.6in TT, one 3.9in/40 gun
(Sunk by enemy aircraft on 28 February 1943)
Seven more French submarines (*Requin, Espadon, Dauphin, Saphir, Turquoise, Circé* and *Henri Poincaré*) were seized at Bizerte in December 1942 or at Toulon but – although receiving 'FR' series hull numbers – were never commissioned into Italian service, being sabotaged after 9 September, or broken up later.

'S' class – 9 submarines
(German built, Type VIICs, 1941/1942)
S.1 / 9
Displ. 769/1,070 tons; length 64.5m; six 21in TT, one 88mm/45 gun
(Transferred from the Kriegsmarine in August 1943 at Danzig, and recommissioned into German service after 9 September 1943 with their original designations of *U 428, U 429, U 430, U 746, U 747, U 748, U 749, U 750* and *U 1161*)

The two *Argo* class submarines (*Argo* and *Velella*), laid down in 1931, had originally been ordered by the Portuguese Navy which was unable to complete the purchase because of financial difficulties. Strong and well-built vessels, they had almost twice the endurance of the '600' class while being only 200 tons heavier. The design of the two *Argo*s proved so successful that the Regia Marina decided to base the boats of the *Flutto* class on their plans, and with some improvements, these turned out to be the best wartime-built Italian submarines. The *Velella* was sunk on 7 September 1943 in the Gulf of Salerno by the British submarine HMS *Shakespeare*; the *Argo*, undergoing an overhaul at Monfalcone when the Armistice was signed, never returned to service and was broken up in 1947, some time after this photograph was taken. (F Petronio collection)

The submarine *Veniero* at Naples at the end of October 1940, just before being deployed to the Atlantic. The *Marcello* class was the largest group of Italian ocean-going submarines, and one of the most successful, being employed in the Mediterranean at first and later in the Atlantic, with four vessels (*Dandolo*, *Emo*, *Mocenigo* and *Veniero*) returning to the Mediterranean in summer 1941. The nine boats built at CRDA, Monfalcone – *Barbarigo*, *Dandolo*, *Emo*, *Marcello*, *Mocenigo*, *Morosini*, *Nani*, *Provana* and *Veniero* – were all named after medieval and renaissance Doges of the Venetian Republic (except *Provana*, which honoured the founder of the Navy of the Kingdom of Savoy in the sixteenth century). The two built at OTO, Muggiano (*Comandante Cappellini* and *Comandante Faà di Bruno*) bore the names of the commanding officers of the ironclads *Palestro* and *Re d'Italia*, killed in action when the two warships were lost at the Battle of Lissa in July 1866 against the Austro-Hungarian Navy. (A Fraccaroli collection)

Alpino Bagnolini in Taranto's Canale Navigabile on 21 June 1940, bound for Mar Piccolo, on her return from her first war patrol during which she sank the light cruiser HMS *Calypso* south of Crete on 12 June. The four *Liuzzi* class boats (*Console Generale Liuzzi*, *Reginaldo Giuliani*, *Alpino Bagnolini* and *Capitano Tarantini*) were 'Cavallini' type submarines, whose design derived from that of the *Brin* class. Two vessels in the class were lost in 1940 (*Liuzzi* in the Mediterranean and *Tarantini* in the Atlantic); *Bagnolini* and *Giuliani*, having been converted into transport submarines, were seized after the Armistice at Bordeaux by the Germans (*Bagnolini*) and by the Japanese at Singapore (*Giuliani* – later transferred to the Kriegsmarine), and both were lost in early 1944 while operating under the German flag. (E Bagnasco collection)

Slightly larger than the *Marcello*, the six 'Bernardis' type *Marconi* class boats (*Maggiore Baracca*, *Michele Bianchi*, *Leonardo da Vinci*, *Alessandro Malaspina*, *Guglielmo Marconi* and *Luigi Torelli*) were among the most successful Italian submarines of the Second World War. All commissioned between January and June 1940, and were initially equipped with a 4in/35 gun, later replaced by a 3.9in/47 gun when these weapons began to be available in sufficient numbers. In the Atlantic and Indian Oceans the *Marconi* class submarines sank thirty-nine ships totalling 213,948 grt, and *Da Vinci* was the highest-scoring Italian boat, with seventeen ships totalling 120,243 grt. Five boats were lost in the Atlantic between 1941 and 1943 and only *Torelli* survived the war, after having been converted into a transport submarine: seized by the Germans after 8 September 1943, she was employed to ferry valuable supplies to and from the Far East. *Torelli*, found at Kobe in September 1945, was broken up in 1946. (E Bagnasco collection)

Ammiraglio Caracciolo in late 1941, soon after commissioning. The four large submarines of the *Cagni* class (*Ammiraglio Cagni, Ammiraglio Caracciolo, Ammiraglio Millo, Ammiraglio Saint Bon* – 87.9m long, displacement almost 2,200 tons submerged) had been designed for oceanic deployments to interdict enemy shipping: thus, they were armed with two 3.9in/47 guns and with an unbelievably large number of torpedo tubes (eight forward and six aft), but whose smaller calibre (17.7in) was deemed sufficient for attacks against unarmoured merchant ships. (F Petronio collection)

Ammiraglio Cagni at Taranto, in summer 1944. The *Cagni* made two war patrols in the Atlantic, the first (6 October 1942 – 20 February 1943) being the longest of any Italian submarine in the Second World War; *Cagni*'s second war patrol came to an abrupt end in early September 1943, when the boat, in the Indian Ocean when the Armistice was signed, went to Durban in compliance with its terms. Later, the *Cagni* returned to Taranto and was broken up post-war. Note that, before her deployment to the Atlantic the low amidships structure above the deck (on which the conning tower originally rested) had been deleted, thus lowering the conning tower itself to deck level. The *Cagni*'s conning tower is now preserved in Taranto's dockyard. (E Bagnasco collection)

A 21in torpedo being loaded aboard *Nichelio* in late 1942. She survived the war and was transferred to the USSR as reparations on 7 February 1949. As *Z 14*, the ex-*Nichelio* served with the Soviet Navy until 1960. (E Bagnasco collection)

Volframio and *Bronzo* (*Acciaio* series of the '600' class) in spring 1942. On 12 July 1943, the *Bronzo* was captured off Syracuse by four British minesweepers that raked her deck with gunfire, killing many officers and men. Commissioned in the Royal Navy as *P 714*, the ex-*Bronzo* was transferred to the Free French Navy in 1944 and – renamed *Narval* – served for a few more years under the French flag, being scrapped in 1948. (A Fraccaroli collection)

The submarine *Vortice* in July 1943; along with the *Marea* she was one of the two *Flutto* class boats that survived the war. In the 1950s, the *Vortice* and the *Acciaio* series *Giada* were rebuilt with snorkels and additional modern equipment, being used to train the submarine crews of the new Marina Militare Italiana before the arrival of the first US built 'fleet boats' of the *Gato/Balao* class transferred from the US Navy. (E Bagnasco collection)

The launch of the transport submarine *Romolo* at the Tosi yard, Taranto on 21 March 1943. Of the 'R' class, only *Romolo* and *Remo* were commissioned before the Armistice, but their design was considered so successful that the Kriegsmarine tried in 1944 to complete the six boats laid down in Northern Italian yards (three at OTO, Muggiano and three at CRDA, Monfalcone), although the attempt was unsuccessful. The 'R' class were the Regia Marina's largest submarines, displacing over 2,600 tons submerged; the conning tower of *R 12* has been preserved and, after having been refurbished, is now kept in Rome and is often exhibited at ceremonies and parades.
(E Bagnasco collection)

The midget submarine *CA 2* on a railway truck at Bordeaux in 1944. *CA 2* had been specifically fitted to attack enemy ports and in September 1942 tests were conducted with the submarine *Leonardo da Vinci* operating as 'battello avvicinatore' (transport submarine). The *Da Vinci* had been modified, forward of the conning tower, to ferry the *CA 2* when submerged and it was planned to transport the *CA 2* in this manner to the waters off New York harbour, where the midget would have attacked US merchant shipping. However, these plans were not realised and the 'CA' boats saw no further service. (A Fraccaroli collection)

The Caproni-designed and -built midget submarines of the 'CB' class were larger and more capable than the 'CAs'; twelve were commissioned into Regia Marina service in 1941 and CB 1–6 were transferred to the Black Sea in 1942, where the *CB 5* was lost. The *CB 3* and *CB 2* sank one Soviet submarine each (the *Sc 213* and *S 32* respectively), with one more Soviet submarine probably sunk by *CB 4*. After the Armistice, the five Black Sea Flotilla 'CBs' were transferred to the Romanian Navy, and the *CB 7–12* served as training boats with the co-belligerent Regia Marina. This photograph shows *CB 10* at Taranto in October 1943. Additional 'CBs' served with the RSI Navy, but saw no further service and all the midgets of this class were scrapped after the end of the war, apart from a few boats preserved in museums in Italy and abroad. (E Bagnasco collection)

Miscellaneous Warships

Gunboats

During the Second World War the Regia Marina had quite a large number of gunboats in commission, but the operational value of this mixed group of ships was rather low: in fact these vessels were in most cases old, several were former yachts or trawlers and between 1940 and 1943 they were employed only in harbour protection or for coastal escort duties. Among Italy's largest gunboats at this time were two ex-Yugoslavian vessels, captured in April 1941: the *Cattaro* was the former Yugoslavian coastal cruiser *Dalmacija*, commissioned as the German cruiser *Niobe* before the First World War (displacement 2,360 tons, armed with four 84mm guns) and the CRDA-built *Zagabria* (567 tons, two 20mm/70 light cannon), which was the former royal yacht *Bjeli Orao*. Following her transfer to an Italian owner, an old Austro-Hungarian yacht was commissioned as the *Aurora* (1.220 tons, two 57mm guns), which was sunk by a German Schnellboot off Ancona on 9 September 1943. The similar but smaller *Illiria* (670 tons) was acquired in France in 1938 and scrapped in 1958. The river gunboat *Ermanno Carlotto* also deserves a mention: built in Shanghai between 1914 and 1922, she served in Chinese waters until seized by the Japanese Navy in 1943; she later served as the *Kiang Kun* of the Chinese Nationalist Navy until her loss in 1949.

The following list gives all other Italian gunboats, as well as their building year, full load displacement and main armament: many were old and varied vessels (mostly former trawlers of First World War vintage, often British or Japanese-built) which in most cases were war losses between 1940 and 1943:

Alula (1917, 430 tons, one 76mm/40 gun)
Camogli (1905, 449 tons, two 76mm/40 guns)
Cirene (1912, 500 tons, two 76mm/40 guns)
Dante de Lutti (1911, 370 tons, two 76mm/40 guns)
Fata (1930, 260 tons, two MG)
Gallipoli (1911, 418 tons, two 76mm/40 guns)
Giovanni Berta (1924, 644 tons, two 76mm/40 guns)
Giuseppe Biglieri (1924, 644 tons, two 76mm/40 guns)
Levanzo (1906, 350 tons, two 76mm/40 guns)
Levrera (230 tons, two MG)
Lido (1902, 250 tons, one 76mm/40 gun)
Mario Bianco (1911, 385 tons, two 76mm/40 guns)
Mario Sonzini (1924, 630 tons, two 76mm/40 guns)
Otranto (1911, 385 tons, two 76mm/40 guns)
Palmaiola (1916, 562 tons, one 76mm/30 gun)
Pellegrino Matteucci (1924, 630 tons, two 76mm/40 guns)
Porto Corsini (1912, 380 tons, two 76mm/40 guns)
Riccardo Grazioli-Lante (1912, 400 tons, two 76mm/40 guns)
Rimini (1912, 420 tons, one 76mm/40 gun)
Rondine (1930, 260 tons, two MG)
Scilla (1904, 470 tons, one 76mm/40 gun)
Valoroso (1913, 434 tons, two 76mm/40 guns)

Auxiliary cruisers

Thirty-six auxiliary cruisers served with the Regia Marina in the Second World War. All merchant ships requisitioned for naval use, most of them had been built in the 1920s and 1930s with the prospect of naval service in mind, positions to mount guns, extra accommodation for additional crewmembers etc. Although it was originally planned to employ them as coastal escorts in home waters, they were in fact used all over the Mediterranean, and each ship took part in an average of 138 escort missions between 1940 and 1943 (a very high figure, if we consider that in the same period torpedo boats served on an average of ninety-nine missions, destroyers forty and the corvettes, of course commissioned late in the war, only nine). Most auxiliary cruisers were armed with 4.7in, 4in, 3.9in and 76mm guns, and many of them also operated as minelayers; several of these vessels were lost in action, many were scuttled soon after 9 September 1943 and very few were left at the end of the war.

The three fast, modern cold storage ships of the Regia Azienda Monopolio Banane – RAMB (the government-owned Royal Banana Monopoly Company), *RAMB I*, *II* and *III*, were particularly active in wartime: *RAMB I*, *II* and *III* operated in the Red Sea and a fourth ship (*RAMB IV*) was

The gunboat *Aurora* on 17 August 1938. Built in Glasgow in 1904 as *Nirvana*, she was later the Austro-Hungarian *Taurus*, becoming the Italian *Marechiaro* after the First World War and, renamed *Aurora* in 1928, she was used as Mussolini's state yacht. (A Fraccaroli collection)

The old gunboat *Lido* at Venice on 11 April 1941. The former Japanese-built trawler *Fukuakau 2 Maru*, she later served as the harbour tug *G 24*. She was seized by the Germans after the Armistice and was sunk at Venice on 21 March 1945 during an Allied air raid. (Photo A Fraccaroli)

converted into an hospital ship, and was seized by the British off Aden on 8 April 1941.

Only twenty-nine of the thirty-six Italian auxiliary cruisers were assigned a hull number (caratteristica ottica) in the 'D X' series, as shown in the following list (which also gives tonnage and main armament):

D 1 *Città di Napoli* (5,418 grt, four 4.7in/45 guns)
D 2 *Città di Tunisi* (same as D 1)
D 3 *Città di Palermo* (same as D 1)
D 4 *Città di Genova* (same as D 1)
D 5 *Arborea* (4,959 grt, four 4in/45 guns)
D 6 *RAMB III* (3,666 grt, four 4in/45 guns)
D 7 *Olbia* (3,514 grt, four 4in/45 guns)
D 8 *Caralis* (same as D 7)
D 9 *Filippo Grimani* (3,431 grt, four 4in/45 guns)
D 10 *Piero Foscari* (same as D 9)
D 11 *Egitto* (3,329 grt, two 4in/45 guns)
D 12 *Francesco Morosini* (2,423 grt, two 4in/45 guns)
D 13 *Brioni* (1,987 grt, two 4in/45 guns)
D 14 *Zara* (same as D 13)
D 15 *Brindisi* (same as D 13)
D 16 *Barletta* (same as D 13)
D 17 *Ipparco Baccich* (884 grt, two 76mm/40 guns)
D 18 *Narenta* (1,362 grt, two 3.9in/47 guns)
D 19 *Loredan* (1,357 grt, two 4in/45 guns)
D 20 *Lorenzo Marcello* (1,413 grt, two 3.9in/47 guns)
D 21 *Lazzaro Mocenigo* (1,404 grt, two 3.9in/47 guns)
D 22 *Lago Tana* (783 grt, two 3.9in/47 guns)
D 23 *Lago Zuai* (same as D 22)
D 24 *Mazara* (984 grt, two 76mm/40 guns)
D 25 *Lero* (1,980 grt, two 4in/45 guns)
D 26 *Cattaro* (former *Jugoslavija*) (2,398 grt, two 3.9in/47, one 76mm/40 gun)
D 27 *Lubiana* (ex-*Ljubljana*, ex-*Salona*) (985 grt, one 57mm/43 gun)
D 28 *Pola* (451 grt, three 20mm/70 cannon)
D 29 *Rovigno* (same as D 28)
Adriatico (1,976 grt, two 4in/45 guns)
Capitano Antonio Cecchi (2,321 grt, four 4in/45 guns)
Città di Bari (3,339 grt, two 4.7in/45 guns)
Attilio Deffenu (3,510 grt, two 4.7in/45 guns)
Egeo (3,311 grt, two 4.7in/45 guns)
RAMB I (same as D 6)
RAMB II (same as D 6)

The M/S *Arborea* as an auxiliary cruiser (D 5) at Bari in April 1942. (E Bagnasco collection)

The auxiliary cruiser D 25 *Lero* at Piraeus on 5 August 1942; note the aft 4.7in/45 gun and depth charge rails astern (Photo A Fraccaroli)

Submarine chasers

Another varied group of auxiliary warships of the Regia Marina was composed of more than 200 small craft, former trawlers, requisitioned yachts and military harbour craft equipped to be used as small or coastal submarine chasers. The general efficiency of most of them was questionable at best as they were only lightly armed and had no sonar, depending on outdated hydrophones which gave them little chance of detecting a submerged submarine. Several of them were former MAS transferred to the Guardia di Finanza (Customs and Revenue Service) which in wartime were also employed as pilot boats, coastal patrol boats and for other auxiliary duties. Two *Guardia di Finanza* ships (the *Maggiore Macchi* and *Generale Turba*, 214 and 303 t displacement respectively), in fact rather similar indeed to many Regia Marina gunboats, were among the largest of the submarine chasers.

The small Guardia di Finanza (Customs and Revenue Service) ship *Generale Turba*, employed as a submarine chaser after Italy's entry into the Second World War. (Author's collection)

The submarine chaser *Vergada* was the ex-Yugoslavian tug *Orao* (built as a minesweeper in Germany during the First World War, she was seized by the Regia Marina in 1941, that initially employed her as a minelayer); in December 1943 she was returned to the Yugoslavian Navy. (M Ghiglino collection)

Mine warfare vessels

Between June 1940 and September 1943, the Regia Marina laid about 49,000 mines, nearly 10 per cent of the total of about 500,000 employed in the Second World War. Unfortunately not all the mines used by the Italian Navy were of modern design, most being of the 'contact' type, with very few being fitted for use in deep waters. There were also no magnetic mines except for a few supplied by the Kriegsmarine late in the war. Nevertheless, Italian minefields scored several successes against British naval and merchant shipping, in particular sinking fourteen submarines before September 1943. Both the Regia Marina and the Royal Navy laid minefields to defend ports and naval bases, as well as against enemy convoys, but the nature of the seabed, sometimes with deep waters near the coast, prevented the effective use of Italian mines in some home waters, for example off Genoa and along the Ligurian coast. The results scored by Italian and British minefields were quite similar, as about 100 ships were lost to mines by each side; at the same time, the movements of merchant and naval ships of both fleets were similarly affected by the presence of minefields, particularly in the central Mediterranean.

The Italian Navy showed a particular interest in minelayers in the inter-war period and, on 10 June 1940, several ships of this type were in commission:

- *Albona* class (*Albona*, *Laurana* and *Rovigno* – former Austro-Hungarian minelayers commissioned after the First World War; displacement 130 tons, 34 mines);
- *Crotone* class (*Crotone* and *Vieste* – German war prize vessels commissioned in 1920; displacement 673 tons, 42 mines);
- *Panigaglia* class (*Panigaglia*, *Buffoluto* and *Vallelunga* – built by Ansaldo-San Giorgio at Muggiano [La Spezia] in 1921–4. They were named after Regia Marina powder depots as they were originally designed as ammunition transport ships; displacement 1,071 tons, 50 mines. The *Buffoluto* had a very long career, not being discarded until 1973);
- *Azio* class (*Azio*, *Legnano*, *Lepanto* and *Ostia* – built by CNR, Ancona and Stabilimento Tecnico Triestino in 1925–7. They were also employed as gunboats and colonial vessels, and *Lepanto* herself spent a long period in China beginning in the mid-1930s, never returning to Italy and being seized by the Japanese, and later by the Communist Chinese Navy; displacement 842 tons, 80 mines. Two more vessels in the class – *Dardanelli* and *Milazzo* – were sold to Venezuela in 1938);
- Eleven additional Yugoslavian minelayers were seized after April 1941. Five were small craft (*Arbe* class – *Arbe*, *Ugliano*, *Solta*, *Meleda* and *Pasman*; displacement 142 tons, 30 mines) and six were larger, tug-like vessels (*Selve* class – *Eso*, *Oriole*, *Selve*, *Unie*, *Zirona* and *Vergada*, the last ship being later used as an auxiliary submarine chaser; displacement 476 tons, 12 mines).

In wartime, the Regia Marina had almost 1,100 minesweepers in commission, but most of them were requisitioned yachts, trawlers and small craft. Of course, the above figure is an overall total and over the year the number of vessels in service at the same time was lower: 490 on 10 June 1940, 678 on 1 January 1942, 645 on 1 January 1943 and 587 on 1 August 1943.

Thirty-seven minesweepers were of the 'RD' class, (displacement 200 tons, one 76mm gun) the building of which started in 1916, ending ten years later; in the inter-war period three small experimental minesweepers were built (*Vigilante*, *Vedetta* and *D 1*), but starting in June 1940 vessels of varying origins (among them many former Guardia di Finanza patrol craft) began to be converted into minesweepers. Later in the war, larger ships were fitted for magnetic minesweeping, and, apart from the 'RD' class, all other small minesweepers were classified in four different categories ('G', 'R', 'B' and 'F' types), according to their dimensions.

It was only in 1942 that the Regia Marina laid down new modern minesweepers, whose design relied heavily on the efficient German 'R' or 'Raumboote' coastal minesweepers: these were the vessels of the 'DV' class, of which fifty were ordered but none were commissioned before 8 September 1943, although some 'DVs' served in auxiliary and hydrographic roles until the mid-1950s.

The minelayer *Buffoluto* in 1942, with a full load of mines. (A Fraccaroli collection)

The *Lepanto* on the Yangtze-Kiang River, near Shanghai, in the late 1930s. Although fitted for minelaying, she spent most of her life in Chinese waters as a river gunboat; the other vessels in the class, on the other hand, saw extensive service as minelayers in the Mediterranean in the Second World War. (Courtesy Cocchi Family)

The First World War vintage minesweeper *RD 7* at Venice on 5 October 1940. (Photo A Fraccaroli)

The *DV 134* (commissioned in 1946) in 1948, as a patrol craft in the Adriatic Sea. Note the radome for the US SO radar and the two 20mm/70 Oerlikons. (E Bagnasco collection)

Landing ships and craft

Although the Regia Marina had shown a certain degree of interest in landing operations and specialised landing craft in the inter-war period, on 10 June 1940 only five ships that could be employed for landing operations were in service. These were the *Adige* (built 1927–9, displacement 846 tons) and the four ships of the *Sesia* class (*Sesia*, *Garigliano*, *Tirso* and *Scrivia*, built 1931–7, displacement 1,460 tons); all were designed as water tankers with additional landing capabilities, being fitted with a bow ramp to put troops and small vehicles ashore.

When the FNS (Forza Navale Speciale) was formed to conduct landing operations (in particular, a proposed invasion of Malta in mid-1942) several small landing craft for troops and small vehicles were built or converted from existing vessels, but the Italian landing force was very small and rather inefficient at best and never had a chance to actually conduct landing operations with these vessels.

In 1942 the Regia Marina acquired the plans of the German produced 'Marinefährprähme – MFP', a rather large landing craft (47m long, displacement 239 tons at full load) built of steel and fitted with a bow ramp, whose dimensions were midway between those of the US LCM and LCT types. The Italian version of the 'MFP' was called the 'Motozattera' ('Motor barge') or 'MZ' and before the Armistice ninety-five were built and commissioned. They were never used for landing operations, but served extensively until May 1943 on the North African routes, particularly ferrying supplies to Tunisia and, later, repatriating personnel shortly before the fall of the last Italian possessions there. Nine 'MZ' remained in service with the Italian Navy after the war and, designated 'Moto trasporti Costieri' – MTC, served for many more years, the last vessel in the class (*MTC 1009*, the former *MZ 800*) not being stricken and broken up until 1984.

A fine side view of the water tanker/landing ship *Garigliano* in late 1940. (A Fraccaroli collection)

The 'Motozattera' *MZ 781* off the Sardinian coast near Castelsardo in 1943. (Courtesy E Buzzo)

Naval auxiliaries

A very large number of auxiliary vessels were operated by the Regia Marina during the war, and the sheer number of ships in this category (so many being small craft and harbour vessels) means there is no room in this book to provide a complete, detailed list of all of them. However, certain of the more important types, such as tenders, hospital ships and transports, are worth describing.

Among these, one of the largest and most interesting craft was the 'pontone armato' (armed pontoon, or floating battery) *GM 194*, the former monitor *Faà di Bruno* built in 1917: armed with a twin 15in/40 turret she saw service mostly in the Genoa and Ligurian area for harbour defence duties, being incorporated in the RSI Navy from the Armistice until the end of the war.

The *Giuseppe Miraglia* (built 1921–2 as a National Railways steamer) was commissioned in 1928 as a seaplane tender and also served extensively as a naval transport until the Second World War. After 10 June 1940 she serviced the Ro.43 seaplanes assigned to battleships and cruisers and was later used for testing the Re.2000 fighters embarked on the *Littorio* class battleships. After the Armistice she was based at Taranto and was scrapped after the war.

The two submarine tenders *Pacinotti* and *Volta* (displacement about 3,000 tons, built in 1924–5 as National Railways steamers, like the *Miraglia*) had different fates: the *Volta* was sunk by mistake by British MTBs in the Aegean on 8 October 1943, while the *Pacinotti* survived the war and was scrapped in 1952. The old submarine salvage ship *Anteo* of 1914 was still in service in 1940, as each of her two 200-ton cranes could lift a submerged load from a depth of 60m; in wartime, the *Anteo* was used for testing depth charges and other equipment and, rescued from one of the inner basins of the La Spezia Dockyard in late 1945, still saw some service post-war, being employed to remove hulks and other debris from the dockyard and from the Gulf of La Spezia.

Twelve hospital ships and seven smaller 'navi soccorso' ('medical aid ships') served as naval auxiliaries, some of them having been requisitioned for this role even before Italy's entry in the war. The larger ships were all former liners or passenger ships operating under the rules of the Geneva Convention; nevertheless, the *RAMB IV*, operational in Italian East African waters in June 1940 but not recognised as such a hospital ship by the British, was captured on 10 April 1941 in the Red Sea by HMS *Kingston* and later recommissioned into British service. Seven hospital ships and three 'navi soccorso' were war losses before 8 September 1943, others were scuttled at the Armistice and three (*Gradisca*, *Principessa Giovanna* and the smaller *Sorrento*) were derequisitioned between 1943 and 1946.

Aquileia (1914, 9.448 grt)
Arno (1912, 8,024 grt)
California (1920, 13,060 grt)
Città di Trapani (1928, 2,467 grt)
Gradisca (1913, 13,870 grt)
Po (1911, 7,289 grt)

Principessa Giovanna (1922, 8,585 grt)
RAMB IV (1937, 3,676 grt)
Sicilia (1924, 9,646 grt)
Tevere (1912, 8,448 grt)
Toscana (1923, 9,442 grt)
Virgilio (1926, 11,718 grt)
(Medical aid ships: *Giuseppe Orlando, Epomeo, San Giusto, Meta, Laurana, Capri, Sorrento*).

In addition, four large modern liners (*Duilio, Giulio Cesare, Vulcania* and *Saturnia*) operated as 'protected ships' between 1942 and 1943, repatriating Italian non-combatants from Italian East Africa via the Cape of Good Hope route, as they were not allowed to use the Suez Canal. For these specific missions, they were painted as provided for by the Geneva Convention: red

A bow-on view of the floating battery *GM 194* at Genoa, in spring 1940, shortly before Italy's entry into the war. The twin 15in/40 turret originally had no armoured roof, so a large steel cap was later fitted. (G Vaccaro collection)

GM 194, camouflaged, at Genoa on 28 August 1943; notice the two 76mm AA guns above the turret. (Photo A Fraccaroli)

crosses and a large national flag on the sides (but no green stripe) and white crosses in light blue circles on the funnels.

The two sail training ships *Cristoforo Colombo* (1926–8) and *Amerigo Vespucci* (1930/31) were both built at the Royal Naval Yard of Castellammare di Stabia (Naples) and served for cadet training throughout the war. The *Colombo* was handed over to the USSR in 1949 as war reparations, but the *Vespucci* still sails as a training ship for the cadets of the Italian Naval Academy, and has recently (2011) celebrated her 80th birthday as well as her 80th year of continuous service.

The only ship classified as a royal yacht was the *Savoia*, a former National Railways steamer displacing over 5,900 tons, launched in 1925 by the La Spezia Dockyard. Luxuriously fitted, she was listed among the gunboats on 10 June 1943 and, without seeing much war service, was scuttled on 9 September 1943.

On 10 June 1940 the Regia Marina had two cable ships in service: the old German-built *Città di Milano* (1905) and the more recent *Giasone*, commissioned in 1930; as the *Giasone* was lost to an Italian mine on 24 October 1940 near Pantelleria, the similar *Giasone II* was built by Ansaldo, Genoa between late 1940 and 1941; in 1943 the much smaller *Rampino* – a former merchant ship – was acquired and commissioned into naval service, not being discarded until 1976.

Only two hydrographic ships were in service in the Second World War: the *Ammiraglio Magnaghi* (displacement 2,111 tons, specifically built for this purpose in 1913/14 by Odero, Genoa) and the *Cariddi*, an old Japanese-built trawler of First World War vintage acquired in 1917 and converted into a hydrographic vessel in 1923. Both were war losses: the *Cariddi* (on 6 April 1943 at Taranto, destroyed in an Allied air raid), and the *Magnaghi* scuttled by her crew on 9 September 1943.

The varied category of naval transport included ships of differing size and dimensions, ranging from the 8,360 and 6,643 tons of the

The seaplane tender *Giuseppe Miraglia* in the early 1930s. Between 1935 and 1938 she was fitted with a 'Hein Mat' device at the stern to recover seaplanes while underway, but the whole equipment (a sort of large tarpaulin towed in the ship's wake) proved unsuccessful and was landed. (Author's collection)

A Reggiane Re.2000 fighter ready to be launched from the bow catapult of the seaplane tender *Giuseppe Miraglia*, in mid-1942. (E Bagnasco collection)

The submarine tender *Pacinotti* at Taranto, modernised after a refit, shortly before the war. (E Bagnasco collection)

Enrichetta and *Pluto*, to the 3,600 tons of the *Cherso*, to even smaller vessels as several steam and motor barges ('bette') in the 100–200 tons range. In 1942 the Regia Marina was to purchase a homogeneous group of transports based on the German 'KT' ('Kriegtransporter') type, but only two ships of this type were commissioned into Italian service (*Montecucco* and *Monte Grappa*, the former German *KT 32* and *KT 10*). A third 'KT' (*Monte Santo*) was sunk at La Maddalena by enemy aircraft while fitting out, and two more vessels (*KT 16* and *KT 20*) were never handed over by the Kriegsmarine because of the impending Armistice.

Similarly, the fifteen tankers that served with the Regia Marina in the Second World War were of different sizes, the largest one being the modern *Sterope*, built in 1939–40 by the Cantiere del Quarnaro, Fiume; nevertheless, other older, smaller tankers such as the *Nettuno*, *Prometeo* and *Brennero* served extensively, mostly operating from the most important dockyards and oil depots in southern Italy. Nine water tankers were in service as of 10 June 1940, and two (*Tanaro* and *Velino*, of 1,443 grt) were built in 1939–41 by Navalmeccanica, Castellammare di Stabia (Naples). The water tankers *Dalmazia*, *Po*, *Isonzo*, *Volturno* and *Velino* survived the war and served for many years with the Marina Militare Italiana, with the *Volturno* being the last wartime-built water tanker to be decommissioned in 1976.

Four rescue tugs (*Ciclope*, *Polifemo*, *Teseo* and *Titano*) were in service on 10 June 1940, and an additional similar vessel (*Instancabile*, the ex-

Yugoslavian *Spasilac*) entered service in 1941. The larger of these five tugs was the *Teseo* (1,423 tons, a former First World War British sloop acquired from a private owner in 1933), and the *Ciclope* was the only one of the group to remain in service after the war, being stricken in 1964. Twenty-one additional oceangoing tugs (*Ausonia*, *Atlante*, *Ercole*, *Atleta*, *Colosso*, *Forte*, *Gagliardo*, *Gigante*,

Robusto, *Tenace*, *Vigoroso*, *Chirone*, *Costante*, *Egadi*, *Luni*, *Marittimo*, *Luigi Ferdinando Marsigli*, *Favignana*, *Montecristo*, *Nereo* and *Porto Empedocle*) soldiered on in a variety of roles during the war and – last but not least – no less than 200 smaller tugs (either naval or requisitioned) served in ports, dockyards and naval bases between 1940 and 1943.

The submarine salvage ship *Anteo* at La Spezia on 16 June 1946, following her refloating after the war. (Photo A Fraccaroli)

The hospital ship *Aquileia* in 1941–2. A former Lloyd Triestino liner launched in 1914, the *Aquileia* was captured by the Germans on 9 September 1943 and was lost in 1944 to a USAAF air raid on Marseille. (E Bagnasco collection)

The former liner *Duilio* as a 'protected ship' in 1942. Note the white painting overall, red crosses but no green stripe on the sides of the hull, and white crosses in light blue circles on both funnels. (E Bagnasco collection)

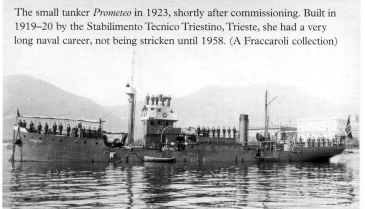

The small tanker *Prometeo* in 1923, shortly after commissioning. Built in 1919–20 by the Stabilimento Tecnico Triestino, Trieste, she had a very long naval career, not being stricken until 1958. (A Fraccaroli collection)

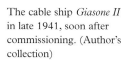

The cable ship *Giasone II* in late 1941, soon after commissioning. (Author's collection)

The sail training ship *Cristoforo Colombo* at Venice in the late 1930s. Sister-ship of the *Amerigo Vespucci*, she was handed over to the USSR in 1949 as reparations. (Photo Baschetti, Venice; Author's collection)

The royal yacht *Savoia* in the Bacino di San Marco at Venice in the late 1930s; her wartime appearance was almost unchanged, although she was camouflaged in a 'standard' scheme in 1942. (Photo Baschetti, Venice; Author's collection)

The hydrographic ship *Ammiraglio Magnaghi* at La Spezia in the late 1920s. The name honoured Italy's most important naval hydrographer of the nineteenth century. (Photo Pucci, La Spezia; author's collection)

The transport *Cherso* at Venice on 3 September 1941, with buoys and other mooring aids aboard. (Photo A Fraccaroli)

Although scheduled to be transferred to the Regia Marina (which would have named her *Monte Cengio*), the 'Kustentransporter' *KT 16* – seen here in summer 1943 – remained under the German flag because of the Armistice. (M Cicogna collection)

The 19,641 grt *Sterope* was the largest Italian naval tanker of the Second World War. In this late-1942 photograph, she has been painted in a 'standard' scheme and, in order to disguise her as a less valuable dry cargo ship, a dummy funnel has been fitted amidships, while the 'real' funnel astern has been merged in a purpose-built structure to make it less conspicuous. (Author's collection)

The small water tanker *Verde* at Taranto in the mid-1930s. (Z Freivogel collection)

The rescue tug *Titano* (displacement 1,075 tons) was commissioned in 1912 and served widely until 9 September 1943, when she was scuttled by her crew following the Armistice. (Z Freivogel collection)

CHAPTER 5
Surface and Underwater Assault Craft

DURING THE SECOND WORLD War, the surface and underwater fast assault craft of the Italian Navy were responsible for some of the most daring operations of the war. The numerical and technological superiority of the Allied navies prevented the 'Siluri a lenta corsa' (SLC – Slow Speed Torpedoes, whose operators sat astride them to guide them to their targets, sometimes referred to as 'human torpedoes'), the explosive 'Barchini' (surface assault craft) and 'Gamma' swimmers from being able to seriously affect the conduct of strategic operations in the Mediterranean: nevertheless, several famous actions inflicted considerable damage to British ships. The Royal Navy found itself forced to deal with embarrassing situations arising from the fact that bases once considered inviolable had been breached by Italian assault craft, as well as from the loss of or serious damage to major units of the Mediterranean Fleet or to merchant ships equally important to the war effort.

The Regia Marina's interest in assault craft with stealthy and innovative features had already had practical results during the First World War. First of all, several series of fast motor torpedo boats, referred to as 'MAS' ('Motoscafo Anti Sommergibili' – 'Anti-submarine motor boats') were built: two of these sank the Austro-Hungarian battleship *Szent Istvan* off the island of Premuda in the Adriatic on 10 June 1918. In

March of that year the four 'Barchini Saltatori' (literally, 'jumping small boats') *Grillo, Cavalletta, Locusta* and *Pulce*, had become operational, the most unique feature of which was a special system of caterpillar tracks which would allow them to

On 29 July 1941, some Royal Navy petty officers examining an 'MT' assault craft (probably *MT 16*) found almost intact after the Xᵃ Flottiglia MAS attack on Malta that came to a disastrous end on the night of 25/26 July. (Malta War Museum via J Caruana)

'Barchini esplosivi' of the second batch of the 'MT' series during exercises early in the war. Note the small dimensions of the craft and the dark paint scheme. (E Bagnasco collection)

'climb' over barriers and obstructions defending ports and attack targets in harbour with their torpedoes. Only the *Grillo*, on 13 May 1918, tried to force the harbour of Pola but she was soon spotted, came under heavy fire from the shore batteries and had to be scuttled by her crew.

It was soon clear that to penetrate the well-protected bases of the Austro-Hungarian fleet, assault craft embodying really revolutionary features were needed. Captain Costanzo Ciano, then-Inspector of all Regia Marina 'MAS', soon ordered the building of a couple of 'Torpedini Semoventi' ('self-propelled torpedoes', later known by the decidedly unwarlike nickname of 'Mignatta', i.e. 'leech') based on two complementary designs, attributed to the Captain of the Genio Navale Raffaele Rossetti and to Lieut. Raffaele Paolucci of the Medical Corps.

The 'Mignatta' was similar to a torpedo in appearance and dimensions, propelled by two coaxial counter-rotating propellers; its forward section consisted of two cylindrical explosive charges that could be detached and either secured to the bilge keels of the target, or placed directly on the sea-bottom beneath its hull. There were two operators, but the instability of the 'Mignatta'

Side view of a 'MT' of the second series, actually used in the attack against Suda Bay in March 1941 (top), and side and deck views of a 'MTM' of the fourth series, built in 1942 (bottom). Note, in the 'MT' drawing, the dotted lines indicating the position of the engine and of the explosive charge. (Line drawing by E Bagnasco)

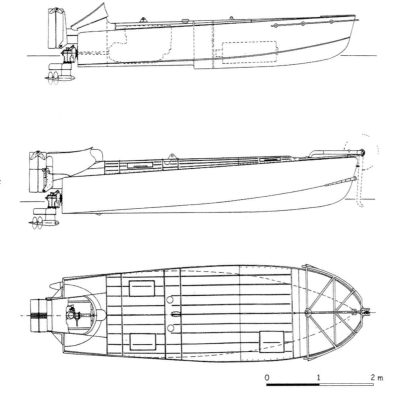

of Gibraltar.

Therefore, the Regia Marina gave new impetus to studies on assault craft by allowing, in particular, the development of a 'self-propelled torpedo' designed by Captains (equivalent to the naval ranks of Lieutenants) Teseo Tesei and Elios Toschi of the Genio Navale. This craft was, in practice, an updated and improved version of the First World War 'Mignatta': a little faster, with increased range and most importantly able to approach and enter enemy naval bases underwater. The two operators steered the 'self-propelled torpedo' much as if riding on horseback, wearing wetsuits and equipped with scuba gear, which had been developed by various specialised companies. Offically called 'Siluri a Lenta Corsa' but soon familiarly and widely known as 'maiali' ('pigs'), they were built in several series by the Officina Siluri San Bartolomeo of the La Spezia Dockyard.

At the same time, developing an idea by Adm. Aimone di Savoia-Aosta, the Regia Marina also began to study a surface assault craft, identified by the acronym 'MT' (Motoscafo Turismo), based on an existing design of a fast sporting motorboat. The hull of these craft, known as 'Barchini Esplosivi' ('explosive motor boats'), had been designed by the Baglietto yard, with a specially-designed transmission between the gasoline engine and the propeller designed by CABI-Cattaneo of Milan, (the same company that actually built most of these very small boats, produced in several versions). Once close to the target, the assault craft operator would set the small boat on its way to the target, and then be catapulted clear into the water, in his floating seat, by a small explosive charge.

In 1938 tests were started in the Bocca di Serchio (on the northern coast of Tuscany), and the submarine *Ametista* was experimentally converted into a 'Unità Avvicinatrice' (delivery

prevented them from steering the craft in the classic 'straddling' position; the crew found it easier to hold on to specially-fitted handles, being 'pulled' along by the 'Mignatta' helped by the craft's low speed (about two knots). With this rudimentary assault craft, surfing the waves while wearing rubberised cloth suits (not completely waterproof), Rossetti and Paolucci managed to enter the naval base at Pola on the night of 1 November 1918, and placed the first explosive charge of their 'Mignatta' on the sea-bottom, directly below at the engine rooms of the battleship *Viribus Unitis* which capsized and sank, at 06.30. Once discovered, Rossetti and Paolucci abandoned the 'Mignatta' with the propellers still turning and, with unbelievable luck, it ended its run under the stern of the steamer *Wien* where the second charge exploded, sinking this second ship as well. With such significant results (which may well have brought forward the Austro-Hungarian surrender), the activities of the Italian assault craft in the First World War came to an end.

During the 1920s and early 1930s, the Italian Navy's efforts were mainly directed towards the construction of capital ships, destroyers and submarines. The debate on the necessity and feasibility of aircraft carriers and naval aviation,

the restrictions imposed by the naval treaties and the decision to keep battleships as the priority in Italian naval planning caused the study and design of assault craft to be largely neglected. However, in 1935, with the start of the Ethiopian war, the strategic balance in the Mediterranean shifted in favour of the Royal Navy, which began to deploy several ships detached from the Home Fleet east

A 'MSMAT' (also known by the briefer form of 'SMA') in the final phases of construction at the CABI factory in Milan, in early 1945. Only three craft of this type were delivered to the Regia Marina before the Armistice, but twenty-five were later in service with the RSI Navy, and others with the Kriegsmarine. In the early post-war years, some 'MSMAT' were also briefly used by the 'Incursori' units of the new Marina Militare Italiana. (F Harrauer collection)

A 'SLC' of the first production series being hoisted aboard a support ship at Bocca di Serchio (near Pisa) in early 1941. (E Bagnasco collection)

vessel) for the transport of the 'maiali' in the vicinity of their targets. From an administrative point of view, the assault craft were assigned to a 'Special Weapons Section' of the 1ª Flottiglia MAS (based in La Spezia) This Flotilla became an autonomous unit in March 1941 being renamed – with Cdr. Moccagatta as Commanding Officer – the Xª Flottiglia MAS. An underwater attack against the British base at Alexandria had already been planned in 1938–9, but in the early months of the war, two such 'special' operations (in August and September 1940) were attempted but not completed, as they ended up with the loss of the 'Sommergibili avvicinatori' *Iride* and *Gondar*, specially fitted to transport three 'SLC' each, in the Gulf of Bomba and a hundred miles west of Alexandria respectively.

On the night of 26 March 1941, six 'Barchini Esplosivi' scored the first success of the Regia Marina's assault craft arm, forcing Suda Bay (Crete): the operation ended with the destruction of the British heavy cruiser *York* and of the tanker *Pericles*, although the six crewmen, all uninjured, were taken prisoner. Although considerable care was taken in the design and operation of such craft for the safety of their crews, once they had abandoned the 'Barchino' or 'Maiale', they had little chance of being recovered and faced the virtual certainty of capture.

On the night of 26/27 July 1941 a complex underwater and surface attack against Malta's Grand Harbour was planned, but the operation, affected by delays and by the sighting of some of the Barchini by British sentries, came to a tragic end with the loss of almost all craft and the deaths of several operators, including Cdr. Moccagatta, Maj. Tesei of the Genio Navale, Petty Officer Diver Pedretti and Lieut. Falcomatà of the Medical Corps.

With the death of Moccagatta and other important members of the unit's original personnel, Xª Flottiglia MAS had to be reorganised: Cdr. Ernesto Forza was made commander, while LtCdr Salvatore Todaro and LtCdr Junio Valerio Borghese were appointed respectively as commander of the Surface and Underwater Sections of the Flottiglia. Directly subordinate to the Underwater Section there was also a special 'Gamma' swimmer unit (who today would be referred to as 'frogmen') trained to attack ships with limpet mines.

On the night of 18 December 1941, the assault craft of the Regia Marina achieved their greatest success, entering the port of Alexandria and seriously damaging the British battleships *Queen Elizabeth* and *Valiant*. Transported close to the harbour by the submarine *Sciré* (CO LtCdr Junio Valerio Borghese), three 'SLC' (manned by de La Penne/Bianchi, Marceglia/Schergat and Martellotta/Marino) penetrated the harbour defences, and their crews managed to place the explosive charges of the 'Maiali' under the hulls of their targets: the two battleships, and the tanker *Sagona*. The submarine *Sciré* (now commanded by LtCdr Bruno Zelich) was lost on 10 August 1942 during an operation against the port of Haifa by 'Gamma' swimmers. Some time earlier, on the night between 13 and 14 July 1942, twelve 'Gamma' swimmers managed to damage four British merchant ships at Gibraltar and were even able to get safely back to Italy through Spain and southern France.

In order to improve the chances of success against targets in the port of Gibraltar, the Regia Marina converted the tanker *Olterra*, which had been interned in the Spanish port of Algeciras in the bay of Gibraltar since the outbreak of war, into a base for underwater assault craft, thus giving the crews a better chance of avoiding capture after their attacks. Unfortunately, the first operation from *Olterra* ('BG5' – 7 December 1942) ended tragically with the death of three men, including Lieut. Licio Visintini. On 8 May 1943 'Maiali' from *Olterra* were more successful, sinking three Allied merchant ships (including a Liberty ship) and on 4 August 1943, another Liberty ship, a Norwegian tanker and a British freighter were sunk. In both operations, all the crews, except for one man taken prisoner during the second attack, got back safely to the *Olterra*.

An 'SLC' of the '200' series, being serviced at the technical facility of the Xª Flottiglia MAS at Bocca di Serchio in mid-1941. (E Bagnasco collection)

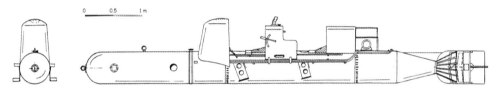

Side and front view of a '100' series 'SLC'. (Line drawing of E Bagnasco)

In another successful operation, on the night of 11 December 1942, the submarine *Ambra* (CO LtCdr Mario Arillo) delivered three 'Maiali' and ten 'Gamma' swimmers to the port of Algiers, where they sank two merchant ships and seriously damaged three more. As in the case of the attack on Alexandria, however, all the men were taken prisoner. The next day, in the harbour of La Galite in Tunisia, the militarised trawler *Cefalo*, equipped to carry 'Barchini Esplosivi', was sunk, having just returned from an operation against the port of Bona. In the attack LtCdr Todaro was killed, having again been assigned to Xª Flottiglia MAS since the summer of 1942, after a tour of duty as CO of the submarine *Cappellini*, operating in the Atlantic from Bordeaux.

This brief survey of the assault craft operations of the Regia Marina between 1940 and 1943, would not be complete without mentioning the actions of the 'Gamma' swimmer, 'Milmart' (Maritime Territorial Militia) Lt. Luigi Ferraro. Operating alone in the neutral ports of Mersin and Iskenderun in Turkey (under the fake identity of a local Italian consular official), Ferraro was able to attack four British merchant ships with limpet mines between June and August 1943, three of which were sunk. After the last attack, Ferraro was able to get back to Italy shortly before the Armistice.

During the Second World War, the surface and underwater assault units of the Regia Marina sank or seriously damaged five warships totalling about 72,000 tons and twenty-three merchant ships totalling over 130,000 grt. The Armistice of 8 September 1943 forestalled even more ambitious operations, one of which even envisaged attacking New York with a midget submarine (of the 'CA' type), that was to have been transported there by the submarine *Leonardo Da Vinci*, which had been adapted for this purpose in the summer of 1942.

Two 'SSB' as captured by the Allies at the end of the Second World War. At left, a British-captured craft at Venice, S Andrea in May 1945 (IWM); at right, a 'SSB' in American hands used for tests in the immediate post-war years. (US Navy)

After the Armistice, the Regia Marina's assault craft were split between the RSI and the pro-Allied Italian forces. In northern Italy, without changing its name and operating under the flag of the RSI Navy, the Xª Flottiglia MAS (now commanded by Cdr. Borghese) suffered both from a lack of assault craft and from a lack of suitable targets, and its personnel often found themselves fighting on land with units of the German Army. The Flotilla's most significant 'classic' action was the attack against the French destroyer *Trombe* on 17 April 1945, which was severely damaged off the western coast of Liguria by a 'Barchino' piloted by Leading Torpedoman (Sottocapo) Sergio Denti.

In southern Italy, an assault craft unit named 'Mariassalto' was reconstituted at Taranto under the command of Cdr. Forza, and operated along with British divers, often using 'Chariots' (the British 'human torpedoes' initially based on captured Italian 'Maiali'). The two most important operations in the 1944–5 period were the attack on the harbour of La Spezia on 21 June 1944 (in which the hulk of the heavy cruiser *Bolzano* was sunk), and the one on the port of Genoa on the

night of 19 April 1945, when two Italian-manned 'Chariots' attacked the hull of the incomplete aircraft carrier *Aquila*.

After the war, several veterans of the Regia Marina's assault craft arm were employed mostly in minesweeping operations, allowing the Italian Navy to retain the valuable experience acquired in 'special' assault operations that, though expressly forbidden by the Treaty of Peace of 1947, in fact never ceased. Indeed, in the 1950s almost all the men who had served in the Second World War formed the Raggruppamento Subacquei e Incursori ('Comsubin') which – named in honour of Teseo Tesei and with its main base at the Fort of Varignano, near La Spezia – is today one of the Marina Militare Italiana's elite units.

Surface Assault Craft

The first two prototypes of a small fast motorboat to be used for surface assault operations were built in 1936 by the Baglietto Yard of Varazze, and according to the original design a S.55 seaplane was to have been able to carry one such craft. Very small (4.70m long) and quite fast (32 knots), the prototypes already had the essential characteristics of the forthcoming operational 'Barchini Esplosivi', with a 300kg explosive charge in the bow and provisions, i.e. a buoyant chair with a small charge to blow it clear of the craft, to allow

the crewman to bail out before impact on the target. The first operational 'Barchini Esplosivi', known as 'Motoscafo Turismo' ('MT' – 'Sport Motorboats') followed in late 1939. Two series of 'MT' – for a total of eighteen craft – were built, and some of them were the first to be employed operationally, with six 'MT' attacking Suda Bay (Crete) and damaging HMS *York* and a tanker on 26 March 1941, and others taking part in the attack against Malta's Grand Harbour on the night of 26/27 July 1941. The 'MT' were 6.15m long with an accentuated 'V'-shaped hull and a now-standard 300kg explosive charge.

The 'MTs' were followed by a modified version, the 'Motoscafo Turismo Modificato' (MTM – 'Modified Sport Motorboat'), again built of wood and in some cases fitted with a 330kg warhead. A six-cylinder, 2,500cc, 90hp Alfa Romeo gasoline engine allowed the 'MTM' to conduct its approach and attack at 31 knots. Late in the war, an improved 'MTM' was built by SIAI, with slightly different characteristics (length 5.80m, four-cylinder engine etc).

In 1941–2, the same CABI-Cattaneo company developed a smaller version of the 'Barchino Esplosivo' (Motoscafo Turismo Ridotto – 'MTR'), the reduced dimensions of which would have allowed it to be transported inside the cylinders fitted on some submarines for the transport of 'SLCs' on a one-for-one basis; later, in 1944–5, the Baglietto and SIAI companies built a rather large

Underwater exercise by 'Gamma' divers near a target's propellers and rudder. Note that the two men are carrying small demolition charges (commonly known as 'Bauletti esplosivi' – 'small explosive trunks'). (E Bagnasco collection)

The submarine *Scirè* in the Gulf of La Spezia in October 1940, fitted with three watertight cylinders for the transportation of 'SLCs'. Note that the conning tower is still in the original configuration as for all the '600' class *Adua* series boats. (A Fraccaroli collection)

stern-launched torpedoes, whose classification was quite similar to that of the assault craft: 'MTS' ('Motoscafo Turismo Silurante' – 'Torpedo-armed fast motorboat'), 'MTSM' and 'MTSMA', where 'M' stood for 'Modificato' ('modified') and 'A' for 'Allargato' ('enlarged').

Between the inter-war years and 1945 the CABI, SIAI and Baglietto companies built the following small craft:

• Two prototypes ('MA' – 1936)
• Eighteen 'MT' (two series – 1938/40)
• One 'MTM' prototype (early 1941)
• About forty 'MTM' (several series – 1941/43)
• About 140 modified 'MTM' (1944/45)
• One prototype and twelve production 'MTR' (1942)
• Three 'MTS' (1940/41)
• Thirty-four 'MTMS' (1941/42)
• About seventy 'MTSMA' (1943/45)

number of modified 'MTMs' that were delivered either to the Kriegsmarine or to the RSI Navy but they did not see much service.

In addition to the 'MT' and 'MTM' series, more traditional small craft began to be developed from late 1939/early 1940 for the specific use of the Xª Flottiglia MAS. These were several series of slightly larger fast vessels armed with one or two

A detail of the two cylinders abaft the conning tower of *Scirè*, with their hatches open, in late 1940. (Ufficio Storico della Marina Militare, Rome)

The submarine *Ambra* (right, fitted with three cylinders for the transportation of 'SLCs') and a German Type VIIC boat (left) at La Spezia's inner dock on 2 April 1942, when a ceremony was held during which decorations were awarded to both Italian and German submariners. (A Rastelli collection)

Underwater Assault Craft

The 'Siluro a Lenta Corsa' ('SLC') was the most effective Italian assault craft, and broadly speaking could trace its origins back to the 'Mignatta' of the First World War. In 1935, two Captains of the Genio Navale, Teseo Tesei and Elios Toschi started working on an idea already developed by Tesei in 1927, when he was still attending the Naval Academy at Leghorn. The plan was to modify a 21in torpedo, in order to transform it into a self-propelled underwater assault craft, manned by two operators wearing scuba gear; in October 1935 the first prototype of what would become the widely-known 'Maiale' was built at the Officina Siluri San Bartolomeo of the La Spezia Dockyard, using spare parts and other gear fortuitously purchased from other workshops of the dockyard, and in November a second craft was built This second prototype was tested in 1936 but, as tension with

Great Britain reduced with the end of the Ethiopian war, plans for further development of underwater assault craft slowed down in 1937, even though further craft were built in the years that followed (with a total of eleven pre-production 'SLCs' available for testing with the 1ª Flottiglia MAS as of August 1939).

By early 1940 the CABI company began production of operational craft, and the first series (identified by the number '100') of eight craft – by now officially designated 'SLC' – was in service when Italy entered the Second World War. The '100' series was followed in 1941 by the more numerous improved craft of the '200' series, and 'SLCs' from both series were employed in most underwater assaults between late 1940 and 1943 (for instance, for the attack against Alexandria of 18 December 1941, one '100' series and two '200' series craft were employed),

The 'SLC' used the main body of a 21in torpedo, whose compressed air machinery was replaced by an electric motor, while enlarged hydroplanes and rudders improved manoeuvrability. The 1.6hp electric motor allowed a maximum speed of 3 knots and a range of 15 nautical miles at a sustained speed of 2.3 knots. It was fitted with two trimming tanks and one ballast tank that could be operated by electrical pumps, and two compressed-air cylinders supplied air at 200 kg/cm. The two operators sat 'in tandem' and were partially protected by fairings also containing the navigational instruments and the controls. On the forward part of the torpedo, a 230kg explosive charge was fitted: the charge could be easily detached from the torpedo's main body while underwater and, although the very first 'SLC' had charges fitted with magnetic plates to be fixed to the underwater hulls of the target, a more practical solution (with an eyebolt and grommets in order to suspend the charge below the hull, using a metal cable and clamps tightened to the bilge keels) was soon adopted for early-production 'SLCs'. Late-production 'SLC' were often equipped with two

charges.

The two 'SLC' operators usually approached the target on the surface, diving only when they got close to it; the 'Maiale' was also equipped to cut, destroy or pass over nets and other barriers protecting the target or an enemy ship's mooring. Once the craft had dived below the target, two clamps were tightened to the bilge keels, and a steel cable was hung between them; the explosive charge was then detached from the 'SLC', connected to the cable and suspended below the enemy ship, just below her keel. After that, the crew were to destroy the 'Maiale' with small demolition charges and then swim ashore and attempt to escape overland, having hidden their wetsuits' etc. In fact, almost all 'SLC' crews were taken prisoner (as well as some being killed), until, as has been mentioned above, for operations against Gibraltar the *Olterra* was employed as a base ship close to the target, giving the crews a reasonable chance to get back safely.

The Regia Marina's 'SLCs' were built in different series, as shown in the following list:
• Two prototypes (1935–6)
• 1st pre-production series (four craft, 1937–8)
• 2nd pre-production series (five craft, 1938–9)
• '100' series (eight craft, 1940)
• '200' series (about thirty craft, 1941–2)

In 1943, studies for a larger and improved assault craft led to the building of the first prototypes of an underwater 'semovente' ('self-propelled craft') called 'SSB', acronym for 'Siluro San Bartolomeo'. The 'SSB' was longer than the 'SLC', of greater diameter (30.7in) and had a larger, semi-enclosed 'cockpit' for the crew. Some 'SSB' prototypes were built in La Spezia and probably also by the Caproni Company in 1944–5 for the RSI Navy, but none saw operational service; nevertheless, the 'SSB' project was used for further development of Italian underwater assault craft for the Marina Militare's 'Incursori' in the 1950s and early 1960s.

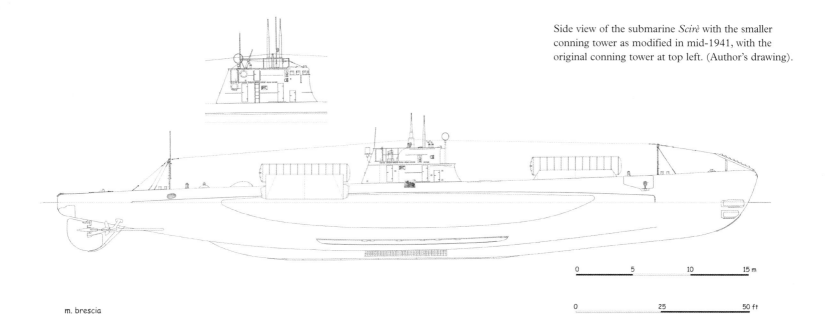

Side view of the submarine *Scirè* with the smaller conning tower as modified in mid-1941, with the original conning tower at top left. (Author's drawing).

m. brescia

0   5   10   15 m

0   25   50 ft

Today, in addition to some 'SSBs' preserved in Italy and abroad, five 'SLCs' can be found in Italian museums, institutions or naval commands: one in both naval museums at La Spezia and Venice, one at the Sacrario delle Bandiere at the Vittoriano in Rome (in the basement of the Monument to the Unknown Soldier), one at the Museo della Scienza e della Tecnica in Milan and one at the Headquarters of the Navy's Subacquei e Incursori force at Varignano, near La Spezia.

Over the years the Regia Marina used a number of ships, craft and submarines as 'Unità avvicinatrici' to transport and support the assault craft of the Xª Flottiglia MAS:

A '200' series 'SLC' now preserved in the Sacrario delle Bandiere at the Vittoriano in Rome, in the basement of the Monument to the Unknown Soldier. (Author's photograph)

- The destroyers *Quintino Sella* and *Francesco Crispi* were fitted to transport six 'MTs' each; both *Sella* and *Crispi* transported a total of six 'MTs' from Stampalia (Astipalea) in the Dodecanese to Suda Bay (Crete), for the attack of 25/26 March 1941.
- The sloop *Diana* was modified as a 'MT' transport in spring 1941, and took part in the ill-fated attack against Grand Harbour, Valletta, on 25/26 July 1941.
- In 1944, the destroyers *Grecale* and *Granatiere* operated as 'MTM' and 'MTSM' transports; in particular, on the evening of 21 June 1944, *Grecale* transported four 'MTSM' and four 'Gamma' swimmers from Bastia to the entrance of the Gulf of La Spezia for an attack against shipping in the area. In the same operation, the torpedo boat *MS 74* ferried two British 'Chariots' that attacked and sank the hulk of the heavy cruiser *Bolzano*.
- The requisitioned trawlers *Sogliola*, *Cefalo* and *Pegaso* were assigned to the Xª Flottiglia MAS to support surface assault craft.
- The submarine *Ametista* was the first Italian boat modified for the transport of underwater assault craft. In early 1940 she was fitted with three 'saddles' on the main deck for three 'SLCs', being employed for tests and training only and soon returning to fleet duty.
- The submarine *Iride* was fitted with four saddles to transport the same number of 'SLCs' and, in this configuration, was torpedoed and sunk on 21 August 1940 in the Gulf of Bomba (Cyrenaica) during a training exercise. Some crewmen and the four 'SLCs' were rescued.
- The submarine *Gondar* was the first Italian boat fitted with three watertight cylinders (one forward of the conning tower and two either side aft of it) for the transport of three 'SLCs'. The *Gondar* was sunk on 30 September 1940 by the destroyer HMAS *Stuart*, other smaller vessels and a 'Sunderland' seaplane, during an attempted mission against Alexandria. By the examination of the *Gondar*'s photographs taken shortly before her sinking, and taking into account the many divers and specialists found among the survivors, the Royal Navy began to suspect that the Regia Marina was developing underwater attack craft and techniques.
- The submarine *Scirè* was the most famous 'avvicinatore': modified similarly to the *Gondar*, she took part in two missions against Gibraltar in 1940 and two in 1941. In December 1941 the *Scirè* transported the 'SLCs' that damaged the

battleships *Valiant* and *Queen Elizabeth* to Alexandria, and was lost off Haifa on 10 August 1942. Unique among Italian submarines, the boat's standard has been decorated with the Medaglia d'Oro al Valor Militare, Italy's highest military award.

- The submarine *Ambra* was converted in early 1942 to operate with the Xª Flottiglia MAS and, similarly to the *Scirè*, she was fitted with three watertight cylinders for 'SLC' transport. The *Ambra*'s most important mission (under her CO LtCdr. Arillo) was against Algiers on 11 December 1942; later she was employed to transport some 'MTRs' for an attempted attack against the Allied-held port of Palermo on 18 July 1943, but she was attacked and damaged by an enemy aircraft off Syracuse. The *Ambra* managed to get back to Naples and was later towed to La Spezia, where she was scrapped after the war.
- The three submarines *Murena*, *Sparide* and *Grongo* (of the *Flutto* class) were to have been

An 'MTM' preserved in the Malta War Museum at Fort St Elmo, Valletta. Although painted black like the 'MT' surface assault craft that, along with 'SLC' underwater craft, attacked Malta's Grand Harbour on the night of 26/27 July 1941, this is a late-war production craft, probably captured by the Allies in Sicily after the landings of summer 1943. (Author's photograph)

fitted from their commissioning with four watertight cylinders – two on each side of the conning tower – to transport either 'SLCs' or 'MTRs'. Only the *Murena* was launched (in April 1943) with the cylinders already in place, and none of the three boats was commissioned before the Armistice. The three submarines were requisitioned by the Germans in mid-September 1943, but – although plans were drafted for possible use either with the Kriegsmarine or the RSI Navy – they never saw service and were lost in an Allied air raid on Genoa in September 1944.

CHAPTER 6

Naval Aviation

DURING THE FIRST WORLD War the Regia Marina developed a large and effective air arm that from late 1916, also began to employ Army personnel (both pilots and airmen) in order to meet the increasingly pressing needs of wartime operations. At the end of the war on 4 November 1918 (when fighting ceased on the Italian front, a week before the official cessation of hostilities on 11 November), the Regia Marina had thirty-five 'Stazioni' (or 'Aeroporti' – 'Naval Air Stations') and twenty-seven smaller air bases ('Aeroscali'), scattered all along the Italian coastline, particularly in the Adriatic; a total of 546 seaplanes, 92 land-based aircraft and 39 airships (of which only 15 were operational) were in service. As for personnel, there were 323 Navy-trained pilots, while an additional 398 pilots had been transferred to the Navy from the Army's Air Service; of the 8,299 airmen on the Navy's payroll on 4 November 1918, 4,049 were Navy and 4,240 former Army personnel: considerable numbers for what was still a rather experimental arm of service. Between 24 May 1915 and 4 November 1918 – the Italian Navy's aircraft and airships flew more than 18,400 missions suffering heavy losses, both in men killed in action and in aircraft destroyed in combat. The rapid demobilisation after the war greatly reduced the size of the Regia Marina's Air Arm and, in June 1920, only 939 men (among them only 58 officers) were assigned to it.

On 28 March 1923 the Italian Air Force (Regia

A Cant Z. 506B (an updated version built in wartime), flying over the coast of Sicily in early 1943. (Courtesy *STORIA militare*)

Aeronautica) was established by law, and all military aviation came under its control. All pilots, other aviation personnel and aircraft were transferred to it, leaving the Navy with neither the means nor the legal basis to develop an independent and specialised naval air arm.

Despite the new regulations of the Regia Aeronautica establishing a specific naval branch, or 'Aviazione per la Regia Marina' that, '... in peace and wartime will be directed by the Navy also for protection of sea-lanes and to defend the coasts of mainland Italy and of the Colonies as well', inter-service rivalry grew and this contributed to the lack of interest in the development of aircraft carriers until the late 1930s, by which time it was too late to develop a genuine and effective naval air arm, whether under the control of the Navy or the Air Force.

In any case, the Regia Marina soon began to devote attention to the establishment and training of the thirty-five Squadriglie ('Squadrons') provided for by a 1925 amendment to the 1923 law; most of the Squadriglie were equipped with land-based aircraft, but six were specifically

Two views of one of the IMAM Ro.43s of the heavy cruiser *Bolzano* in the late 1930s. The 'clocks' on the front side of the structure between the tripod's legs indicate wind speed, the ship's course and other data for both the pilot and the crewmen manning the catapult. (Left: E Bagnasco collection. Right: courtesy G Apostolo Archive)

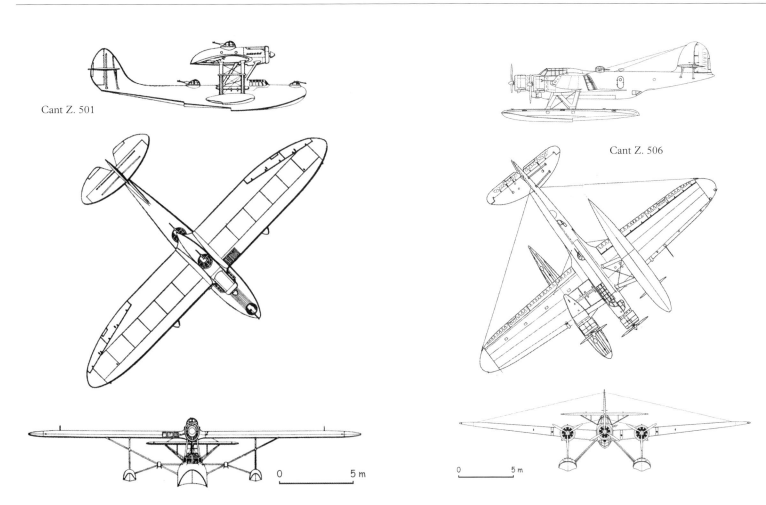

Cant Z. 501

Cant Z. 506

0   5 m

0   5 m

established to support ship-based seaplanes. A new law in 1931 gave new regulations to the Regia Aeronautica, whose control over aircraft and airships was enhanced: by now, the 'Aviazione per la Marina' was to consist only of reconnaissance squadrons, with seaplanes embarked aboard ships (battleships and cruisers). In brief, while in the late 1920s a genuine naval air arm had been envisaged (and, originally, torpedo bomber squadrons and even ship-based fighter squadrons had been allowed), after 1931 the 'Aviazione per la Marina' was greatly reduced in its effectiveness, with serious consequences for the Navy's operations between 1940 and 1943. Moreover, the 1931 law did not specify the exact number of squadrons allotted for naval service, and this brought new and fiercer arguments between the Air Force and the Navy: the Regia Aeronautica, much better supported by the Fascist regime than the Navy, feared that too many 'auxiliary' branches would weaken its primary fighter, bomber and air superiority commitments, and the consequences of this very pernicious quarrel may be seen not only in the reduced interest devoted to the development of aircraft carriers in wartime, but also in the unbelievably late decision to establish an independent Italian naval air arm, not taken until 1988.

The 1931 law allowed naval officers to man Regia Aeronautica aircraft only as 'Osservatori' ('Reconnaissance specialists') and, as of 10 June 1940, 173 of them were available: 100 commissioned officers, 58 former warrant officers and 15 naval reserve officers. At the same date, twenty-one Squadriglie da Ricognizione Marittima of the Regia Aeronautica, plus six smaller units called Sezioni ('Sections'), were operational in mainland Italy and abroad. A single Squadriglia usually numbered eleven aircraft, while the Sezione had from two to four planes, and on Italy's entry into the Second World War the units of the 'Aviazione per la Marina' were stationed as follows:

Northern Tyrrhenian Sea
Two Squadriglie (twenty-two aircraft)
Two Sezioni (seven aircraft)

Sardinia
Four Squadriglie (forty-two aircraft)
One Sezione (four aircraft)

Southern Tyrrhenian Sea
Two Squadriglie (twenty-two aircraft)

Sicily
Five Squadriglie (fifty-three aircraft)

Ionian and Southern Adriatic Seas
Four Squadriglie (thirty-four aircraft)
One Sezione (four aircraft)

Northern Adriatic Sea
One Squadriglia (eleven aircraft)

Libya
One Squadriglia (eleven aircraft)
One Sezione (three aircraft)

Aegean
Two Squadriglie (twenty-two aircraft)
One Sezione (two aircraft)

This made a total of twenty-one Squadriglie, with the six Sezioni being equivalent to another three Squadriglia, for a total of twenty-four, much less than the thirty-five envisaged in 1925, and even fewer than the forty-five that the Regia Marina had deemed absolutely necessary in 1929. A Generale di Brigata Aerea of the Regia Aeronautica was appointed as Inspector of Naval Aviation: the first being (from 15 November 1939) Generale di Brigata Aerea Francesco Marini, who became a member of Supermarina subordinate to the Navy's CinC. On 10 June 1940 this Inspectorate was renamed 'Comando Superiore dell'Aviazione per la Marina'.

During the war, the most important Air Stations were located at La Spezia, Leghorn, Elmas (Cagliari), Santa Giusta (Oristano, Sardinia), Terranova Pausania (today Olbia, Sardinia), Nisida (near Naples), Stagnone (Marsala), Augusta, Syracuse, Taranto, Brindisi, Pola, Leros (Dodecanese) and Menelao (Gulf of Bomba in Cyrenaica, Libya). Additional smaller stations were established later in Sardinia, Corsica, Libya, the Aegean and on the coast of Dalmatia.

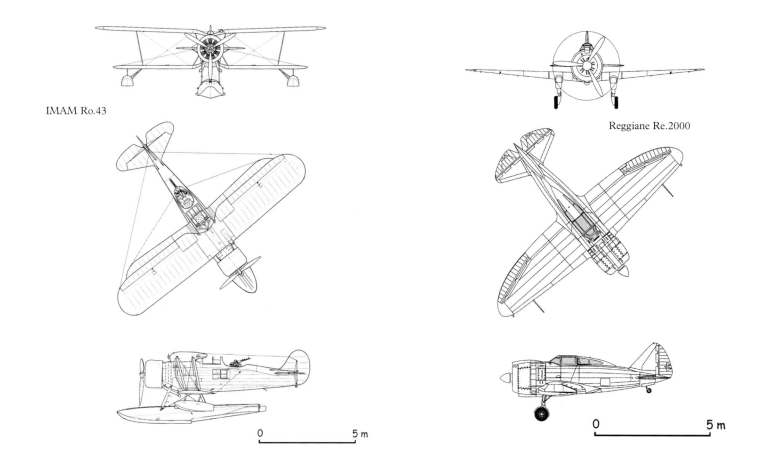

IMAM Ro.43

Reggiane Re.2000

0   5 m

0   5 m

One of the few navalised Reggiane Re.2000 fighters employed aboard Italian battleships from mid-1942 onwards, ready to be launched from the catapult of *Vittorio Veneto* in September 1942. (Courtesy *STORIA militare*)

The Cant Z. 501 was the standard seaplane of the Aviazione per la Marina in the Second World War: obsolescent and slow, it paid a heavy price in action, with many being downed by RAF and FAA fighters. Nevertheless, it served extensively in the reconnaissance and search and rescue roles until the end of the war, and the last four 501s served with the 183ª Squadriglia at Cagliari Elmas until the late 1940s, being scrapped in 1950. (Courtesy G Apostolo Archive)

On 10 June 1940, 163 land-based seaplanes were in service (although 237 were deemed necessary): for the most part they were of the single-engined Cant Z. 501 type, only twenty of the more modern, three-engined Cant Z. 506 seaplanes being operational; additional 506s were built between 1940 and 1942. Between 1935 and 1943, more than 200 single-engined IMAM Ro.43 reconnaissance seaplanes were built, and these aircraft equipped all of the Italian light and heavy cruisers, as well as the three battleships of the *Littorio* class. Previously, until the mid-1930s when the Ro.43 came into service, the cruisers of the Regia Marina embarked one or two older Cant 25 seaplanes, in the 'AR' ('Ali Ripiegabili', i.e. 'folding wings') version.

In late 1942, the three *Littorio*s embarked a maximum of two or three Reggiane Re. 2000 each in place of the same number of Ro.43s: the Re. 2000 was a land-based fighter modified for catapult launch and intended to supply a skeleton CAP (Combat Air Patrol) to these battleships, but none ever saw action in this role. They were intended to return to airstrips on shore at the end of their missions, retaining their normal wheeled undercarriage for this purpose.

Between 1940 and 1943 the command structure of the Aviazione per la Marina varied according to operational needs and to the loss of territories once under Axis control (for instance, the Aviazione per la Marina unit of Tripoli was abolished on 29 January 1943, and the number of Squadriglie in the Aegean was greatly reduced by June 1943). Throughout the war, the 501s and 506s of the Regia Aeronautica served extensively in the search-and-rescue role, with specific units based at La Spezia, Orbetello, Nisida, Elmas, Syracuse, Stagnone, Brindisi, Leros and – later in the war – Toulon (Southern France), Ajaccio (Corsica) and Prevesa (on western coast of Greece).

On 1 March 1942 the units of the Aviazione per la Marina were stationed as follows:

Northern Tyrrhenian Sea
Four Squadriglie (forty-three aircraft, twenty-two combat-ready)

Sardinia
Three Squadriglie (twenty-four aircraft, twelve combat-ready)

Southern Tyrrhenian Sea
Three Squadrglie (twenty-four aircraft, twelve combat-ready)

Ionian and Southern Adriatic Seas
Four Squadriglie (twenty-nine aircraft, fifteen combat-ready)

Northern Adriatic Sea
Three Squadriglie (twenty-three aircraft, thirteen combat-ready)

Mainland Greece
Two Squadriglie (twenty-eight aircraft, twelve combat-ready)

Aegean
One Squadriglia (ten aircraft, eight combat-ready)

On the same date, 181 seaplanes were in service: eighty-four Cant Z. 501, fifty-eight Cant Z. 506 and thirty-nine Fiat RS 14 (a twin-engined seaplane of modern design intended to replace the 501, but only built in very small numbers). In addition to these, there were fifty–sixty IMAM Ro.43, both land-based and aboard warships. Between 10 June 1940 and 8 September 1943, the Regia Aeronautica employed 248 seaplanes for naval service, in addition to those already available at the beginning of the war: a very small number indeed, and absolutely insufficient to meet the demands of the naval war in the Mediterranean. One hundred and sixty-three aircraft were available when war was declared and 181 (not so surprisingly, the same number as on 1 March

A Cant Z. 506 of a reconnaissance Squadriglia of the Aviazione per la Marina, with dark-green camouflage overall, in mid-1942. Only twenty 506s were operational on 10 June 1940, but additional aircraft were built during the war. (Courtesy G Apostolo Archive)

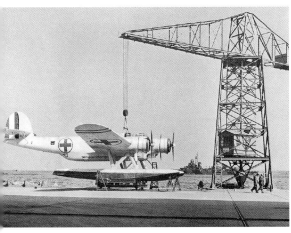

Directly derived from the 506B, the 506S ('S' for Sanitario, i.e. 'ambulance') was built in wartime for search-and-rescue and air ambulance duties. Although painted with Red Crosses and sporting civilian markings, such aircraft were never officially considered as operating under the Geneva Convention, and enemy fighter aircraft took a heavy toll of them. This Cant Z. 506S is shown in a southern Italian base in summer 1943: notice the camouflaged light cruiser *Scipione Africano* in the background. (Courtesy G Apostolo Archive)

1942) on 8 September 1943; seventy-four seaplanes were destroyed by enemy action, and more than 200 were lost to other causes (engine failures, weather, fire etc.). Pilots of the Regia Aeronautica were often replaced and transferred to other duties (when their skills and experience in naval operations were badly needed), but this in turn often led to reductions in training levels for pilots newly assigned to their units: a problem particularly felt aboard ships, whose seaplanes were often unable to perform their reconnaissance and spotting tasks satisfactorily.

As for naval flying personnel, 446 Osservatori served during the war (more than 260 being trained as such in wartime), and 112 were listed as killed or missing in action: among them nine were awarded the Medaglia d'Oro al Valor Militare and more than 300 others were recipients of lesser decorations.

Cant Z. 501 Gabbiano
(first flight 1934)
Single-engined, high-wing, central hull seaplane
Length: 14.3m
Wingspan: 22.5m
Weight: 3,850kg
Max take-off weight: 7,050kg
Engine: One Isotta Fraschini Asso XI.RC, liquid-cooled, V12 (880hp)
Maximum speed: 275km/h (170 mph)
Range: 2,400km
Service ceiling: 7,000m
Armament: Three 7.7mm Breda-SAFAT MG; bombs 640 kg
Crew: 4/5

Cant Z. 506 Airone
(first flight 1935)
Three-engined, low-wing, twin float seaplane
Length: 19.4m
Wingspan: 26.5m
Weight: 8,300kg
Max take-off weight: 12,300kg
Engine: Three Alfa Romeo 126 RC34 (75hp each)
Maximum speed: 365km/h (227 mph)
Range: 2,745km
Service ceiling: 7,850m
Armament: One 12.7mm Breda-SAFAT MG, three 7.7mm MG Breda-SAFAT; bombs 1,200kg
Crew: 5

IMAM Ro.43
(first flight 1934)
Single-engined, biplane, single float seaplane
Length: 9.7m
Wingspan: 11.6m
Weight: 1,760kg
Max take-off weight: 2,400kg
Engine: One Piaggio P.XR 9 (700hp)
Maximum speed: 300km/h (186 mph)
Range: 1,500km
Service ceiling: 6,600m
Armament: Two 7.7mm Breda-SAFAT MG
Crew: 2

Reggiane Re.2000
(first flight 1939)
Single-engined, all-metal, low-wing monoplane fighter
Length: 7.0m
Wingspan: 11.0m
Weight: 2,200kg
Max take-off weight: 2,979kg
Engine: One Piaggio P.XI RC 40 (1,000hp)
Maximum speed: 505km/h (320 mph)
Range: 545km
Service ceiling: 11,200m
Armament: Two 12.7mm Breda-SAFAT MG
Crew: 1

The first Ro. 43 of the first production series at Vigna di Valle on 24 April 1936: notice that the aircraft of the first series had – like the prototypes – an enclosed cockpit, later replaced by a sliding canopy. (Courtesy G Apostolo Archive)

CHAPTER 7

Italian Naval Camouflage in the Second World War

THE REGIA MARINA HAD conducted tests on naval camouflage during the First World War, and several ships, mainly in the Adriatic, were painted with various camouflage schemes in 1917/1918. Most of these made extensive use of dazzle patterns and were heavily influenced by British and US schemes then used in the Atlantic (*Mackay*, *Warner* and *Toch*), although the Italian Navy also developed some schemes on its own, and some destroyers and torpedo boats had broad, irregular stripes painted in alternate shades of light and dark grey on their hull and superstructures.

After the end of the war, the Regia Marina's warships were painted dark grey overall, in a shade very similar to that of the USN's Measure 1 (1939/40) and both horizontal and vertical surfaces were painted this way. In most cases wooden decking was left in its natural colour. In 1931 the Navy issued new regulations on the painting of ships and, after that date, Italian warships had steel decks (wooden decks remained natural) and horizontal surfaces painted dark grey, with all vertical surfaces light grey (this colour was known as 'grigio cenerino chiaro', i.e. 'light ash

grey'); this colour was a bit lighter than the USN's Measure 13 Haze Grey. Italian warships began the war with this scheme, with a few modifications being introduced soon after:

- Removal of black funnel bands indicating the Squadriglia which each destroyer or torpedo boat belonged to.
- Funnel caps, originally painted black, were in most cases repainted light grey to make the ships less conspicuous.
- Soon after the Battle of Punta Stilo (during which Italian ships were actually attacked by their own aircraft, luckily without suffering any damage), a new means for identification from the air was introduced. Red and white stripes, 7–15ft wide, were painted diagonally from port to starboard. They stripes began at the extreme bow and extended aft up to the breakwater (mostly in destroyers) or up to the barbette of 'A' turret (in some cruisers and battleships). The stripes were maintained until the Armistice: sometimes they were painted on the aftermost part of the deck, but very few cases are well

documented (the destroyer *Aviere* being one of these).

In August 1940, Major (i.e. LtCdr) Luigi Petrillo, of the Genio Navale, was tasked by the Navy's Headquarters to begin studying naval camouflage: Petrillo's small group of technicians and experts looked first at US and British schemes from the First World War, but also created original schemes of their own. Their studies produced two proposals: a 'dazzle' pattern and a 'fishbone' pattern that were to find practical application some time later.

The first tests were carried out during the early months of 1941. A full dazzle pattern (probably a 'Petrillo' one) was applied to the heavy cruiser *Fiume* whilst the destroyers *Aviere* and *Camicia Nera* received schemes designed to deceive enemy rangefinders as to the length of the ship. Very few photographs of *Fiume* in dazzle pattern (and all of them of very poor quality) have been located up to now: *Fiume*'s hull and superstructure sides were painted with splotches of dark and light grey, blue and blue-green. *Aviere*'s hull sides were dark grey

The destroyer *Fabrizi* in mid-1925, in formation with similar ships. She is painted dark grey overall, with white identification letters on the bows and on both sides of the stern; funnel bands (indicating her rank in the flotilla she belongs to) are white. In a few cases, with this dark grey scheme the identification letters on destroyers and torpedo boats were red instead of white. *Fabrizi* and all other three-stackers of First World War vintage were reclassified as torpedo boats on 1 October 1929. (Fotocelere; Author's collection)

The destroyer *Libeccio* in the late 1930s, with light grey ('grigio cenerino chiaro') on all vertical surfaces: most Italian warships began the war painted in this scheme. Funnel bands (three black stripes) show the rank of *Libeccio* in the 10th Destroyer Flotilla, but all such bands were removed before June 1940. The identification letters on the bows and at the stern are red. (E Bagnasco collection)

The destroyer *Granatiere* of the 'Soldati' class, in a floating dry-dock at Brindisi in the second half of 1940. This image clearly shows the colours of the paint scheme in use early in the war: light grey vertical surfaces and hull sides with red lettering, black boot-topping and green anti-fouling paint on the underside of the hull. In the left lower background, a small part of the battleship *Impero*'s port side is just visible: when the war broke out, *Impero* was being towed from Genoa to Trieste to complete fitting-out but for security reasons it was decided to temporarily moor the ship in the harbour at Brindisi. She remained there until January 1942, when she was towed to Venice where it was hoped to complete her fitting out. (Author's collection)

The battleship *Littorio* 'taking it green' over her bows on 1 September 1940, while returning to Taranto after the Regia Marina's unsuccessful attempt to oppose the Royal Navy's Operation 'Hats'. Note, on the forecastle deck, the broad red and white diagonal air recognition stripes painted up after the Battle of Punta Stilo. In the far distance, steaming on the same heading, the cruisers of the 1st and 3rd Divisions can be seen. (E Bagnasco collection)

In October 1941, at the end of the naval camouflage experiments conducted by the Regia Marina, the light cruiser *Giovanni delle Bande Nere* was painted in a dazzle scheme, almost identical on both sides, with straight-edged dark grey bands on a light grey background. This scheme proved to be quite effective, and led to the 'standard' schemes applied to most Italian warships from early 1942 onwards. This photograph was taken in February 1942, when *Bande Nere* was escorting a convoy bound for Tripoli. Note how *Bande Nere*'s disruptive scheme makes her identification difficult when compared with the heavy cruiser *Gorizia* – still painted light grey overall – in the background. (E Bagnasco collection)

and her superstructure light grey, with the extreme bows painted light grey. *Camicia Nera*'s vertical surfaces were dark grey with the extreme bow and stern light grey. At the naval base of Pola, the torpedo boats *Audace* and *Insidioso* and the gunboat *Aurora* were painted with experimental dazzle patterns using light grey, dark grey, black and, for *Aurora* only, shades of green.

Further camouflage schemes for ships were devised by the noted naval artist Rudolf Claudus. Claudus was born an Austro-Hungarian, but after the First World War, he obtained Italian citizenship, as he had always been an admirer of Italy and of the Regia Marina. His most famous paintings were produced during and after the Second World War and show Italian warships as well as his interpretations of naval actions in the Mediterranean. At the outbreak of the war, Claudus was co-operating with the Italian Navy on the matter of camouflage and, very soon, his recommendations began to be put into practice. Claudus' schemes tended to alter a ship's general appearance, (as in the case of USN Measures 32 and 33); at the same time there were also obvious attempts to make ships look shorter and to be moving faster than they were by the use of false bow waves. Most of these schemes show typical 'sawtooth' patterns and many colours were used, although not all together: dark and light grey, white, black, light blue, light green and even yellow. Steel decks were always dark grey. From mid-1941 onwards 'Claudus' schemes were applied to the battleships *Cesare* and *Doria*, the heavy cruiser *Trento*, the light cruisers *Attendolo* and *Garibaldi* and the destroyers *Ascari* and *Nicolò Zeno*. By the first months of 1942, all of the schemes suggested by Claudus began to be replaced by official standard Navy schemes.

Another experimental pattern was the 'Petrillo' fishbone design applied to a few major surface warships, (the battleships *Duilio*, *Littorio* and *Vittorio Veneto* and the light cruiser *Duca d'Aosta*) in 1941. Steel decks were always dark grey and any wooden decks were overpainted with this colour; all vertical surfaces were dark grey with superimposed triangles painted with a very light shade of yellow-green (very similar to the 'Sky type S' colour used for the undersides of the Royal Navy's FAA aircraft in the 1950s). These triangles were placed in patterns very similar to that of a fishbone but, as for the 'Claudus' schemes, they were also discontinued at the beginning of 1942.

During the early months of 1942 more detailed regulations on the matter of camouflage were issued by the Regia Marina's Technical Department. By mid-1942 practically all Italian warships were camouflaged in dazzle patterns that in most cases required only two colours, 'grigio cenerino chiaro' (light ash grey) and 'grigio scuro' (dark grey). Deck colours remained as before (i.e. dark grey), and red and white recognition stripes remained in use as well.

The interesting fact is that no 'designs' for general use on specific ship classes existed, and each ship had her own pattern. In wartime, this could possibly help to confuse an observer even more but, for today's researchers, it is almost impossible to know what a single ship looked like if no photographs are available. Official 'camouflage leaflets' for each ship were released by the Navy's Technical Department or by the navy yards themselves: they were used by the ship's company to paint the upperworks during overhauls or when repainting was needed. Almost complete collections of these leaflets still exist, but one will always have to refer to photographs as in most cases the leaflets' instructions were followed rather loosely; patterns were also modified during overhauls following the first painting, depending also on types and quantities of paint available.

If we consider the vertical surfaces of a ship painted light grey overall, camouflage was created by superimposing dark grey figures whose 'style' can be classified – as we will see later on – as three main designs:

1) Lobed patterns.
2) Straight edged patterns.
3) 'Splotch' patterns.

Demarcations between light and dark grey were always clean and distinct as the colours never 'blended'; without making a comparison between colours, lobed patterns resembled those of Measure 16 and straight-edged patterns those of USN Measures 32 and 33. Demarcation between the colours in 'splotch' patterns was quite similar to the appearance of USN Measure 12, but it must

The light cruiser *Emanuele Filiberto Duca d'Aosta* mooring at Taranto, on 17 February 1941. She was the first Italian ship painted with the experimental 'fishbone' pattern deriving from work by Major Petrillo's study group. All vertical surfaces were dark grey with superimposed triangles painted with a very light shade of yellow-green. (F Bargoni collection)

be pointed out that Italian naval camouflage schemes never had the purpose of blending a ship into the horizon. Regia Marina camouflage patterns used the same colours extensively on the sides of both the hull and the superstructure. In such 'official' schemes, the extreme bows and stern were often painted white, but by mid-1942, light grey replaced these white areas, white having been found to be too conspicuous in Mediterranean conditions, particularly during spring and summer.

In some cases, light green (the heavy cruiser *Trieste*, the light cruiser *Attilio Regolo*, the destroyer *Legionario* and the torpedo-boats *Stocco* and *Pilo*) or light blue (the battleship *Duilio* and the destroyer *Da Recco*) were used to paint some areas, along with light and dark grey. In 1942, the pattern of the torpedo boat *San Martino* used light and dark blue instead of light and dark grey. Italian ships taken over by the Kriegsmarine after the Armistice often kept their Italian camouflage schemes or, in some cases, were repainted with German patterns. Most Italian ships fighting on the Allied side after September 1943 were repainted (starting in 1944), with US or British schemes very similar to the USN's Measure 22 or its Royal Navy counterparts ('Admiralty standard schemes' etc.). Such Allied schemes were maintained until 1949/1951, when Italian ships reverted to the colours in use before the war. With very few exceptions, light grey for vertical surfaces and dark grey for decks are still in use today

aboard the ships of the Marina Militare Italiana. Boot topping was always black and, for painting the submerged part of the hull, red or (more often) green anti-fouling paint was used.

At the beginning of the war submarines were usually painted black or blue-black overall and tests on submarine camouflage were carried out in Pola, La Spezia and Taranto by the end of 1940: at the end of such tests precise regulations on submarine painting were published. The upper-works were painted with a very light blue-grey overall, with irregular splotches of 'greenish' dark brown painted on top (after the tests, geometric forms of the same colour were discontinued). Boats operating on the Allied side reverted to black or were painted, later in the war, with USN schemes.

Most Italian ships operational between early 1942 and the autumn of 1943 were thus camouflaged with a two-colour 'standard' scheme, that used light grey and dark grey and – until mid-1942 – a greyish white (referred to in Italian as 'bianco sporco,' or 'dirty white') both on the bows and on the stern. However, while the US Navy (widely) and the Royal Navy (at least in some cases) adopted camouflage schemes whose patterns were quite similar even for ships of different types or belonging to completely different classes, every Regia Marina warship had a unique pattern of her own, although it always used both 'standard' colours. This was attributable to several reasons, that varied from a conscious effort to make the identification of individual ships as difficult as possible, to a certain margin of creativity that the Navy left to the technical employees and experts who developed camouflage, as well as to the workers of naval yards who actually painted the ships.

Despite the wide latitude the Regia Marina allowed in creating individual ship camouflage schemes, when comparing the various 'standard' schemes and patterns used by the Italian Navy in

The battleship *Caio Duilio* during gunnery trials in the Gulf of Taranto in June 1941. She was painted with the 'fishbone' camouflage system during a refit in Genoa in early 1941; in the same period, the battleships *Littorio* and *Vittorio Veneto* and the light cruiser *Aosta* (see previous photographs) were also camouflaged in a very similar pattern. (A Fraccaroli collection)

The light cruiser *Muzio Attendolo* at Taranto late in 1941, wearing a camouflage scheme devised by the noted naval artist Rudolf Claudus. Colours are light grey, black and white. In the background, the cruiser *Aosta*'s superstructure (with a 'fishbone' scheme) may be seen, as well as the seaplane tender *Miraglia*'s funnels further in the background. ('A Maj' Library, Bergamo, Occhini bequest)

After an overhaul in the La Spezia dockyard, the destroyer *Ascari* returned to service in December 1941 painted in a 'Claudus' scheme with black panels (some of 'sawtooth' design) over a light grey background; areas in white on both lower bows were applied to simulate high speed. During the overhaul, a single shielded 4.7in gun mount was fitted atop the midships deckhouse, in place of a previous illuminating howitzer. (E Bagnasco collection)

This photograph of the battleship *Andrea Doria* was taken on the afternoon of 17 December 1941, while she was steaming towards the British ships escorting the tanker HMS *Breconshire*; the subsequent clash between Italian and Royal Navy ships would become known as the First Battle of Sirte. Shortly before, in October, *Doria* was painted in this 'Claudus' scheme – the same on both sides – whose colours were light grey, black, greyish white and light blue (on the bows, lower stern quarters and with small panels on the superstructure). (E Bagnasco collection)

1942–3 it is nevertheless possible to find some specific and common arrangements and patterns that marked the camouflage schemes of several ships. There were, in effect, some schemes that presented common features across various types of ships, from battleships to corvettes, as shown by the fact that despite rather wide divergences in the various designs some guidelines were nevertheless borne in mind and, in some cases, were in fact applied.

One pattern was based on broad curved bands (mainly in dark grey) with smooth contoured edges with the curves facing either up or down. It is highly likely that such schemes originated from the design originally conceived for the 'Navigatori' class destroyer *Da Mosto*, which was the same on both sides of the ship: it is highly probable that this particular scheme was not properly evaluated because of the very short time that elapsed since its adoption (autumn 1941) and the ship's sinking (1 December 1941).

Similar curved bands also appeared on the battleship *Andrea Doria*, on the light cruisers *Aosta* and *Montecuccoli* and on the destroyer *Pigafetta* of the 'Navigatori' class. It should be noted that on *Montecuccoli* the bands were 'in negative' (i.e. painted light grey), and on the port side only. The destroyer escort *Orione* sported a scheme with curved bands as well, but in this case the edges of the bands were wavy and rather irregular. The scheme of the light cruiser *Eugenio di Savoia* was quite similar to *Orione*'s, with bands (also with irregular edges) that almost seemed to be semi-circles or semi-ellipsoids in dark grey on a light grey background.

Dark grey areas and panels were, in most cases, polygonal designs either with straight or curved edges and there were only a few ships with 'standard' camouflage with irregular edges for the dark grey areas. These were:

- the battleship *Littorio*;
- the cruisers *Eugenio di Savoia*, *Attilio Regolo* (in her third scheme) and *Scipione Africano*;
- the destroyers *Turbine*, *Da Noli* (first 'standard' scheme), *Usodimare*, *Vivaldi*, *Strale*, *Grecale*, *Oriani*, *Bersagliere*, *Camicia Nera*, *Carabiniere*, *Corazziere*, *Fuciliere*, *Granatiere*, *Bombardiere*, *Mitragliere* and *Sebenico*:
- the torpedo boats *Abba*, *Dezza*, *Mosto* (first 'standard' scheme), *Stocco*, *Cascino*, *Prestinari*, *San Martino*, *Solferino*, *Monzambano*, *Antares*, *Aretusa*, *Lince*, *Partenope*, *Sagittario* and *T5*;
- the destroyer escorts *Orione* and *Ardimentoso*;
- the gunboat *Cattaro*.

The destroyer *Pigafetta* ('Navigatori' class) manoeuvring in the port of Piraeus, Greece, on 18 August 1942, with curved dark grey bands on a light grey background, white areas fore and aft, and red identification letters. (A Fraccaroli photograph)

Camouflage schemes

Colour artwork by Paola Zaio

The destroyer *Vivaldi* and other similar vessels in the Gulf of Naples on 5 May 1938, steaming in column during the 'H Review', at the time of Hitler's visit to Italy. (Life)

The destroyer *Libeccio* at the 'H Review' on 5 May 1938; notice the *Trento* class heavy cruiser in the far distance. (Life)

The destroyer *Folgore* in 1940, with the pre-war paint scheme of all Regia Marina ships: light grey on vertical surfaces, dark grey decks, black boot-topping and medium green anti-fouling paint.

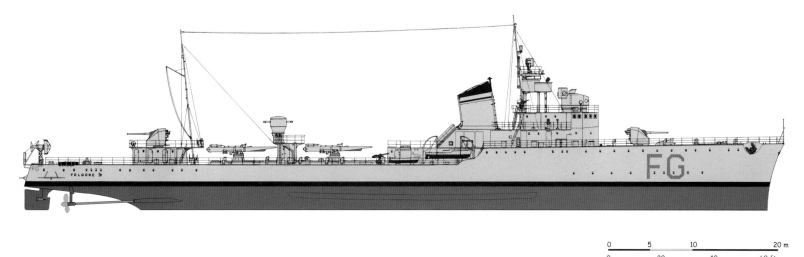

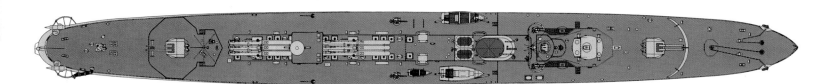

A very rare colour image of the destroyer *Legionario* in the Gulf of Naples, in spring 1945. *Legionario* has dark grey hull and light grey superstructures; notice the bedspring antenna of the German 'De.Te' radar fitted on the top of the bridge. (USAF, 57th Fighter Group)

In one of the very few good colour photographs showing Italian warships in the Second World War, the hulk of destroyer escort *Tifone* (shown at Korbus, in the Gulf of Tunis, after she was scuttled on 5 May 1943) sports her 'standard' dark and light grey scheme, with red lettering on the starboard bows. (US National Archives)

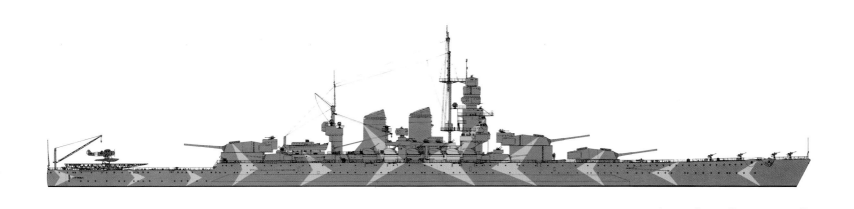

| 0 | 10 | 20 | 40 m |
| 0 | 30 | 60 | 120 ft |

The battleship *Littorio* as painted in March 1941, with a 'fishbone' design devised by the team directed by Major Petrillo of the Naval Engineering Corps. Of the four ships camouflaged with this scheme, only *Littorio* had the same pattern on both sides, while the starboard pattern on *Vittorio Veneto*, *Duilio* and *Aosta* differed slightly from the port one. The deck view below shows dark grey horizontal surfaces and the diagonal red and white identification stripes, applied after July 1940.

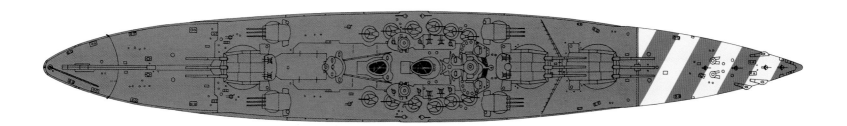

The complex camouflage scheme of the light cruiser *Muzio Attendolo*, drafted by naval painter Rudolf Claudus, was applied in July 1941. In November 1941, *Garibaldi* was similarly camouflaged, with additional green areas on the port side.

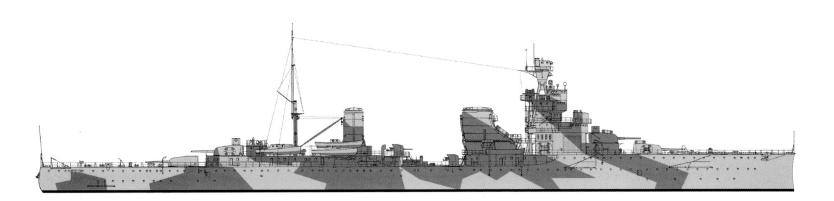

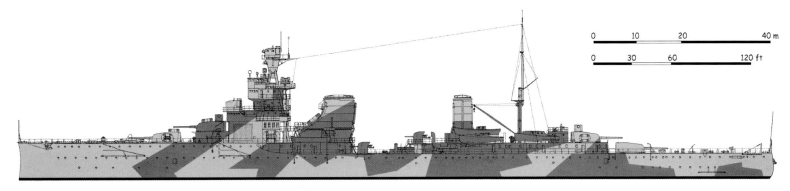

This scheme applied to the light cruiser *Bande Nere* in November 1941 was the last of the experimental designs tried out by the Italian Navy and may be considered the prototype of all 'standard' camouflages used by the Regia Marina from spring 1942 onwards. When sunk on 1 April 1942, *Bande Nere* was still painted like this.

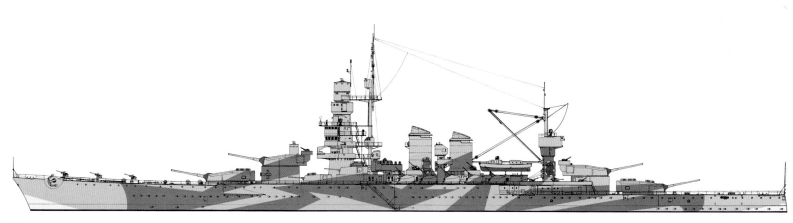

The 'standard' camouflage of the battleship *Caio Duilio* (April 1942), with additional wide light blue areas on the hull and the superstructure.

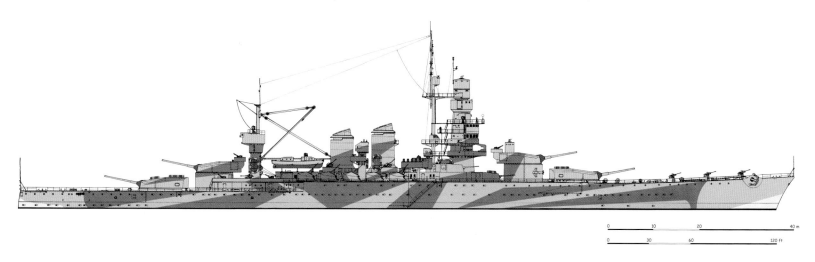

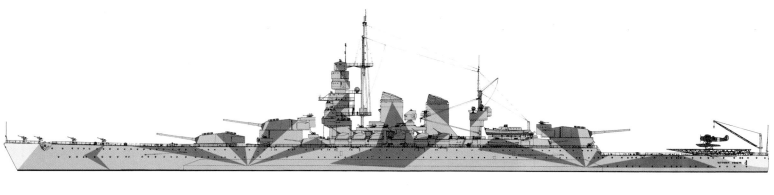

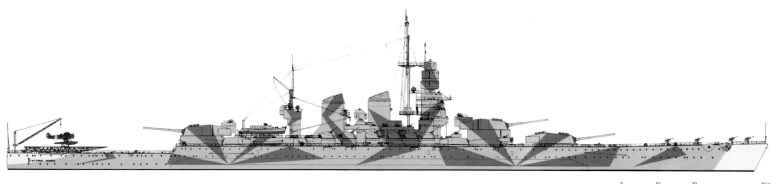

In March 1942, the battleship *Vittorio Veneto* was painted with this 'standard' scheme of wide triangular panels with a radiating or 'sunburst' arrangement. White areas at the bow and at the stern were overpainted with light grey in August 1942, and *Veneto* kept this scheme until after the Armistice, being repainted – the same as *Littorio* – light grey overall with a dark grey rectangular area amidships during her internment at the Great Bitter Lake.

The destroyer *Zeno* was camouflaged with a complex 'Claudus' scheme, the same on both sides, in October 1941; notice the use of yellow and the attempt to simulate a bow wave. In late 1942 *Zeno* was repainted in a 'standard' light and dark grey scheme.

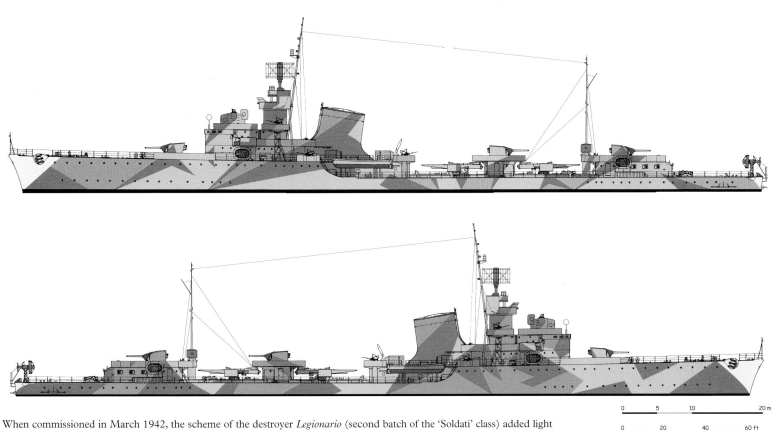

When commissioned in March 1942, the scheme of the destroyer *Legionario* (second batch of the 'Soldati' class) added light green to the usual 'standard' colours of whitish-grey, light grey and white. By the end of the year, green and white areas were overpainted with light grey. Also the light cruiser *Attilio Regolo*, after having been camouflaged at her commissioning in May 1942 with the same four colours as *Legionario*, reverted to light and dark grey even earlier, in August 1942.

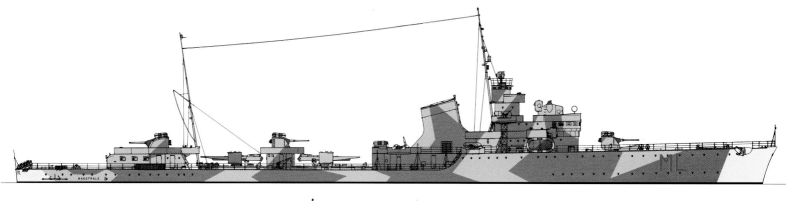

The destroyer *Maestrale*, as camouflaged in spring 1942.

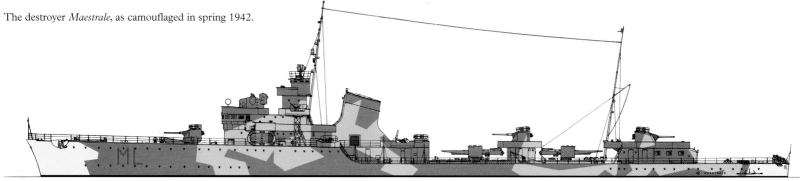

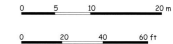

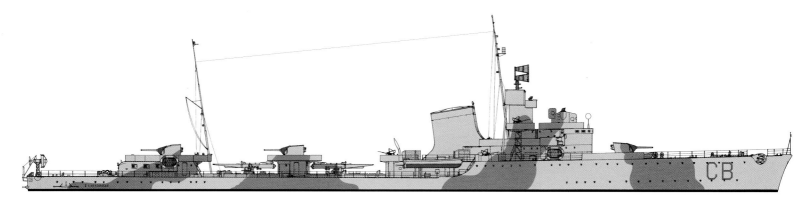

It was not until January 1943 that the destroyer *Carabiniere* was camouflaged with 'standard' colours.

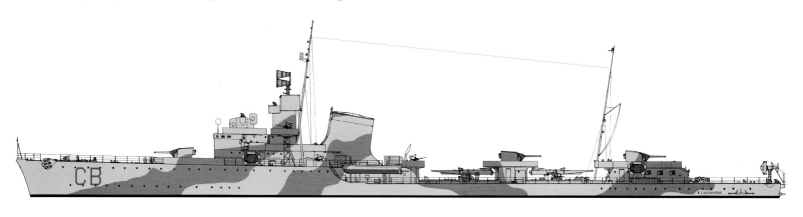

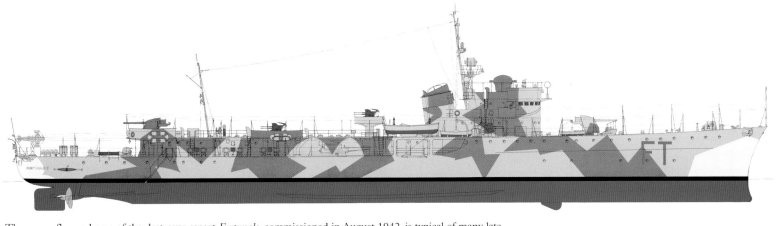

The camouflage scheme of the destroyer escort *Fortunale*, commissioned in August 1942, is typical of many late-war Italian ships, with rather complex polygonal dark grey areas over a light grey background.

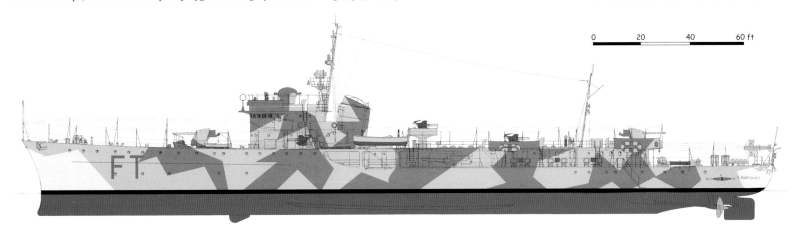

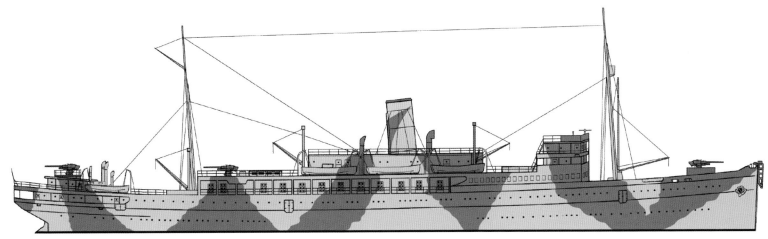

The auxiliary cruiser *Arborea* (a former Tirrenia Line ship in service on Sardinian routes), was camouflaged in 1942 with a '4A' merchant ship scheme on the starboard side and '3B' on the port side.

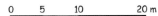

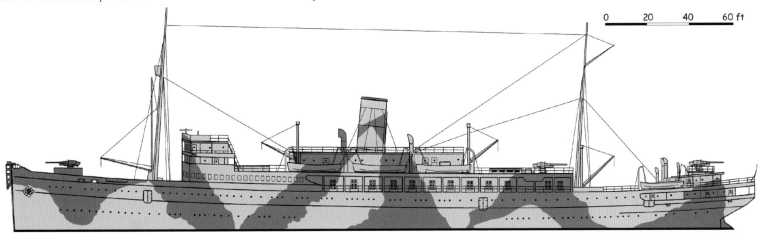

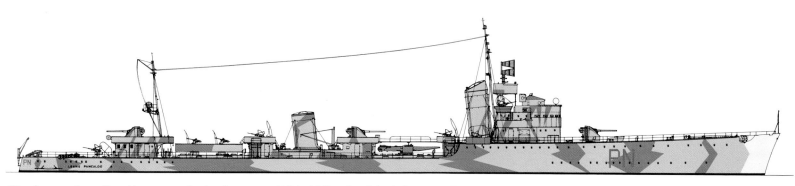

The destroyer *Leone Pancaldo* was torpedoed at Augusta on 10 July 1940 and sank in shallow water. By the end of the month she was salvaged and towed to Genoa, where repairs lasted until November 1942; she was fitted with a E.C. 3/ter 'Gufo' radar at La Spezia dockyard, and was recommissioned on 12 December wearing this 'standard' camouflage scheme.

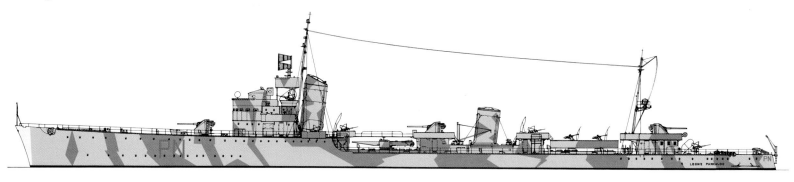

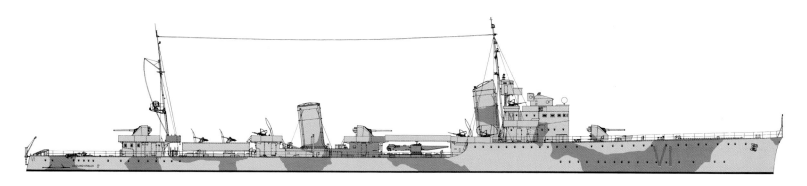

The destroyer *Ugolino Vivaldi*, of the 'Navigatori' class, in early 1943: 'standard' camouflage, with irregular edges for the dark grey areas.

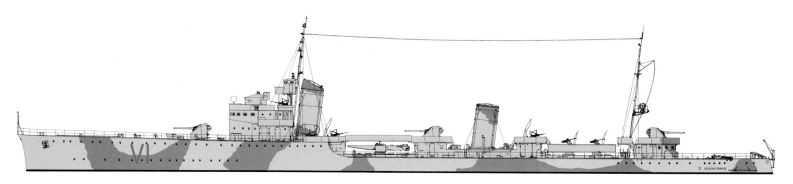

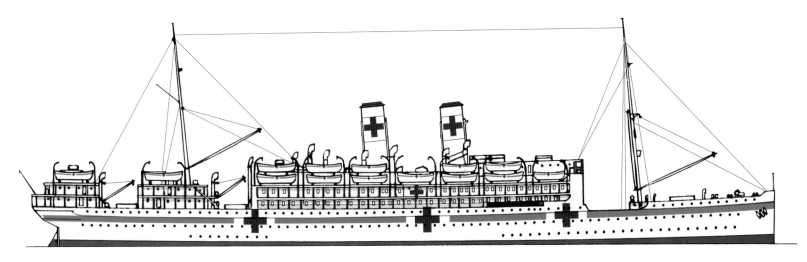

The hospital ship *Gradisca*, like all other Italian hospital ships, was painted white with red crosses and a green band on the hull sides as required by the Geneva Convention.

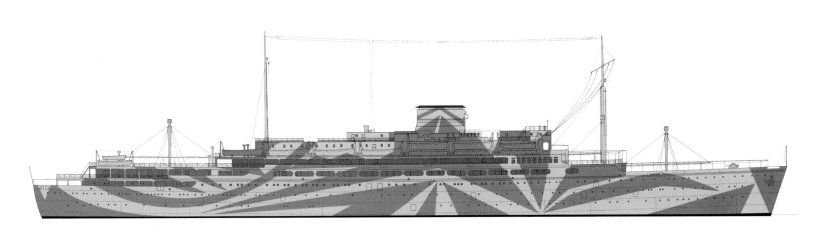

The liner *Oceania*, pressed into war service as a troop transport like several other passenger ships, was camouflaged with a scheme resembling those of large surface combatants. *Oceania*'s pattern, particularly on the port side, brings to mind the 'sunburst' camouflage of the battleship *Vittorio Veneto*.

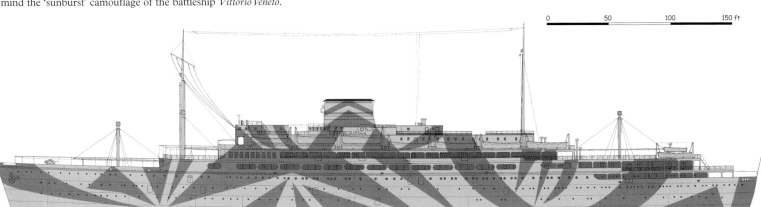

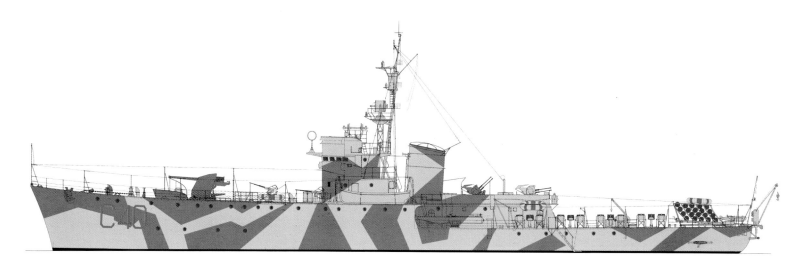

The 'standard' scheme of the corvette *Persefone* in November 1942.

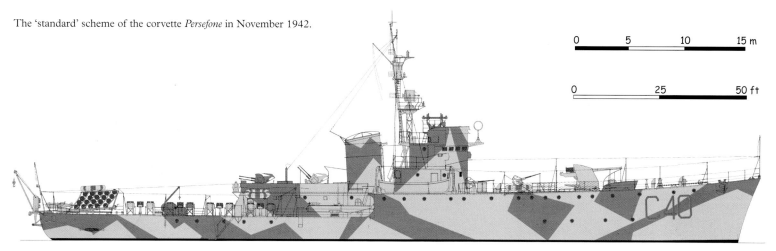

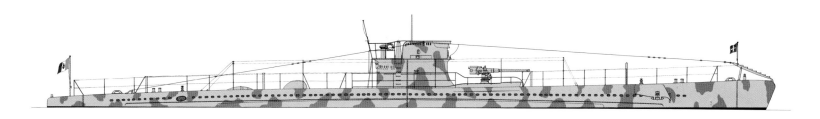

The submarine *Asteria* in 1942, with the 'official' colours for submarines (light blue-grey overall, with irregular splotches of 'greenish' dark brown painted on top).

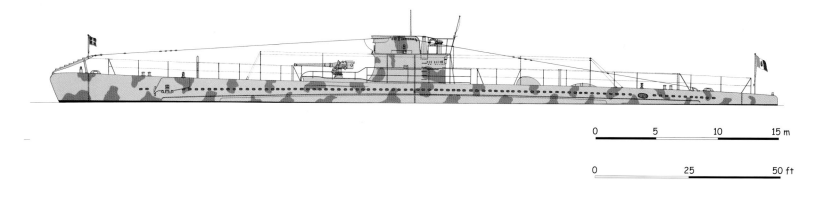

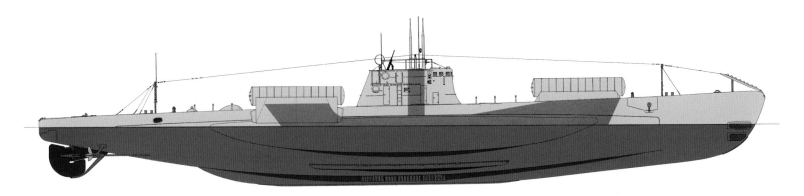

The submarine *Scirè*, modified in 1940 for the transportation of human torpedoes, was painted in late summer with a peculiar scheme, probably devised by her CO, Lt.Cdr. Borghese, (top). The hull and conning tower sides were painted in a very light green, with a superimposed dark grey shape resembling a fishing boat. *Scirè* sailed on only one combat mission painted this way, at the end of September 1940. After having been painted again in the pre-war very dark grey overall for some time, in mid-1941 *Scirè* was refitted, and camouflaged with what was almost a 'standard' scheme for submarines (below). During the overhaul the conning tower was reduced in size to make the boat less conspicuous.

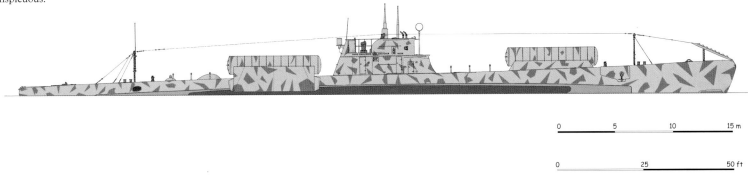

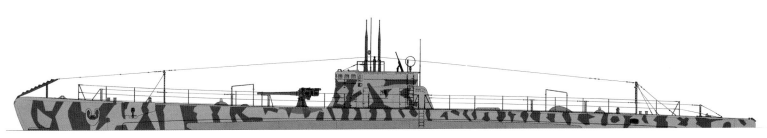

The non-standard scheme of the submarine *Perla*, as derived from photographs of the boat taken on her arrival in Bordeaux, from East Africa, on 27 May 1941. Only the port side is fully known, while the few existing photographs only show portions of the starboard side.

In the second half of summer 1942, the submarine *Leonardo Da Vinci* was modified to transport a small 'CA' type midget submarine: it was planned that *Da Vinci* sail to New York, where the 'CA' would have been released to enter the harbour and attack US shipping there. This operation never got beyond the planning stage and by the end of the year *Da Vinci* was restored to her former configuration. By mid-1942 onwards, Italian boats operating in the Atlantic were hardly ever camouflaged, being painted dark grey overall.

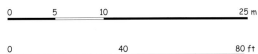

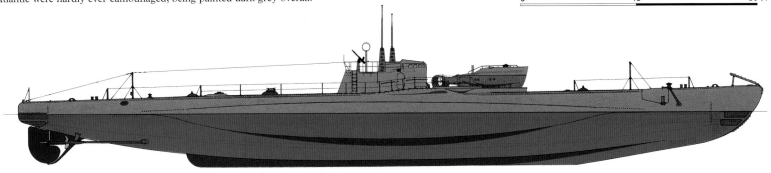

A rare colour photograph of the port of Tripoli in early January 1943. From left to right, the M/S *D'Annunzio* (which would be sunk a few days later off Lampedusa, on 16 January, by British ships), the M/S *Sestriere* and the steamer *Marocchino*. Note the two Cant Z. 506 seaplanes near the *D'Annunzio*'s port side. (G Apostolo collection)

Steaming at high speed with 8in gun turrets trained to port, *Fiume* is seen here on 5 May 1938 in the Gulf of Naples during the 'H Review'. This original colour photograph is part of a series taken by the German photographer Hugo Jaeger, who accompanied the Führer during his state visit to Italy. (*LIFE*)

An IMAM Ro.43 of a Squadriglia based in mainland Italy in the early stages of the war. During the war, the Ro.43s assigned to naval ships had markings on both sides of the fuselage indicating the ship and the Naval Division she belonged to: for instance, number '712' indicated the second aircraft of the first ship – in this case the cruiser *Eugenio di Savoia* – of the 7ª Divisione navale. (Courtesy G Apostolo Archive)

The current flag of the Marina Militare Italiana, with the emblem of the four Maritime Republics and the 'crown of rams' (a crown decorated with the rams of Roman galleys), seen here aboard the sail training ship *Palinuro* in April 2001. (Author's photograph)

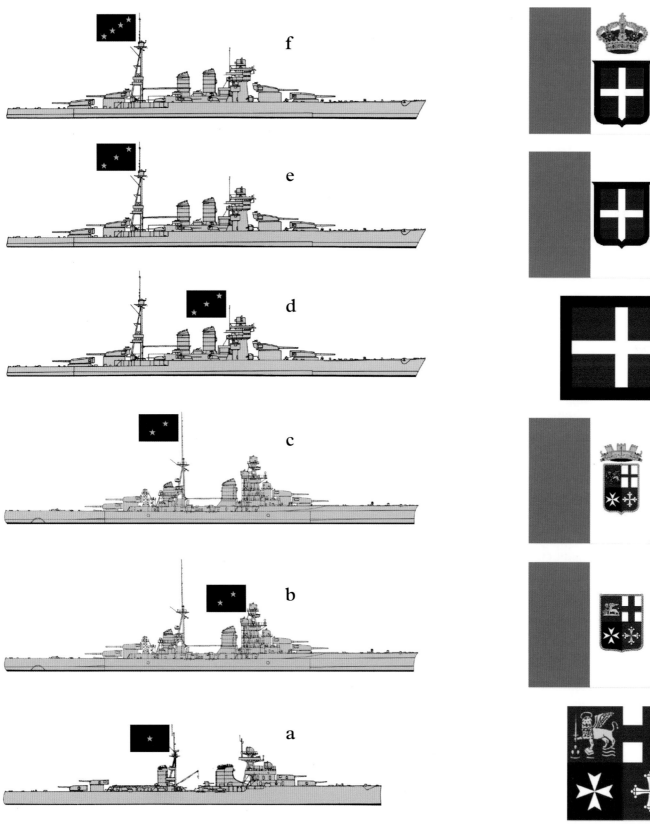

Positions of the 'rank flags' for admirals as used in wartime, according to Regia Marina regulations issued on 13 December 1926 and effective from 1 January 1927. From bottom to top:

a – Contrammiraglio (Commodore or Rear Admiral, lower half of the US Navy): one star at main mast.
b – Ammiraglio di Divisione (Rear Admiral): two stars at fore mast.
c – Ammiraglio di Squadra (Vice Admiral): two stars at main mast.
d – Ammiraglio designato d'Armata (no corresponding RN rank): three stars at fore mast.
e – Ammiraglio d'Armata (Admiral): three stars at main mast.
f – Grande Ammiraglio (Admiral of the Fleet): four stars at main mast.
(in brackets, the corresponding Royal Navy or US Navy ranks)
Note that in wartime, the rank flags for Ammiraglio di Squadra (c) and Ammiraglio d'Armata (e) were commonly hoisted at the foremast instead of at the mainmast.

1-3: Italian naval flags, 15 April 1861 – 2 June 1946
(1: naval ensign; 2: national flag and merchant marine ensign; 3: jack).
4-6: Italian naval flags, since 1 January 1948
(4: naval ensign; 5: merchant marine ensign; 6: jack)

One of the two colour pages of the *Almanacco Navale 1941* (published by the then Press and Public Relations Office of the Regia Marina) showing several flags for naval use. (From top to bottom and from left to right):
- top: masthead pennant ('Fiamma');
- second row: Royal Imperial Standard and Royal Princes Pennant;
- third row: Prime Ministerial Flag, Minister of the Navy and State Undersecretary of the Navy;
- fourth row: Commander-in-Chief of Naval Fighting Force (similar to naval jack), Capo di Stato Maggiore della Marina Flag and Grande Ammiraglio Flag;
- fifth row: Capitano di Vascello (Captain) acting as Division Commander, Senior commanding officer and commanding officer of a destroyer or torpedo boat flotilla;
- bottom: commanding officer of a destroyer flotilla; commanding officer of a torpedo boat flotilla; commanding officer of a submarine flotilla; commanding officer of a motor torpedo boat flotilla.

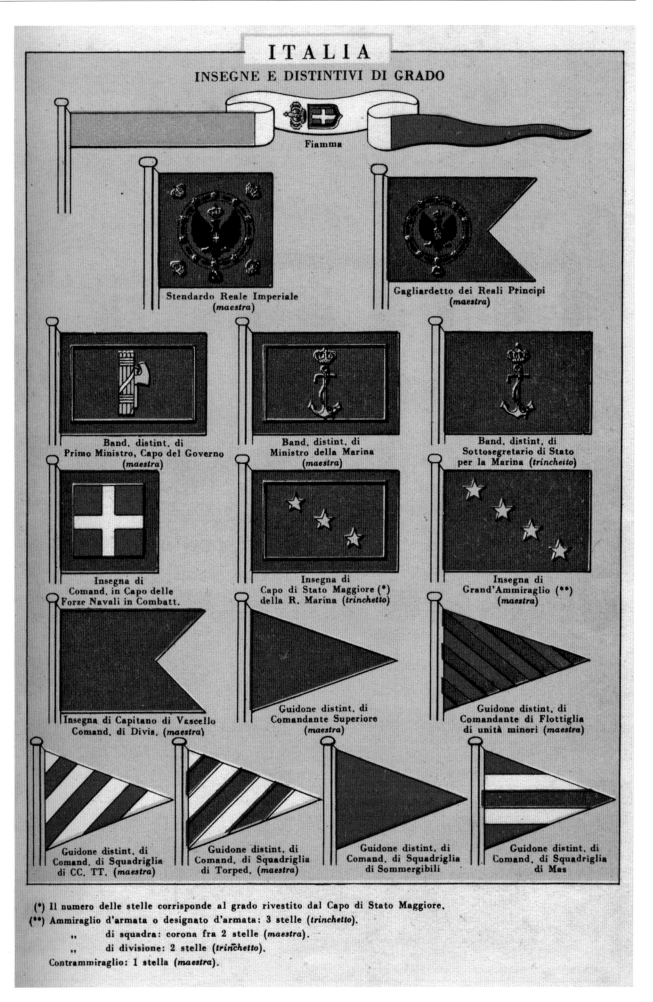

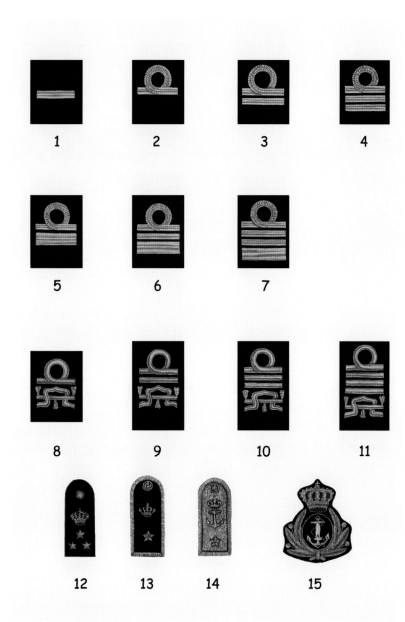

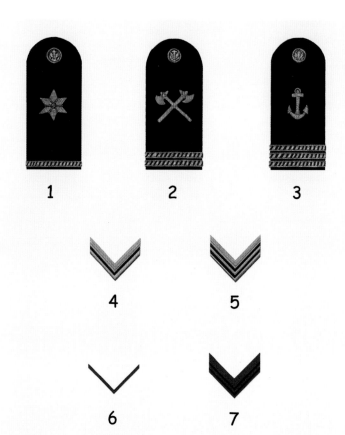

Sleeve insignia for Officers
1 – Aspirante Guardiamarina
2 – Guardiamarina
3 – Sottotenente di Vascello
4 – Tenente di Vascello
5 – Capitano di Corvetta
6 – Capitano di Fregata
7 – Capitano di Vascello
8 – Contrammiraglio
9 – Ammiraglio di Divisione
10 – Ammiraglio di Squadra and Ammiraglio Designato d'Armata
11 – Grande Ammiraglio
Shoulder insignia for Officers (selection)
12 – Tenente di Vascello
13 – Capitano di Corvetta
14 – Contrammiraglio
15 – Peaked cap badge for Officers: this example is for an Officer of the Ordnance Corps (Armi Navali), with a sword superimposed on the anchor at the centre of the badge.

Sleeve insignia for Petty Officers, upper half
1 – Capo di 1ª Classe, Furiere (Yeoman)
2 – Capo di 2ª Classe, Carpentiere (Carpenter Mate)
3 – Capo di 3ª Classe, Nocchiere (Quartermaster's Mate)
Rank chevrons for Petty Officers, lower half, and Ratings
4 – Sergente
5 – 2° Capo
6 – Comune di 1ª Classe
7 – Sottocapo

The most important Italian military decorations and awards:
1- Medaglia d'Oro al Valor Militare (Gold Medal for Valour, equivalent to the British Victoria Cross or the US Medal of Honor)
2 – Medaglia d'Argento al Valor Militare (Silver Medal for Valour)
3 – Medaglia di Bronzo al valor Militare (Bronze Medal for Valour)
4 – Croce di Guerra al Valor Militare
5 – Croce al Merito di Guerra
(1, 2 and 3 show the Gold, Silver and Bronze Medals for Valour as issued by the Kingdom of Italy until 2 June 1946. 4 and 5 show the Croce di Guerra al Valor Militare and Croce al Merito di Guerra as issued by the Italian Republic for merit awarded during the Second World War; the two corresponding decorations issued by the Kingdom of Italy until 2 June 1946 had a crown inside the upper bar of the cross).

The 'standard' scheme on the port side of the light cruiser *Raimondo Montecuccoli* was similar to *Pigafetta*'s scheme, but this pattern appears to have its colours inverted, with light grey curvilinear bands over dark grey background. *Montecuccoli* was camouflaged in May 1942; at the end of the year the white areas fore and aft were removed and the ship was repainted in an 'Allied' scheme with dark grey hull and light grey superstructures after the Armistice, late in 1943. (A Barilli collection)

Along with the 'standard' camouflage schemes, in some cases other colours were used in addition to the two shades of grey and 'dirty white': the battleship *Caio Duilio*'s scheme (applied in April/May 1942) had light blue panels both on the sides of the hull and on the superstructure, and other ships had, for a short period, panels or splotches in a light shade of green (the light cruisers *Attilio Regolo* and *Taranto*, the destroyer *Legionario*, the torpedo boats *Stocco* and *Pilo* and the destroyer escort *Tifone*).

The camouflage schemes of the battleship *Vittorio Veneto*, the heavy cruiser *Bolzano* and – partially – of the destroyer *Riboty* consisted of wide triangular panels in a radiating or 'sunburst' arrangement. Another very peculiar pattern (used

The destroyers *Alpino* (left) and *Lanciere* (right) at Messina in mid-March 1942. This is the only known image showing *Lanciere*'s port side camouflaged and is probably the last showing of this ship before her loss on 23 March, in a gale 120nm east of Malta, after the Second Battle of Sirte, during which the destroyer *Scirocco* also capsized and foundered. In the background the cruisers *Trento* (still in pre-war light grey) and *Bande Nere* (already camouflaged) can be seen. (G Vaccaro collection)

only on three ships, the cruiser *Cadorna* and the destroyers *Aviere* and *Geniere*) had the colours reversed on one side of the ship from the other, a concept more often used, for example, in Kriegsmarine camouflage schemes. Furthermore, the 'standard' schemes of the torpedo boat *Audace* and of the escort ship (former torpedo boat) *Insidioso* were the 'negative' or reverse of each other as a direct consequence of the early studies of naval camouflage carried out at Pola in 1941.

In the specific field of camouflage patterns for escort ships, many common points can be found among the schemes of a number of ships. The upper bows of the torpedo boats *Circe* (in her first 'standard' camouflage), *Polluce* and *Sirio* and of the destroyer *Euro* sported a unique oblong and rounded panel in dark grey whose upper side coincided with the stringer of the forecastle deck. On the starboard bows of the torpedo boats *Calliope* and *Cassiopea* (in her second 'standard' scheme), a straight-sided panel resembling an 'M' is easily identifiable, and this element – with several variations – can be found on several other ships.

When examining the camouflage schemes of *Spica* class torpedo boats (and likewise for the destroyer *Crispi*), we find that *Cassiopea*'s first scheme, and *Lira*'s and *Sirio*'s second schemes were quite different from the schemes of all other ships in their class, as their patterns were composed of very large dark grey panels each one measuring about one-third of the ship's length.

The schemes of *Gabbiano* class corvettes were very different from each other, but all of them clearly originated from a common concept: they all showed patterns with very small dark grey panels, whose dimensions were smaller when compared to the dark areas in other escort and destroyer camouflages. There was a greater density of these dark grey panels on the *Gabbiano*s, and the design of each panel was more complex and irregularly shaped. Corvettes *Gabbiano* and *Cicogna* had a very typical elliptic element on their sides, while other ships in the class (*Berenice*,

Minerva, *Sibilla* etc.) had – particularly on their bows – characteristic elements of a 'split-polygon' design. As most *Gabbiano* class corvettes were commissioned rather late in the war, only *Artemide* had the lower bows painted in greyish white ('dirty white').

Identification Letters and Hull Numbers

During the Second World War Italian ships did not have individual hull numbers. Battleships, heavy and light cruisers had no distinctive letters or numbers at all. Destroyers, destroyer-escorts, torpedo boats and gunboats had two large red letters painted on the bows, which were repeated, in smaller size, on both sides of the stern. Corvettes had a red 'C' followed by a number on both bows. When the same letters were applied to two different vessels, the difference was found in the number of funnels; (i.e.: the destroyer *Aquilone* and the torpedo boat *Aldebaran* had both the letters 'AL', but *Aquilone* had two funnels, while *Aldebaran* had only one). The letters were generally the first and one other of the ship's name. When a ship was named after a person, the letters were chosen from those of the family name and, in fact, in the Italian Navy such ships are generally known with a 'shortened' name referring to their family name (for instance: *Gioberti* for *Vincenzo Gioberti*, *Da Recco* for *Nicoloso Da Recco*, *Abruzzi* for *Luigi di Savoia Duca degli Abruzzi* etc.).

The distinctive letters were not used for scouts: thus, *Mirabello*, *Leone*, the 'Navigatoris' and (for a short period) *Maestrale* class ships did not have these letters until they were reclassified as destroyers on 5 September 1938.

Identifying letters and hull numbers for Italian destroyers, torpedo boats, destroyer escorts, corvettes and sub-chasers are given in the list below (when the same letters apply to two different vessels, the number of funnels is shown in brackets):

AA	*Albatros*
AB	*Giuseppe Cesare Abba* (3), *Alabarda* (1)
AC	*Giovanni Acerbi* (3), *Alcione* (1)
AD	*Audace* (2), *Andromeda* (1), *Ardente* (1)
AE	*Ariel, Ariete* (both 1 funnel, but *Ariel* was sunk before *Ariete* was commissioned. The same applies for all other duplicates.)
AF	*Vittorio Alfieri*
AG	*Auriga*
AI	*Ascari*
AL	*Aquilone* (2), *Aldebaran* (1)
AM	*Animoso*
AN	*Antares*
AO	*Airone, Arturo* (both 1)
AP	*Alpino*
AR	*Artigliere, Ardito* (both 1)
AS	*Aliseo*
AT	*Altair, Ardimentoso* (both 1)
AU	*Aretusa*
AV	*Aviere*
AZ	*Ardimentoso* (letters given when *Altair* was still afloat)
BA	*Comandante Baroni*
BG	*Bersagliere*
BL	*Balestra*
BO	*Baleno, Comandante Borsini* (both 1)
BR	*Borea* (2), *Bombardiere* (1)
BS	*Angelo Bassini*
BT	*Cesare Battisti*
C	initial letter for corvettes
C11	*Gabbiano*
C12	*Procellaria*
C13	*Cormorano*
C14	*Pellicano*
C15	*Cicogna*
C16	*Folaga*
C17	*Ibis*
C18	*Gru*
C19	*Antilope*
C20	*Gazzella*
C21	*Camoscio*
C22	*Capriolo*
C23	*Alce*
C24	*Renna*
C25	*Ape*
C26	*Vespa*
C27	*Lucciola*
C28	*Grillo*
C29	*Cicala*
C30	*Calabrone*
C31	*Cavalletta*
C32	*Libellula*
C33	*Scimitarra*
C34	*Baionetta* (former *Partigiana*)
C35	*Colubrina*
C36	*Spingarda*
C37	*Carabina*
C38	*Bombarda*
C39	*Artemide*
C40	*Persefone*
C41	*Euterpe*
C42	*Minerva*
C43	*Driade*
C44	*Danaide*
C45	*Pomona*
C46	*Folaga*
C47	*Sfinge*

C48	*Chimera*
C49	*Sibilla*
C50	*Fenice*
C51	*Tuffetto*
C52	*Marangone*
C53	*Strolaga*
C54	*Ardea*
C55	*Daino*
C56	*Cervo*
C57	*Stambecco*
C58	*Crisalide*
C59	*Farfalla*
C60	*Maggiolino*
C61	*Cocciniglia*
C62	*Scure*
C63	*Clava*
C64	*Zagaglia*
C65	*Urania*
C66	*Berenice*
C67	*Egeria*
C68	*Melpomene*
C69	*Tersicore*
C70	*Euridice*
CA	*Corsaro* (1), *Giacinto Carini* (3), *Canopo* (1)
CB	*Carabiniere*
CC	*Circe*
CD	*Giosuè Carducci* (1), *Castelfidardo* (2)
CE	*Generale Antonio Cantore* (3), *Climene* (1)
CF	*Confienza*
CG	*Cigno*
CH	*Generale Antonio Chinotto*
CI	*Generale Antonio Cascino* (3), *Calipso* (1), *Ciclone* (1)
CL	*Fratelli Cairoli* (3) *Clio* (1)
CM	*Calatafimi*
CN	*Camicia Nera, Comandante Casana* (both 1, and both intended to be afloat at the same time)
CO	*Centauro*
CP	*Calliope* (1) *Francesco Crispi* (2)
CR	*Francesco Crispi* again (2), *Corazziere* (later changed to CZ to avoid confusion with *Carrista*) and *Carrista* (both 1)
CS	*Enrico Cosenz* (3), *Cassiopea* (1)
CT	*Curtatone* (2), *Castore* (1)
CZ	*Corazziere* (later)
DA	*Dardo* (later)
DC	*Comandante De Cristofaro*
DG	*Daga*
DL	*Comandante Dell'Anno*
DM	*Alvise Da Mosto*
DN	*Antonio Da Noli*
DR	*Dardo* (1, earlier), *Nicoloso Da Recco* (2), *Dragone* (1)
DV	*Giovanni Da Verazzano*
DZ	*Giuseppe Dezza*
ED	*Eridano*
ER	*Euro*
ES	*Espero*
FA	*Comandante Fontana*
FB	*Nicola Fabrizi*
FC	*Fuciliere*
FG	*Folgore*
FI	*Fionda*
FL	*Fulmine*
FR	*Freccia*
FT	*Fortunale*
GB	*Vincenzo Gioberti*
GE	*Geniere*

GH	*Ghibli*
GL	*Gladio*
GN	*Granatiere*
GP	*Groppo*
GR	*Grecale*
GV	*Ernesto Giovannini*
ID	*Indomito*
IM	*Impavido*
IP	*Impetuoso*
IS	*Insidioso*
IT	*Intrepido*
LA	*Lubiana*
LB	*Libra*
LC	*Lince*
LE	*Leone*
LF	*Giuseppe La Farina*
LG	*Legionario*
LI	*Libeccio*
LM	*Giuseppe La Masa*
LN	*Lanciere, Lancia* (both 1)
LP	*Lampo* (1), *Lupo* (1, but in 1938 *Lupo* was relettered LU, to avoid confusion)
LR	*Lira*
LU	*Lupo*
MA	*Daniele Manin* (2), *Comandante Margottini* (1)
MB	*Monzambano*
MD	*Giacomo Medici*
MI	*Carlo Mirabello*
MN	*Generale Carlo Montanari*
MO	*Lanzerotto Malocello*
MS	*Giuseppe Missori* (3), *Monsone* (1)
MT	*Antonio Mosto* (3), *Mitragliere* (1)
NB	*Nembo*
NL	*Francesco Nullo*
OA	*Alfredo Oriani*
ON	*Orione*
OR	*Vincenzo Giordano Orsini*
OS	*Orsa*
OT	*Ostro*
PA	*Generale Achille Papa* (3), *Pantera* (2)
PC	*Polluce*
PD	*Pallade* (1), *Premuda* (2, but not actually used)

PG	*Pegaso*
PI	*Antonio Pigafetta*
PL	*Rosolino Pilo* (3), *Pleiadi* (1)
PN	*Leone Pancaldo* (2), *Partenope* (1)
PR	*Generale Marcello Prestinari* (3), *Procione* (1)
PS	*Perseo* (1), *Emanuele Pessagno* (2)
PT	*Palestro*
PU	*Pugnale* (1), *Premuda* (2)
RG	*Rigel*
RI	*Augusto Riboty*
RU	*Comandante Ruta*
SA	*Saetta*
SB	*Sebenico*
SC	*Scirocco*
SD	*Spada*
SE	*Quintino Sella*
SF	*Simone Schiaffino*
SG	*Sagittario*
SI	*Sirio*
SL	*Solferino*
SM	*San Martino*
SO	*Francesco Stocco*
SP	*Spica*
SQ	*Squadrista*
SR	*Giuseppe Sirtori* (3), *Stella Polare* (1)
ST	*Strale*
SU	*Nazario Sauro*
TA	*Luca Tarigo*
TB	*Turbine*
TF	*Tifone*
TI	*Tigre*
TO	*Comandante Toscano*
TU	*Stefano Turr*
UR	*Uragano*
US	*Antoniotto Usodimare*
VG	*Vega*
VI	*Ugolino Vivaldi*
VL	*Velite*
ZE	*Nicolò Zeno*
ZF	*Zeffiro*

Below: The cruiser *Abruzzi* at La Spezia, on 4 July 1942, at the end of an overhaul in dock to repair torpedo damage sustained in November 1941. The 'standard' scheme is similar, but not identical, on both sides; *Abruzzi* was one of the few surface combatants painted with this scheme, whose straight and rather simple bands were more widely used for auxiliaries and ships taken up from trade.
(E Bagnasco collection)

A well-known photograph of the battleship *Roma*, seen in Trieste harbour on 21 August 1942 at the beginning of her move to Taranto to complete crew training and fitting-out. 'Standard' camouflage scheme, with dark grey polygonal panels over light grey background; white areas would be overpainted with light grey by the end of the year. (E Bagnasco collection)

A detail of the destroyer *Lampo* manoeuvring in the port of Genoa in May 1942. Note the white areas on the funnel and on the bridge sides; the dark panels were much denser on the starboard side. (E Bagnasco collection)

The corvette *Driade* on 14 January 1943, painted in a typical late-war 'standard' camouflage pattern with no white areas on the bows and at the stern and dark grey polygonal panels. (Foto Mioni, Trieste)

The destroyer escort *Impavido* soon after her launch, at Cantieri del Tirreno – Riva Trigoso (near Genoa), on 24 February 1943. Note *Impavido*'s high freeboard, with camouflage also carried on areas that will be covered by anti-fouling painting and black boot-topping at the end of fitting-out. (G Parodi collection)

From December 1941, most Italian merchant ships were camouflaged according to regulations that established common schemes based on six or seven patterns. The tanker *Illiria* is shown in 1943 with a scheme known as '2B': notice the false funnel amidships, with the real funnel astern 'merged' in a temporary structure simulating an enlarged deckhouse. (Author's collection)

M/S *Calino* off Piraeus on 6 September 1942: the camouflage pattern is a very modified '3A' scheme for merchant ships, with white on the bows. The two other colours are the 'standard' dark and light grey. (A Fraccaroli photograph)

MAS 534 and *MAS 535* at Piraeus, Greece, on 11 December 1941. Both are painted in a non-standard medium grey; notice the red and white diagonal stripes on *534*'s forecastle. (A Fraccaroli photograph)

Italian submarines began to be painted according to precise regulations issued in early 1941, with upperworks in a very light blue-grey overall, with irregular splotches of 'greenish' dark brown on top. Initially, the shapes and forms of such splotches were left to the inventiveness of the dockyard workers, as shown in this picture of *Emo* at Souda Bay, Crete, in late summer of 1941: the splotches are rather small and with quite irregular contours. *Emo* is moored on the starboard side of the auxiliary cruiser *Barletta*. (Author's collection)

The destroyer *Velite* in April 1947, with dark grey hull sides, light grey superstructure and red identification letters. In 1948 *Velite* was transferred to France as reparations; the Marine Nationale renamed her *Duperrè* but decommissioned her in 1951, after only a few years of service. (E Bagnasco collection)

Allied schemes were maintained by Italian warships until 1947–8, when they started to be painted with pre-war light grey again. The battleship *Andrea Doria* is in the channel between Mar Piccolo and Mar Grande at Taranto in late 1947. (Foto de siati, Taranto)

The submarine *Asteria* at Monfalcone on 27 November 1941, a few weeks after her commissioning. Her camouflage pattern is the correct 'standard' scheme for submarines, with large, rounded 'greenish' dark brown splotches. (E Bagnasco collection)

CHAPTER 8

Flags

THE ITALIAN NATIONAL FLAG ('Il Tricolore') features three equally-sized vertical pales of green, white and red, with the green at the hoist side. Although this flag has only been in use in its current form since 19 June 1946, being formally adopted on 1 January 1948, the three colours were earlier used in revolutionary flags of the late eighteenth century, and the official use of the Tricolore dates back to the reign of Piedmont and Sardinia from 1848.

The first state to use a white, red and green flag was the Cispadane Republic of 1797, established in Northern Italy after Napoleon's first Italian campaign. During this period, several Jacobin-inspired republics supplanted former Italian absolute principalities, and almost all of them used flags with three bands of equal size (green, white and red from hoist outwards), clearly inspired by the French revolutionary flag of 1790. However, the Cispadane Republic's flag also referenced the colours of the flag of the City of Milan (red and white) and green was the main colour of the uniforms of Milan's Civic Guard.

It was during the period of the unification of Italy (less Venice, Rome, Trento and Trieste which joined the Kingdom of Italy later, between 1866 and 1918) from 1848 to 1861, known as the 'Risorgimento' ('resurgence') when the Tricolore

became the flag that symbolized the efforts of the whole Italian people towards freedom and independence.

The Tricolore, with the coat of arms of the House of Savoy in the white field, enclosed in a 'Samnite shield' with blue borders. was first adopted as the battle flag of the Kingdom of Piedmont and Sardinia in 1848, at the beginning of the first Italian War of Independence. In fact, King Carlo Alberto declared that '... In order to show more clearly with exterior signs the commitment to Italian unification, we want that our troops ... have the Savoia shield placed on the Italian tricolour flag.' In the same year, the Grand Duchy of Tuscany promulgated a constitution and discontinued the use of the Austrian flag (with the superimposed Austria-Lorraine coat of arms), adopting the Italian tricolour; in 1859 the Grand Duchy joined the Duchies of Modena and Parma to form the United Provinces of Central Italy, whose flag was again a tricolour Italian flag, with no emblems, until it was annexed to the Kingdom of Piedmont and Sardinia the following year.

In 1848, a rebellion broke out in the Austrian-ruled possessions of Lombardy and the Veneto, and provisional governments were established in Milan and Venice; tricolour flags were used until 6 and 24 August 1849 respectively, when Austrian

troops re-established Habsburg rule. In 1849, the new Roman republic adopted the Italian Tricolore bearing the legend 'Dio e Popolo' ('God and People') in the white pale. This flag was in use for four months only, during which the Papal State was in abeyance.

In the meanwhile, the Tricolore with the Savoy arms had been adopted as the state flag and merchant marine flag of the Kingdom of Piedmont and Sardinia; in the naval flag, the coat of arms was surmounted by a crown. On 15 April 1861 these flags became respectively the state (and merchant marine as well) and the naval flag of the Kingdom of Italy – established by a decree of the Turin parliament on 17 March – and remained in use until 2 June 1946, when the results of a referendum led to the birth of the Italian Republic.

The naval jack was instituted by royal decree on 22 April 1879, to be hoisted at the bowsprit of

The 'Bandiera di Combattimento' ('Battle Flag') of the battleship *Vittorio Veneto* in wartime, flying from the mainmast gaff. The 'Bandiera di Combattimento' is a naval ensign, usually woven from fine fabric, that is donated to a ship soon after her commissioning by a Veterans' association, a city council or a body otherwise affiliated to the ship. The 'Battle Flag' is hoisted only when action is imminent and, if possible, should be saved in the event of the ship's sinking. (E Bagnasco collection)

The flag of the Regia Marina, as used on Italian naval vessels from 15 April 1861 until 2 June 1946, in a photograph from the 1930s. (Author's collection)

every ship at anchor; use of the naval jack at sea was allowed only if the ship was fully dressed. The naval jack was of squared design, being based on the coat of arms of the House of Savoy (a white cross on a red field with a blue border), and, as with the national and naval flags, remained in use until 2 June 1946.

In 1889, a Royal Decree of December provided 'rank flags' for admirals: several of these flags were issued, all blue and rectangular, with varying numbers of six-pointed yellow stars disposed diagonally, according to the rank of the admiral to which they referred. With the 1926 revision of the highest ranks of the Italian armed forces, new 'rank flags' were issued – now with five-pointed stars, in the by-now usual diagonal disposition:

• Grande Ammiraglio (Admiral of the Fleet): four stars.
• Ammiraglio d'Armata e Designato d'Armata (Admiral): three stars.
• Ammiraglio di Squadra e Ammiraglio di Divisione (Vice Admiral and Rear Admiral): two stars.
• Contrammiraglio (Commodore): one star.

The difference between Ammiraglio di Squadra and Ammiraglio di Divisione was shown by the flag's position: hoisted at the mainmast for the first, and at the foremast for the second (a complete chart showing the flags' position is on page XIV of the colour section).

The 1861 naval flag and jack, and the 'rank flags' for admirals, were thus used by Regia Marina ships between 1940 and 1945. Along with these flags, others were used: a 'masthead pennant' ('Fiamma' in Italian) to be hoisted by all ships whose CO is a commissioned officer, a 'Royal Standard' to be hoisted when the King boarded a ship (squared blue flag, with a black eagle inscribed in a golden rosette, and the coat of arms of Savoy at the centre) and – between 1927 and 1943 – the 'Prime Ministerial Flag'. This flag (dark blue, rectangular, with a golden 'Fascio Littorio' at the centre inscribed in a golden border) was hoisted when Mussolini officially visited a ship or when he boarded a naval vessel taking part in a naval review. Another specific flag was used by the Capo di Stato Maggiore della Marina: this was dark blue, of rectangular form, with three yellow stars disposed diagonally inscribed in a golden border.

Between 1943 and 1945 the Repubblica Sociale Italiana (RSI) in Northern Italy adopted the 'plain' Tricolore with no emblems in the white pale, but the RSI's war flag – and the flag of its small navy – had an eagle in the centre, with outspread wings and holding a 'Fascio Littorio' in its claws.

In 1923, specific pennants for the leaders of destroyer, torpedo boat, motor torpedo boat and submarine flotillas were established. The commanding officer of a destroyer or torpedo boat flotilla hoisted a triangular pennant – with alternate red and blue diagonal stripes – at the starboard outer halyard of the fore mast; the pennant of a submarine flotilla commander was

The cruisers *Trento* (left) and *Trieste* moored at Naples in spring 1940. The Italian naval flag is flying at the ensign staff of *Trieste*; the four flags of the International Code of Signals at her mainmast's port halyard spell 'ICJU', probably her radio call sign. (E Bagnasco collection)

The Italian naval jack from 1861 to 1946 was the coat of arms of the House of Savoia – a white cross on a red background – with a blue border. The naval jacks of the four destroyers of the 10th Destroyer Flotilla (10ª Squadriglia Cacciatorpediniere), at Genoa in late May 1938. From top to bottom: *Maestrale*, *Grecale*, *Scirocco* and *Libeccio*. (Author's collection)

The destroyer *Leone Pancaldo* moored at Gaeta in April 1943; the naval flag can clearly be seen on the mainmast.
Note the Ec3 ter 'Gufo' radar atop the wheelhouse. (E Bagnasco collection)

triangular and red overall, while a motor torpedo boat flotilla commander hoisted a triangular pennant, with five horizontal sectors – red, white, blue, white and red respectively from top to bottom.

With the proclamation of the Italian Republic, royal emblems were removed from all Italian flags and initially the naval flag and jack were a simple Tricolore. A decree issued by the Italian President on 9 November 1947 established new naval flags (still in use today), using the Italian Navy's coat of arms, that had already been proposed and adopted between 1939 and 1940, 'purged' of the fascist and royal features originally provided. This is a 'Samnite shield' with the emblems of the four most important Italian Maritime Republics of the Middle Ages inscribed in a stylized rope: in more detail – clockwise from upper left – Venice, Genoa, Amalfi and Pisa may be found (see drawing on page XIV of the colour section); the shield has a 'rammed' crown superimposed, i.e. a crown of Roman inspiration, with towers on the top, two rams of Roman galleys at the sides and an anchor in front. The coat of arms itself, now square and with no border or crown, was adopted as the naval jack, and both flags officially entered into use on 1 January 1948.

Finally, it must be pointed out that the same decree of 9 November 1947 also established the merchant marine flag. This flag has no 'rammed crown' and – in its Maritime Republics coat of arms – Venice's Leone di San Marco has his right foreleg on an open Gospel. The coat of arms in the current Italian naval flag is slightly different, as Leone di San Marco holds a sword with his right foreleg and the Gospel is not present.

Below: The 'Bandiera di Combattimento' of the battleship *Giulio Cesare*, on 16/17 December 1941 during the First Battle of Sirte. Note the initials 'SPQR' near the left edge of the green pale, standing for the well-known Latin phrase 'Senatus Populusque Romanus' ('The Senate and the People of Rome'), associating the ship with the ancient Rome of her namesake, Julius Caesar. However, it must be pointed out that no lettering was (nor is) officially allowed for use on Italian naval flags, so the presence of this acronym is possibly the idea of the crew – certainly not authorised but allowed by the ship's Commanding Officer. (P Solimano collection, via 'Società Capitani e Macchinisti Navali', Camogli [Genova])

Above: The launch of the destroyer *Granatiere* (of the 'Soldati' class) at Cantieri Navali Riuniti's Palermo yard, on 1 February 1939. Note the merchant marine flag (the Italian *tricolore* with the Savoy coat of arms, but no crown), as the ship has not yet been commissioned into naval service. (Author's collection)

Left: The light cruisers *Montecuccoli* and *Garibaldi* at Naples in late 1946. Note that the naval ensign (as well as the naval jack at the bow, not visible in this photograph) is now a plain Italian Tricolore, as the Savoy coat of arms was removed from the naval ensign (and the jack itself changed) soon after 2 June 1946, with the proclamation of the Italian Republic. These 'simplified' naval flags remained in use until 9 November 1947, when a decree issued by the Italian President established the new naval ensign and jack, which officially went into use from 1 January 1948. (S Cioglia collection)

CHAPTER 9

Uniforms, Ranks, Insignia and Decorations

The uniforms of the officers and ratings of the Regia Marina in the Second World War were the results of regulations issued on 1 February 1936 which modified items in use since the First World War or the 1920s.

Uniforms

Winter service dress for officers and petty officers consisted of a dark blue jacket and trousers; the jacket had two vertical rows of three golden buttons, with an anchor and a crown in relief on each button. The peaked cap had a blue cover in winter, and a gold badge on the front with an anchor encircled by laurel leaves and a superimposed crown; in spring and summer, when the dark blue service dress was still in use, the blue cap cover could be replaced by a white one. In addition to the peaked cap, there was a blue 'field cap' (berretto da navigazione) with matching cloth peak and, on the right side (according to the original 1938 regulations), rank badges similar to those worn on the cuffs, but smaller. For summer dress in home waters, the white cap cover was worn, along with a breasted white tunic with stand-up collar and fly front, with white lace on the collar, front, skirt and pocket openings, and on the cuffs (the white tunic for

petty officers, on the other hand, had open patch pockets). It was worn with blue shoulder straps for rank badges, blue trousers and black shoes; although in particularly hot climates white trousers and white canvas shoes were worn.

Ratings' winter full dress consisted of a blue sweater (replaced by a white T-shirt at the end of winter and in spring), blue trousers, and a blue jumper with mid-blue collar edged with two white stripes and two five-pointed stars on the lower side; a black scarf and a white lanyard were worn under the collar, knotted on the front. Shoes were black and the cap cover blue: the blue sailor's cap had a black silk ribbon with the name of his installation or ship in yellow or gold block letters, and the ship's name was preceded by 'R.N.', i.e. 'Regia Nave' (the equivalent of 'HMS' for the Royal Navy). For security purposes, in wartime the ship name was in most cases replaced by the words 'Regia Marina' in the same style. In summer, the blue jumper and cap were replaced by white items of similar design, all other uniform elements remaining the same. The basic winter working dress for ratings was a blue jumper and trousers, with a similarly dark blue beret (basco); in summer, the blue jumper was replaced by a white T-shirt, and the beret by a classic white canvas working cap, quite similar to that worn by USN ratings at the time; trousers were often grey or in a shade of lighter blue.

In winter, a double-breasted pea coat with two rows of three brass buttons was issued to ratings, while officers and petty officers wore a longer overcoat with similar buttons; working dress for officers and petty officers was of various types and sizes, the most common being a white overall with pockets on the sides. Battle dress was – for both ratings and higher ranks – similar to the working dress, with the addition of a steel helmet with a yellow crowned anchor painted on the front.

During the war – in the Mediterranean and in the tropics as well – many officers adopted a khaki drill jacket with four pockets on the front (two on the breast and two lower down) and a single row of three buttons. Submarine crew often wore

One Guardiamarina (left) and two Sottotenenti di Vascello aboard the battleship *Cesare* in winter 1940/41. Note that the officers on the left and right wear the light blue sash indicating that they are acting as Ufficiale di Guardia. Because of their age, it is likely they are Ufficiali di Complemento, i.e. recalled reservists. (Author's collection)

Submarine crew on parade in winter 1940/41: from left to right, officers, petty officers and ratings can be seen, all wearing their corresponding winter dress. Note that the three officers wear a light blue sash obliquely on the jacket, a distinctive indication of their rank during official ceremonies or when acting as Ufficiale di Guardia (Officer of the Deck). (Author's collection)

Two officers of a MAS Flotilla in a small port in the Dodecanese in summer 1940. The Guardiamarina (equivalent to the USN rank of Ensign) on the left is wearing the khaki drill jacket issued since the beginning of the war; the officer on the right – probably a *Sottotenente di Vascello* (Lt.jg. in the USN) – has a white version of the same jacket. (A Petrina collection)

specific, warm clothing (sometimes of German origin) such as leather jackets, 'turtleneck' sweaters, leather boots etc.

Following the Armistice, officers and petty officers of the co-belligerent Navy often adopted Allied uniforms and other clothing, while ratings in most cases kept their pre-September 1943 uniforms. At the same time several changes were made to the uniforms of the RSI Navy. In particular, the crown on the cap badge was replaced by a winged eagle, and the five pointed stars on the ends of the collar (that since Italian unification, and still today, for all the members of the Italian Armed Forces indicate the military

Taranto, 25 June 1942: Mussolini, along with admirals Arturo Riccardi and Angelo Iachino, reviewing the crew of the battleship *Littorio*. The service dress for officers, petty officers and ratings is the usual summer dress, with blue trousers, white jacket or jumper and white cap covers. Mussolini is wearing the uniform of 'Primo Caporale d'Onore della Milizia', an honorary rank indicating his position of chief of the 'Milizia Volontaria Sicurezza Nazionale – MVSN', the Fascist Party's paramilitary organisation (notice Aldo Vidussoni, Secretary of the Fascist Party, with black jacket and grey breeches). It is also interesting to note that – in spite of the time of year and the temperature – the petty officer partially visible on the left is wearing the winter service dress with white peaked hat cover. (Istituto Luce, Rome)

Regia Marina	Royal Navy	US Navy
Flag officer		
Grande Ammiraglio	Admiral of the Fleet	Fleet Admiral
Ammiraglio d'Armata	Admiral	Admiral
Ammiraglio designato d'Armata	No corresponding rank	No corresponding rank
Ammiraglio di Squadra	Vice Admiral	Vice Admiral
Ammiraglio di Divisione	Rear Admiral	Rear Admiral (upper half)
Contrammiraglio	Commodore	Rear Admiral (lower half)
Line officers, upper half		
Capitano di Vascello	Captain	Captain
Capitano di Fregata	Commander	Commander
Capitano di Corvetta	Lieutenant Commander	Lieutenant Commander
Line officers, lower half		
Tenente di Vascello	Lieutenant	Lieutenant
Sottotenente di Vascello	No corresponding rank	Lieutenant, junior grade
Guardiamarina	Sub-Lieutenant	Ensign
Aspirante Guardiamarina	Midshipman	Midshipman
Petty officers, upper half		
Capo di 1ª Classe (Chief petty officer, 1st Class)		
Capo di 2ª Classe (Chief petty officer, 2nd Class)		
Capo di 3ª Classe (Chief petty officer, 3rd Class)		
Petty officers, lower half		
2° Capo (2nd Chief – Petty officer, lower half)		
Sergente (Sergeant)		
Ratings		
Sottocapo (Leading seaman)		
Comune di 1ª Classe (1st class seaman)		
Comune di 2ª Classe (2nd class seaman		

condition of those wearing them), were replaced by a 'gladio', i.e. the Roman short sword. Minor changes affected rank badges and lace rings on caps; the traditional sailor's hat was replaced by a blue beret, with a small metal anchor on the front.

Men of the Reggimento San Marco (the naval infantry) mostly wore Army service dress, with naval cap and cuff badges; in North Africa, khaki drill berets and dress replaced the former items, and, after September 1943, men of the Xª Flottiglia MAS of the RSI received a special dark green uniform, with a green beret and jacket with a single row of four buttons on the front.

Ranks and Insignia

Ranks were as shown in the list above (for flag and line officers the corresponding Royal Navy and US Navy ranks are indicated).

Ranks were indicated by red inverted chevrons for ratings and by gold ones for Sergente and 2° Capo; petty officers had from one to three gold lace stripes on the jacket's *passants* and on the shoulder straps.

Lower half officers had one to three medium gold lace stripes with a curl (colloquially known as 'giro di bitta') on the top one, either on the cuffs and field cap's sides; one to three medium gold lace rings were on the peaked cap band, and one to three five-pointed gold stars with a gold crown

were on the shoulder straps.

Similarly, upper half officers had one wide and from one to three medium gold lace stripes with a curl on the top one on the cuffs and field cap's sides; the peaked cap band had one medium and from one to three smaller lace rings, and the shoulder straps were edged with gold.

Flag officers' rank had a gold-embroidered 'Greca' (a 'Greek key' design), with one to four gold-embroidered lace stripes above, with a curl on the top one; the peaked cap band conformed accordingly and shoulder straps were gold laced, with a gold embroidered crown and one to four five-pointed golden stars.

Only line officers were known by naval ranks and wore the curl on the rank distinction lace; the officers of the other corps were known by Army-style ranks and used different colours in the centre of the cap badge and as backing of the cap rings and cuff stripes; at the centre of the cap badge a different item for each service branch was superimposed on the anchor. Commissioned warrant officers (Corpo Reale Equipaggi Marittimi – CREM) had neither curl nor coloured rank backing, but a metal badge showing the branch they belonged to before receiving their commission.

The above items are summarised in the table below:

The red branch badges for ratings (more than forty different specialisations, varying from quartermasters to gunners, from divers to signalmen, from carpenters to musicians just to mention some of them) were worn above rank

Branch	Colour	Badge
Line	Uniform cloth	Anchor
Aides to Flag Officers	Uniform cloth	Five pointed star inside curl
Genio Navale (Construction)	Dark red	Helmet on crossed hammer and axe
Armi Navali (Ordnance)	Brown	Sword
Corpo Medico (Medicine)	Turquoise	Geneva cross
Farmacisti (Pharmacists)	Green	Æsculapius staff
Commissariato (Supply Corps)	Scarlet	Five pointed star
Capitanerie di Porto (Port Captaincy)	Grey-green	Fouled anchor
Cappellani (Chaplaincy)	Purple	Gold cross

chevrons; petty officers' branch badges were the same as those of ratings, but golden instead of red and were worn above the Sergente and 2° Capo's chevrons or on the jacket cuffs for petty officers. Naval pilots and observers wore gilt metal wings; crews of submarines were authorised to place a circular gilt metal badge – with a dolphin inside and the word 'Sommergibili' – above the medal ribbons on the left breast.

Decorations

Italy's most important medals were (and still are) the following:

- Medaglia d'Oro al Valor Militare (Golden Medal for Valour, equivalent to the British Victoria Cross or the US Medal of Honor).
- Medaglia d'Argento al Valor Militare (Silver Medal for Valour).
- Medaglia di Bronzo al Valor Militare (Bronze Medal for Valour).

Only 121 Medaglia d'Oro al Valor Militare were awarded to naval personnel during the Second World War, several posthumously; the Silver and Bronze Medals were more numerous, with several hundred awarded between 1940 and 1943.

The Croce di Guerra al Valor Militare is the lesser decoration awarded for a single action and, also in this case, was awarded in great numbers; it is to be distinguished from the Croce al Merito di Guerra, that is not awarded for a single specific action, but is intended as a recognition for prolonged war service.

The working dress for officers and petty officers was an overall (with two pockets on the breast), usually white or grey, as in the case of this Sottotenente di Vascello aboard a '600' class submarine in summer 1941. (Author's collection)

Below: A detail of the stern of the avviso scorta (destroyer escort) *Ciclone* in summer 1942. The officers on the right are in the normal summer service dress, while the crewmen lined up on the main deck and atop the deckhouse in front of the gun have the white T-shirt and grey trousers of the ratings' summer working dress; nevertheless, they don't wear the white canvas hat usually seen with the working dress, but the white summer full dress cap: this was usually worn during moorings and other operations in important naval bases or in the presence of admirals or other high-ranking officials. The life jacket was usually khaki or grey. (E Bagnasco collection)

Below: Deck crew of the battleship *Vittorio Veneto* at work on the forecastle in June 1940, with the *Littorio* and a *Cesare* class battleship in background. The ratings wear summer working dress, with white canvas hat, T-shirt and grey trousers. (E Bagnasco collection)

Two gunners aboard a cruiser early in the war, showing the two versions of summer working dress: the white T-shirt with light grey trousers (left), and the light grey working jumper and trousers (right). Both men are wearing the white canvas hat. (Istituto Luce, Rome)

LUCE

CHAPTER 10

'Who's Who' of the Italian Navy in the Second World War

THIS LIST IS MADE up of short biographical notes on the most important figures of the Regia Marina from 1930 to 1945, with a particular emphasis on those who played specific roles in the Second World War and who, in many cases, are cited in the book.

The list is divided into two groups, the first for flag officers and the second for line officers, petty officers or ratings; as most were recipients of the Medaglia d'Oro al Valor Militare, this is indicated by one asterisk (⋆) when the decoration was awarded when the recipient was still alive or by two (⋆⋆) when the award was posthumous.

Flag Officers

Carlo BERGAMINI (⋆⋆) (1888–1943) – Served in the war against Turkey and in the First World War aboard the battleship *Regina Elena*, the cruiser *Vettor Pisani* and the armoured cruiser *Pisa*. As a Captain, was the commander of the cruisers *Bande Nere* and *Duca d'Aosta* in 1934–6; later (1937) he served in the Regia Marina's Naval Weapons Directorate. During the Second World War commanded the 4ª, 5ª and 9ª Divisioni Navali and was appointed commander of the Forze Navali on 5 April 1943. He died, along with all his staff, in the sinking of the battleship *Roma* off Asinara Island, on 9 September 1943.

Luigi BIANCHERI (1891–early 1950s) – Fought in 1912 against Turkey and in the First World War. At the beginning of the Second World War he was the CinC of the Naval Command in the Dodecanese and was in direct charge of the defence of Castelrosso; later, he commanded the 12ª Divisione Navale and the 8ª Divisione Navale.

Bruno BRIVONESI (1886–1970) – He was one of the first Italian naval pilots and flew both aircraft and airships in Libya during the war against Turkey and later in the Adriatic in the First World War. His assignments in the 1930s include the command of the scout *Zeno*, a liaison post at Regia Aeronautica headquarters and the naval command in Libya, held from the late 1930s until early 1941, when he was appointed commander of the 3ª Divisione Navale. The destruction, in November 1941, of the 'Duisburg' convoy (escorted by the 3ª Divisione) led to his removal from this post; later, Adm. Brivonesi was CinC of the Sardinian Naval command ('Marisardegna') and retired in 1946.

Inigo CAMPIONI (⋆⋆) (1878–1944) – Until 9 December 1940 Ammiraglio di Squadra Campioni commanded the Squadra Navale and was aboard the battleship *Cesare* at the Battle of Punta Stilo on 9 July 1940. His partial responsibility for the Regia Marina's failures in the early months of the war led to his removal on 9 December 1940, being replaced by Adm. Iachino. Later, he was appointed Governor of the Dodecanese and, after 8 September 1943, having decided not to co-operate with the Germans and the RSI government, was arrested, tried for treason and executed at Parma along with Adm. Mascherpa and others on 24 May 1944.

Carlo CATTANEO (⋆⋆) (1883–1941) – Served in the war against Turkey and in the First World War, being awarded several decorations. As a Captain, between 1933 and 1935 was the CO of the light cruiser *Alberto di Giussano* and – as a Contrammiraglio – commanded the 3ª Divisione Navale (flying his flag in the heavy cruiser *Trento*) at the Battle of Punta Stilo. In December 1941 Adm. Cattaneo became the commander of the 1ª Divisione Navale and was killed in action aboard the heavy cruiser *Zara* at the Battle of Cape Matapan, on the night of 28/29 March 1941.

Domenico CAVAGNARI (1876–1966) – Served in the war against Turkey and in the First World War in the Adriatic. In 1929–32 commanded the Naval Academy at Leghorn and in 1934 was appointed Capo di Stato Maggiore della Marina, also acting as Sottosegretario di Stato per la Marina with the rank of Ammiraglio d'Armata. He held this post until 8 December 1940 when, following the first failures of Regia Marina operations, he resigned and was replaced by Adm. Arturo Riccardi.

Alberto DA ZARA (1889–1951) – Joined the Navy in 1907 and, during the First World War, served aboard the destroyer *Ippolito Nievo*. Promoted to Captain in 1933, he was the first CO of the new cruiser *Duca d'Aosta* and, in 1937, was appointed CO of the similar *Raimondo Montecuccoli*. Promoted to Contrammiraglio (equivalent to the USN Rear Admiral, lower half) in January 1939 and Ammiraglio di Divisione (Rear Admiral, upper half) shortly after, became the commander of the 7ª Divisione Navale (the cruisers *Montecuccoli*, *Eugenio*, *Aosta* and *Attendolo*) on 5 March 1942, fighting at Pantelleria ('Mezzo giugno') and at 'Mezzo agosto'. From 1 August 1943 commanded the 5ª Divisione Navale and on 11 September 1943, he became CinC of the Italian battle fleet, at Malta, after Adm. Bergamini's death. Da Zara retired in 1946 and, before his death five years later, wrote the famed memoir *Pelle d'ammiraglio*.

Raffaele DE COURTEN (1888–1978) – As with most Italian admirals of this period, he attended the Naval Academy in the first decade of the twentieth

Ammiraglio di Squadra (Vice Admiral) Inigo Campioni aboard the battleship *Cesare* at the battle of Punta Stilo, 9 July 1940. (Ufficio Storico della Marina Militare)

Taranto, 21 June 1942. Aboard the battleship *Littorio*, Mussolini reviewing the ship's crew, followed – from left to right – by Aldo Vidussoni (Secretary of the Partito Nazionale Fascista), by Adm. Arturo Riccardi (Capo di Stato Maggiore della Regia Marina) and by Adm. Angelo Iachino (CinC of the Squadra Navale). (Istituto Luce, Rome)

June 1946 and retired to Buenos Aires, where he died in 1948.

Mario FALANGOLA (1880–1967) – As a Lieutenant, was the CO of the submarine *F.7* during the First World War; in 1935 was among the first Italian flag officers to back the development of the new underwater assault craft. Vice Admiral from 1939, Falangola was the CinC of the Regia Marina's submarine force (Squadra Sommergibili) as of 10 June 1940, a post held until the end of 1941, when he became the CinC of the Port Captaincy Corps. After the Armistice, Adm. Falangola joined the Repubblica Sociale Italiana in northern Italy, later becoming the president of the RSI's Consiglio Superiore di Marina. For his involvement with the RSI, Adm. Falangola was tried for collaboration after the war.

Emilio FERRERI (1894–1981) – As a Captain, was the Naval attaché at the Italian embassy in France in the mid-1930s and, at the beginning of the war, was appointed to the Ufficio Traffico Oltremare ('Overseas Shipping Office') at Supermarina. During the war was promoted to Contrammiraglio and Ammiraglio di Divisione and, after the Armistice, Ferreri co-ordinated the resistance by the naval personnel to the German occupation of the Italian capital. After the war, with the rank of Vice-Admiral, he held the post of Capo di Stato Maggiore della Marina Militare from 4 November 1948 until 10 August 1955, playing a fundamental role in the Italian Navy's post-war reconstruction.

century and fought in the 1911–12 war against Turkey and in the First World War. From 1933 to 1936 De Courten was Naval attaché at the Italian embassy in Germany and between 1941 and early 1942 was the commander of the 7ª Divisione Navale and, later, of the 8ª. After the fall of the Fascist regime, on 27 July 1943 he was appointed Minister of the Navy in the newly-established Badoglio government and two days later Capo di Stato Maggiore della Regia Marina with the rank of Ammiraglio di Squadra. De Courten distinguished himself in the difficult task of leading the Italian Navy in the eventful co-belligerancy period and in the immediate post-war months but, disagreeing with the conditions imposed on the Italian Navy by the peace treaty, resigned from his post on 31 December 1946.

Aimone DI SAVOIA-AOSTA (1900–48) – Ensign in 1916 and LtCdr. in 1933, he organised scientific expeditions; later (1935), as a Captain was the commander of the Italian destroyers in the Red Sea. After marrying Princess Irene of Greece in 1939, was appointed King of Croatia on 18 May 1941 but, after disagreements with the

Croatian Nationalist Party, he never exercised his royal powers and abdicated in October 1943. After unsuccessful attempts to obtain a peace agreement with the Allies, Adm. Aimone di Savoia-Aosta commanded the naval base at Taranto in the last months of the Second World War. He left Italy after the proclamation of the Italian Republic on 2

Bordeaux, 5 October 1940. From left to right: LtCdr. Aldo Enrici (CO of the submarine *Faà di Bruno*), an unidentified LtCdr., LtCdr Mario Leoni (CO of the *Malaspina*), Rear Admiral Angelo Parona (commander of the Italian submarines in the Atlantic) and Cdr. Aldo Cocchia, then commanding officer of the *Torelli* and a future chief of staff of 'Betasom'. (E Bagnasco collection)

Ammiraglio di Squadra Carlo Bergamini, who died in the explosion of the battleship *Roma* on 9 September 1943. (Ufficio Storico della Marina Militare)

Antonio LEGNANI (1888–1943) – After fighting in the war against Turkey and in the Regia Marina's submarine arm in the First World War, as a Captain was the CO of the cruiser *Pola* during the Spanish Civil War. As a Rear Admiral, commanded the 8ᵃ Divisione Navale in the clash off Gaudo and – by the end of 1941 until the Armistice – was the CinC of the Regia Marina's submarine force (Squadra Sommergibili). Adm. Legnani joined the RSI, accepting the post of Sottosegretario alla Marina, but soon after (October 1943) died in a car-crash near Vicenza.

Francesco MAUGERI (1898–1978) – Promoted to Captain in 1937, commanded the cruisers *Bande Nere* and *Bolzano* and took part in the battle of Punta Stilo. Contrammiraglio in 1941, served on the staff of the Stato Maggiore della Regia Marina, with special responsibility for naval intelligence and covert operations, particularly in Rome during the German occupation. In early 1945 Maugeri was promoted to Rear Admiral (Ammiraglio di Divisione) and commanded the northern Tyrrhenian naval department in the first post-war years and – as Vice-Admiral – relieved Admiral De Courten as Capo di Stato Maggiore della Marina, holding the post from 1 January 1947 until 4 November 1948 and retiring in 1955.

Angelo PARONA (1889 – late 1960s) – Almost his entire naval career was spent in the Navy's submarine arm, beginning with operations in the Adriatic during the First World War. He was the first CinC of the Italian submarine force in the Atlantic, operating from the 'Betasom' base of Bordeaux, then commanded the 3ᵃ Divisione Navale at the Battle of 'Mezzo giugno' and later the 7ᵃ Divisione Navale. He retired from active service in 1951, with the rank of Vice Admiral.

Admiral Alberto Da Zara (right), with Admiral Andrew Cunningham at Malta on 11 September 1943, at the end of the talks that led to the agreement between the Regia Marina and the Allies on the disarming and internment at Malta of the Italian warships, following the Armistice of 8 September. (E Bagnasco collection)

Giuseppe FIORAVANZO (1891–1975) – As an Ensign, served in the war against Turkey in 1912 and, as a Captain, was CO of the light cruiser *Armando Diaz* in 1936. As a Rear Admiral, he oversaw the preparations for 'Operation C3' (the projected landings on Malta), in March 1943 became the commander of the 8ᵃ Divisione Navale and on 8 September 1943 he was the CinC of the Taranto Naval command. Between 1950 and 1959 (and from 1953 as a Vice Admiral), Giuseppe Fioravanzo was the head of the Ufficio Storico della Marina Militare – USMM, the Italian Navy's Historical Dept. He may be considered one of the most prominent Italian writers and researchers in the naval field for the 1920s–1940s period.

Angelo IACHINO (1889–1976) – Sometimes also referred to as 'Jachino', was a Lieutenant in the First World War and commanded the gunboat *Ermanno Carlotto* in Chinese waters and the light cruiser *Armando Diaz* in the 1930s. Vice Admiral in September 1939, Iachino commanded the 2ᵃ Squadra at the Battle of Cape Teulada on 27 November 1940 and, on 9 December, replaced Adm. Campioni's post as CinC of the Squadra Navale, bringing Italian warships into action at the Battles of Matapan and First and Second Sirte. In early April 1943 (in the meantime promoted to Ammiraglio designato d'Armata) was relieved by Adm. Bergamini; in 1954, having attained three-star rank, retired from active service. Later, he wrote several famous books on the Italian naval involvement in the Second World War and, before his death he donated to the township of Taranto the monument dedicated to all Italian sailors, located on the eastern side of the 'Canale Navigabile'.

Adm. Raffaele De Courten, Capo di Stato Maggiore of the Italian Navy from 29 July 1943 until 31 December 1946. (*LIFE*)

Umberto PUGLIESE (1880–1961) – Appointed as an Ensign in 1898, in 1901 took his degree in naval engineering at the Scuola Superiore Navale of Genoa and, the following year, joined the Genio Navale. From 1925 to 1931 he was the director of the Royal Naval Yard of Castellammare di Stabia (Naples) and later, at La Spezia was in charge of the fitting-out of the cruisers *Zara* and *Armando Diaz*. Promoted to the rank of General, Pugliese drafted the design of the *Montecuccoli* and *Duca d'Aosta* class cruisers and of the *Littorio* class battleships, for which last vessels he devised an innovative underwater protection system. Because of his Jewish origins, Pugliese was discharged from the Regia Marina in 1938 but, in November 1940, was hastily recalled to duty to oversee the refloating of and repairs to the battleships damaged at Taranto by the British torpedo bombers attack on the 11th of that month. He finally left the Navy in January 1945 and after the war was the Director of the National Institute for Studies and Experiences on Naval Architecture until 1961.

Arturo RICCARDI (1878–1966) – After a brilliant career between the early 1900s and the late 1930s, in February 1938 became the commander of the 1ª Squadra Navale and, after the first six months of the war (having been nominated in the meanwhile a Senator of the Kingdom), on 8 December 1940 was nominated Sottosegretario di Stato per la Marina and Capo di Stato Maggiore della Marina as well, cultivating strong political relationships in the meanwhile. Ammiraglio d'Armata (Admiral) Riccardi was relieved by Adm. De Courten as CinC of the Regia Marina on 27 July 1943.

Luigi SANSONETTI (1888–1959) – Adm. Sansonetti commanded the 7ª Divisione Navale early in the war and the 3ª Divisione Navale in Operation 'Gaudo' and at Matapan. Later he was appointed Vice CinC of the naval staff (Sottocapo di Stato Maggiore della Regia Marina) and maintained the organisation of the Navy's command in Rome soon after the Armistice, later reaching the co-belligerent naval forces in southern Italy and leaving active service in 1951.

Vittorio TUR (1882–1969) – Fought in Libya during the war against Turkey, and in the First World War was with the naval infantry on the River Piave. He was the commander of the 7ª Divisione Navale in the late 1930s and during the war of the Forza Navale Speciale initially formed for the invasion of Malta, and of the Comando in Capo del Dipartimento del Basso Tirreno, with headquarters at Naples. Adm. Tur retired from active service in 1945.

Other Personnel

Mario ARILLO (*) (1912–2000) – As a Lieutenant, was the CO of the submarines *Fieramosca* and *Ambra* and, with this second boat (in the rank of LtCdr.), accomplished important missions transporting underwater assault craft and 'Gamma' divers, the most important being the attack on the port of Algiers in December 1942. After the Armistice, joined the RSI Navy and after the war was promoted to the ranks of Captain and Vice Admiral in the naval reserve.

Gino BIRINDELLI (*) (1911–2008) – Trained as an underwater operator of the Xª Flottiglia MAS, took part in an ill-fated action against enemy warships at Gibraltar ('BG2') on the night of 30 October 1940, being taken prisoner. He returned to active service following the Armistice and served for many years after the war: as a Captain, was CO of the cruiser *Montecuccoli* during the ship's cruise around the world in 1956–7, his last appointments, with the rank of Vice Admiral, being those of CinC of the Squadra Navale and Allied Naval Commander for southern Europe until his retirement, in 1973.

Junio Valerio BORGHESE (*) (1906–74) – As a Lieutenant commanded the submarine *Vettor Pisani* and – promoted LtCdr. in August 1940 – was appointed as CO of the submarine *Scirè*, operating with the underwater assault craft of the Xª Flottiglia MAS; as a Cdr., became the Flottiglia's commander and, after 8 September 1943, joined the RSI Navy in northern Italy.

Costantino BORSINI (**) (1906–40) – Promoted to LtCdr. in early 1940, became the CO of the destroyer *Francesco Nullo* operating in the Red Sea. On 21 October 1940, near the Island of Hamil, engaged a strong British naval group composed of destroyers and cruisers. While the *Nullo* was sinking at the end of this unequal action, LtCdr. Borsini refused to leave his ship and sank with her, along with his orderly **Vincenzo CIARAVOLO** (**) (1919-1940) who – having

LtCdr. Junio Valerio Borghese, commanding officer of the submarine *Scirè* and later, commander of the Xª Flottiglia MAS. (E Bagnasco collection)

already been rescued – got back aboard the *Nullo* to die with him.

Giuseppe BRIGNOLE (*) (1906–92) – Between 1928 and 1933 served in the Regia Marina retiring as a Sottotenente di Vascello (equivalent to USN's Lt.jg.). Recalled to duty in 1935, as a Lieutenant was in command of the torpedo boat *Calatafimi* at the beginning of the war; on 14 June 1940 he boldly attacked a French naval group bombarding the Savona-Genoa area. Later, he kept command of the *Calatafimi* in the Aegean until 8 September 1943: having refused to co-operate with the Kriegsmarine or the RSI Navy, was interned in Germany, returning to Italy after the end of the war, retiring from the Navy as a LtCdr. in 1947.

Giuseppe CIGALA FULGOSI (*) (1910–77) – On 22 May 1941, commanding the torpedo boat *Lupo* with the rank of Lieutenant, attacked a strong British naval group off Crete thus defending the convoy of small motor-sailers that he was escorting. Promoted LtCdr., when the Armistice was signed was the CO of the torpedo boat *Impetuoso*: to avoid the internment of his ship in Spain, he ordered the *Impetuoso* to be scuttled off the Balearics. He retired in 1946 as a Cdr., being later promoted to the rank of Captain in the naval reserve.

Aldo COCCHIA (*) (1900–68) – Commanding officer of the submarine *Torelli* in the Atlantic, as a Captain was Capo di Stato Maggiore of the Italian

LtCdr. Junio Valerio Borghese and (right) Cdr. Ernesto Forza at the Bocca di Serchio technical facility of the Xª Flottiglia MAS in 1941. (E Bagnasco collection)

Atlantic Submarine Command ('Betasom') at Bordeaux. In December 1942 he fought with the 14ª Squadriglia Cacciatorpediniere at the Skerki Bank, being seriously injured (and being later awarded the Medaglia d'Oro al Valor Militare for his behaviour in the action). After the war, as a Vice-Admiral, he was the editor of the Italian Navy's official magazine *Rivista Marittima* and the Chief of the Navy's Historical Dept from 1960 to 1963.

Luigi DURAND DE LA PENNE (★) (1914–92) – Upon his promotion to Lieutenant, in late 1940 was included in the underwater operators team of the Xª Flottiglia MAS and, on the night of 18 December 1941, took part in the famous attack on Alexandria during which the battleships HMS *Valiant* and HMS *Queen Elizabeth* and the tanker *Sagona* were damaged. De La Penne was taken prisoner and returned to Italy in 1944; after the war, he attained the rank of Captain and retired from the Italian Navy in the late 1950s, being later elected several times as a Member of the Italian Parliament. For the attack against Alexandria, Lieut. De La Penne was rewarded with the Medaglia d'Oro al Valor Militare along with the other five 'SLC' operators that took part in the action: *Emilio BIANCHI* (★) (b. 1912: still alive as of June 2012), *Vincenzo MARTELLOTTA* (★) (1933–73), *Mario MARINO* (★) (1914–82), *Antonio MARCEGLIA* (★) (1915–92) and *Spartaco SCHERGAT* (★) (1920–96).

Luigi FAGGIONI (★) (1909–91) – As a Lieutenant, was the highest-ranking officer that took part in the surface assault craft action of the Xª Flottiglia MAS against Suda Bay, on the night of 26 March 1941, during which six 'barchini esplosivi' irreparably damaged the cruiser HMS *York* and the tanker *Pericles*. The other five operators taking part in the action were *Angelo CABRINI* (★) (1917–87), *Emilio BARBERI* (★)

(1917–2002), *Lino BECCATI* (★) (1913–99), *Alessio DE VITO* (★) (1906–82) and *Tullio TEDESCHI* (★) (1910–87).

Carlo FECIA DI COSSATO (★) (1908–44) – After several tours of duty aboard various submarines, in December 1940 became the CO of the submarine *Tazzoli* operating in the Atlantic and, while in command of this boat, sank eighteen enemy merchant ships totalling over 96,000 grt, becoming the Regia Marina's top submarine ace for the number of ships sunk. In February 1943 was appointed commander of the 3ª Squadriglia Torpediniere and – on 9 September 1943, as CO of the torpedo boat *Aliseo* – fought brilliantly off Bastia (Corsica) against an overwhelming force of seven German warships. He followed the Italian fleet to Malta after the surrender, but the events following the Armistice deeply troubled his conscience, and he killed himself at Naples on 27 August 1944.

Ernesto FORZA (★) (1900–75) – In June 1941 was appointed as commander of the 22ª Flottiglia MAS and, in October, was assigned to the Xª Flottiglia MAS for which unit he planned several surface and underwater assault actions. After the Armistice, in southern Italy, with the rank of Captain he reconstituted the assault craft speciality ('Mariassalto') for the co-belligerent Regia Marina. After the war he attained the rank of Rear Admiral and commanded the 1ª Divisione Navale at La Spezia and the autonomous naval command of Sicily, being honourably discharged in 1960.

Gianfranco GAZZANA PRIAROGGIA (★★) (1912–43) – On 10 June 1940, as a Lieutenant, was in command of the submarine *Malachite*; after acting as Tenente (i.e. second in command) of the submarines *Durbo* and *Tazzoli*, became the CO of the *Archimede* and then of the *Da Vinci* from 10

August 1942. During his patrols he sank and damaged several Allied merchant ships totalling over 90,000 grt; while returning to Bordeaux from a successful mission in the southern Atlantic and Indian Oceans (during which he was promoted for meritorious service to LtCdr.), on 23 May 1943 the *Da Vinci* was sunk with all hands off Vigo by the combined action of the destroyer HMS *Active* and the frigate IIMS *Ness* of the Royal Navy.

Primo LONGOBARDO (★★) (1901–42) – In command of the submarines *Sirena*, *Galilei*, *Ferraris* and *Calvi* in the 1930s, was promoted to Cdr. in 1938. During the Second World War initially commanded the submarines *Torelli* and *Toti*, then was again CO of the *Calvi* from 1942. Cdr. Longobardo's last mission began on 2 July 1942: on the 15th, the *Calvi* was attacked in the Atlantic by the destroyer escort HMS *Lulworth* and the Italian boat, after a long and unequal surface action, was sunk with Cdr. Longobardo refusing to abandon his submarine.

Giovanni MARABOTTO (1891–1975) – As a Captain, was the CO of the light cruiser *Alberto di Giussano* when she was sunk along with the *Da Barbiano* off Cape Bon on the night of 13 December 1941. Served throughout 1942–3 as Caposcorta for several Africa-bound convoys and,

Teseo Tesei, Captain of the Genio Navale (rank equivalent to Lieutenant for line officers), with a diver's suit early in the war. (Ufficio Storico della Marina Militare)

LtCdr. Mario Arillo aboard the submarine *Ambra* in 1942. (Ufficio Storico della Marina Militare)

after the Armistice, without joining the RSI remained in northern Italy performing important intelligence work and maintaining contacts between the Regia Marina in southern Italy, the RSI Navy and independent partisan formations.

Carlo MARGOTTINI (★★) (1899–1940) – In the late 1930s, upon his promotion to Captain, was appointed as the Naval attaché of the Italian embassy in Paris. Soon before Italy's entry into the war, became the commander of the 11ᵃ Squadriglia Cacciatorpediniere, taking part in the Battle of Punta Stilo. On 12 October 1940, as CO of the destroyer *Artigliere*, engaged a British squadron composed of destroyers and cruisers. In the ensuing combat, *Artigliere* was heavily damaged, and Capt. Margottini died aboard his ship, finally sunk the following morning by the gunfire of HMS *Ajax*.

Francesco MIMBELLI (★) (1903–78) – In December 1940, as a Cdr., was appointed as commander of a Squadriglia Torpediniere and, in the Aegean on the night of 22 May 1941, aboard the *Sagittario*, engaged in combat a greatly superior British force while escorting a convoy bound for Crete. In March 1942 Mimbelli was in the Black Sea, commanding a MAS Squadriglia and, after the war, was promoted several times. Commanded the Naval Academy in 1953–54 and then the Squadra Navale between 1959 and 1961, being honourably discharged in 1964.

Livio PIOMARTA (★★) (1908–41) – LtCdr.

Piomarta commanded the submarine *Ferraris* during the long two-ocean voyage undertaken to reach Bordeaux from Massawa, after the fall of that base. In 1941 became the CO of the *Guglielmo Marconi*, sinking six merchant ships in the Atlantic totalling over 16,000 grt. On 5 October 1941 the *Marconi* left Bordeaux to attack a British convoy that had left Gibraltar, but never returned to 'Betasom', being lost to unknown causes, probably 300 miles west of Gibraltar, between the end of October and early December 1941.

Danilo STIEPOVICH (★★) (1912–41) – He was the chief engineer of the submarine *Cappellini* from the beginning of the war, with the rank of Lieutenant of the Genio Navale. On 12 October 1941, in the Atlantic Ocean, the *Cappellini* engaged in a gunfire action a British auxiliary cruiser and, in the ensuing combat, Lieut. Stiepovich was mortally wounded, asking his CO to be able to see the enemy ship sinking as he died, and with the national flag laid on him.

Teseo TESEI (★★) (1909–41) – As an officer of the Genio Navale, together with Elios Toschi he designed and tested the innovative underwater assault craft later known as 'SLC' or 'Maiale'. Assigned to the underwater operational unit of the Xᵃ Flottiglia MAS, died while piloting an 'SLC' in the ill-fated attack against Malta's Grand Harbour on the night of 25/26 July 1941.

Salvatore TODARO (★★) (1908–42) – LtCdr, as commanding officer of the submarine *Cappellini*,

was one of the leading Italian submariners and distinguished himself for particular humanity towards the crew of the ships sunk by his boat. In November 1941 he was transferred to the Xᵃ Flottiglia MAS and took part in operations in the Black Sea, particularly in the Sevastopol area. LtCdr. Todaro was killed in action during an air raid off La Galite (Tunisia) on 12 December 1942, at the end of a surface assault craft mission.

Salvatore TOSCANO (★★) (1897–1941) – Promoted to Captain in 1937, before the war was the CO of the cruiser *Cadorna*, of the battleship *Duilio* during her reconstruction and of the cruiser *Duca degli Abruzzi*. In March 1941 was detached aboard the destroyer *Alfieri* as commander of the 9ᵃ Squadriglia Cacciatorpediniere and died aboard his ship when she was sunk by British gunfire during the night action of Cape Matapan, refusing to abandon her.

Licio VISINTINI (★★) (1915–42) – In 1940 requested to be assigned as an underwater operator to the Xᵃ Flottiglia MAS and, after being promoted Lieutenant in 1941, was sent aboard the tanker *Olterra* interned in the Spanish port of Algeciras to plan assault operations against Gibraltar. During his second mission with a 'SLC' (on the night of 7/8 December 1942), after overcoming the obstructions protecting the battleship *Nelson*, was killed in action along with his crewman *Giovanni MAGRO* (★★) (1916–42) when he was about to place the craft's charge under the hull of the British battleship.

Selected Bibliography

Ufficio Storico della Marina Militare – USMM

No study of the activities of the Regia Marina in the Second World War can ignore the series of volumes – covering all Italian naval operations between 1940 and 1945 – published by the Italian Navy's Historical Dept. (Ufficio Storico della Marina Militare – USMM, Rome) between the mid-1950s and the mid-1970s (and in several cases reprinted more recently). This 21-volume series is known as *La Marina Italiana nella seconda guerra mondiale* ('The Italian Navy in the Second World War'):

USMM staff, vol. I: *Dati statistici* (1972, 1st ed. 1950).
USMM staff, vol. II: *Navi militari perdute* (1977, 1st ed. 1951).
USMM staff, vol. III: *Navi mercantili perdute* (1997, 1st ed. 1952).
Fioravanzo, G, vol. IV: *La Guerra nel Mediterraneo – Le azioni navali: dal 10 giugno 1940 al 31 marzo 1941* (1976, 1st ed. 1959).
_____, vol. V: *La Guerra nel Mediterraneo – Le azioni navali: dal 1° aprile 1941 all'8 settembre 1943* (1970, 1st ed. 1960).
Cocchia, A, vol. VI: *La difesa del Traffico con l'Africa Settentrionale: dal 10 giugno 1940 al 30 settembre 1941* (1977, 1st ed. 1958).
_____, vol. VII: *La difesa del Traffico con l'Africa Settentrionale: dal 1° ottobre 1941 al 30 settembre 1942* (1976, 1st ed. 1962).
Fioravanzo, G, vol. VIII: *La difesa del Traffico con l'Africa Settentrionale: dal 1° ottobre 1942 alla caduta della Tunisia* (1964).
Lupinacci, P F, vol. IX: *La difesa del traffico con l'Albania, la Grecia e l'Egeo* (1965).
_____, vol. X: *Le operazioni in Africa Orientale* (1976, 1st ed. 1961).
_____, vol. XI: *Attività in Mar Nero e Lago Ladoga* (1972, 1st ed. 1962).
Mori-Ubaldini, U. vol. XII: *I sommergibili negli oceani* (1976, 1st ed. 1963).
Bertini, M, vol. XIII: *I sommergibili in Mediterraneo*, two volumes (1972, 1st ed. 1967).
De Risio, C, vol. XIV: *I mezzi d'assalto* (1972, 1st ed. 1964).
Fioravanzo, G, vol. XV: *La Marina dall'8 settembre 1943 alla fine del conflitto* (1971, 1st ed. 1962).
Levi, A, vol. XVI: *Avvenimenti in Egeo dopo l'armistizio* (1972, 1st ed. 1957).
De Risio, C, vol. XVII: *I violatori di blocco* (1972, 1st ed. 1963).
Lupinacci, P F, vol. XVIII: *La guerra di mine* (1988, 1st ed. 1966).
Franti, M, vol. XIX: *Il dragaggio* (1969).
Fioravanzo, G, vol. XXI: *L'organizzazione della Marina durante il conflitto*, three volumes (1972–8).
Rauber, V, vol. XXII: *La lotta antisommergibile* (1978).
(The projected Volumes XX [about Italo-German naval relations] and XXIII [Navy and Army activities on rivers and lakes] have never been published.

Another important series of books published by the USMM is *Le Navi d'Italia* ('Ships of Italy'): each volume is related to a specific type of ship (battleships, cruisers, submarines etc.), obviously covering a wider time-span than the 1930s-1940s period.

Bagnasco, E, *I MAS e le motosiluranti italiane* (1969, 1st ed. 1967).
Bargoni, F, *Esploratori, fregate, corvette e avvisi italiani* (1974).
Giorgerini, G, and A Nani, *Le navi di linea italiane* (1973, 1st ed. 1962).
_____, *Gli incrociatori italiani* (1971, 1st ed. 1964).
Pollina, P M, *Le torpediniere italiane* (1974, 1st ed. 1964).
_____, *I sommergibili italiani* (1971, 1st ed. 1963: the third edition currently on sale is a two-volume set published in 2010, by A Turrini, O O Miozzi and M M Minuto).
USMM staff, *I cacciatorpediniere italiani* (1971, 1st ed. 1966).

Some of the above volumes have recently been re-published in revised and expanded versions:

Bagnasco, *M.A.S. e mezzi d'assalto di superficie italiani* (1996).
_____, *Unità veloci costiere italiane* (1998).
Bargoni, F, *Esploratori italiani* (1996).
_____, and F Gay, *Corvette e pattugliatori* (2004).

The following USMM books are very useful for their detailed, comprehensive and often tabulated data:

Bargoni, F, *Tutte le navi militari d'Italia (1861-1986)* (1987).
Giorgerini, G, and A Nani, *Almanacco Storico delle Navi Militari Italiane (1861-1995)* (1996, 1st ed. 1978).

Series 'Orizzonte Mare'

Between 1972 and 1983 the publisher Bizzarri of Rome (incorporated in 1977 into Edizioni dell'Ateneo e Bizzarri), produced the 'Orizzonte Mare' series of detailed and well-illustrated booklets. filled with drawings, data, photographs and comprehensive text.

Andò, E, *Incrociatori leggeri classe 'Montecuccoli'*, vols I & II (1982).
_____, *Incrociatori leggeri classe 'Duca d'Aosta'*, vols I & II (1985).
_____, F Bargoni, and F Gay, *Incrociatori pesanti classe 'Trento'*, vols I & II (1975).
Bargoni, F, and F Gay, *Corazzate classe 'Conte di Cavour'* (1972).
_____ _____, *Corazzate classe 'Duilio'* (1972).
_____, *Corazzate classe 'Littorio'*, vols I & II (1973).
Gay, F, *Incrociatore corazzato San Giorgio* (1977).
_____, *Incrociatori pesanti classe 'Zara'*, vols I & II (1977).
_____, *Incrociatori leggeri classe 'Di Giussano'*, vols I & II (1979).
_____, *Incrociatori leggeri classe 'Cadorna'* (1981).

The second batch of the 'Orizzonte Mare' series was published between 1994 and 1997 by Albertelli, Parma.

Andò, E, *Incrociatori leggeri classe 'Capitani Romani'* (1994).
Bagnasco, E, *Cacciatorpediniere classe 'Soldati'*, vols I & II (1993).
_____, and M Brescia, *Cacciatorpediniere classi 'Freccia/Folgore', 'Maestrale' e 'Oriani'*, vols I & II (1997).
Brescia, M, *Cacciatorpediniere classe 'Navigatori'* (1995).
Gay, F, *Incrociatori leggeri classe 'Duca degli Abruzzi'*, vols I & II (1993).
Rastelli, A, *Torpediniere (ex CT) tipo 'Pattison' e 'Orlando'* (1994).

Italian Warships and Naval Construction

Books
Bagnasco, E, *I sommergibili della seconda guerra mondiale* (Albertelli Parma, 1973; reprinted 2005).
_____, *Le motosiluranti della seconda guerra mondiale* (Albertelli, Parma, 1977).
_____, *Le armi delle navi italiane nella seconda guerra mondiale* (Albertelli, Parma, 1978; reprinted 2003).
_____, *La portaerei nella Marina italiana*, supplement to *Rivista Marittima* (Dec 1989).
_____, and E Cernuschi, *Le navi da guerra italiane* (Albertelli, Parma, 2003; 2nd ed. 2005, 3rd ed. 2009).
_____, and A De Toro, *Le navi da battaglia classe 'Littorio' 1937-1948*

(Albertelli, Parma, 2008; revised edition 2010).

_____, and M Brescia, *La mimetizzazione delle navi italiane 1940-1945* (Albertelli, Parma, 2006).

_____, and M Spertini, *I mezzi d'assalto della X Flottiglia MAS 1940-1945* (Albertelli, Parma, 1991, 1993, 1997 and 2005).

Borghese, J V, *Decima Flottiglia MAS. Dalle origini all'armistizio* (Garzanti, 1950; republished by *STORIA militare*, Parma, 2005).

Cosentino, M (with E Bagnasco), *Le portaerei italiane* (Albertelli, Parma, 2011).

De Risio, C, *L'Aviazione di Marina* (Ufficio Storico della Marina Militare, Rome, 1995).

Giorgerini, G, *Le navi da battaglia della seconda guerra mondiale* (Albertelli, Parma, 1972; reprinted 2003).

_____, *Gli incrociatori della seconda guerra mondiale* (Albertelli, Parma, 1974).

STORIA Militare's staff, *Le navi ospedale italiane 1935-1945* (Albertelli Edizioni Specialil, Parma, 2010).

Articles

Bagnasco, E, 'Le motozattere italiane nella seconda guerra mondiale', *Rivista Marittima* (Apr 1969).

_____, 'I caccia classe Comandanti', *Rivista Marittima* (Jan 1987).

_____, 'Le torpediniere di scorta classe Orsa', *STORIA militare* (Oct 1993 & Nov 1993).

_____, and F Bargoni, 'Cacciasommergibili', *STORIA militare* (Sep 2009).

Curami, A, and G Garello, 'L'aviazione ausiliaria per la Regia Marina tra le due guerre (1923-1940)', *Rivista Marittima* (Aug/Sep 1985).

_____, and A Rastelli, 'La Forza Navale Speciale', *STORIA militare* (Dec 1993 & Jan 1994).

The Regia Marina in the Second World War

Books

Bagnasco, E, *Aldo Fraccaroli, fotografo navale, sessant'anni di storia della Marina italiana attraverso le immagini* (Albertelli, Parma, 1996).

_____, *In guerra sul mare* (Albertelli, Parma, 2005; reprinted 2011).

_____, and A Rastelli, *Sommergibili in guerra, centosettantadue battelli italiani nella Seconda guerra mondiale* (Albertelli, Parma, 1989; last edition 2005).

Benussi, G, *Treni armati e treni ospedale 1915-1945* (Albertelli, Parma, 1983).

Bernardi, G, *Il disarmo navale tra le due guerre mondiali (1919-1939)* (Ufficio Storico della Marina Militare, Rome, 1975).

_____, *La Marina, gli armistizi e il trattato di pace (set. 1943-dic. 1951)* (Ufficio Storico della Marina Militare, Rome, 1979).

Bragadin, M A, *Il dramma della Marina Italiana 1940-1945* (Mondadori, Milan, 1982).

Brescia, M (with G Vignati), *I fotografi navali – tra cronaca e storia dall'800 ai nostri giorni*, supplement to *Rivista Marittima* (Dec 2008).

Clerici, C, *Le difese costiere italiane nelle due guerre mondiali* (STORIA militare, Parma, 1996).

Del Giudice, V and E, *La Marina Militare italiana, uniformi, fregi e distintivi dal 1861 a oggi* (Albertelli, Parma, 1997).

Fraccaroli, A, *Marina Militare 1946* (Albertelli, Parma, 1994; facsimile reprint of the original book published in Milan by Hoepli in 1946).

Gabriele, M, *Operazione C 3 Malta* (Ufficio Storico della Marina Militare, Rome, 1990).

Galuppini, G, *Le uniformi della Marina Militare*, two vols (Ufficio Storico della Marina Militare, Rome, 1997–9).

Giorgerini, G, *La battaglia dei convogli* (Mursia, Milan, 1977).

_____, *Da Matapan al Golfo Persico, la Marina Militare italiana dal fascismo alla repubblica* (Mondadori, Milan, 1989).

_____, *La guerra italiana sul mare. La Marina italiana tra vittoria e sconfitta* (Mondadori, Milan, 2001)

_____, *Uomini sul Fondo* (Mondadori, Milan, 2003).

_____, *Attacco dal mare* (Mondadori, Milan, 2007).

Iachino, A, *Gaudo e Matapan* (Mondadori, Verona, 1946).

_____, *Le due Sirti* (Mondadori, Verona, 1953).

_____, *Operazione Mezzo Giugno* (Mondadori, Verona, 1955).

_____, *La sorpresa di Matapan* (Mondadori, Verona, 1957).

_____, *Il punto su Matapan* (Mondadori, Verona, 1969).

Mattesini, F, *Il giallo di Matapan* (Edizioni dell'Ateneo e Bizzarri, Rome, 1985).

_____, *La battaglia aeronavale di Mezz'agosto* (Edizioni dell'Ateneo e Bizzarri, Rome, 1986).

_____, *La battaglia di Punta Stilo* (Ufficio Storico della Marina Militare, Rome, 1990).

_____, *L'operazione Gaudo e lo scontro notturno di Capo Matapan* (Ufficio Storico della Marina Militare, Rome, 1998).

_____, *Betasom la guerra negli oceani (1940-1943)* (Ufficio Storico della Marina Militare, Rome, 1999)

_____, *La battaglia di Capo Teulada* (Ufficio Storico della Marina Militare, Rome, 2000).

_____, *La Marina e l'8 settembre* (Ufficio Storico della Marina Militare, Rome, 2002).

Rapalino, P, and G Schivardi, *Tutti a bordo!* (Mursia, Milan, 2009).

Santoni, A, *Il vero traditore* (Mursia, Milan, 1981).

_____, *La seconda battaglia della Sirte* (Edizioni dell'Ateneo e Bizzarri, Rome, 1982).

_____, and F Mattesini, *La partecipazione aeronavale tedesca alla guerra nel Mediterraneo (1940-1945)* (dell'Ateneo e Bizzarri, Roma, 1980; reprinted by *STORIA militare* in 2005).

Articles

Bagnasco, E, 'Mariassalto (1943-1954)', *STORIA militare* (May 1995).

_____, 'Le 'prede' della Regia Marina (1940-1945), *STORIA militare* (Feb & Mar 1966).

_____,'La Marina del trattato di pace', *STORIA militare* (Nov 2000).

Berezhnoy, S, 'Navi italiane all'URSS', *STORIA militare* (Aug 1995).

Cernuschi, E, 'La Marina Repubblicana 1943-1945', *STORIA militare* (May 2009 & Jun 2009).

Colliva, G, 'La squadra da battaglia italiana e il problema dei combustibili (1940-1943)', *Bollettino d'Archivio dell'Ufficio Storico della Marina Militare* (Dec 1999).

Books and Articles by British or US Publishers

Andò, E, 'Capitani Romani', *Warship*, Nos 7 & 8 (1978).

_____, 'The Gabbiano Class Corvettes', *Warship*, Nos 34 & 35 (1985).

Bagnasco, E, 'The Comandanti Class Destroyers of The Italian Navy 1942-1943', *Warship International*, No 3 (1990).

_____, *Submarines of Second World War* (Arms & Armour Press, London, 1977; US Naval Institute, Annapolis (Maryland), 1977).

_____, E Cernuschi and V P O'Hara, 'Italian Fast Coastal Forces: Development, Doctrine and Campaigns, – 1914-1986: *Warship*, 2008 and 2009

_____, and A De Toro, *The Littorio Class. Italy's Last and Largest Battleships 1937-1948* (Barnsley, Seaforth Publishing, 2011; Naval Institute Press, Annapolis (Maryland), 2011).

_____, and M Grossman, *Regia Marina – Italian Battleships of WW II* (P H Publishing, Missoula (Montana), 1986).

Bragadin, M A, *The Italian Navy in World War II* (US Naval Institute, Annapolis (Maryland), 1957).

Fraccaroli, A, *Italian Warships of World War II* (Ian Allan, London, 1968).

_____, 'The *Littorio* Class', *Warship*, No 1 and No 2 (1977).

Giorgerini, G, 'The *Cavour* and *Duilio* Class Battleships', *Warship*, No 16 (1980).

Hervieux, P, '*Marconi* Class submarines', *Warship*, Nos 30 and 31 (1984).

Mallet, R *The Italian Navy and Fascist Expansionism 1935 – 1940* (Frank Cass, London, 1998).

Mollo, A, *Uniforms & Insignia of the Navies of World War II* (US Naval Institute, Annapolis (Maryland), 1991).

_____, M McGregor, *Naval, Marine and Air Force Uniforms of World War 2* (Blandford Press, Poole, 1975).

Sadkovich, J, *The Italian Navy in World War II* (Greenwood Press, Westport (Connecticut), 1994).

Note

For a general and complete overview on Italian naval bibliography for the 1930–45 period, the standard work is Enrico Cernuschi's *La Marina italiana nella seconda guerra mondiale – una bibliografia critica (1944-2009)*, published in January 2010 as a supplement to the Italian Navy's monthly magazine *Rivista Marittima*.

Notes on the Photographic Sources

Since the 1920s, the ships and activities of the Regia Marina have been documented photographically by both professional and amateur photographers based in the main dockyards of La Spezia and Taranto, as well as in Genoa, Leghorn, Naples, Palermo, Brindisi, Ancona, Venice and (after 1918) Trieste and Pola.

The most important of the numerous naval photographers of La Spezia is Studio Pucci, whose prints, often in standard postcard format, were very popular between the late nineteenth century and the early 1930s. The Pucci archive, now sadly broken up, included thousands of images of virtually all Regia Marina ships of the period. Most photographs had an identifying number in Pucci's archive, which appears on both the negative and the prints. These pictures, with their unmistakeable and highly-appreciated style, were taken either from the shores of the Gulf of La Spezia or more commonly from boats which allowed the studio's photographers to produce images that are not only of technical and documentary value, but also of high visual impact. One minor transgression by the Studio, however, was that in a very small number of photographs, the identification letters of destroyers and torpedo boats were altered, in order to fill gaps in the collection.

However, Studio Pucci was not the only one active in La Spezia during that 'golden age' for Italian naval photography. The prints and postcards that can now be found only on antique stalls bear the names of Cavalca, Barr, Falzone and CM, photographic studios which, besides more traditional work related to weddings, etc, consistently documented almost all naval activities in the Gulf and the Dockyard.

The 1920s and 1930s were the period in which the 'cartolina illustrata' (postcard), gained its maximum splendour and widespread use, in Italy as well as elsewhere. In Turin, the Studio Fotocelere distinguished itself by creating and marketing a number of cards being part of a series called *Le Navi d'Italia* ('The Ships of Italy') which, in a compact 9cm x 14cm format, are still among the best examples from the point of view of reproduction and printing of naval photography for those years.

At the same time, the activities of several local photographers (Agosto and Calì in Genoa, Baschetti in Venice and Miniati in Leghorn) are well documented, as well as those of further firms in other cities, but Taranto and Trieste hosted some of the most famous and enduring studios of that period, that in some cases went on working until after the Second World War.

The naval photographers of Taranto are well known not only to the students of naval history but, also, to all those who from the 1930s to the 1970s served in the navy there. Paolo De Siati and G Priore, in particular, created huge collections in which were preserved not only their own glass plates and negatives, but also those of other firms that over the years had ceased working. Today, unfortunately, nothing remains of these important collections, although many images taken by these two important naval photographers are still preserved in the private archives of several Italian historians and collectors .

The important Studio Mioni at Trieste was the direct heir of the many photographers who - when the city belonged to the Austro-Hungarian Empire - had an important role in documenting the activities of the K.u.K. Marine in that area. In particular, the images of 'Mioni' (whose quality is due to the use of excellent photographic equipment combined with advanced developing and printing techniques) depict virtually all the ships of the Regia Marina launched by CRDA and other yards up to 1943, and are thus one of the more definitive sources for determining the appearance, specific fittings or camouflage of a large number of Italian warships of that period. The photographers of Studio Mioni took many photographs during the sea trials of ships in the Gulf of Trieste, therefore increasing the emotional and dynamic value of shots that may be considered as a true part of the history of world naval photography. Yet again, however, once the studio closed down, this important collection was broken up with only some of its images being preserved in the archives of a few shipyards and of other institutions.

Finally, in the 1930s and during the Second World War , the photographers and technicians of the 'Istituto Luce' of Rome (established in 1924), along with those of some official naval photographers of the Regia Marina, allowed a large number of images to be produced related to naval operations and of the more 'routine' wartime activities of Italian warships and their crews.

Index